Introduction to Islamic Theology and Law

MODERN CLASSICS IN NEAR EASTERN STUDIES

Introduction to Islamic Theology and Law

BY IGNAZ GOLDZIHER

Translated by ANDRAS and RUTH HAMORI

With an introduction and additional notes by Bernard Lewis

Princeton University Press, Princeton, New Jersey

Published by Princeton University Press, Princeton, New Jersey
In the United Kingdom: Princeton University Press, Guildford, Surrey

Library of Congress Cataloging in Publication Data will be found on the last printed page of this book
Publication of this book has been aided by a grant from the National Endowment for the Humanities
This book has been composed in V-I-P Bembo
Clothbound editions of Princeton University Press books are printed on acid-free paper, and binding materials are chosen for strength and durability
Printed in the United States of America by Princeton University Press, Princeton, New Jersey

Translated from the German, *Vorlesungen über den Islam* (Heidelberg, 1910)

The translation and preparation of this volume were made possible through a grant from the translation program of the National Endowment for the Humanities, to which we would like to express our deep appreciation.

Contents

Introduction

On 16 May 1906 Ignaz Goldziher noted in his diary, "I have received an invitation from America to give a series of six lectures for the Society for Lectures on the History of Religion, at eight universities, on the history of Islam. Honorarium $2,500. This will give me something to think about for many nights."[1]

Goldziher obviously thought to some purpose. On 8 September 1907 he noted in his diary, "On 22nd June I was able to bring my American lectures to completion: six chapters, rich in content, in which I dealt exhaustively with the history of the development of Islam."[2]

In fact, however, the lectures, though completed in little more than a year, were never delivered. The explanation normally given in the past was that he was prevented by ill health from making the necessary trip to America. His diary reveals that this was not the whole story. An entry dated 2 April 1908 reads, "I am getting the English translations of my lectures in installments. Miserable work, especially the ones I got from Berlin through the intermediary of Yahuda. On top of that I am again seriously ill, and cannot expose myself to stress and strain, but can only work in my usual routine. I am now wondering whether it would not be in the interest of my health to give up the American plan, even now, almost at the last moment. The comparison of the botched English job with my own original, successful in form as in content, causes me terrible distress, which will become permanent if I continue to collate them. I haven't the strength for this. It grieves my heart when I observe the mangling of my fine work from line to line. How can I put this in order?"[3]

It was presumably at this time or shortly after that Goldziher decided not to go to the United States to deliver his lectures, but instead to publish them in book form, in the original German. An entry in his diary dated 15 August 1909 notes, "I am devoting the summer holiday mainly to completing the notes and excursuses to the Islam lectures, the publication of which, under pressure from the publisher Winter in Heidelberg, I can unfortunately not postpone for very much longer. So I am working

[1] Ignaz Goldziher, *Tagebuch*, edited by Alexander Scheiber (Leiden, 1978), p. 251

[2] *Ibid.*, p. 257.

[3] *Ibid.*, pp. 258-59.

through a whole lot of new reading, especially the new volumes of Ibn Sa'd,[4] which are very fruitful."[5]

There are two more entries in the diary about the lectures, one dated 5 March 1910, noting that the printing is proceeding rapidly,[6] and a final one dated 31 December 1910, in which the author proudly notes that "my lectures have appeared and received the approval of Nöldeke and Snouck."[7]

The approbation of Theodor Nöldeke and Christiaan Snouck Hurgronje, the two major Islamicists of the time apart from Goldziher himself, was well deserved, and the *Vorlesungen über den Islam* (Lectures on Islam) immediately took its place as a major classic of Islamic studies. It was published in 1910, when Goldziher was sixty years old and at the height of his intellectual powers. A number of translations followed—Russian 1911, Hungarian 1912, French 1920, Arabic 1946, and Hebrew 1951. An English version by Kate Chambers Seelye, entitled *Mohammed and Islam*, was published by the Yale University Press in February 1917, with a preface by Morris Jastrow claiming that "the present translation into English is authorized by the distinguished author." This is presumably the English translation on which Goldziher commented in his diary. Not surprisingly, the book was withdrawn by the publisher at Goldziher's request, when it was brought to his attention. No English translation has since appeared. A second German edition, edited and adapted by Franz Babinger, was published in Heidelberg in 1925. Although Babinger was able to make use of Goldziher's own annotated copy, his somewhat idiosyncratic adaptation makes his edition unreliable, and the following translation, like all the others, is based on the first edition, the only one approved by the author.

Goldziher was born on 22 June 1850 in the town of Székesfehérvár in Hungary. He began his scholarly career at a strikingly early age. At five he was reading the Hebrew text of the Old Testament, at eight the Talmud; at twelve, he wrote and published his first monograph, on the origins and classification of the Hebrew prayers. At sixteen, while still a schoolboy, he attended courses in classics, philosophy, and oriental languages, including Persian and Turkish, at the University of Budapest, where he continued his studies after leaving school. With the help of his teachers, he obtained a scholarship from the Hungarian Minister of Edu-

[4] On Ibn Sa'd, see below, Ch. IV, Sec. 2.

[5] *Tagebuch*, pp. 262-63.

[6] *Ibid.*, p. 264.

[7] *Ibid.*, p. 268.

cation and embarked on a comprehensive program of study and research designed to equip him for a university appointment. His first period abroad was in Germany at the Universities of Leipzig and Berlin, where he took his doctorate at the age of nineteen. In the following year, he was approved as an occasional lecturer—Privatdozent—in the University of Budapest.

From Germany, he went to Holland and spent six months in Leiden, then the foremost school of Islamic studies in Europe. Goldziher's previous work in Hungary and Germany, though ranging widely, had been mainly in the fields of Judaic and Semitic studies, the latter of course including Arabic. His experience in Leiden, as he notes in his diary, made Islam in the broadest sense the main focus of his scholarly work.[8]

This new direction was confirmed when Goldziher went on his first and only trip to the Middle East, from September 1873 to April 1874. His time was spent mainly in Damascus and in Cairo, where he obtained permission—the first non-Muslim to do so—to enroll as a student in the mosque university of al-Azhar. Goldziher's diary reveals the impact of his Middle Eastern experience, which he describes as the best, the happiest, and the most fruitful time of his life; it also reflects his deep feeling of sympathy with Islam, and of kinship with the Muslims.

His stay in Cairo was cut short by bad news from home—his father was dying, the family business was in a bad way, and a new mood in the Ministry of Education, and, indeed, in the country, was putting his academic future in doubt.

Despite these difficulties, his scholarly reputation was growing, and in 1874 he published work in the proceedings of the Imperial Academy in Vienna. This marked the beginning of a career of outstanding distinction which brought him international recognition as one of the great masters of oriental scholarship and a founder of the modern science of Islamics.[9]

For all his achievements and reputation, however, Goldziher was not able to make an academic career in his native land. This was a time of mounting anti-Semitism in Hungary, and Jews were barred from most academic appointments. Though elected as an Extraordinary Member of the Hungarian Academy in 1876 and as an Ordinary Member in 1892, he was not given the title of Professor until 1894, the year in which the legis-

[8] *Ibid.*, p. 50.

[9] See, for example, C. H. Becker in *Der Islam*, XI (1922), 214-22; reprinted in *idem.*, *Islamstudien*, II (Leipzig, 1932), 499-513. Other appreciations are listed in J. D. Pearson, *Index Islamicus 1906-1955* (Cambridge, 1958), p. 11.

lative assembly formally recognized Judaism as equal to the three Christian denominations existing in the country. Even then he received only the title, but without faculty privileges and without salary—this in spite of the fact that in 1889 the Eighth International Congress of Orientalists had awarded him its gold medal for his scholarly publications, and that in 1894 he had received and refused an invitation to a chair at Cambridge University, in succession to W. Robertson Smith.

Having no salaried academic appointment, he turned for his livelihood to the Jewish community, and for thirty years, from 1876 to 1905, served it as secretary. This was no sinecure, but an exacting and sometimes disagreeable job, which left him only his evenings, weekends, and holidays for his scholarly work. It was not until 1904 that he was finally appointed to a genuine professorship in the University of Budapest, at first in Semitics, and then, from 1914, in the Chair of Muslim Law and Institutions in the Faculty of Laws. He died on 13 November 1921.

The *Lectures on Islam* are, inevitably, a product of their time. In a few matters, mostly of detail, Goldziher's findings must be modified in the light of new evidence that has become known since his day or new insights attained by subsequent research. The book also reflects in a number of ways the very different political and intellectual world of its time. Unlike the modern Western writer on Islamic or other Asian and African topics, Goldziher and his contemporaries had no need to take thought of a possible Muslim reader, but addressed themselves exclusively to a Western audience. Along with virtually all Western writers up to and including his time, he ascribes the authorship of the Qur'ān to Muhammad, and cites and discusses it accordingly. For the Muslim, to whom the Qur'ān is of divine authorship, this is sacrilege or blasphemy, and the Muslim custom is invariably to cite God as the author and to introduce a Qur'ānic quotation with the words, "God said." Modern orientalist scholarship has adopted an intermediate position, and cites the Qur'ān as itself: "the Qur'ān says." This has two advantages. It avoids shocking Muslim sensitivity, without committing the writer to a Muslim theological position. It also avoids confusion with Muslim tradition concerning the sayings of the Prophet (hadith), which in Muslim practice is cited with the formula, "Muhammad said."[10]

Goldziher's unself-conscious reference to Muhammad's authorship of the Qur'ān is paralleled by his calm and open discussion of another sub-

[10] Where Goldziher's text could be modified without changing his meaning, it has been amended to take account of this point.

ject that has since become sensitive and delicate—the pre-Islamic and foreign influences in the Qur'ān and hadith. From a strictly Muslim point of view, to speak of foreign influence in Qur'ān and hadith is to speak of foreign influences on God, and is self-evidently absurd and blasphemous. Modern orientalists, while for the most part not accepting Muslim doctrines, have taken care to avoid offending Muslim feelings, and this has made their discussion of such topics cautious and sometimes insincere. To modern readers, therefore, accustomed to this kind of delicacy, Goldziher's language, though normal in the early years of this century, may come as a surprise.

But these are in reality trivial matters, involving little more than conventions of expression. Of much greater significance is his profoundly sympathetic attitude to Muslim beliefs and achievements. If he lacks the anxious propitiation of writers of our time, he also is free—and this is surely far more important—from both the condemnation and condescension with which most of his contemporaries in Europe treated the Muslims, their scriptures, their religion, and their civilization. Although Goldziher was a product of the age of empire and mission, there is little trace in his works of either. On the contrary, he is at some pains to defend the authenticity and originality of Islam against its detractors from outside, and against those who were seeking to distort or undermine it from within. He protests against the one-sided rationalism of Christian scholars who, while safeguarding the sacrosanct character of their own scriptures and beliefs, subject those of the Muslims to rigorous and even captious criticism. At the same time he is concerned to preserve Islam from the pettifogging and casuistry of some jurists whom he sees as corrupting and distorting the true character of the faith.

In both of these respects, Goldziher was undoubtedly influenced by his Jewish origins and education. At that time a European Jew, particularly among the less assimilated communities of Central and Eastern Europe, was much better placed than his Christian compatriots to study Islam and to understand the Muslims. A knowledge of Hebrew smoothed and speeded the study of Arabic. To know rabbinic law and submit to its rules make it easier to understand the Holy Law of Islam and those who obey it. And Jews too were familiar with the hostile "higher criticism" that bared and lacerated their most cherished beliefs while preserving intact those of their critics. Even in his defense of Islam against its own pedants and reactionaries, Goldziher is clearly reflecting the protest of a Jewish liberal against the narrow obscurantism of some traditionalist and fundamentalist rabbis. In all this, Goldziher was able to achieve an immediacy of understanding, an intuitive sympathy, that eluded most of his Christian colleagues and contemporaries.[11]

But sympathy and understanding are not in themselves enough. They were underpinned and sustained by his vast learning, disciplined by his mastery of scholarly method, and illuminated by his creative imagination. In this book, based almost entirely on primary sources, he selects and presents material to illustrate and exemplify the salient features of Islam, with due emphasis but without distortion, and with extraordinary lucidity and architectonic skill. The result is a masterpiece at once of perception, of construction, and of exposition. Since its first publication, there have been other presentations of Islam for the Western reader, some of them of great merit. For the most part, however, they are either elementary and therefore, inevitably secondary, or specialized, and limited to one or another aspect of the Islamic heritage. As a guide to Muslim faith, law, doctrine and devotion, at once comprehensive and documented, Goldziher's lectures remain without equal.

The following translation is based on the first edition, with a few addenda derived from the second where these are clearly based on Goldziher's own notes. Some additional notes have been provided where this seemed necessary to correct or to clarify Goldziher's remarks in the light of later developments, evidence, and research. Goldziher's notes are numbered; the additional notes are lettered.

Goldziher's own notes present special difficulties that have called for some modification. His references to his sources are usually brief, and often cite manuscripts or superseded editions, many of them now rare and inaccessible. Printer's errors are also not uncommon, and the result is to limit the usefulness of a valuable part of the book, particularly for the nonspecialist. Lawrence I. Conrad has performed the exacting but invaluable task of identifying and recasting Goldziher's often cryptic references into a standard modern format, and of adding further elucidatory comments, most of which indicate translations of secondary material and better or more readily accessible editions of primary sources. To avoid unnecessary cluttering of the notes, the reader's attention is not drawn to cases where modification involves simple standardization, or correction of misspellings and errors in page and volume references. Any substantial

[11] On this point, see further B. Lewis, *Islam in History* (London, 1973), pp. 112-37.

changes, however, and all supplementary references and comments, have been set off in square brackets to distinguish them from Goldziher's own material. With the exception of a few unsigned articles and brief notes quoted from the *Revue du monde musulman*, notes citing a modern author without title refer to book reviews, and most of those omitting the author's name are studies by Goldziher himself. Any difficulties encountered in using the notes can be resolved by reference to the bibliography, also prepared by Mr. Conrad, which lists all texts and abbreviations used in this book, with the exception of classical and rabbinical works and articles from the *Encyclopaedia of Islam*. These works present no difficulties in identification or location of references.

BERNARD LEWIS
July 1979

TRANSLATORS' NOTE

This is a translation of the first edition (Heidelberg, 1910) of the Vorlesungen über den Islam. *Only the passage on the Zaydīs (Ch. V, Sec. 18) is taken from the second edition; it is clear from the French translation by F. Arin that this passage was written by Goldziher, and in its revised form it rounds out Goldziher's picture of the Shīʿī imamate.*

We retained Goldziher's interpretation of Qur'ān verses that some scholars understand differently. Occasionally, where in the German a hadith appears between quotation marks but has been turned into oratio obliqua, *we put it back into the looser form of the Arabic, as this did not affect the sense. We changed the numbering of Qur'ān verses to conform to the usage of modern Arabic editions and Western translations. In some instances we supplied the Arabic for words or phrases translated in the text. All our additions are in square brackets.*

In a very few places, we decided that the reader would be best served by an explanatory translation. For example, where Goldziher writes about ʿAbd al-Malik's Hauspfaffe, *we thought that "chaplain" would be perplexing, and wrote "confidential jurisconsult" instead, going back to Goldziher's source, Ibn Qutayba.*

Once in a great while we found that the exact rendering of sense did not require in English as cluttered a sentence as Goldziher wrote in German. An example is the first sentence of Chapter V.

Some common terms and names are written without diacritics. Imam is spelled with a capital I *when it means, in the Shīʿī sense, a successor of the Prophet; with a lower case* i *when it means the founder of a school of law or theology, or a prayer leader.*

The Arabic and Hebrew translations of the Vorlesungen *were both useful: the Arabic because in it the Arabic originals of most quotations are ready to hand, the Hebrew because of its massive updating of scholarly references.*

ANDRAS AND RUTH HAMORI
July 1979

Introduction to Islamic Theology and Law

I. *Muhammad and Islam*

1. What is the psychological source of religion?[a] Various answers have been suggested since religion first became the subject of an independent branch of knowledge. C. P. Tiele, the Dutch historian of religion, surveyed and scrutinized a number of them in one of his Gifford lectures at Edinburgh.[1] Some propose man's innate awareness of causality or his sense of dependency, others the awakening of a consciousness of the infinite or the renunciation of the world as the dominant state of mind that served as the seedbed of religion.

Religion, as I believe, is so complex a phenomenon in the psychology of mankind that its workings cannot be properly ascribed to a single impulse. It never appears as an abstraction free from specific historical conditions. Advanced or primitive, religion exists in concrete forms that vary with social conditions. We may assume that in each of these forms a particular religious impulse—one of those mentioned above or one of any number of others—predominates, but not to the exclusion of other components. At its earliest stage of development the character of a religion is already defined by the predominance of a particular motif, and that motif retains its ascendancy over all others as the religion evolves and passes through its historical existence. This is equally true of religions born of illumination experienced by an individual.

The principal feature and the essential character of the religion whose history forms the topic of these lectures are seen in the very name that its founder gave it at the beginning and under which, fourteen centuries later, it still runs its course in history.

Islam means submission, the believer's submission to Allah.[b] The word

[a] For general historical accounts of the development of the Islamic religion, see Michelangelo Guidi, *La Religione dell'Islam*, in *Storia delle Religioni*, edited by P. Pietro Tacchi-Venturi (Turin, 1949), II, 303–437; H.A.R. Gibb, Mohammedanism, an Historical Survey, 2nd ed. (New York, 1962); Fazlur Rahman, *Islam* (London, 1966). A selection of translated texts is provided by Arthur Jeffery, *Islam, Muhammad and His Religion* (New York, 1958). On the background and development of some of the basic Islamic concepts, see M. M. Bravmann, *The Spiritual Background of Early Islam: Studies in Ancient Arab Concepts* (Leiden, 1972).

[1] *Inleiding tot de Godsdienstwetenschap*, 2nd series, 9th lecture (Dutch edition, Amsterdam, 1899), pp. 177ff. [translated as *Elements of the Science of Religion* (Edinburgh and London, 1897-1899), II, 208ff.].

[b] This has for long been the usual explanation of the word Islam. It is based on a passage

expresses, first and foremost, a feeling of dependency on an unbounded omnipotence to which man must submit and resign his will. It expresses, better than any other, Muhammad's idea of the relation between the believer and the object of his worship. Submission is the dominant principle inherent in all manifestations of Islam: in its ideas, forms, ethics, and worship. Submission is the distinguishing feature that determines the specific character of the education of man that Islam intends to accomplish. Islam is the most cogent example for Schleiermacher's thesis that religion is rooted in a sense of dependency.

2. The task we have set ourselves in these lectures does not require a description of the details of the religious system of Islam. Rather, we must stress the factors that contributed to its historical evolution; for Islam as it appears in its mature aspect is the product of various influences that had affected its development as an ethical world view and as a system of law and dogma before it reached its definitive, orthodox form. Moreover, we must discuss the factors that directed the flow of Islam into its various channels; for Islam does not have the uniformity of a church. Its historical life reveals itself in the very diversity that it has brought forth.

Two kinds of influence determine the history of an institution. Some are internal: impulses that spring from the nature of the institution and whose driving force propels it along its historical course. Others are intellectual influences from the outside, enriching and fecundating the original nucleus of ideas, and thus bringing about its historical evolution. Impulses of the former kind were not lacking in Islam, but the most important stages in its history were characterized by the assimilation of foreign influences. The dogmatic development of Islam took place under the sign of Hellenistic thought; in its legal system the influence of Roman law is unmistakable; the organization of the Islamic state as it took shape during the 'Abbāsid caliphate shows the adaptation of Persian political ideas; Islamic mysticism made use of Neoplatonic and Hindu habits of thought. In each of these areas Islam demonstrates its ability to absorb

---

in the Qur'ān itself and is commonly accepted among Muslims. Recently, however, scholars have attempted to find other explanations for the term. See, for example, M. Lidzbarski, "Salām und Islām," *Zeitschrift für Semitistik*, I (1922), 88; M. Abdel Razek, "Le Mot Islam, son sense primitif et son évolution," *Actes du 18e Congrès International des Orientalistes* (Leiden, 1932), pp. 225-26; H. Ringgren, *Islam, 'Aslama and Muslim* (Lund, 1949); M. M. Bravmann, *The Spiritual Background of Early Islam*, pp. 7-25; D.Z.H. Baneth, "What Did Muhammad Mean when He Called His Religion 'Islam'? The Original Meaning of Aslama and Its Derivatives," *Israel Oriental Studies*, I (1971), 183-90.

and assimilate foreign elements so thoroughly that their foreign character can be detected only by the exact analysis of critical research.

With this receptive character Islam was stamped at its birth. Its founder, Muhammad, did not proclaim new ideas. He did not enrich earlier conceptions of man's relation to the transcendental and infinite. None of this diminishes, however, the relative value of his religious achievement. When the historian of civilization appraises the effect of an historical phenomenon, the question of originality does not claim his principal attention. In an historical evaluation of Muhammad's work the issue is not whether the contents of his revelation were a completely original, absolutely trail-blazing creation of his soul. The Arab Prophet's message was an eclectic composite of religious ideas[2] and regulations. The ideas were suggested to him by contacts, which had stirred him deeply, with Jewish, Christian, and other elements,[3] and they seemed to him suited to awaken an earnest religious mood among his fellow Arabs. The regulations too were derived from foreign sources; he recognized them as needed to institute life according to the will of God. The thoughts that so passionately roused him in his heart of hearts he conceived to be a divine revelation of which he was to be the instrument. External impressions and experiences confirmed this sincere conviction.

It is not our task to inquire into the pathological causes that awakened and confirmed Muhammad's sense of revelation.[c] Harnack's profound words come to mind about "diseases that only strike supermen who then draw from them new life never before suspected, energy that levels all hindrances in its path, and the zeal of the prophet or apostle."[4] We have

[2] This syncretistic character was most recently demonstrated by K. Vollers in an analysis of the Khaḍir legend in which he found, besides Jewish and Christian elements, late echoes also of Babylonian and Greek mythology. *Archiv für Religionswissenschaft*, XII (1909), 277ff.

[3] Recently Hubert Grimme stressed the influence of South Arabian ideas, especially in his *Mohammed* (Munich, 1904; Weltgeschichte in Karakterbildern, 2nd part) and in "Der Logos in Südarabien," *Nöldeke Festschrift*, I, 453ff.

[c] Here Goldziher is arguing against the view, still current in his time, that Muhammad's inspiration was in some sense pathological. An early form of this may be found in the medieval legend that the Prophet was an epileptic. This story, common in Byzantine and medieval Western writers, survived into modern times, when it was given a new and superficially scientific form allegedly derived from the "psychology of mysticism." For a discussion of this, see Tor Andrae, *Mohammed, the Man and His Faith*, translated by Theophil Menzel (London, 1936), pp. 67ff: for a discussion of more recent literature, see Maxime Rodinson, "Bilan des études mohammadiennes," *Revue Historique*, CCXXI (1963), 210-11.

[4] Adolf von Harnack, *Die Mission und Ausbreitung des Christentums in den ersten drei Jahrhunderten* (Leipzig, 1902), p. 93 top [4th ed. (Leipzig, 1924), I, 152; translated as *The Mission and Expansion of Christianity in the First Three Centuries* (London and New York, 1908), I, 126].

before us the vast historical effect of the Call to Islam, in the first place its effect on the milieu at which Muhammad's message was directly aimed. Its lack of originality is outweighed by the fact that for the first time, and with a tenacious solicitude, Muhammad proclaimed such teachings to be of an intimate concern to all; that he persisted, with a self-sacrificing endurance, in propagating them in the teeth of the arrogant scorn of the masses. For no history had been made by the quiet protest that religiously inclined men before Muhammad had expressed, more in their lives than their words, against the pagan Arab conception of life.[d] We do not know what kind of message was proclaimed by Khālid ibn Sinān, for example, the prophet whom "his people allowed to perish." The first historically effective reformer among the Arabs was Muhammad. Therein lies his originality, no matter how eclectic much of his prophecy may be.

The business he pursued in the first half of his life had brought him into various contacts. From these he acquired ideas that, in a period of contemplative retreat, he inwardly assimilated. He was a man given to somber brooding, and these ideas violently roused his conscience against his compatriots' ways in religion and ethics. The society into which he was born had its roots in Arab tribal life and customs. Its moral level was not appreciably raised by a primitive and yet bleak polytheism.[e] Mecca, the city where Muhammad was born and where he lived, played an outstanding role in the quasi-fetishist cult: it was one of its chief meeting places, for the Ka'ba, with the "black stone" in it, was a national sanctuary.

In addition, the dominant traits of the Meccan patricians were materialism and a plutocratic arrogance. Guardianship of the sanctuary was no mere religious privilege for them; it was also a major economic interest. The Qur'ān complains of the oppression of the poor; of greed; of dishonest dealing; of an ostentatious indifference to man's higher concerns and duties in life, to what is "good and enduring" in contrast to the "glitter of the world" (18:46). To these disquieting observations Muhammad now applied the impressions derived from earlier lessons still vivid in his

[d] This refers to the well-known group of people in pre-Islamic Arabia, described by the Muslim tradition, who were dissatisfied with ancient Arabian paganism yet unwilling to accept either Judaism or Christianity. They are seen as a kind of prefigurement of the advent of Islam. For a discussion, see H.A.R. Gibb, "Pre-Islamic Monotheism in Arabia," *Harvard Theological Review*, LV (1962), 269–80.

[e] Some scholars have taken a more positive view of pre-Islamic paganism. See, for example, Tor Andrae, *Mohammed*, pp. 167ff.

mind. He was forty years old. He was in the habit of retiring to the caverns of the mountains near Mecca, and in their desolation he felt the call of God ever more imperiously bidding him in vision, waking dream, and hallucination, to go among his people and warn them of the ruin to which their conduct must lead. He was now irresistibly driven to become the moral teacher of his people, the one to "warn and exhort them."

3. At the beginning of his career these meditations found release in eschatological images whose grip on his mind ever grew in intensity. They were, so to speak, the *idée mère* of his prophecy. He had heard of the judgment that would some day burst upon the world, and what he had heard he now applied to the circumstances that filled his soul with dread. Against the unconcerned and arrogant conduct of the overbearing Meccan plutocrats, to whom humility was unknown, Muhammad proclaimed the prophecy of approaching Doomsday, resurrection and last reckoning, all painted in fiery brushstrokes. His enthusiast's visions offered a terrifying picture of the details. God is the judge of the world, the sole ruler of the day of judgment, who in His mercy leads forth from the wreck of the destroyed world the small company of those who obeyed, who did not confront the warner's anguished cry with scorn and ridicule but repented, ceased to glory in the power that accrues from earthly possessions, and hastened to recognize their dependence on the boundless might of the one God of the world. Muhammad's call to repentance and submission derives, first and foremost, from his eschatological ideas.[5]

It was a consequence, not a cause, of this visionary consciousness that Muhammad rejected the polytheism of the pagans; for polytheism fragments and diminishes the limitless omnipotence of God. The beings thought of as Allah's associates "cannot benefit and cannot harm." There is but one Lord of the Last Day; He alone pronounces judgment, without associates, circumscribed by nothing and accountable to no one. A feeling of such absolute dependency as Muhammad was gripped by could be owed only to one being: the one God, Allah. But the terrifying images of judgment—most of whose features were furnished by ideas current in the Apocrypha—are not balanced by hopes of an approaching kingdom of heaven. Muhammad warns of the end of the world, the *dies irae*. His eschatology is entirely pessimistic in its vision of the world. Not until they enter Paradise will the elect see the brighter side. For this world no ray of hope remains.

[5] "Die Religion des Islams," *Die Orientalischen Religionen* (Berlin and Leipzig, 1906; Part I, Section iii, 1, in Paul Hinneberg's *Die Kultur der Gegenwart*), p. 94:12-23 from bottom.

Thus it was with borrowed blocks that Muhammad built his eschatological message. He made use of Old Testament history (mostly in haggadic form), citing from it admonitory examples of the fate of ancient peoples who opposed and scoffed at the warners sent to them. Muhammad now placed himself at the end of this chain of prophets; he was its final link.

The pictures, painted with a fiery palette, of the end of the world and the last judgment, the admonitions to prepare for these events by forsaking godlessness and worldliness, the stories of the fate of ancient peoples and of their behavior toward the prophets sent to them, the invitation to consider the creation of the world and the wondrous manner in which man is fashioned as proofs of the omnipotence of God and of the dependency of His creatures whom He can annihilate and bring back to life as He sees fit—these are contained in the oldest part of the book of revelations known to world literature by its Arabic name as the Qur'ān (Recitation). The whole book comprises 114 sections (suras) which vary greatly in length. Approximately a third of the 114 stem from the first decade of Muhammad's prophetic activity, from the period of his work in Mecca.

4. I shall not recount the details of his successes and failures. The first turning point in the history of Islam was the year 622. Derided by the people of his tribe and his city, Muhammad emigrated to the northern city of Yathrib, where the population, of south Arabian stock, appeared more receptive to religious ideas. Because of a sizable Jewish population in Yathrib, the ideas of Muhammad's prophecy were more familiar, or at least not quite as alien, to these Arabs, as they had been to the Meccans. In consequence of the help and welcome that the people of Yathrib extended to Muhammad and his companions, Yathrib became Medina, "The City (of the Prophet)." It has been known by that name ever since. It was here that the Holy Spirit continued to inspire Muhammad, and the great majority of the suras of the Qur'ān bear the stamp of his new home.

He did not cease to feel and practice the vocation of "warner" in his new surroundings, but prophecy took a new course. The Prophet was no longer a mere apocalyptic visionary. New circumstances had turned him into a fighter, a conqueror, a statesman. He organized the new and ever-growing community. Islam as an institution received new form in Medina: it was here that the first lineaments of Islamic society, law, and political order began to appear.

The revelations Muhammad proclaimed in Mecca did not yet establish a new religion; they created a religious mood within a small circle of people. They nourished a world view that was devout but not amenable to precise definition, and whose forms and doctrines showed as yet no fixed outline. Pious mood found expression in ascetic practices that could be encountered among Jews and Christians as well: in devotions (recitations with genuflections and prostrations), voluntary privations (fasting), and acts of charity. But there was as yet no body of rules to determine the form, time, and extent of these activities. Nor were the boundaries of the community of believers clearly drawn. It was in Medina that Islam became an institution. It also became a fighting organization whose trumpet has echoed through all the later history of Islam. Only yesterday Muhammad had been resigned and long-suffering, preaching patience and perseverance to his handful of faithful companions who had to endure the scorn of the Meccan patricians. Now he organized military expeditions. He had disdained earthly possessions; now he set about regulating the distribution of plunder and fixing the laws of inheritance and property. He did not, it is true, cease to speak of the vanity of earthly things. But in the meantime laws were laid down; institutions were created for religious practices and for the most pressing circumstances of social life. The rules of conduct that served as the foundation of later jurisprudence found their definite form here, although some of them had been prepared by the Meccan revelations and brought in rudimentary form to the north Arabian date-palm oasis by the Meccan immigrants.[6]

Islam proper was born in Medina: its historical aspects took shape here. Whenever in Islam a need has been felt for religious reconstruction, people have looked to the *sunna* (traditional usage) of Medina, the Medina in which Muhammad and his Companions first began to give palpable form to life in the spirit of Islam. We shall have occasion to return to this subject.

Thus in the history of Islam the date of the Hijra (emigration to Medina) was of importance in other ways besides marking a change in the outward destinies of the community. The year 622 is not merely the date after which the Prophet's small band of adherents, having found safe haven, could turn upon their opponents and take the offensive in the struggle—a struggle crowned with the conquest of Mecca in 630, and with the subsequent submission of all Arabia. The year 622 signaled a turning point in the evolution of Islam as a religion.

The Medinese period also brought an essential change in the Prophet's

[6] *Ibid.*, p. 95:12 from bottom ff.

sense of his own character. In Mecca he saw himself as a prophet summoned to take his place alongside the Biblical prophets and, as they had done, to warn his fellow men and rescue them from perdition. In Medina his goals changed with his circumstances. The background was no longer what it had been in Mecca; in his prophetic vocation new considerations came to the fore. He now demanded recognition as the renewer of Abraham's religion, as its restorer from distortion and decay. His prophecy became interwoven with Abrahamic traditions. The form of worship he instituted had been established, so he saw it, by Abraham; it had in time become corrupt and at length taken an idolatrous course. Muhammad's goal was now to reestablish the *dīn* of the one God, in the Abrahamic spirit; in fact his very mission was to reaffirm (*muṣaddiq*) what God had made known in previous revelations.[7]

Muhammad's sense of his position and tasks as a prophet was now greatly influenced by his charge that the old revelations had been falsified and obscured. Time-serving converts no doubt reinforced his view that the adherents of the older religions had distorted their scriptures and suppressed passages in which prophets and evangelists had predicted his future coming. This accusation has its seeds in the Qur'ān, and bears abundant fruit in later Islamic literature. Polemics against Jews and Christians occupy a large part of the Medinese revelations. If in earlier passages the Qur'ān acknowledges that monasteries, churches, and synagogues are true places of worship (22:40), the later passages attack Muhammad's original teachers, the Christian *ruhbān* (monks) and the Jewish *aḥbār* (scholars of scripture). The Qur'ān expresses displeasure at the undeserved but nearly divine authority they exercise over their followers (9:31), self-seeking men though they are who divert people from the way of God (9:34). On another occasion, however, the Qur'ān sees merit in the humble conduct of the ascetic *ruhbān*, and finds that they have a fellow feeling for the Muslims and stand nearer them than the Jews do who reject Islam absolutely (5:82). The Qur'ān reproaches the Jewish *aḥbār* for their additions to the divine law (3:78).

[7] This development was demonstrated by C. Snouck Hurgronje in his first publication, *Het Mekkaansche Feest* (Leiden, 1880), [pp. 29ff. = *Verspreide Geschriften*, I, 22ff.; translated in *Oeuvres choisies de C. Snouck Hurgronje* (Leiden, 1957), pp. 186ff. This thesis by Snouck Hurgronje acquired some notoriety when it was set forth by another Dutch scholar, A. J. Wensinck, in the article "Ibrāhīm," in *EI*[1]. This brought denials and denunciations from some Muslims who saw it as an attack on their faith, and also some scholarly criticism from scholars who were not convinced by Snouck Hurgronje's arguments. For a discussion of the question and the literature to which it has given rise, see the article "Ibrāhīm" (by R. Paret) in *EI*[2]].

In sum, the decade in Medina was a time of defense and assault, with word and sword.

5. The change in Muhammad's prophetic character unavoidably left its mark on the style and rhetoric of the Qur'ān. With sound intuition, the earliest transmitters of the book already drew a clear distinction between the two component parts—Meccan and Medinese—of the 114 suras into which the matter of the Qur'ān is arranged.

Such a chronological distinction is on the whole justified by a critical and esthetic examination of the Qur'ān. To the Meccan period belong the revelations that express the creations of the Prophet's fiery tumult in a visionary style, in speech that flows from his very soul. In these he has no sword to rattle, no warriors and subjects to address. To the host of his adversaries he avers his passionate conviction of the unbounded omnipotence of Allah in His creation and government of the world. He assures them of the approach of the dreadful day of judgment and the end of the world, the visions of which leave him no rest. He bears witness to the chastisement of bygone nations and tyrants who set themselves against the warners God had dispatched to them.

In the Medinese revelations the primal prophetic power gradually goes slack. At times they sink to the level of everyday prose, their rhetoric rendered colorless by the commonplace character of the matters with which they have to deal. The Prophet is shown as calculating and deliberating with care. He becomes subtly cautious and wise in the ways of the world as he agitates against the internal and external opponents of his aims. He organizes the faithful, he promulgates (as I have mentioned already) a civil and religious law for the organization that is taking shape, he provides rules for the practical circumstances of life. At times even his own personal and domestic concerns are drawn into the scope of revelation.[8] It does not make up for the flagging of rhetorical vigor that these parts of the Qur'ān employ *saj'*, the technique of rhyming clauses within long prose sentences. The old diviners too had made their utterances in that style. No Arab would have acknowledged them as coming from a

[8] This peculiarity did not go unnoticed by the Muslims themselves. Characteristic of it is the following report, attributed to Abū Ruhm al-Ghifārī, a Companion of the Prophet. During one campaign, he was riding his camel next to the Prophet's, and at one point the two animals came so near each other that the rough rim of Abū Ruhm's sandal scraped against the Prophet's thigh, causing him great pain. The Prophet gave expression to his displeasure, and struck Abū Ruhm's foot with his crop. Abū Ruhm was seized with anxiety. "I feared," he reported, "that a Qur'ān passage would be revealed about me because of the enormity of what I had done." Ibn Sa'd, *Ṭabaqāt*, IV, i, 180:4-9.

divine source if they had been cast in any other form. Muhammad affirmed to the end the divine origin of his utterances. But what a difference between the *saj'* of the early Meccan and the Medinese utterances! In Mecca Muhammad's visions find expression in a *saj'* whose segments follow one upon the other like the feverish beating of his heart. In Medina the literary form of the revelation is the same, but it no longer has the same verve and power, not even when it comes back to deal with the topics of the Meccan prophecy.[9]

Muhammad himself declared that the Qur'ān was an inimitable work. Muslims recognize no gradations of value in the style of the book,[10] but consider it a miracle of God communicated by the Prophet: the supreme miracle proving that his was a truly divine mission.

6. The Qur'ān is thus the foundation of the religion of Islam, its scripture, its revealed document. In its entirety, it represents an amalgam of the two essentially heterogeneous periods that form the infancy of Islam.

Neither their cast of mind nor their way of life was likely to fix the eyes of the ancient Arabs on otherworldly values. But the triumphs that the Prophet and his first successors gained against the adversaries of Islam strengthened the Arabs' belief in him and his mission. The Arabs were not a nation: they were splintered into tribes. They were not a religious group: such central places of worship as existed merely assured a loose linking of the local cults, each cult going its own way. The immediate historical effect of the early triumphs of Islam was to bind together more firmly a large part of these divergent groups, although it is wrong to think (as is still often done) that success brought about the

[9] Cf. Theodor Nöldeke, *Geschichte des Qorāns* (Göttingen, 1860), p. 49; new ed. by Friedrich Schwally et al. (Leipzig, 1909-1938), I, 63. [In his discussion of the Qur'ān, Goldziher is following the view sketched by Nöldeke and developed by Schwally, which has reigned among Orientalists until our own time. More recently, it has been challenged on three fronts—by Muslim scholars, by Soviet Marxists, and by a new wave of Western critical scholarship. On the background and earlier history of this field of study, see R. Blachère, *Introduction au Coran*, 2nd ed. (Paris, 1959), especially pp. 247ff.; N. A. Smirnov, *Očerki Istorii Izučeniya Islama v SSSR* (Moscow, 1954; abridged translation and analysis in *Islam and Russia*, with an introduction by A.K.S. Lambton, London, 1956); for more recent views, see J. Wansbrough, *Qur'ānic Studies* (London, 1977); John Burton, *The Collection of the Qur'ān* (Cambridge, 1977).]

[10] Muslim theologians do not, however, disallow the possibility that certain parts of the Qur'ān may be more important in their contents than others. This view, accepted also by the orthodox, is set forth by Taqī al-Dīn ibn Taymīya (whose name will be mentioned again in the course of these lectures) in a special work: *Jawāb ahl al-īmān fī tafāḍul āy al-Qur'ān* (Cairo, A.H. 1322). Cf. *GAL*, II, 104, no. 19 [not mentioned in the 2nd ed.; see *GAL*, SII, 122, no. 35].

complete unification of the Arabs.[11] The Prophet set up the ideal of amalgamation into a single ethical and religious community. The Qur'ān taught that the group should be held together by its sense of dependency on Allah, the one God. "O you who believe! Fear God as is His due, and do not die except as Muslims. Hold fast, all of you together, to Allah's rope, and do not separate. Remember Allah's beneficence to you, for you were enemies but He composed your hearts so that by His favor you have become brothers" (3:102-103). From now on, fear of God was to give one man precedence over another; genealogy and tribal considerations would have no role to play. The range of this idea of unity widened more and more after the Prophet's death. It was extended by conquests whose success it is difficult to match in world history.

7. If any part of Muhammad's religious achievement may be called original, it is the part of his prophecy directed against the status quo. It did away with all the barbarous abominations in the cult and society of the pagan Arabs, in their tribal life, in their world view. It put an end to the *jāhilīya*, "barbarism,"[f] as the Qur'ān calls pagan, as opposed to Islamic, ways. On the other hand, the Prophet's doctrines and institutions were, as we have seen, of an eclectic character. Judaism and Christianity furnished constituent elements in equal measure. I cannot now discuss these in detail.[12] It is well known that there are five points that in their

[11] Cf. R. Geyer in *WZKM*, XXI (1907), 400.

[f] The term *jāhilīya* is commonly translated "The Age of Ignorance," from the Arabic root *j-h-l*. Goldziher's rendering of this term by the word barbarism instead of ignorance is justified by him in an excursus to his *Muhammedanische Studien*, I, 219-28 (= *Muslim Studies*, I, 201-208).

[12] For the Jewish elements, now see A. J. Wensinck's dissertation *Mohammed en de Joden te Medina* (Leiden, 1908) [translated as *Muhammad and the Jews of Medina* (Freiburg im Breisgau, 1975)]. Primarily concerned with later developments, but instructive also for the earliest period, is C. H. Becker, *Christentum und Islam* (Tübingen, 1907; Religionsgeschichtliche Volksbücher, Mohr, Series 3, Fascicule 8) [= *Islamstudien*, I, 386ff.; translated as *Christianity and Islam* (London, 1909)].

[The whole question of external influences in Islam has formed the subject of an extensive literature. Some scholars stress the importance of Jewish influences; others of Christian influences; others again dismiss both. For a discussion of some of the literature on the subject, see Maxime Rodinson, "Bilan," pp. 211ff.

More recently there has been a certain reaction even among Western scholars against the tendency to attribute everything in Islam to pre-Islamic—Jewish, Christian, or other—origins, and several articles by Western scholars have reasserted the originality of the Islamic revelation. See, for example, Johannes Fück, "Die Originalität des arabischen Propheten," *ZDMG*, XC (1936), 509-25, and Gustave von Grünebaum, "Von Muhammed's Wirkung und Originalität," *WZKM*, XXIV (1937), 29-50. Goldziher himself is quoted as remarking, "What would be left of the Gospels if the Qur'ānic method were applied to them?"]

fully developed form serve as the foundation pillars of the Muslim religion. Their first outlines—the liturgical and humanitarian ones—began to appear in the Meccan period, but they received fixed form only in Medina. The five are: 1) the profession of faith in the one God, and the acknowledgment that Muhammad is the messenger of God; 2) the ritual of the prayer service (which began in the form of vigils and recitations that show a link to the traditions of eastern Christianity, as do such accompanying features as genuflection, prostration, and preliminary washing); 3) alms, which had originally been a matter of voluntary charity, but later became a contribution payable in fixed amounts toward the needs of the community; 4) fasting, originally on the tenth day of the first month (in imitation of the Jewish Day of Atonement, *'āshūrā*), later during Ramaḍān, the ninth month in the lunar calendar; 5) pilgrimage to the Ka'ba, the house of God, the old Arab national sanctuary in Mecca.[13] This last element the Qur'ān retains from the pagan cult, but gives it a monotheistic turn and reinterprets it in the light of Abrahamic legends.

The Christian elements of the Qur'ān reached Muhammad mostly through the channel of apocryphal traditions and through heresies scattered in the eastern Church. In the same way, more than a few elements of eastern Gnosticism are represented in Muhammad's message. He was receptive to all sorts of ideas brought his way by the superficial contacts of business dealings, and he turned these ideas to account in a largely unsystematic way. How different from his customary conception of God is the mystical tone of the utterance known to Muslims as the "light-verse" (24:35)![14] A Gnostic tendency (prevalent among Marcionites, etc.) to

[13] For this summary statement of the five principal obligations, cf. Bukhārī *Īmān* no. 37, *Tafsīr* no. 208, which also contains the oldest formulation of the Muslim creed. It would contribute to our knowledge of the earliest development of the doctrine of Islamic obligations to examine which obligations are listed in the ancient documents, from period to period, as pillars of faith and religious practice. Here we will mention only one example. In a saying ascribed to Muhammad, a sixth is added to the five points enumerated in the text and recognized from an early age as the roots of Islam: "Do to people what you would have them do to you; keep from doing to people what you would dislike being done to you" (Ibn Sa'd, VI, 37:12ff.; Ibn al-Athīr, *Usd al-ghāba*, Cairo, A.H. 1285-1286, III, 266, cf. p. 275 of the same group). This last doctrine frequently occurs elsewhere as well, without being linked to other themes, as a self-contained maxim of the Prophet. No. 13 in the *Forty Traditions* [*Al-Arba'ūn ḥadīthan*, various numbered editions] of Nawawī (after Bukhārī and Muslim [see A. J. Wensinck, *Concordance et indices de la tradition musulmane*, I, 407]): "No one among you is a believer until he desires for his brother what he desires for himself." Cf. Ibn Qutayba, *Kitāb al-ma'ārif*, edited by Ferdinand Wüstenfeld (Göttingen, 1850), p. 203:13 [edited by Tharwat 'Ukāsha (Cairo, 1960), p. 399]. For a similar saying of 'Alī ibn Ḥusayn, see Ya'qūbī, *Ta'rīkh*, edited by M. T. Houtsma (Leiden, 1883), II, 364:6.

[14] Now cf. Martin Hartmann, *Der Islam* (Leipzig 1909), p. 18.

look down on Mosaic law as an emanation of the stern God who has turned away from kindness filters through the Qur'ānic view of the Jews' God-given laws: God imposed dietary laws on the Jews in punishment for their disobedience. Almost all these dietary laws are abrogated by Islam. God has not ordered the believers to abstain from any tasty thing. Those statutes were burdens and shackles that God had laid on the Israelites (2:286, 4:160, 7:157). This echoes Marcionite speculations, although it is not identical with them. Moreover the theory of a pure primeval religion which it is the Prophet's task to reestablish, and the assumption that the scriptural texts have been tampered with, are very close to, although more rudimentary than, the complex of ideas related to the Marcionite speculation and known from Clement's homilies.

Besides Jews and Christians, Zoroastrians (*majūs*, Magians) also came under Muhammad's observation, and the Qur'ān groups the Zoroastrians with them rather than with the pagans. This religion too did not fail to leave its mark on the receptive mind of the Arab Prophet. One important stimulus he received from Zoroastrianism was to deny that the Sabbath was a day of rest.[g] The Qur'ān institutes Friday as the day of weekly assembly, but while it accepts the idea of creation in six days, it firmly rejects the notion that God rested on the seventh. Therefore the sixth and not the seventh day was instituted as the day of congregation. Since it was not a day of rest, it was permissible after the conclusion of the religious service to engage in all manner of secular business.[15]

8. If we now wish to view Muhammad's achievement in its entirety and to speak of its intrinsic value from the point of view of its moral effects, we must banish from our minds all apologetic and polemical considerations. Even modern authors are tempted in their descriptions of Islam to disparage its religious worth, because they apply criteria of value preconceived as absolute, and they judge Islam by its relation to that ab-

[g] Goldziher's attribution of this idea to Persian influence, tacitly assumed in this text and defended at length in the article cited in the following note, is no longer generally accepted by scholars. The notion that the Creator did not rest on the seventh day, which should not therefore be treated as a day of idleness, is to be found in the Syrian St. Ephraim as well as in some of the Western church fathers. See V. Aptowitzer, "Arabisch-Jüdische Schöpfungstheorien," *Hebrew Union College Annual*, VI (1929), 239 n. 117; Heinrich Speyer, *Die biblischen Erzählungen im Qoran* (Gräfenhainichen n.d.; repr. Hildesheim, 1961), p. 23. See further S. D. Goitein, *Studies in Islamic History and Institutions* (Leiden, 1966), chapter V, "The origin and Nature of the Muslim Friday Worship," pp. 111-25.

[15] Cf. my essay "Die Sabbathinstitution im Islam," *Gedenkbuch zur Erinnerung an David Kaufmann* (Breslau, 1900), pp. 89, 91 [partial French translation in *Arabica*, VII (1960), 237ff.].

solute. Such people call the Islamic conception of God primitive because it inflexibly rejects the notion of immanence. They find Islamic ethics perilous because in it the principle of obedience and submissiveness (as evidenced by the very name Islam) prevails. Such people would seem to believe that because of the Muslim's conviction that he is subject to an inviolable divine law, and because of his belief in the utter otherness of God, he is kept from drawing closer to God and from being brought into God's mercy through faith, virtue, and good works (Qur'ān 9:99). They think that religio-philosophical formulas can serve to classify and analyze the inward devotion of the pious worshiper, humbly conscious of his dependency, weakness, and helplessness, as he lifts up his soul in prayer toward the almighty source of all power and perfection.

Those who appraise the religions of others by their subjective yardstick of values should be reminded of the wise words of the theologian A. Loisy (1906): "It may be said of every religion that it has an absolute value in the consciousness of its adherent, and a relative value in the mind of the philosopher and the critical observer."[16] This has often been overlooked in evaluations of the effect of Islam on its believers. Further, people have unjustly held Islam answerable for moral defects or instances of intellectual backwardness that in fact stem from the situation of the peoples among whom Islam has spread.[17] Islam bridled the rude habits of those peoples; it certainly did not cause them. Moreover, Islam is not an abstraction that can be pried loose from its manifestations and effects. These have varied with the periods of its historical evolution, with the geographic areas of its expansion, and with the ethnic characters of its adherents.

To prove the slight moral and religious worth of Islam, people have also adduced facts about the language in which the teachings of Islam were first cast. It has been said, for example, that Islam lacks the ethical concept we call "conscience," and it has been offered in evidence that "neither in the Arabic itself nor in any other Muḥammadan language is there a word which *properly* expresses what we mean by *conscience*."[18] In other areas, too, such reasoning can easily mislead. The assumption has

[16] *Revue critique d'histoire et de littérature*, new series, LXII (1906), 307.

[17] See C. H. Becker's excellent remarks in the article "Ist der Islam eine Gefahr für unsere Kolonien?" *Koloniale Rundschau* (May 1909), pp. 290ff. [= *Islamstudien*, II, 156ff.]. Cf. also "L'Islam et l'état marocain," by Ed. Michaux-Bellaire, *RMM*, VIII (1909), 313ff., for a refutation of the widespread assumption that the principles of Islam present an obstacle to political progress.

[18] William Tisdall, *The Religion of the Crescent*, 2nd ed. (London, 1906), p. 62.

proved prejudiced that a word is the only reliable witness to the existence of a concept. "Lack of a thing in language is not necessarily a sign that the thing is lacking in the heart."[19] Were it not so, one could cogently assert that the concept of thankfulness was unknown to the authors of the Vedas, because the verb "to thank" does not occur in Vedic.[20] Already in the ninth century, the Arab scholar al-Jāḥiẓ refuted a remark by a dilettante friend who thought he could find proof of the Greeks' avaricious character in the alleged lack of a Greek equivalent for *jūd* (generosity). He also showed the fallacious reasoning of others who argued that the absence of a word for "sincerity" (*naṣīḥa*) from the Persian language was an infallible demonstration of the innate Persian affinity for deceit.[21]

The evidence of ethical maxims, of principles reflecting ethical consciousness, must be regarded as more conclusive than the evidence of a word or technical term; and there are indeed Islamic maxims that bear on the question of conscience. The following is cited in the *Forty Traditions* (actually forty-two) of al-Nawawī, a book intended as a compendium of the essentials of religion for the true Muslim. It is no. 27, a saying taken from the most reliable collections: "In the name of the Prophet. Virtue is (the sum of) good qualities. Sin is that which perturbs the soul and which you do not want other people to know about you." Wābiṣa ibn Maʿbad relates: "Once I came to the Prophet and he said: 'You have come to ask me about virtue' [*birr*]. I said 'Yes.' He said: 'Question your heart [lit. ask your heart for a *fatwā*, a legal opinion]. Virtue is that which brings heart and soul tranquillity and sin is that which throws perturbation into the soul and makes the heart flutter, no matter what people may say.' " "Lay your hand on your chest and question your heart. Whatever disquiets your heart you should keep from doing." According to Islamic tradition, Adam imparted the same teaching to his children before his death, concluding with ". . . as I approached the forbidden tree I felt a perturbation

[19] G. M. Sproat, *Scenes and Studies of Savage Life* (London, 1868), [p. 165], quoted in Edvard A. Westermarck, *The Origin and Development of the Moral Ideas* (London, 1906-1908), II, 160, with many examples. From the lack of an equivalent to the word "interesting" in Turkish and Arabic, the equally unjustifiable conclusion has been drawn that "intellectual curiosity" is lacking in the peoples who speak these languages. See Duncan B. MacDonald, *The Religious Attitude and Life in Islam* (Chicago, 1909), p. 121; and *ibid.*, p. 122, the quotation from *Turkey in Europe* by Odysseus [published in London, 1900 by Sir Charles Eliot under this pseudonym; MacDonald quotes from p. 98].

[20] Hermann Oldenberg, *Die Religion des Veda* (Berlin, 1894), p. 305:9 [translated as *La Religion du Véda* (Paris, 1903), p. 259].

[21] *Kitāb al-bukhalā'*, edited by G. van Vloten (Leiden, 1900), p. 212:3ff. [edited by Ṭaha al-Ḥājirī (Cairo, 1971), pp. 195-96].

in my heart," which is as much as saying "my conscience troubled me."

Fairness demands the admission that in the teachings of Islam, as of other religions, there is "a force working for the good:" that a life lived in the spirit of Islam can be an ethically impeccable life, demanding compassion for all God's creatures, honesty in one's dealings, love, loyalty, the suppression of selfish impulses, and all the other virtues that Islam derived from the religions whose prophets it acknowledges as its teachers. A true Muslim will lead a life that satisfies stringent ethical requirements.

To be sure, Islam is also a law; it requires from the believer the performance of ceremonial acts. But it is declared already in the earliest, fundamental, Islamic document, the Qur'ān—and not only in the traditional maxims that reflect the subsequent evolution of Islam—that the intention behind an act is the criterion for the religious value of the act, and that it is of little worth to observe the letter of the law without accompanying acts of compassion and charity toward one's fellow men. "Piety [*birr*] is not the turning of your faces east and west. He is pious who believes in Allah and the Last Day and the angels and the Book and the prophets, who for love of Him (*'alā ḥubbihi)*[h] gives his wealth to (poor) relatives, to the orphans and the needy, to travelers and supplicants, and to set captives free; who observes the prayer service and pays the levy for the poor. And those who keep their treaty if they conclude one, who are patient in suffering, adversity, and time of fearfulness. Such are those who are sincere; such are those who fear God" (2:177).

When the Qur'ān speaks of the rites of the pilgrimage that it institutes (that is, retains from the traditions of the heathen Arabs) because "we [Allah] have established sacrificial rites for every nation so that they may remember the name of Allah over the sustenance He has granted them," it stresses above all the devotion of mind that must accompany the ritual. "Their flesh and blood do not come to Allah; your fear of God comes to Him" (22:34, 37). The highest value is ascribed to *ikhlāṣ*, unclouded purity of heart (40:14); *taqwā al-qulūb*, "piety of heart" (22:32); *qalb salīm*, "a whole heart" (26:89) (which corresponds to the *lēbh shālēm* of the Psalms). Such are the criteria by which the believer's religious worth is assessed. As we shall see, these convictions are didactically elaborated in the maxims of tradition. They are extended over the entire range of reli-

[h] In the second edition of Goldziher's lectures, the editor—whether on the basis of Goldziher's notes is not clear—offers a different translation of the Qur'ānic text. In this the pronominal suffix is referred to the wealth instead of to God. The note refers to Sir Charles Lyall, "The Meaning of *'Alā ḥubbihi* in Qur. II, 172," *JRAS*, 1914, pp. 158–63.

gious life by the doctrine that *nīya*, the disposition or intention behind a religious act, serves to gauge the value of that act. According to this doctrine, a tincture of selfish or hypocritical motive deprives any good work of its value. Thus no unprejudiced observer will accept the Reverend Tisdall's dictum that "it will be evident that purity of heart is neither considered necessary nor desirable: in fact it would be hardly too much to say that it is impossible for a Muslim."[22]

Moreover, what is the "steep path" (perhaps to be compared to Matt. 7:13, the "straight gate" that leads unto life) trodden by the "companions of the right hand," that is to say, those who will obtain the delights of Paradise? That path does not mean merely a life sanctimoniously spent in ceremonial acts and in the observance of all rites and formalities of external worship. It also requires, insofar as good works are concerned, "to free a captive, to feed on the day of hunger a closely related orphan or a poor wretch lying in the dust; moreover, to be one of those who believe and exhort one another to perseverance and exhort one another to mercy: these are the companions of the right hand" (90:13-18, a version of Isaiah 58:6-9).

In the next chapter we shall discuss the way in which the teachings of the Qur'ān are supplemented and further developed in a large number of traditional maxims. These are essential for a characterization of the spirit of Islam, even though they do not in fact go back to the Prophet himself. We have already made use of some of them in our discussion. Since the task of this first introductory chapter has taken us beyond the Qur'ān, to the ethical evaluation of Islam as a historical phenomenon, we must not neglect this opportunity to show that the principles set forth in the Qur'ān in rudimentary but sufficiently distinct form were developed in more definite fashion in a large number of later maxims that were ascribed to the Prophet.

Muhammad teaches Abū Dharr the following: "A prayer in this mosque (in Medina) equals a thousand prayers performed in any other except the one in Mecca. A prayer performed in the mosque in Mecca is worth a hundred thousand times more than a prayer in any other mosque. But there is something worth more than all these: the prayer spoken by a person in his own house where no one but Allah sees him, without any purpose other than his desire to approach God" (cf. Matt. 6:6). Elsewhere Muhammad is cited as saying: "Shall I tell you what is of

[22] Tisdall, *Religion of the Crescent*, p. 88.

higher worth than all praying, fasting, and alms-giving? It is reconciling two enemies." 'Abdallāh ibn 'Umar says: "If you bow in prayer so much that your body becomes crooked as a saddle, and fast so much that you become thin as a bowstring, God will not accept it from you until you have joined humility to these things." "What is the best kind of Islam?" The Prophet replies: "The best kind of Islam is that you should feed the hungry and spread peace among those you know and those you do not know (that is, in the whole world)." "What use is abstention from food and drink when somebody fails to abstain from falsehood?" "No one wrongs his fellow man and enters Paradise." Abu Hurayra relates: "Someone told the Prophet of a woman famed for prayer, fasting, and alms-giving, who however often injured people with her tongue. 'She is bound for Hell,' the Prophet declared. The same man then told of another woman, notorious for neglecting prayer and fasting, but who was in the habit of giving *laban* (coagulated sour milk) to the needy and never injured anyone. 'She is bound for Paradise.' "

It would be easy to compile a large number of such sayings. They are not the private views of ethically disposed people, but represent the common feeling of Islamic didacticism, and were perhaps intended polemically against the rising tide of sanctimonious, outward piety. They nowhere suggest that salvation depends only on compliance with legal formalities. Time and time again, the life that is pleasing to God is summed up as "belief in God and works of piety," meaning works of love for one's fellow man. When details of formally fixed religious conduct are mentioned, little else is emphasized besides *ṣalāt*, that is, the communal liturgy expressing submission to the omnipotence of Allah, and *zakāt*, help with the concerns of the commonwealth by material participation in the obligatory alms-tax.

Among those concerns, it was chiefly care for the poor, for widows, orphans, and wayfarers that stirred the lawgiver's sense of duty. To be sure, in its later development, under foreign influence, Islam allowed casuist subtleties and theological hairsplitting to be grafted onto it; it permitted speculative cleverness to strain and distort its faith and God-fearing piety. In the next two chapters (II and III) we shall witness the course of such developments. Later on, however, we shall once again encounter efforts and aspirations that represent a reaction in Islam against such excrescences.

9. Now some remarks about the less attractive side. Were Islam to keep strictly to the testimony of history, there is one thing with which it could

not provide the faithful on their moral journey through life: an *imitatio* of Muhammad. But it is not the historical picture that works on the believers' imagination. Very early on, historical fact was supplanted by the idealized Muhammad of pious legend. Islamic theology conformed to the postulate that the picture of the Prophet must show him as more than a mechanical organ of divine revelation and of its expansion among the unbelievers. He must appear as a hero and a prototype of supreme virtue.[23] Muhammad himself, it appears, wished nothing of the sort to hap-

[23] It is the most fervent aspiration of pious Muslims to imitate, in every least detail, Muhammad, whom legend has endowed with every perfection. Originally this imitation was concerned not so much with ethical issues as with the forms of ritual and the formal aspects of habitual acts. 'Abdallāh ibn 'Umar, who imposed it on himself thus to imitate the Prophet in all things (he was regarded as the most scrupulous follower of *al-amr al-awwal,* "the state of affairs at the beginning," Ibn Sa'd, IV, i, 106-22), made an effort in his travels always to make a stop where the Prophet used to, to pray wherever the Prophet had performed a prayer, and to make his camel kneel at the places where the Prophet had done the same. There was a tree under which the Prophet was said to have rested on one occasion. Ibn 'Umar used to water this tree, taking care that it should remain alive and should not wither (Nawawī, *Tahdhīb al-asmā'*, edited by Ferdinand Wüstenfeld, Göttingen, 1842-1847, p. 358). In the same spirit, people endeavor to imitate the habits of the Prophet's Companions. Their conduct is a model for the believers (Ibn 'Abd al-Barr al-Namarī, *Jāmi' bayān al-'ilm wa-faḍlihi*, edited by Aḥmad 'Umar al-Maḥmaṣānī, Cairo, A.H. 1326, p. 157). Such imitation is, indeed, the principle of all *sunna*. The theologians' picture of the Prophet's life assumes that the Prophet had himself held the view that every minute detail of his conduct in matters of religious practice would be regarded as *sunna* for the future. For this reason he once abstained from a certain action, lest the believers make it into *sunna* (Ibn Sa'd, II, i, 131:19).

It is only natural that Muhammad soon came to be regarded as an ethical model as well. On this there is an extensive literature. The Cordovan theologian Abū Muḥammad 'Alī ibn Ḥazm (d. 456/1069), known for his inflexible traditionalist position in theology and law, sums up this ethical requirement in his tractate on "The Conduct of Life and the Healing of Souls" (*Kitāb al-akhlāq wa'l-siyar fī mudāwāt al-nufūs*), which also deserves some attention because its author includes some *confessiones* in it: "If someone aspires to felicity in the next world and to wisdom in this, to righteousness in his conduct, to the encompassing of all good qualities, and to becoming adapted for all excellences, he should follow the example of the Prophet Muhammad and copy in practice, as much as possible, the Prophet's character and conduct. May God aid us with His favor that we might follow this example" (edited by Maḥmaṣānī, Cairo, 1908, p. 21).

People went even further. We may mention in this connection—although drawing on a sphere of ideas proper to a trend that we shall discuss in a subsequent section—that at a higher evolutionary stage of Islamic ethics, under the influence of Sufism (Chapter IV), it is set up as an ethical ideal that in his conduct man should strive to assimilate the qualities of God (*al-takhalluq bi-akhlāq Allāh*). Cf. τῷ θεῷ κατακολουθεῖν; *la-halōkh aḥar middōtāv shel haqqādōsh bārūkh hū* (Bab. *Sōṭā* 14a), *hiddabbēq bi-derākhāv* (*Sifrē*, Deuteronomy ‡ 49, edited by Meir Friedmann 85a:16).

Already the early Sufi Abū'l-Ḥusayn al-Nūrī sets this up as an ethical goal (Farīd al-Dīn 'Aṭṭār, *Tadhkirat al-awliyā'*, edited by R. A. Nicholson, London, 1905-1907, II, 55:1). It is as

pen. He was sent by God "as a witness, a messenger of good news and a warner, as a summoner to God by His permission, as a bright lamp" (33:45–46). He leads the way but he is no model except in hopefully looking to God and the last day, and in his diligent devotion (vs. 21). He seems to have been frankly aware of his human weaknesses. He wanted his believers to regard him as a man with all the defects of the common mortal. His work was more significant than his person. He did not feel that he was a saint and did not wish to be regarded as one.[i] We shall have occasion to return to this when we discuss the dogma of Muhammad's sinlessness. Perhaps it was his awareness of human weaknesses that caused Muhammad to have nothing to do with working miracles, for at his time and in his environment miracles were seen as a necessary attribute of saintliness. In studying Muhammad's character, we must examine how he went about accomplishing his mission, particularly in the Medinese period, when circumstances transformed the long-suffering ascetic into head of state and warrior. It is the merit of the Italian scholar Leone Caetani to have set in relief the secular aspects of the earliest history of Islam. In his great work, *Annali dell'Islam*, he performed a comprehensive critical examination of the Islamic historical sources, in a much more exact fashion than had been done previously. He has thus

---

an aspect of the imitation of God that Ibn 'Arabī requires the virtue of doing good to one's enemies ("The Lives of 'Umar Ibnu'l-Farid and Muhiyyu'ddin Ibnu'l-'Arabi," edited by R. A. Nicholson, *JRAS*, 1906, p. 819:10 [= Ibn al-'Imād, *Shadharāt al-dhahab* (Cairo, A.H. 1350-1351), V, 198]). In the introduction to his *Fātiḥat al-'ulūm* (Cairo, A.H. 1322), Ghazālī cites as a hadīth the maxim *takhallaqū bi-akhlāq Allāh*. Influenced by his Sufi view of religion, Ghazālī advances, as a summary of extensive previous discussion, the following doctrine: "The perfection and happiness of man consist in his endeavor to assume the qualities of God, and in his adorning himself with the true meaning of God's attributes." This is what lends importance to the profound study of the meaning of the divine names (*al-asmā' al-ḥusnā*); cf. Ghazālī's *Al-Maqṣad al-asnā* (Cairo, A.H. 1322), pp. 23ff. What Ismā'īl al-Fārīnī (ca. 1485) says about this in his commentary on al-Fārābī's *Al-Fuṣūṣ fī'l-ḥikma* (edited by M. Horten, *ZA*, XX, 1907, 350), is only a copy of Ghazālī's exposition. Incidentally, this formulation among Sufis of man's ethical goal is probably influenced by the Platonic view that the desired escape from the θνητὴ φύσις consists in ὁμοίωσις θεῷ κατὰ τὸ δυνατόν (*Theaetetus* 176b, *Republic* 613a). Following later Greek models, the Arab philosophers state that the practical aim of philosophy is "becoming like (*tashabbuh* = ὁμοίωσις) the Creator, in proportion as the powers of man allow." See al-Fārābī's *Risāla fīmā yanbaghī an yuqaddama qabla ta'allum al-falsafa*, edited by Friedrich Dieterici in *Alfārābīs philosophische Abhandlungen* (Leiden, 1890), p. 53:15, and frequently in the writings of the Ikhwān al-Ṣafā'. Sufism, however, goes one step further in its definition of the *summum bonum*, to which in due course we shall return. (See below, Ch. IV, Sec. 6 near the end.)

[i] For a major study of the progressive mythologization of Muhammad in the Muslim community, see Tor Andrae, *Die Person Muhammeds in Lehre und Glauben seiner Gemeinde* (Stockholm, 1917).

permitted us to make several essential modifications in our views of the Prophet's activity.

It is clear that the saying "more slayeth word than sword" cannot be applied to his work in the Medinese period. Emigration from Mecca put an end to the time when he was to "turn away from the idolaters" (15:94) or merely summon them "to the way of God through wisdom and good admonition" (16:125). It was now time for a different watchword: "When the sacred months are over, kill the idolaters wherever you find them; take them prisoner, lay siege to them, and wait for them in every ambush" (9:5); "fight in the way of God" (2:244).

From visions of the catastrophic end of this evil world Muhammad now evolved, with an abrupt transition, the conception of a realm that was of this world. The change was in some ways detrimental to his character. The great success of his mission, which changed the political complexion of Arabia, and the part he played as leader, rendered this inevitable. He brought the sword into the world; he did not merely "smite the earth with the rod of his mouth, and with the breath of his lips slay the wicked." The trumpet of war he sounded was real enough. Real blood clung to the sword he wielded to establish his realm. An Islamic tradition asserts that in the Torah Muhammad is given the epithet "Prophet of Struggle and War."[24] This is a correct assessment of his career.

The circumstances of the society upon which he felt divinely summoned to act were not of a sort to lull him into a relaxed confidence that "Allah will fight on your behalf; you may remain silent." To assure acknowledgment of his mission and even more of the supremacy of that mission, he had to go through a down-to-earth, matter-of-fact war. This down-to-earth, matter-of-fact war was the legacy his successors fell heir to. There was now no preference for peace: "O you who believe! Obey Allah and obey the messenger and do not cause your actions to come to nothing. . . . Do not weaken and invite (the unbelievers) to make peace when you hold the upper hand; and Allah is with you and will not reduce (the reward for) your deeds" (47:33, 35).

The struggle must go on until "God's word is supreme." To stay out of this struggle is an act of indifference to the will of God. A peaceable attitude toward the heathen, who keep people from the way of God, has nothing virtuous about it: "Those among the believers who sit still (that is, stay out of the fighting), other than those suffering from a disability,

[24] See "Neutestamentliche Elemente in der Traditionslitteratur des Islam,." *Oriens Christianus*, II (1902), 392 [= *Gesammelte Schriften*, IV, 317].

are not the equals of those who engage their wealth and their lives in zealous fight in the way of Allah. Allah has given a higher rank to those who fight, engaging their wealth and their lives, than to those who sit still. To all Allah has promised good, but He has distinguished those who fight zealously above those who sit still, with a great reward, degrees of rank from Him, and forgiveness, and mercy" (4:95-96).

10. This involvement with worldly concerns, this continued war footing that formed the setting of the second half of Muhammad's career not only drew the Prophet's character down into the sphere of worldliness, but also had an influence on the shaping of the higher concepts of his religion. War and victory had become the means and end of his prophetic vocation, and they did not fail to color the idea of God that he now wished to render supreme by military means. Certainly, it was in the mighty attributes proper to a monotheistic concept of divinity that his thought grasped the God "in whose way" he waged his wars and whose diplomacy he conducted. In this God absolute omnipotence, unlimited power to reward and punish, and severity toward obdurate malefactors join the attribute of compassion and clemency (*ḥalīm*). God is indulgent with sinners and forgiving to the repentant. "He has made compassion (*al-raḥma*) an inviolable law for Himself" (6:54). The following tradition seems a kind of commentary on this Qur'ān verse: "When God had completed creation, He wrote in the book that is kept by His side on the heavenly throne: 'My compassion overcomes my wrath.' "[25] Although He reaches with His punishment whom He will, His mercy encompasses all things (7:156). Nor is love missing from the attributes of God in the Qur'ān; Allah is *wadūd*, "loving." "If you love God, follow me, and God will love you and forgive your sins." However, "God does not love the unbelievers" (3:32).

But He is also the God of the struggle that, at His bidding, His Prophet and His Prophet's believers wage against the enemy. This attribute inevitably blended some petty mythological motifs into the Qur'ānic conception of God. It is as if the almighty Warrior needed to be on His guard against the intrigues and perfidious tricks of His enemies' malice, and needed constantly to defy them with means of the same mold, but more powerful. For according to an old Arabic proverb, "to wage war is to be crafty." "They devise stratagems—and I (too) devise stratagems" (86:15,

[25] Bukhārī, *Tawḥīd* nos. 15, 22, 28, 55. J. Barth cites this saying in a compilation of midrashic elements in Muslim tradition. *Berliner Festschrift*, p. 38, no. 6.

16). God calls the manner of punishment He uses against those who deny His revelations a "powerful stratagem:" "Those who call our revelations a lie—we will gradually bring them down, without their noticing it. I give them rein, for my stratagem is powerful" (68:44-45 = 7:182-83). In these examples the Arabic word is *kayd*, an innocuous kind of trickery and intrigue.[26] A stronger expression is *makr*, denoting a graver degree of cunning. Palmer translates it as "craft," "plot," or "stratagem" but the word also encompasses the notion of intrigue: "They intrigue, and Allah intrigues, and Allah is the best of intriguers" (8:30). This is the case not only in Muhammad's own time, with the enemies of God and His message who make known their hostile disposition by their resistance to, and persecution of, Muhammad. God is said to have behaved in like manner toward the heathen nations of the past who had scorned the prophets sent to them: toward the people of Thamūd who had rejected the messenger Ṣāliḥ (27:51), or toward the Midianites to whom Shu'ayb, the Biblical Jethro, had been sent (7:97-99).

It is not to be thought, of course, that the Qur'ān really represents Allah as a guileful intriguer. The likeliest sense of the cited threats is that God gives measure for measure,[27] that against God all human deviousness is futile, that God frustrates all acts of ill faith and dishonesty, and protects His faithful from cunning and treachery, by anticipating the wicked schemes of their enemies.[28] "God protects (against evil) those

[26] Some commentators understand in this sense Sura 13, vs. 13: *wa-huwa shahīd al-miḥāl*. Cf. Qālī, *Al-Amālī* (Būlāq, 1324), II, 272.

[27] Cf. Hermann Hupfeld, *Die Psalmen*, 2nd ed. edited by Eduard Riehm (Gotha, 1867-1871), commentary to Ps. 18:27.

[28] Such is the explanation of the frequent saying *Allāh yakhūn al-khā'in*, "Allah betrays the betrayer," Cf. *khada'atni khada'ahā Allāh*, "she has deceived me, may Allah deceive her": Ibn Sa'd, VIII, 167:25. In a menacing address to the mutinous Iraqis, Mu'āwiya, so it is reported, said: "Allah is mighty in onslaught and retribution; He deceives those who deceive him (*yamkuru bi-man makara bihi*)"; Ṭabarī, I, 2913:6.

While *makr* and *kayd*, thus ascribed to God, are meant to express nothing more than the baffling of the tricks of antagonists, the phrase *makr Allāh* has passed from the Qur'ān into Islamic linguistic usage and is used, without hesitation, in contexts to which this explanation cannot apply. A favorite Muslim supplication is: "We seek refuge with God from the *makr Allāh*," *na'ūdhu billāh min makr Allāh* (Shaykh al-Ḥurayfīsh, *Kitāb al-rawḍ al-fā'iq fī'l-mawā'iẓ wa'l-raqā'iq*, Cairo, A.H. 1310, pp. 10:16, 13:26). This belongs in the group of prayers by which one seeks God's help against God (*a'ūdhu bika minka*, cf. 'Aṭṭār, *Tadhkirat al-awliyā'*, II, 80:11; *minka ilayka*, see "Ueber eine rituelle Formel der Muhammedaner," *ZDMG*, XLVIII, 1894, 98f. [= *Gesammelte Schriften*, III, 345f.; partial French translation in *Arabica*, VII (1960), 249f.]). Among the prayers of the Prophet, whose text the believers are encouraged to use, the following entreaty is cited: "Help me, and do not help against me;

who believe; God does not love any treacherous unbeliever" (22:38). As the Qur'ān describes it, the fashion in which the Lord of the world reacts to the intrigues of malefactors mirrors Muhammad's own political approach to the obstacles in his way. His own disposition and his own method for combating internal enemies[29] are projected onto God who wages His Prophet's wars: "If you fear treachery from a people, fling it back at them in equal measure. Indeed, Allah does not love the treacherous. Do not think that the unbelievers will gain the advantage; they cannot weaken Allah" (8:58-59).[j]

This terminology shows, at all events, the attitude of mind of a diplomat carefully weighing matters rather than a man of meek perseverance. It must be emphasized that this terminology exerted no influence on Islamic ethics, which strictly rejects treachery (*ghadr*) even against unbelievers.[30] Nonetheless, Muhammad's conception of God did suffer the growth of some mythological excrescences once Allah had been lowered from His transcendental heights, to act as the collaborator of His Prophet caught up in the battles of this world.

Thus with the external progress of Muhammad's work a transition occurred. At the beginning of his prophetic career somber apocalyptic images had dominated his soul and message. These yielded to vigorous worldly aspirations which became dominant during the course of his successes. Thus historical Islam was stamped with the character of a combative religion, in contrast to the early years when there could be no envisioning a lasting polity in a world doomed to destruction. Muhammad left his immediate achievements within his Arabian sphere as a testament for the future of his community: to fight the unbelievers, to extend not so

---

practice *makr* to my benefit, and do not practice *makr* to my harm," *wa-mkur lī wa-lā tamkur 'alayya.* Nawawī, *Al-Adhkār* (Cairo, A.H. 1312), p. 175:6; cf. the hadith in Tirmidhī, *Ṣaḥīḥ* (Cairo, A.H. 1292), II, 272 [*Birr* no. 27; see Wensinck, *Concordance*, VI, 246]. This formula occurs in an even stronger version in the Shī'ī prayer book *Al-Ṣaḥīfa al-kāmila* (cf. *Nöldeke Festschrift*, I, 314 bottom [= *Gesammelte Schriften*, V, 43, referring to the edition of Lucknow, A.H. 1312; see *GAL*, SI, 76, no. 3]), p. 33:6—*wa-kid lanā wa-lā takid 'alaynā wa-mkur lanā wa-lā tamkur binā*. Cf. further the following saying: "Were one of my feet already planted in Paradise but the other still outside, I would not yet feel secure from the *makr Allāh*" (Subkī, *Ṭabaqāt al-shāfi'īya al-kubrā*, Cairo, A.H. 1324, III, 56:7 from bottom). Cf. 'Aṭṭār, *Tadhkirat al-awliyā'*, II, 178:21. The Muslims themselves understand these expressions to mean nothing more than the inexorable and severe punishment of God.

[29] Cf. particularly Ibn Sa'd, II, i, 31:14.

[j] A variant reading of this Qur'ānic verse would give the translation: "Let not the unbelievers think," etc. See Arthur Jeffery, *Materials for the History of the Text of the Qur'ān* (Leiden, 1937), pp. 44ff.

[30] Ibn Sa'd, IV, i, 26 top.

much the faith as the territory dominated by the faith, which was also the territory dominated by Allah. The warriors of Islam had as their immediate concern the subjugation, rather than conversion, of the unbelievers.[31]

11. Contradictory answers have been proposed to the question: were Muhammad's immediate intentions limited to his Arabian homeland, or did he hold a more comprehensive idea of his prophetic vocation? In other words, did he feel summoned as a prophet to his people or to the world?[32] In my view there is reason to incline toward the latter assumption.[33] There can of course be no doubt that the call he inwardly heard, the dread he felt at the damnation of the unrighteous, at first concerned his immediate environment, the contemplation of which had first made him sense his prophetic vocation. He heard God bid him "Warn your tribe of close kin" (26:214). He was sent "to warn the mother of cities and those who dwell around it" (6:92). There is no doubt, however, that already at the outset of his mission his mind's eye swept wider reaches, even though his limited geographic horizons could hardly enable him to surmise the outlines of a world religion. From the beginning, his view of his mission was that Allah sent him *raḥmatan li'l-'ālamīna*, "out of mercy to the worlds" (21:107). In the Qur'ān it is a stock description of God's teaching that it is *dhikrun li'l-'ālamīna*, "a reminder to the worlds" (εἰς τὸν κόσμον ἅπαντα. . . . Πάσῃ τῇ κτίσει, Mark 16:15). Cf. Qur'ān 12:104; 38:87; 68:52; 81:27.

The word *'ālamūn*, "worlds," is always used in the Qur'ān in an all-encompassing sense. God is "Lord of the *'ālamūn*." He has instituted the differences among the languages and colors of mankind as an instructive sign for the *'ālamūn* (30:22). Clearly all mankind is meant. Analogously, Muhammad saw his vocation as extending to all that, to his knowledge, this word defined. Naturally, the first objective had to be his own people and land. Near the end of his career, ambitions that passed beyond the world of Arabia appeared in his desire to establish relations with foreign powers, as well as in the military expeditions he ordered. As Nöldeke

[31] The earliest wars of Islam are seen from this point of view in Leone Caetani, *Annali dell'Islam* (Milan, 1905-1926), II, *passim*.

[32] Cf. now also Henri Lammens, *Études sur le règne du calife omaiyade Mo'āwia Ier* (Beirut, 1908), p. 422; also in *MFO*, III (1908), 286. Lammens rejects the theory of the original conception of Islam as a world religion.

[33] I agree in this with Nöldeke's view; cf. his review of Caetani's work, *WZKM*, XXI (1907), 307. Nöldeke stresses the Qur'ān passages in which Muhammad already senses in Mecca that he is a messenger and warner, *kāffatan li'l-nās*, "to all mankind."

remarks, his goals included areas where he could be sure to meet the Byzantines as enemies. The last campaign he bade his warriors undertake was a raid into Byzantine territory. There is no better commentary on Muhammad's own wishes than the great conquests embarked upon immediately after his death, and carried out by men who had best known his intentions.

In a varied series of sayings of the Prophet, Islamic tradition itself expresses Muhammad's awareness of having a mission to all mankind, "the red and the black."[34] The universal character of his mission is extended as far as possible.[35] Tradition represents the Prophet as expressing in so many words the thought of conquering the world, and as foreshadowing that conquest in symbolic acts. Tradition will go to the extent of recognizing in Qur'ān 48:16 an annunciation of the imminent conquest of the Iranian and Byzantine empires.[36] We cannot go so far. But even though we appraise the Muslim theologians' exaggerations critically, we may on the whole agree with them, on the strength of the indications I have referred to, that Muhammad already saw Islam as a power that would embrace a large portion of humanity, far beyond the borders of Arabia.

Its triumphant course in Asia and Africa began immediately after the passing of its founder.

12. It would be a great error if, in a comprehensive characterization of Islam, we considered the Qur'ān our most important source, and an even greater error if we based our opinion of Islam exclusively on the holy book of the Muslim community. The book covers at most the first two decades of the evolution of Islam. It remained, during the entire history of Islam, the fundamental work for the adherents of Muhammad's religion, held in awe as the speech of God. No other written book in the world is likely to have had such a share of admiration.[37] It is natural

[34] I.e., Arabs and non-Arabs; cf. *Muhammedanische Studien*, I, 269 [= *Muslim Studies*, edited by S. M. Stern (London, 1967-1971), I, 243f.]. But already the early commentator Mujāhid takes the expression "the red" to mean people and "the black" to mean the *jinn* (Aḥmad ibn Ḥanbal, *Musnad*, Cairo, A.H. 1311, V, 145 bottom). [On the significance of these terms, see B. Lewis, *Race and Color in Islam* (New York, 1971).]

[35] Tradition gives this universality a scope even larger than all mankind: not only the *jinn* are included but, in a certain sense, also the angels. An extensive statement of Muslim views on this question is found in Ibn Ḥajar al-Haytamī, *Al-Fatāwā al-ḥadīthīya* (Cairo, A.H. 1307), pp. 114ff.

[36] Ibn Sa'd, II, i, 83:25.

[37] Judgments of the Qur'ān's literary value may vary, but there is one thing even prejudice cannot deny. The people entrusted, during the reigns of Abū Bakr and 'Uthmān, with the redaction of the unordered parts of the book occasionally went about their work in a very clumsy fashion. With the exception of the earliest Meccan suras, which the Prophet

enough that in the course of later developments Muslims constantly referred back to the Qur'ān, measured the products of all historical periods by its words, and believed themselves to be in harmony with them or at least strove to be so. But we must not overlook that the Qur'ān by itself will not at all suffice for an understanding of Islam as an historical phenomenon.

---

had used before his emigration to Medina as liturgical texts, and which consist of self-contained pieces so brief as to make them less vulnerable to editorial confusion, the parts of the holy book, and particularly certain Medinese suras, often display a disorder and a lack of coherence that caused considerable difficulty and toil to later commentators who had to regard the established order as basic and sacrosanct. If scholars undertake one day "a real critical edition of the text, reflecting all the results of scholarly research"—a project recently urged in these words by Rudolf Geyer, *Göttingische Gelehrte Anzeigen*, 1909, p. 51—they will have to pay attention to the transposition of verses out of their original contexts and to interpolations (cf. August Fischer, "Eine Qorān-Interpolation," *Nöldeke Festschrift*, I, 33ff.). The fact of editorial confusion appears clearly from Nöldeke's survey of the arrangement of individual suras (*Geschichte des Qorāns*, 1st ed., pp. 70-174; 2nd ed., I, 87-234).

The assumption of inapposite interpolations can on occasion help us get around difficulties in understanding the text. I would like to illustrate this by an example.

Sura 24 (from verse 27 on) deals with the way virtuous people visit one another, how they should announce themselves, greet the people of the house, how women and children are to behave on such occasions. The rules for such situations became confused because in verses 32-34 and 35-36 two digressions, only loosely related to the main theme, were interpolated (cf. *Geschichte des Qorāns*, 2nd ed., I, 211). Then in verse 58 the theme of announcing one's visit is reintroduced, and discussed through verse 60. Then verse 61 reads: "There is no restriction on the blind, no restriction on the lame, no restriction on the sick, nor on yourselves, if you eat (in one of) your houses, or the houses of your fathers, or the houses of your mothers, or the houses of your brothers, or the houses of your sisters, or the houses of your paternal uncles, or the houses of your paternal aunts, or the houses of your maternal uncles, or the houses of your maternal aunts, or in one whose keys you hold or in one belonging to your friend. It will not render you guilty of a sin, whether you eat together or apart. And when you enter houses, greet one another with a greeting from Allah, a blessed and goodly one."

In this passage Muhammad permits his followers to join their relatives at table without any restriction, and even to go as guests to the houses of female blood relations. One cannot fail to notice that the first words of verse 61, which extend this freedom to the blind, lame, and sick, do not fit the natural context very well.

A writer on medicine in the Qur'ān took this juxtaposition very seriously, and offered the critique that while the dinner company of the halt and the blind is unobjectionable, "a meal in the company of a sick man may be dangerous for one's health; Muhammad would have done better not to combat the aversion to it" (Karl Opitz, *Die Medizin im Koran*, Stuttgart, 1906, p. 63).

On closer study we see that the passage out of place in this context strayed into it from another group of rules. Its original reference is not to taking part in meals at the houses of others, but to taking part in the military campaigns of early Islam. In Sura 48, verses 11-16, the Prophet inveighs against "the Arabs who were left behind," those who did not participate in the campaign just undertaken. He threatens them with severe divine punishments. He appends to this verse 17: "It is no compulsion for the blind (*laysa . . . ḥarajun*), no com-

His own inner development and the circumstances he encountered forced Muhammad himself to pass beyond certain revelations of the Qur'ān; he did so, to be sure, with new divine revelations. He was forced to admit that upon divine command he had to abrogate what had been revealed to him, only a short while ago, as the word of God.[k] It is easy to imagine what the time would bring when Islam had crossed its Arabian borders and set about becoming an international power.

Without the Qur'ān Islam cannot be understood, but the Qur'ān alone is not nearly adequate for a complete understanding of Islam as it has unfolded in history.

In our next lectures we shall examine more closely the forces that affected the development of Islam beyond the Qur'ān.

---

pulsion for the lame, and no compulsion for the sick"—the text agrees literally with 24:61—i.e., people handicapped in these or other serious ways may be excused if they abstain. This phrase was inserted into the other context, to which it is foreign. It evidently influenced the redaction of the verse, whose original beginning cannot be reconstructed with certainty. Muslim commentators too have attempted, naturally without assuming an interpolation, to explain the words in keeping with their natural sense as an excuse for the abstention from war of those bodily unfit for service, but they had to accept the rejection of such an explanation for the reason that if the words were so understood, "they would not be in harmony with what precedes and follows them." See Bayḍāwī, *Anwār al-tanzīl wa-asrār al-ta'wīl*, edited by H. O. Fleischer (Leipzig, 1846–1848), II, 31:6.

[k] The Qur'ān deals explicitly with this question in 2:100ff. For a discussion, see the article "Koran" in *EI*[1], section 3 (by F. Buhl).

II. *The Development of Law*

1. In Anatole France's story "Sur la pierre blanche," a group of educated gentlemen who happen to be interested in the destinies of the world of antiquity voice, in the form of casual conversation, serious thoughts about the history of religions. In the course of this discussion one of the characters pronounces the maxim: "Qui fait une religion ne sait pas ce qu'il fait," that is, the founder of a religion is rarely aware of the impact that his achievement will have on history.

Muhammad is very much a case in point. True, we may suppose that after the military triumphs he lived to see, the Prophet had an intimation that force of arms would carry the power of Islam far beyond the boundaries of its homeland. But the institutions he had created could in no sense provide for the vastly enlarged circumstances that triumphant Islam was very soon to face. Indeed, Muhammad's thought was always occupied, first and foremost, with the immediate conditions of the moment.

Internal consolidation and military expansion had already, during the rule of the first caliphs, the Prophet's immediate successors, contributed to a change in the nature of the community. A Meccan religious congregation had become in Medina a rudimentary political structure. Now it was on its way to world empire.

In the conquered provinces and at home, every day fresh circumstances required regulation. The bases of the administration of state had to be laid.

Religious ideas as well were contained in the Qur'ān only in germ, with their growth yet to come as wider horizons opened. The great events that brought Islam into contact with other spheres of thought threw open, for thinking believers, doors to reflection on religious issues, which had been shut in Arabia itself. Moreover, there were questions of how everyday life was to be lived in the spirit of the religious law, what were the lawful forms of ritual? Only the barest essentials of these things were regulated; they were uncertain and unstable.[a]

[a] Goldziher's studies on Islamic law were resumed and considerably extended by J. Schacht, notably in his two major works, *The Origins of Muhammedan Jurisprudence*, 4th ed. (Oxford, 1967), and *An Introduction to Islamic Law* (Oxford, 1964). For a general histori-

The unfolding of Islamic thought, the fixing of the modalities of Islamic practice, the establishment of Islamic institutions—all these resulted from the work of subsequent generations. These things did not come about without internal struggle and compromise. It is still often thought today that in all these respects Islam "enters the world as a rounded system."[1] Nothing could be further from the truth. The Islam of Muhammad and of the Qur'ān is unfinished, awaiting its completion in the work of generations to come.

To begin with, we shall consider only a few of the practical demands of secular life. Muhammad and his helpers had looked after the most immediate needs. We may put credence in the tradition that the Prophet had established a proportional rate for the levying of taxes.[2] In the circumstances of his time it must already have appeared imperative to change the *zakāt* from a rudimentary form of collective alms-giving to an obligatory tax levied in fixed amounts by the state.

Such regulations, because of their intrinsic necessity, moved increasingly into the foreground after Muhammad's death. The warriors, dispersed in distant provinces, and especially those who had not come from the religious sphere of Medina, had no clear knowledge of the modalities of religious practice. More urgent yet were the political needs.

Continued war and increasing conquests demanded the establishment of legal criteria for the conduct of war. Statutes were needed to deal with the conquered peoples: to clarify their position in the state, as well as to regulate the economic situation created by the new conditions. It was in particular the vigorous caliph 'Umar, the true founder of the Islamic state, whose great conquests in Syria, Palestine, and Egypt prompted the first fixed regulations in such constitutional and economic matters.

2. Details of these regulations cannot concern us here. What matters

---

cal account, see N. J. Coulson, *A History of Islamic Law* (Edinburgh, 1964). On Islamic law at the present time, see also G. H. Bousquet, *Du Droit musulman et de son application effective dans le monde* (Algiers, 1949); J.N.D. Anderson, *Islamic Law in the Modern World* (London, 1959); and M. Khadduri and H. J. Liebesny, eds., *Law in the Middle East: I, Origin and Development of Islamic Law* (Washington, D.C., 1955). Among numerous works devoted to the substantive law of the various schools, one of the best is David Santillana, *Istituzioni di diritto musulmano malichita con riguardo anche al sistema sciafiita* (Rome, 1926-1938).

[1] Abraham Kuenen, *National Religions and Universal Religions* (Hibbert Lectures; London, 1882), p. 293.

[2] See, for example, Ibn Sa'd, IV, ii, 76:25. For early traditions about the tax rate, see *Muhammedanische Studien*, II, 50 n. 3, 51 n. 3 [= *Muslim Studies*, II, 58, notes 1 and 4]. Besides the list of rates, the tax collectors (*muṣaddiq*) would also be given written instructions requiring them to be considerate in the practical application of the tax rate; Ibn Sa'd, VI, 45:16.

for our purpose is simply to recognize that in Islam legal development commensurate with public need began immediately after the Prophet's death.

I must, however, single out one aspect of these details, because of its importance for understanding the character of this early period. It is undeniable that, in this earliest phase of the development of Islamic law, the spirit of tolerance permeated the instructions that Muslim conquerors were given for dealing with the subjugated adherents of other religions.[3] What today still resembles religious toleration in the constitutional practice of Islamic states—features in the public law of Islam often noted by eighteenth-century travelers—goes back to the principle of the free practice of religion by non-Muslim monotheists, stated in the first half of the seventh century.

Tolerance in early Islam had the support of Qur'ān verse 2:256, "there is no compulsion in religion."[4] The verse was resorted to in later times, too, in occasional cases of apostasy by people who had been forcibly converted to Islam, to avert from them the severe punishment the law would otherwise have demanded for renouncing the faith.[5]

[3] "In the earliest times the Arabs were not fanatic; their intercourse with their Christian Semitic cousins was nearly fraternal. But soon, when these Christians too had become Muslims, they introduced into the pale of the new religion the same intransigence, the same blind hostility to the faith of Byzantium, by which they had previously stunted the growth of eastern Christianity." Leone Caetani, "Das historische Studium des Islams," lecture held at the International Historical Congress in Berlin (Berlin, 1908), p. 9.

[4] Cf. 'Umar's application of this principle to his Christian slave; Ibn Sa'd, VI, 110:2. No desire to hunt after proselytes is attributed to Muhammad, either: "If they convert to Islam it is well; if not, they remain (in their previous religion); indeed Islam is wide (or: broad)." *Ibid.*, VI, 30:10.

[A somewhat different interpretation of this verse and consequently of the whole problem of early Islamic tolerance is given by Rudi Paret, who understands it not as an injunction of tolerance but as an expression of resignation. See R. Paret, "*Sure 2, 256: Lā ikrāha fī d-dīni*, Toleranz oder Resignation?", *Der Islam*, XLV (1969), 299ff. On the general question of tolerance in Islam, see further *idem*, "Toleranz und Intoleranz im Islam," *Saeculum*, XXI (1970), 344–46, and Francesco Gabrieli, *Arabeschi e studi Islamici* (Naples, 1973), pp. 25-36, chapter 32, "La Tolleranza nell'Islam."]

[5] Qifṭī (*Ta'rīkh al-ḥukamā'*, edited by Julius Lippert, Leipzig, 1903, p. 319: 16ff.) relates the following about Maimonides. It is alleged that shortly before his emigration from Spain he was compelled ostensibly to accept Islam. In Egypt, where he stood at the head of the Jewish community, he was harassed by a Muslim fanatic of Spanish origin, Abū'l-'Arab, who denounced him to the government as an apostate (*murtadd*). According to the law, the punishment for apostasy is death. However, 'Abd al-Raḥīm ibn 'Alī, known as *al-qāḍī al-fāḍil*, judged that "the profession of Islam under compulsion has, according to religious law, no validity," and thus there was no ground for the charge of apostasy. Near the end of the seventeenth century the same judicial opinion was pronounced by the *muftī* of Istanbul concerning the Maronite Emir Yūnus, who had been forced by the Pasha of Tripoli to accept

Reports from the first decades of Islam furnish a number of examples for the religious toleration practiced by the first caliphs toward the adherents of the old religions. The instructions to the leaders of armies setting out for the wars of conquest are usually very illuminating. One model may have been the agreement concluded by the Prophet with the Christians of Najrān, guaranteeing the preservation of Christian institutions;[6] another the rule of conduct given by the Prophet to Mu'ādh Jabal, who was about to march to the Yemen: "No Jew is to be troubled in the practice of Judaism."[7] The same high standards ruled the peace treaties granted to the subjected Christians of the Byzantine Empire as it continued to crumble in favor of Islam.[8] In exchange for the payment of a "toleration tax" (*jizya*) they were allowed to practice their religions undisturbed.[b] To be sure, public display of their religious ceremonies was in some ways restricted, but we may stress that a historical scrutiny of the sources[9] leads to the conclusion that several such restrictions, projected back into this earlier period, did not come into play until later times that were more conducive to fanaticism.[10] Such is the case, specifically, with the prohibition against building new churches or repairing old ones. The partisan, narrow-minded 'Umar II, it seems, was the first who seriously

Islam, but soon after openly renewed his profession of Christianity. The *muftī* handed down the decision that profession of Islam made under duress was null and void. The sultan endorsed the *muftī*'s decision. The contemporary patriarch of Antioch, Stephanus Petrus, writes concerning the matter in a circular: "Postea curavit (Yūnus) afferri sibi litteras ab ipso magno Turcarum Rege atque Judicum sententias, quibus declarabatur negationem Fidei ab ipso per vim extortam irritam esse et invalidam." See Jean de la Roque, *Voyage de Syrie et du Mont Libanon* (Paris, 1722), II, 270f. Cf. also Moulavi Cherágh Ali, *The Proposed Political, Legal, and Social Reforms in the Ottoman Empire* (Bombay, 1883), pp. 50-58, on the question of the treatment of apostasy in Islam.

[6] Wāqidī [actually Ibn Sa'd], edited by Julius Wellhausen in *Skizzen und Vorarbeiten*, IV (Berlin, 1889), text, 77:1 [= Ibn Sa'd, I, ii, 85].

[7] Balādhurī, *Futūḥ al-buldān*, edited by M. J. de Goeje (Leiden, 1866), p. 71:12.

[8] Cf. M. J. de Goeje, *Mémoire sur la conquête de la Syrie*, 2nd ed. (Leiden, 1900), pp. 106, 147.

[b] *Jizya* is the Islamic technical term for the poll tax levied on the non-Muslim subjects of the Muslim state.

[9] About such contracts, and for a critical assessment of them, see Caetani, *Annali dell'Islam*, III, 381, 956-59.

[10] For example, the assumption that immediately after the conquest of Syria the Christians were prohibited from sounding the clappers (*nāqūs*) of their churches is irreconcilable with an anecdote about the caliph Mu'āwiya related in Ibn Qutayba, *'Uyūn al-akhbār*, edited by Carl Brockelmann (Berlin, 1900-1908), II, 238:11ff. [edited Cairo, 1343-1349/1925-1930, I, 198]. The noise of these clappers disturbs the sleep of the aging caliph; he sends an emissary to Byzantium to have the noise halted. For the building of churches, see "Zur Literatur des Ichtilāf al-maḏâhib," *ZDMG*, XXXVIII (1884), 674 [= *Gesammelte Schriften*, II, 142].

set about carrying out such measures, which the 'Abbāsid ruler Mutawakkil and others of like disposition then adopted. The very fact that such bigoted rulers found occasion to proceed against the religious buildings that non-Muslims had erected since the conquest proves that previously there had been no obstacle to the erection of such places of worship.

Just as the principle of toleration ruled in matters of religion, forbearance and moderation were to have the force of law in the treatment of non-Muslims in the areas of civil law and economic relations. Oppression of non-Muslims under the protection of Islam (*ahl al-dhimma*) was condemned by the believers as a sinful excess.[11] When the governor of the province of Lebanon used great severity against the populace that had revolted because of an oppressive tax-collector, that governor could be warned with a reminder of the Prophet's teaching: "On the Day of Judgment I myself will act as the accuser of any man who oppresses a person under the protection of Islam, and lays excessive burdens on him."[12] In the neighborhood of Bostra the site of the "House of the

[11] Ṭabarī, I, 2922:6ff.'Umar disapproves of taking harsh measures against the subject populace on account of the *kharāj*. He cites the hadith according to which the Prophet said, "If someone causes people to suffer in this world, God will cause him to suffer on the Day of Judgment." Ya'qūbī, *Ta'rīkh*, II, 168:11. Cf. the instructions given to the governor of the Emesa district; Ibn Sa'd, IV, ii, 14:8.

[12] Balādhurī, *Futūḥ*, p. 162. It is probably such sayings that the Shaykh al-Islām Jamāl al-Dīn had in mind when, with reference to the new Turkish constitution that accorded equal rights to different religions, he declared to the correspondent of the *Daily News* (8 August 1908): "You may rest assured, no matter how liberal the constitution is, Islam is even more liberal."

But fanaticism against those professing other religions also managed, in a way we shall have to discuss, to bring to bear sayings in which the Prophet favors the uncharitable treatment of non-Muslims. The Prophet's command that the *salām*-greeting be withheld from non-Muslims, and that a Muslim should, when so greeted by a non-Muslim, return the greeting in a punning, ambiguous fashion, has been considered authentic and included even in collections of well-attested hadiths (Bukhārī, *Jihād* no. 97, *Isti'dhān* no. 22, *Da'awāt* no. 67; cf. Ibn Sa'd, IV, ii, 71:6; V, 393:26). It is clear, however, from Ibn Sa'd, V, 363:26, and VI, 203:3ff., that not everyone found this to be in keeping with the spirit of Islam. Other sayings of this sort are rejected as apocryphal. For example, the following is thrown out by Ibn Ḥajar al-Haytamī (*Al-Fatāwā al-ḥadīthīya*, p. 118) as a forgery without any foundation (*lā aṣla lahu*): "When someone shows a friendly face to a *dhimmī* (a Jew or Christian under the protection of Islam), it is as if he struck me in the ribs." The next hadith is branded as *khabar bāṭil* in Dhahabī, *Mīzān al-i'tidāl* (Lucknow, A.H. 1301), II, 232 [edited by 'Alī Muḥammad al-Bajāwī (Cairo, 1382/1963), III, 197], and in a longer version, *ibid.*, p. 275 [III, 299]: "The Prophet once met the angel Gabriel, greeted him, and offered him his hand, but the angel would not take it. He said: 'O Gabriel, what prevents you from taking my hand?' Gabriel said: 'You have touched the hand of a Jew; perform the ritual ablution, O Prophet of Allah.' Then the Prophet offered him his hand again, and the angel took it." *Ibid.*, II, 575

Jews" was still pointed out to travelers in recent times. Here, according to the story Porter tells in his *Five Years in Damascus*, had stood a mosque that 'Umar ordered demolished because his governor had forcibly expropriated the house of a Jew in order to build the mosque in its place.[13]

3. The most immediate task in laying down new regulations was to develop a legal view of the relations between Islam, the conqueror, and the subject peoples. But all the ramifications of religious and legal life within Islam also demanded regulation. Muslim soldiers were a single religious community, but they had been dispersed into distant lands before the religious practices had been conclusively fixed. They needed well-defined rules for ritual obligations and for all contingencies that might arise in connection with such obligations. What was rather more difficult, they needed rules for legal circumstances, most of which were wholly unfamiliar to the conquerors from Arabia. In Syria, Egypt, and Persia, the Muslims had to contend with ancient local customs, based on ancient civilizations. To some extent they had to smooth over the conflict between inherited rights and newly acquired rights. In a word, Islamic legal practice, religious and civil alike, had to be subjected to regulation. Such guiding principles as the Qur'ān itself could supply were not sufficient, for the Qur'ānic statutes could not take care of the unforeseen conditions brought about by conquest. The provisions made in the Qur'ān were occasional and limited to the primitive conditions of Arabia. They were not adequate for dealing with the new situation.

[IV, 368f.]: "If someone (a Muslim) enters into a partnership with a *dhimmī* and acts humbly towards him, on the Day of Resurrection a river of fire will be set between them and it will be said to the Muslim: 'Ford it so you can settle your accounts with your partner.' " Contracts of partnership between Muslims and Jews were in fact very frequent at the time when this saying arose. The resulting circumstances are a frequent theme of the legal reflections of Jewish theologians; see Louis Ginzberg, *Geonica* (New York, 1909), II, 186. The purpose of the fanatic hadith is to furnish a severe admonition from the Islamic point of view against such business partnerships.

Every attitude of mind in Islam found expression in Prophetic sayings made to order. People like the Ḥanbalites, who reject the basic forms of social toleration even in their relations to Muslims of other views (see "Zur Geschichte der ḥanbalitischen Bewegungen," *ZDMG*, LXII, 1908, 12ff. [= *Gesammelte Schriften*, V, 146ff.; partial French translation in *Arabica*, VII (1960), 137]) are naturally no less harsh toward those who profess other faiths. They prefer to rely on the invidious sayings, while they try to undermine those that support tolerant doctrines. According to a characteristic report (presumably first put about by his disciples), the *imām* Aḥmad ibn Ḥanbal rejected as inauthentic the well known hadith: "When someone causes pain to a *dhimmī*, it is as if he caused pain to me." See Subkī, *Ṭabaqāt*, I, 268:6 from bottom. The prevalent teaching of Islam has always rejected such attitudes, as well as the documents on which their representatives have relied.

[13] Josias L. Porter, *Five Years in Damascus*, 2nd ed. (London, 1870), p. 235.

Especially in the heyday of the Umayyad dynasty, the secular authorities, busy enhancing the external splendor of the new empire, did not much bother their heads about such needs. They were not indifferent to the religious character of Islam, but their interest lay more in political consolidation than in canonical organization: their chief attention went to maintaining what had been gained by force of arms, and to assuring the privileges of the Arab stock. To deal with day-to-day legal problems, they relied on common usage. To deal with questionable cases there was only the wisdom, and at times the arbitrary judgment, of those who administered justice. Moreover, they did not always hold strictly even to such rules as had already been laid down in the time of the first pious caliphs.

Such a state of affairs could not satisfy the pious, whose aim was to establish a new life in accordance with a religious law willed by God and consonant with the Prophet's intentions. In all matters, religious as well as civil, the will of the Prophet must be ascertained and followed as a practical rule of conduct. The Prophet's Companions were the best source for learning his will: the people who lived their lives in his company, witnessed his actions, and heard his judgments. As long as one had a "Companion" at hand, one could learn from his reports what pious usage required and what the details of the divine law were. After the passing of this first generation, one had to be content with information that members of the next generation had received from the first from time to time, as problems had arisen. In this manner, transmission from generation to generation continued down to the latest periods. Conduct and judgment were considered correct and their legitimacy was established if a chain of reliable transmission ultimately traced them back to a Companion who could testify that they were in harmony with the Prophet's intentions. On the strength of such traditions, certain customs in ritual and law were established as the usage of the authoritative first believers of Islam, and as having been practiced under the Prophet's own eyes. As such, they acquired a sacred character.[14] They are called *sunna*, sacred custom. The form in which such a usage is stated is hadith, tradition. The two concepts are not identical. Hadith is the documentation of *sunna*. Through a chain of reliable authorities who handed down pertinent information from generation to generation, hadith shows what the Com-

[14] The question of whether it is permitted to remove a corpse from the place of death to some other place is decided by Zuhrī in the light of the precedent that the body of Sa'd ibn Abī Waqqāṣ was brought from al-'Aqīq to Medina. Ibn Sa'd, III, i, 104f.

panions, with the Prophet's approval, held to be exclusively correct in matters of religion and law, and what could therefore properly serve as a norm for practical application.[c] One can see how in Islam, as in Judaism, a theory of an extrascriptural sacred law could emerge, a theory admitting both a written law and an orally transmitted law.[15]

Since the *sunna* is the embodiment of the views and practices of the oldest Islamic community,[16] it functions as the most authoritative interpretation of the text of the Qur'ān. That text cannot answer each and every eventuality; it comes alive and becomes effective through the *sunna*. The value placed upon the *sunna* is well illustrated by the following saying, reputedly 'Alī's instruction to 'Abdallāh ibn 'Abbās, whom he sent to negotiate with the rebels: "Do not use the Qur'ān as you contend with them, for the Qur'ān can be interpreted in various ways and has different aspects (*ḥammāl dhū wujūh*). Fight them with the *sunna*; that will leave them no avenues of escape."[17] This cannot be regarded as an authentic saying of 'Alī's, but it does come from an early period and mirrors the thinking of early Islam.

We should not rule out the possibility that hadiths which we know from the transmission of later generations now and then contain a nu-

[c] Goldziher's studies on hadith, summarized here, are presented at greater length and with full documentation in the second volume of his *Muhammedanische Studien* (= *Muslim Studies*, II, 17-251). They were taken up again by the late Joseph Schacht in a series of studies, notably in his classic work *The Origins of Muhammedan Jurisprudence*, and by Robert Brunschvig in various articles, some of them collected in his *Études d'Islamologie* (Paris, 1976). More recently there has been a reaction against the critical approach of Goldziher and his successors among Muslim scholars. For a critique of the critical approach and a defense of the authenticity of the main body of hadith material, see Fazlur Rahman, *Islam*, chapter 3 (pp. 43ff.); *idem*, "Sunnah and Hadith," *Islamic Studies*, I (1962), 33ff.; Fuat Sezgin, *Geschichte des arabischen Schrifttums*, I (Leiden, 1967), 53-84. On recent Egyptian discussions of the subject, see G.H.A. Juynboll, *The Authenticity of the Tradition Literature: Discussions in Modern Egypt* (Leiden, 1969).

[15] See "Kämpfe um die Stellung des Ḥadīṯ im Islam," *ZDMG*, LXI (1907), 863ff. [= *Gesammelte Schriften*, V, 89ff.; partial French translation in *Arabica*, VII (1960), 5f.]

[16] It appears from Ibn Sa'd, II, ii, 135:19ff., a passage important for the concept of the *sunna*, that in the first century there were still Muslims in whose opinion only the attested actions of the Prophet, not of the Companions, could be regarded as *sunna*. But this restriction could not prevail.

[17] *Nahj al-balāgha* (orations and sayings ascribed to 'Alī), edited by Muḥammad 'Abduh (Beirut, A.H. 1307), II, 75:7 [*Bāb al-kutub wa'l-rasā'il*, no. 77; see Ibn Abī'l-Ḥadīd. *Sharḥ nahj al-balāgha*, edited by Muḥammad Abū'l-Faḍl Ibrāhīm (Cairo, 1959-1964), XVIII, 71]. In the text the word for "avenues of escape" is *maḥīṣan*. Clément Huart, *Textes persans relatifs à la secte des Houroûfîs* (E.J.W. Gibb Memorial Series, IX; Leiden and London, 1909), texts, p. 76:17, misread this word as *makhṣīyan*, deriving the remarkable meaning (translations, p. 120:23): "car ils ne trouveront pas personne qui en soit châtrée."

cleus of ancient material, material that may not stem directly from the mouth of the Prophet, but that does stem from the earliest generation of Muslim authorities. On the other hand, it is easily seen that as spatial and temporal distance from the source grew, the danger also grew that people would devise ostensibly correct hadiths with chains of transmission reaching back to the highest authority of the Prophet and his Companions, and employ them to authenticate both theoretical doctrines and doctrines with a practical goal in view. It soon became evident that each point of view, each party, each proponent of a doctrine gave the form of hadith to his theses, and that consequently the most contradictory tenets had come to wear the garb of such documentation. There is no school in the areas of ritual, theology, or jurisprudence, there is not even any party to political contention, that would lack a hadith or a whole family of hadiths in its favor, exhibiting all the external signs of correct transmission.

The Muslims themselves could not remain ignorant of this, and Muslim theologians created an extremely interesting scientific discipline—that of hadith criticism—in order to sift authentic traditions from apocryphal ones whenever contradictions resisted all attempts at harmonization.

It is easy to grasp that the points of view taken by this criticism were not the same as ours, and that our criticism will often raise doubts where its Muslim counterpart believes that it has found undoubtedly authentic material. The concluding achievement of Muslim critical activity came in the seventh century after the Hijra, when six collections of hadith were recognized as canonical. In these works, a few third-century theologians selected, out of a nearly limitless chaos of traditions, those hadiths that appeared genuine to them. Once recognized as canonical, these texts were elevated to the rank of decisive sources for ascertaining the Prophet's *sunna*. Of these six collections, the two most revered sources of prophetic *sunna* are the two "Sound Ones," so named because of the formally unassailable information that they contain. Their authors are al-Bukhārī (d. 256/870) and Muslim (d. 261/875). Joined to them, as further authoritative sources, are the collections of Abū Dāwūd (d. 275/888), al-Nasā'ī (d. 303/915), al-Tirmidhī (d. 279/892), and finally and not without some resistance, Ibn Māja (d. 273/886). Mālik ibn Anas had earlier codified the usage of Medina, the home of all *sunna*, but he had not ordered his work according to the principles of hadith collection.

Thus a new set of texts took their place alongside the Qur'ān as fountainheads of religion. Their significance in Muslim learning and Muslim life has been of the highest order.

4. Since our concern here is with the evolution of religion, our interest is claimed by the growth of hadith, rather than by the final form of hadith as a fixed text. Questions of authenticity and age pale in significance when we realize that hadith is a direct reflection of the aspirations of the Islamic community, and furnishes us with an invaluable document for the development of Islamic religious goals beyond the Qur'ān.

For not only law and custom, but theology and political doctrine also took the form of hadith. Whatever Islam produced on its own or borrowed from the outside was dressed up as hadith. In such form alien, borrowed matter was assimilated until its origin was unrecognizable. Passages from the Old and New Testaments, rabbinic sayings, quotes from apocryphal gospels, and even doctrines of Greek philosophers and maxims of Persian and Indian wisdom gained entrance into Islam disguised as utterances of the Prophet. Even the Lord's Prayer occurs in well-authenticated hadith form. This was the form in which intruders from afar became directly or indirectly naturalized in Islam. An interesting example is the parable, well known in world literature,[18] of the cripple who climbs on a blind man's back to steal the fruit hanging on a tree, and the application of this parable to the shared moral responsibility of body and soul. The story appears in Islam as a hadith, with a precise chain of transmittors: Abū Bakr ibn 'Ayyāsh→Abū Sa'īd al-Baqqāl →'Ikrima→Ibn 'Abbās.[19] The parable and its application were also known to the rabbis. In the Talmud it is ascribed to R. Yehudah ha-Nasi; he uses it to allay the misgivings of the emperor Marcus Aurelius.[20] The story may have entered Islam from that direction. In this fashion, a whole treasury of religious legends penetrated into Islam. As a result, examining these various elements within the traditional material, we can distinguish in Islamic as in Jewish religious literature halakhic and haggadic components.

The eclecticism that marked the infancy of Islam only now reached its

[18] Moritz Steinschneider, *Die hebräischen Übersetzungen des Mittelalters und die Juden als Dolmetscher* (Berlin, 1893), p. 852 n. 43; the same author's *Rangstreit-Literatur* (Sitzungsberichte der Kaiserlichen Akademie der Wissenschaften, Philosophisch-Historische Klasse, CLV; Vienna, 1908), p. 58. For copious references to studies of this motif, cf. Émile Galtier, *Foutouḥ al-bahnasâ* (Mémoires publiés par les membres de l'Institut français d'archéologie orientale du Caire, XXII, 1909), p. 20 n. 1.

[19] In Ibn Qayyim al-Jawzīya, *Kitāb al-rūḥ* (Haydarabad, A.H. 1318), p. 294.

[20] Bab. *Sanhedrīn* 91a bottom.

full fertility. It is among the most fascinating problems of research for those who devote their attention to this province of religious literature to track down the widely different sources from which this motley material springs, and to understand the trends and aspirations that it documents.

In this manner hadith formed the framework for the earliest development of religious and ethical thought in Islam. Hadith gives expression to a continued development based on the moral teaching of the Qur'ān. It is also the voice of those more delicate stirrings of moral consciousness to which the tumultuous beginnings and constant early struggles of Islam had not been favorable. Hadiths contain the definitions of a higher piety—evidence of which we have already had occasion to see—that was not satisfied with mere formalism. There is a predilection for the chords of mercy—God's and man's alike. "God created a hundred parts of mercy. He kept ninety-nine of them for Himself, and left one part for the world. This one part is the source of all acts of forbearance among His creatures."[21] "If you hope to obtain my mercy," says God, "be merciful to my creatures." He who comes to the aid of the widow and orphan is considered an equal of him who in holy war dedicates his life to the way of God, or of him who spends his days in fasting and his nights in prayer."[22] "He who strokes the hair of an orphan will receive, for every hair that his hand has touched, a light on the day of resurrection." "There is a key to everything. The key to Paradise is the love of children and of the poor." There are hadiths in which the Prophet gives such counsels to individual Companions, and recommends the cultivation of moral and humane virtues as the true heart of religion. There are many examples of such individual instruction, but none more worthy of retelling than the one bestowed upon Abū Dharr, of the tribe of Ghifār, a once dissolute fellow who converted to Islam and at the time of the first revolutions was one of the most striking figures in the pious party. Abū Dharr relates, "My friend (the Prophet) gave me a sevenfold admonition: 1) love the poor and be near them; 2) look to those who are beneath you and do not regard those who are above you; 3) never request anything from anyone; 4) be loyal to your relations even when they rouse you to anger; 5) speak nothing but the truth, even when it is bitter; 6) do not let the abuse of those who abuse you frighten you off from the way of God; 7) exclaim often: 'There is no might and no power except what comes from God,' for this is from the treasure hidden beneath the throne of God."[23]

[21] Bukhārī, *Adab* no. 18.
[22] *Ibid.*, nos. 24, 25.
[23] Ibn Sa'd, IV, i, 168 bottom.

The seriousness of formal religion is heightened by demands that are first stated in hadiths. As I have already mentioned, the value of works is determined according to the intention that prompts them: this is one of the supreme principles of religious life in Islam. One may infer the importance of this principle for the Muslim from the fact that a statement of it is inscribed over one of the main entrances of al-Azhar, the mosque in Cairo that is the much-visited center of theological learning in Islam. It reminds all who enter, whether their mind is set on study or devotion: "Deeds are judged according to intentions; each man's accounts are drawn up according to his intentions." This hadith rose to be the guiding thought of all religious action in Islam. "God says: Come, meet me with your intentions, not with your deeds."[24] This is a late hadith but it was nurtured by the believers' conviction, and it characterizes their sense of religious values. The development of hadith also enhanced the moral effect of theological doctrines. I will offer just one example; it is of the greatest importance for an assessment of religious thought in Islam. For the monotheism of the Qur'ān, the greatest of sins is *shirk*, the association of other gods with God. *Shirk* is the sin for which God has no forgiveness (31:13, 4:116). The evolution of this earliest theological concept, as seen through the hadith, goes beyond mere condemnation of straightforward failure to believe in the oneness of God; it brands as *shirk* all worship of God that is not an end in itself. A number of moral defects were subsumed under the sin of *shirk*. Hypocritical piety, calculated to gain the approval or admiration of others, is *shirk*, for in it not only God but also people are taken into account.[25] Hypocrisy and true monotheism do not go together. Pride, too, is a kind of *shirk*. For these reasons, Islamic ethics could delineate the category of the "lesser *shirk*" (*al-shirk al-aṣghar*) or "hidden *shirk*" (hidden in the depths of the soul, *al-shirk al-khafīy*).

The goals of religious life were now pitched higher than they had been in the earliest days of Islam. We come upon voices that would be in perfect harmony with the mysticism that was yet to come. An example is the following speech of God to Muhammad: "My servant approaches me steadily through voluntary works of piety, until I come to love him; and when I love him I am his eye, his ear, his tongue, his foot, his hand.

[24] Ibn Taymīya, *Majmū'at al-rasā'il al-kubrā* (Cairo, A.H. 1323), II, 342.

[25] Cf. Ibn Ḥajar al-'Asqalānī, *Al-Iṣāba fī tamyīz al-ṣaḥāba*, edited by Aloys Sprenger et al. (Calcutta, 1856-1888), II, 396 [edited Cairo, A.H. 1323-1325, III, 197, no. 3851, Shaddād ibn 'Awf]: "In the time of the Prophet we regarded hypocrisy (*al-riyā'*) as the lesser *shirk*."

He sees through me, he hears through me, he speaks through me, he moves and feels through me." This hadith is accepted by the best Muslim authorities, and included in a compendium of the forty-two most important traditions. It is not regarded as disputable or apocryphal.[26]

The Prophet's authority was invoked by every group for every idea it evolved: for legal precepts couched in the form of tradition, as well as for maxims and teachings of an ethical or simply edificatory nature. Through solid chains of tradition, all such matters acquired an unbroken tie to the "Companions" who had heard those pronouncements and statutes from the Prophet or had seen him act in pertinent ways. It took no extraordinary discernment on the part of Muslim critics to suspect the authenticity of much of this material: some reports were betrayed by anachronisms[27] or other dubious features, some contradicted others. Moreover, certain people are named outright who fabricated and spread abroad traditions to support one trend or another. Not a few pious persons admitted, as the end of life neared, how great their contribution to the body of fictive hadiths had been. To fabricate hadith was hardly considered dishonorable if the resulting fictions served the cause of the good. A man honorable in all other respects could be discredited as a traditionist without having his religious reputation tarnished or his honor as a member of society called into question. It was, of course, possible to assert, on the Prophet's authority, that the bottomless pit awaited those who fraudulently ascribed to Muhammad utterances that he never made. But one could also try to save the situation by vindicatory maxims, in which the Prophet had supposedly recognized such fictions in advance as his own spiritual property: "After my death more and more sayings will be ascribed to me, just as many sayings have been ascribed to previous prophets (without their having really said them). When a saying is re-

[26] Nawawī, *Al-Arbaʿūn ḥadīthan*, no. 38 [see Wensinck, *Concordance*, VI, 529:13f.].

[27] On occasion the critics had a sharp eye for anachronisms. But they also made an effort not to reject formally well-attested sayings on account of difficulties of content. Thus they easily found ways to accept, in early hadiths, the anticipation of later circumstances. In the *Musnad* of Aḥmad ibn Ḥanbal there is a hadith in which a woman named Umm al-Dardā' reports that the Prophet once saw her in the street and asked her from where she was coming. She answered, "From the bath (*ḥammām*)." Ibn al-Jawzī, who wrote a book himself about forged hadiths, unhesitatingly and absolutely rejected the hadith and the doctrine conveyed in its garb, on the ground that at that time no baths had existed in Medina. But others, in spite of the anachronism, found ways to settle Ibn al-Jawzī's doubts; see Ibn Ḥajar al-ʿAsqalānī, *Al-Qawl al-musaddad fi'l-dhabb ʿan al-Musnad* (Haydarabad, A.H. 1319), p. 46. [See Aḥmad ibn Ḥanbal's *Musnad*, VI, 362, for the hadith in question.]

ported and attributed to me, compare it with God's book. Whatever is in accordance with that book is from me, whether I really said it or no." Further: "Whatever is rightly spoken was spoken by me."

The fabricators of tradition, as we see, laid their cards on the table. "Muhammad said" in such cases merely means "it is right, it is religiously unassailable, it is even desirable, and the Prophet himself would applaud it." One is put in mind of the Talmudic maxim of R. Joshua ben Levi, that all the ideas that discerning scholars will ever expound have already been imparted to Moses on Sinai.[28]

5. The pious fraud of the inventors of hadith was treated with universal indulgence as long as their fictions were ethical or devotional. But the more rigorous theologians found it a graver matter when a ritual practice or a legal opinion was to be based on fraudulent hadiths. Their apprehension was all the greater as partisans of differing viewpoints had mustered contradictory hadiths. Such could not be the sole foundation for determining religious ritual and custom, law and the administration of justice.

Such scruples played an important role in the emergence of a trend that had already existed at the beginning of the development of jurisprudence. The representatives of this trend made use of such traditions as they admitted to be sound, but they also made use of tools of deduction in ascertaining religious norms, and thought that they could best regulate newly arising circumstances by reliance on analogy, inference, or even the subjective assessment of the case. Hadith was not rejected when it seemed to offer firm footing, but alongside hadith the free exercise of the intellect was admitted, even demanded, as a justifiable method of arriving at the law.

It is not astonishing that foreign cultural influences had an effect on the evolution of this legal method and on various details of its application. Islamic jurisprudence shows undeniable traces of the influence of Roman law both in its methodology and in its particular stipulations.

This cultivation of jurisprudence, which reached its prime as early as the second Islamic century, contributed a new element to the intellectual world of Islam: *fiqh*, the science of religious law, a science which, perverted by casuistry, was soon to become disastrous for religious life and religious learning. A political event that reoriented the spirit of Islamic society played an important part in the development of *fiqh*: the fall of the Umayyad dynasty and the rise to power of the 'Abbāsids.

In previous essays I have had occasion to discuss the driving forces that directed the acts of government under these two dynasties, and to point out the influences that, quite independently of dynastic considerations, brought about that theocratic turn which characterizes the 'Abbāsid epoch, and contrasts it with the century of Umayyad rule. Here I would only recall in brief that the upheaval which placed the 'Abbāsids upon the caliphal throne was no mere political revolution. More than a change of dynasties, it also meant a profound transformation in religious respects. A theocratic regime,[d] with an ecclesiastical policy, supplanted the Umayyads, whom pietistic circles had condemned for worldliness and who, in their desert palaces and in their capital city of Damascus, had cultivated the ancient Arab ideals and traditions. The 'Abbāsids derived their right to rule from the fact that they descended from the Prophet's family. In further justification, they proclaimed that upon the ruins of a government which the pious had denounced as ungodly, they, the 'Abbāsids, were establishing a regime in harmony with the *sunna* of the Prophet and the requirements of divinely revealed religion.[29] This was an appearance the 'Abbāsids strove to maintain and foster, for it was the pillar of their claim. Thus they wished to be not merely kings, but primarily princes of the church. Unlike the Umayyads, they conceived of their

[28] Pal. Talmud, *Ḥagīgā*, 1, 8, near the end.

[d] The German text has the word *kirchenpolitisch*, literally "church-political." The present practice among scholars is to avoid the use of such terms as church, clergy, or ecclesiastical when speaking of Islamic religious institutions and persons. These words are of specifically Christian origin and connotation, and their use in connection with Islam would imply a resemblance which, in fact, does not exist. Islam has no ordination, no sacrament, no priesthood, and no separate hierarchic structure concerned with religious affairs. Goldziher was, of course, well aware of this and by using such terms did not mean to convey that there was an Islamic church. The European and Christian paradigm that he had in mind was not the church as an institution, but the states of the church as a political entity, exercising the normal attributes of government, but with a religiously based sovereignty and authority.

The use of the term theocracy has in recent years been a matter for dispute between Muslim and non-Muslim scholars. Orientalists have commonly used the term theocracy to denote a state in which, in principle, the ultimate sovereignty belongs to God and the effective sovereign power is exercised by God's representative on earth, administering God's law. In this acceptation of the word, the classical Islamic state of the caliphate was undoubtedly conceived as a theocracy. Present-day Muslim scholars have taken the term theocracy to mean a state governed by the church and the priesthood, and have rightly pointed out that since Islam has neither church nor priesthood, an Islamic theocracy in this sense is a contradiction in terms. Since the word theocracy is commonly used in Western languages in either or both of these senses, both sides to the argument may claim to be right.

[29] Dealt with in part in my "Die Religion des Islams," p. 108:7ff.; cf. *Muhammedanische Studien*, II, 52ff. [= *Muslim Studies*, II, 59ff.].

caliphate as a state of the church, in the government of which the divine law was the sole guideline. The 'Abbāsids came to power having outmaneuvered the family with the legitimate title. Unlike the Umayyads, they wished to be seen as doing justice to the claims of that very family, and they displayed the utmost unctuousness in restituting the sanctity of the memory of the Prophet. Indeed, their symbol of office is an alleged mantle of the Prophet. They spoke with ostentatious piety, to make a show of the contrast between their predecessors and themselves. The Umayyads had shunned hypocritical humbug. Though, as we shall see, their consciousness was imbued with their Muslim faith, they had no use for posturing, and did not feign to give pride of place to the religious aspect of their office. Only one among that dynasty's rulers can be found rejecting the notion that government is constituted to see to the secular needs of the state. He was 'Umar II, a prince educated in pious company in Medina, whose blindness to the demands of politics helped prepare the overthrow of his house. Muslim writers found it entirely credible, for instance, that when the governor in Emesa reported to 'Umar II that the city lay in ruins and a certain allocation of money was needed to rebuild it, the caliph instructed him: "Fortify it with righteousness and cleanse its streets of injustice."[30] This is not the Umayyads' language. Under the 'Abbāsids, however, notwithstanding their increased predilection for all the pomp and ostentation of the Sassanid monarchs, pious talk was the order of the day. The Persian ideal of rule, in which church and state are conjoined,[31] was clearly the 'Abbāsid program. Now religion was not only a matter of interest to the state; it was the state's chief business.

It is easily imagined that the stock of theologians rose at court and in the state. Since state, law, and the administration of justice were to be ordered and built up according to the precepts of religion, preference had to be given to people who practiced and studied the *sunna*, or who used scholarly methods to ascertain the divine law. With the rise of the new dynasty the time had come, after scanty and modest beginnings, for Islamic law to blossom and flourish.

To pay attention to traditions of the Prophet, to seek them out and hand them down, was now no mere act of theoretical piety, but a practical matter of exceptional importance. Not only the rules for the ritualistic

[30] Bayhaqī, *Al-Maḥāsin wa'l-masāwī*, edited by Friedrich Schwally (Giessen, 1902), p. 392 = Pseudo-Jāḥiẓ, *Al-Maḥāsin wa'l-'aḍdād*, edited by G. van Vloten (Leiden, 1898), p. 181 top.

[31] See "Zur Geschichte der ḥanbalitischen Bewegungen," p. 2 n. 1 [= *Gesammelte Schriften*, V, 136 n. 1].

aspects of life were now based on religious law, but also the institutions of the state. The administration of justice in all kinds of transactions, down to the simplest statutes of civil law, must fulfill the requirements of the divine law. Consequently those requirements must be discovered down to the minutest detail. This was the age of the development and fixing of the law, the age of *fiqh* and of the scholars of jurisprudence, the *fuqahā'*. The *qāḍī* is the man who matters. In Medina, the true birthplace of Islam and home of the *sunna*, pious opposition to the secular power had always fostered a spirit of religious legalism. But now, in the shadow of the theocratic caliphate, the study of jurisprudence developed even more intensely in the new centers of the empire in Mesopotamia, and radiated from there east and west, to the most remote regions of the state. Hadiths were carried and handed about; new postulates and rules were derived from received material. On occasion the results were contradictory. Points of view and methods also led to differences. Some lawyers deferred to hadith. But contradictory hadiths would furnish contradictory answers to a question. One would have to determine in such cases which hadith outweighed the other. Because of the dubiousness of proof from hadith, other lawyers wanted freedom in legal reasoning, and refused to be much inconvenienced by received material. Deeply rooted local usage and customary law could not be simply done away with. Gradations between these opposing tendencies gave rise to scholarly factions and schools that differed mostly in particular details of legal rulings, but were also at variance on some points of method. They are called *madhāhib* (singular: *madhhab*), that is, "directions," or "rites"—certainly not "sects."

From the very beginning, representatives of these divergent schools maintained a steadfast conviction that they all stood on the same ground, and served the same cause, with equal right. They therefore extended proper esteem to one another.[32] Harsh words between overly zealous fol-

[32] For understanding this attitude, the saying of Yaḥyā ibn Sa'īd (d. 143/760) is very important: "The people of (religious) knowledge are people of generous minds (*ahlu tawsi'atin*). There are always differences of opinion among those who must pronounce decisions (*al-muftūna*): what one declares licit the other holds to be forbidden. Nevertheless they are far from reproving one another. Each feels that every question presented to him weighs upon him like a mountain, and when he sees a door open (to its solution) he exclaims, 'What relief!' " See Dhahabī, *Tadhkirat al-ḥuffāẓ*, (Haydarabad, A.H. 1315), I, 124 [edited Haydarabad, 1375/1955, I, 139]. Yaḥyā's saying brings to mind that of El'āzār ibn Azaryā (Bab. *Ḥagīgā* 3b) about differences of opinion in Jewish law (with reference to Ecclesiastes 12:11): "Although some declare clean what others declare unclean, some permit what others forbid, some declare lawful what others declare unlawful . . . all of them (all these

lowers of different schools were a rarity. Signs of fanatically partisan feeling about *madhāhib* first appeared with the growing self-glorification of the *fuqahā'*, and serious theologians have always condemned such partisanship.[33] Mutual tolerance coined the hadith formula, traced back to the Prophet: "Difference of opinion within my community is a (sign of divine) mercy." There are indications that this principle represents a reaction to attacks, mounted by internal and external antagonists, to which Islamic legal practice was exposed by its multiform and indeterminate character.[34]

Thus to this day the view has prevailed that when the practices of the various legal schools diverge, they must all be acknowledged as orthodox in the same measure, provided that support is found for them in the doctrine and practice of men recognized as authoritative teachers, *imāms*, by the consensus of believers (a matter to which I shall presently return). To switch from one *madhhab* to another—a shift of allegiance that simple expediency may on occasion inspire—brings with it no change in a person's religious status and requires no formality. A theologian who lived in the fifth century of the Hijra, Muḥammad ibn Khalaf (d. ca. 1135), received the sobriquet "Ḥanfash" because he belonged successively to three of the legal rites I am about to discuss. He was originally a Ḥanbalite, then he joined the schools first of Abū Ḥanīfa, and then of Shāfiʿī. The nickname Ḥanfash is a phonetic portmanteau of the names of these three *imāms*.[35] Different schools of law may claim the allegiance of different members of a single family, even of fathers and sons. There is

---

contradictory opinions) have been given by one shepherd. One God has given them . . . for it is written, 'God spoke all these words' (Exodus 20:1)." It is also taught specifically about the differences of opinion between the rival schools of Shammai and Hillel that "both these and those are the words of the living God" (Bab. *'Ērūbhīn* 13b). In contrast, R. Simon b. Yōḥai considers that such differences of opinion in matters of law are a sign of forgetting the Torah (*Sifrē Deuteronomy* §48, edited by Friedmann 84b:11).

[33] We find a most remarkable statement, from a later period, against the *madhhab*-fanaticism of the *fuqahā'* in Tāj al-Dīn al-Subkī, *Muʿīd al-niʿam wa-mubīd al-niqam*, edited by David W. Myhrman (London, 1908), pp. 106-109. It is also evidence of the widespread fanaticism among the jurists of Syria and Egypt in the author's time (d. 771/1370).

[34] On this principle, see my *Die Ẓāhiriten: Ihr Lehrsystem und ihre Geschichte* (Leipzig, 1884), pp. 94ff. [translated as *The Ẓāhirīs: Their Doctrine and Their History* (Leiden, 1971), pp. 89ff.]. That the diversity of legal practice was very early an object of censure, one can see from Ma'mūn's discussion of it in Ibn Abī Ṭāhir Ṭayfūr, *Kitāb Baghdād*, edited by Hans Keller (Leipzig, 1908), p. 61, and from an extremely important passage in the epistle to the caliph ascribed to Ibn al-Muqaffaʿ: see the Arabic periodical *Al-Muqtabas*, III (1908), 230 = Muḥammad Kurd ʿAlī, ed., *Rasā'il al-bulaghā'* (Cairo, 1908), p. 54 [= *Risāla fī'l-ṣaḥāba* (*"Conseilleur" du Calife*), edited and translated by Charles Pellat (Paris, 1976), pp. 41ff.].

[35] Dhahabī, *Mīzān al-iʿtidāl*, II, 370 [III, 528].

an anecdote—from a relatively late period, as a matter of fact—that a pious inhabitant of Damascus prayed that God might give him four sons, so that they might each follow a different one of the four *madhāhib*. The prayer, our source adds, did not go unheard.[36] It is a recurrent motif in biographies that famous theologians framed their legal opinions (*fatwā*) in conformity with two different, ostensibly divergent, schools of thought.[37] To do so was not at all regarded as absurd on principle.

Of the different schools of legal thought, with their minor divergences in matters of ritual and law, four have survived to this day, and one or an other predominates in most parts of the Islamic world. The initial dominance of a legal trend in any one area hinged, in large measure, upon personalities: upon disciples who would bring with them the views peculiar to the trend they followed, and whose reputation enabled them to found a school. In this way, the school of the Imām al-Shāfi'ī (d. 204/820) attained paramountcy in parts of Egypt, in East Africa, in South Arabia, and expanding from there, in the Malay Archipelago. The school of the great Medinese *imām*, Mālik ibn Anas (d. 179/795) struck root in other parts of Egypt, in all North Africa, and in German and British West Africa. It also was the *madhhab* of Muslim Spain. The population of the Turkish regions both in the west and in Central Asia, as well as the Muslims of the Indian subcontinent, opted for the school of Abū Ḥanīfa (d. ca. 150/767). This *imām* may be considered the founder and first codifier of the speculative school of law. Finally, the school of the *imām* Aḥmad ibn Ḥanbal (d. 241/855) is represented today in relatively the smallest numbers. That school, occupying an extreme position with respect to the zealous observance of the *sunna*, had, until the fifteenth century or so, counted among its adherents many of the inhabitants of Mesopotamia, Syria, and Palestine. With the rise of the Ottomans as the dominant power in the Islamic world, the intolerant Ḥanbalite school gradually lost ground in those areas that the Ottomans ruled, while the influence of the Ḥanafite school increased accordingly.[38] Nevertheless, we shall have occasion to speak of a renaissance, in the eighteenth century, of the Ḥanba-

[36] Muḥibbī, *Khulāṣat al-athar fī a'yān al-qarn al-ḥādī 'ashar* (Cairo, A.H. 1284), I, 48, Ibrāhīm ibn Muslim al-Samādī (d. 1662).

[37] Cf. Ibn al-Qalānisī, *Dhayl ta'rīkh Dimashq*, edited by H. F. Amedroz (Beirut, 1908), p. 311 (6th century A.H.): the *qāḍī* mentioned there as an example gives *fatwās* according to the Ḥanafite and Ḥanbalite schools. Compare the frequent epithet *muftī al-firaq*, meaning *muftī* of the different parties, able to pronounce decisions that apply to each party according to the doctrines of its *madhhab*.

[38] Cf. "Die Religion des Islams," p. 104:13-29.

lite school. The Muslims of the Philippines (a possession of the United States) follow the Shāfi'ite *madhhab*.[e]

6. I must now turn to a momentous principle which, more than any other, characterizes the development of Islamic law, and which has furnished a means for smoothing over divisions that resulted from the development of separate schools of law. In the midst of theoretical uncertainty about matters of usage, this principle came to prevail among Muslim theologians, and, in its various applications, has prevailed ever since. It is expressed in a statement ascribed to the Prophet: "My community will never agree on error (*ḍalāla*)" or, in more recent form, and expressed cluster-style: "Allah has granted you protection (*ajārakum*) from three things: your Prophet lays no curse upon you, lest you utterly perish; the party of falsehood among you will never triumph over the party of truth; you will never agree on a false doctrine."[39]

These sentences state the doctrine of the infallibility of the *consensus ecclesiae*.[40] This fundamental concept of Islamic orthodoxy is embodied in the Arabic technical term *ijmā'*, "agreement," a word that we shall encounter frequently in the course of this essay. *Ijmā'* is the key to a grasp of the historical evolution of Islam in its political, theological, and legal aspects. Whatever is accepted by the entire Islamic community as true and correct must be regarded as true and correct. To turn one's back on the *ijmā'* is to leave the orthodox community.

That this fundamental principle came into being only after various developments had occurred within Islam appears from the difficulty that attended attempts to derive it from the Qur'ān. According to an academic anecdote, the great al-Shāfi'ī—for whom the principle of consensus was one of the decisive criteria for establishing the soundness of a law—when asked for a Qur'ān passage that supported that doctrine, had to request three days' time to think. After the grace-period had passed, he appeared before his students, sick and enfeebled, with swollen hands and feet, and with a bloated face; so strenuous an effort had been required to demonstrate that the doctrine of consensus was founded on Sura 4 verse

[e] The Philippine Islands were acquired by the United States from Spain in 1898. They became independent on July 4, 1946.

[39] Muttaqī, *Kanz al-'ummāl* (Haydarabad, A.H. 1312-1314), VI, 233, no. 4157, from the *Musnad* of Aḥmad b. Ḥanbal [see Wensinck, *Concordance*, I, 398:19ff.].

[40] *Inna ijmā'ahum lā yakūnu illā ma'ṣūman*, "their consensus cannot but be protected from error"; *fa-ijmā'uhum ma'ṣūm*: Ibn Taymīya, *Rasā'il*, I, 17:3, 82:10. *Ma'ṣūm*, "protected, immune," means roughly the same as infallible; the same expression is used to denote the infallibility of prophets and *Imāms* (see below, Ch. V, Sec. 10).

115: "If a person separates from the messenger (of Allah) after right guidance has been made clear to him, and follows a way other than the believers', We shall turn away from him as he has turned away, and we shall heat Hell with him[41]—a bad journey's end."[42] It is all the easier to find supporting passages among hadiths that are regarded as the Prophet's own teaching.[43]

Thus, all that is approved by the sense of the community of believers is correct, and can lay claim to obligatory acknowledgment, and it is correct only in the form that the sense of the community, the consensus, has given it. Only such interpretations and applications of Qur'ān and *sunna* are correct as are accepted by consensus; in this sense, consensus is the true possessor of the *auctoritas interpretativa*. Only such theological formulas are in conformity with the faith as consensus has settled on, often after sharp contention. Those forms of religious service and legality that consensus has approved are no longer open to any theoretical fault-finding. Only those men and those texts are regarded as authoritative that the consensus of the community has acknowledged as such, not in synods or councils, but through a nearly unconscious *vox populi*, whose collective character safeguards it from error. We shall have occasion to study more closely the application of this principle as a criterion of orthodoxy. We shall see that only the continued effectiveness of this principle, throughout the history of Islam, explains that certain religious phenomena gained the stamp of orthodoxy because they had gained general acceptance, although in theory they should have been censured as being contrary to Islam. They had become established in the consensus and therefore, regardless of grave theological scruples about them, at length had to be granted approval, and on occasion even accepted as obligatory.

[41] *wa-nuṣlihi*. E. Palmer translates: "we will make him reach Hell," assuming that only the first, and not the fourth, form of the verb *ṣalā* has the sense of cooking, burning, heating. Bayḍāwī too notes the difference (I, 230), and for the commonly used reading (fourth form) he assigns the sense of *adkhala*, "to cause to enter." It is, however, clear from the information in *Lisān al-'Arab*, XIX, 201, s.v., that the fourth form can also bear the sense we prefer.

[42] Subkī, *Ṭabaqāt*, II, 19 bottom. On other occasions Shāfi'ī did not seem to have quite so much trouble in hitting upon proofs from the Qur'ān. For example, in Sura 98 vs. 5, he found the most forceful proof against the Murji'ite doctrine (Subkī, *Ṭabaqāt*, I, 227)—which is rather farfetched. In later times other Qur'ānic proofs were found for the doctrine of the *ijmā'*. So, for example, Fakhr al-Dīn al-Rāzī deduced it from Sura 3 vs. 109 (*Mafātīḥ al-ghayb*, Cairo, A.H. 1278, III, 38). For other scriptural proofs, cf. C. Snouck Hurgronje, "Le Droit musulman," *RHR*, XXXVII (1898), 17 [= *Verspreide Geschriften*, II, 298].

[43] Abū Dāwūd, *Sunan* (Cairo, A.H. 1280), II, 131 [*Fitan* no. 1]; Tirmidhī, II, 25 [*Fitan* no. 7]; Baghawī, *Maṣābīḥ al-sunna* (Cairo, A.H. 1294), I, 14.

The extent of this *ijmā'* was initially more a matter of the sense of the community than of hard and fast theological definition. Futile attempts were made to delimit it with respect to time and place, and to define as *ijmā'* whatever proved to be the consensus of the Companions of Muhammad, or of the men of authority in early Medina. But later developments had made such limitations unworkable. On the other hand, rigorous theology could not be content freely to surrender *ijmā'* to the instinctive sense of the masses. At last a formula was found and *ijmā'* defined as the concordant doctrines and opinions of those who are in any given period the acknowledged doctors of Islam. They are the men with the power "to bind and to loosen"; it is their office to interpret and deduce law and theological doctrine, and to decide whether law and doctrine are correctly applied.

Clearly, this principle provides Islam with a potential for freedom of movement and a capacity for evolution. It furnishes a desirable corrective against the tyranny of the dead letter and of personal authority. It has proved itself, at least in the past, an outstanding factor in the adaptability of Islam. One wonders what its consistent application may bring in the future.

7. From the principle of consensus, let us now return to the differences of opinion that emerged as the law evolved.

The points on which the above-mentioned legal rites are at variance tend to be fairly trivial. It is easy to see why such differences would not lead to sectarian faction. Many formal differences come into play, for example, in the manner prescribed for the ritual prayer: whether certain formulas are to be spoken in a loud or a low voice; how high, relative to the shoulders, one is permitted to raise one's extended hands when the *Allāh akbar*, "God is great," is pronounced at the beginning of prayer; whether during prayer one should let one's arms hang straight down (Mālik) or cross them; whether, if one does cross them, they are to be crossed above or below the area of the navel. There are also differences in the minor formal details of genuflection and prostration. There are interesting differences of opinion whether a prayer may be considered valid if there is a woman next to the praying man or in the row in which the worshipers are aligned to pray. On this issue, the school of Abū Ḥanīfa assumes a resolutely antifeminist position, in contrast to the other schools. One point of difference, among the many minute ones, has always impressed me, because it appears to have far-reaching religious significance. The ritual language of Islam is Arabic. All religious formulas are uttered in the language of the Qur'ān. The question arises: if a person has no Arabic, may he use his native tongue to recite the *fātiḥa*, the prayer that introduces the Qur'ān and that has been called "the Lord's Prayer of Islam"? Only the school of Abū Ḥanīfa, himself of Persian extraction,[f] is unequivocally in favor of the admissibility of languages other than Arabic for the recitation of this holy text. As a result, his opponents have accused him of harboring Zoroastrian sympathies.

In other details of ritual practice, too, there are occasional differences that involve fundamental assumptions. Such are, for example, the differences relating to supplementary fasting and the breaking of the fast. While Abū Ḥanīfa is lenient toward unintentional infringements of the laws of fasting, according to Mālik and Ibn Ḥanbal a day's fast is rendered invalid by any violation through error of the strict law of fasts, and a compensation, prescribed by law, is required. Compensation is also required when, for reasons of health, failure to fast is unavoidable. Moreover, a repentant renegade who returns to the pale of Islam must, by supplementary fasting on days for which no special observance is prescribed, make up all the fast days missed during his apostasy. Abū Ḥanīfa and Shāfi'ī forgo such an arithmetical interpretation of the law of fasts.

The treatment, in the old traditions, of dietary regulations prompted some diversity in that area of the law. Most importantly, differences of opinion are caused by the subjective criterion of admissibility that the Qur'ān sets up for eating the flesh of animals (*al-ṭayyibāt*, "tasty things," cf. Ch. I, Sec. 7). Such differences are probably most prominent in the case of horseflesh, which is permitted by some *madhāhib* and prohibited by others.[44] These differences of opinion are often a mere matter of casuistry,[45] for in many cases they concern animals that would not, in

[f] There has been some argument about the ethnic origins of Abū Ḥanīfa. According to the traditional biographies, his grandfather was brought as a slave from Kabul in Afghanistan to Kufa in Iraq, where he was liberated by an Arab of the tribe of Taym. The grandfather's name is given as Zūṭā or Zuṭrā, an Aramaic word meaning small. This, together with some hints in the tradition, have led some scholars to assume an Aramaic or possibly Jewish origin.

[44] On this question, and on the relevant Qur'ānic material, cf. C. Snouck Hurgronje's critique of Van der Berg's *Beginselen van het Mohammedaansche Recht*, 1st article, pp. 26-27 in the offprint [= *Verspreide Geschriften*, II, 59ff.]. Further, T. W. Juynboll, *Handbuch des islamischen Gesetzes* (Leiden, 1908), pp. 175ff.

[45] Cf. the casuistic, in part quite absurd, questions put to al-Sha'bī in Jāḥiẓ, *Kitāb al-ḥayawān* (Cairo, 1323-1325), VI, 52 [edited by 'Abd al-Salām Muḥammad Hārūn, 2nd ed. (Cairo, 1385-1389/1965-1969), VI, 170]. Relying on Sura 6 vs. 145 ("In that which has been revealed to me, I find nothing forbidden to eat except . . . "), he declares that eating the meat of elephants is admissible.

any case, be eaten.[46] To adduce at least one illustration of the subject, I will mention that Mālik, contrary to the other schools, considers the eating of predators permissible. To be sure, this difference of opinion is in practice smoothed over for him as well, for while he excludes the eating of such animals from the category of the forbidden (*ḥarām*), he does stigmatize it as deserving of reprobation (*makrūh*). I should note here that many of the disagreements are over the varying degrees of approval or disapproval accorded to an action, over the obligatory or merely desirable character of an act of commission or omission.[47]

But the conduct of life in conformity to the law includes more than ritual. For in Islam, religious law encompasses all legal branches: civil, criminal, and constitutional. Not one chapter of the code could escape regulation according to the religious law. All aspects of private and public life fall within the province of the religious ethics by which the lawyer-theologians meant to assure that the lives of the believers were fully in harmony with the demands of their religion. There is hardly a topic in jurisprudence in which no differences of opinion appear among the various orthodox schools. The disputed issues are not always peripheral; some have considerable bearing on family life. I shall mention only one such question: it concerns the extent of the authority a woman's legal guardian (*walī*) may exercise over her entrance into marriage. The schools disagree about the cases in which the *walī* is entitled to raise a legal objection against an impending marriage, as well as about the extent to which the intervention of the *walī* is indispensable for the legal validity of a marriage.

Legal disagreements include the discrepant position, much debated in the early period, of Abū Ḥanīfa and some other teachers on an important question of judicial procedure. These teachers opposed the practice, based on a mass of traditions, that in cases of litigation over property, an oath by the plaintiff might make up for the lack of one of the two witnesses that the rules of judicial procedure require for the corroboration of a claim. They followed the strict regulation of the Qur'ān (2:282), and demanded the testimony of two men, or one man and two women, in favor of the allegation made by the party who bore the burden of proof.

[46] In Damīrī's zoological encyclopedia (*Ḥayāt al-ḥayawān*), at the end of each entry there is a discussion of how the law regards the animal, and how the *madhāhib* differ.

[47] Concerning these categories, cf. *Die Ẓāhiriten*, pp. 66ff. [= *The Ẓāhirīs*, pp. 63ff.]; Juynboll, *Handbuch des islamischen Gesetzes*, pp. 56ff.

They did not accept any other means of proof as a substitute for the testimony of witnesses.[48]

An important branch of juristic theology in Islam is devoted to the study of the doctrines that divide the schools of law, of the arguments that representatives of opposing views can marshal in support of their theories and practices, and of the critique of these arguments, made from the vantage point of one's own school. These issues have always furnished opportunities for the display of scholarly acumen, in a field of the greatest religious interest for standard Islam. In keeping with the importance attached to this area of inquiry, ever since the earliest period of legal study an abundant literature has dealt with such matters.[49]

8. The general tendency that prevails in the development of Islamic jurisprudence holds more interest for us than the particulars on which opinions differ from school to school. We must at this point assume that those who wish to become familiar with the religion of Islam have some interest in questions of hermeneutics. Whenever a religion derives its beliefs and practices from definite sacred texts, the exegesis devoted to those texts illustrates at once the legal and dogmatic development of the religion. In such cases, the history of religions is also a history of the interpretation of scripture. This is especially true of Islam, whose inner history is reflected in the methods applied in the interpretation of its sacred texts.

One fact may be mentioned before we undertake a characterization of the overall tendency followed by the jurisprudential efforts described above. The scholars of *fiqh* did not intend to embitter the life of the Muslim by imprisoning him in a stockade of legal restraints. From the very beginning they stressed compliance with the words of the Qur'ān: "Allah has laid no difficulty upon you in religion" (22:78). "The wish of Allah is your ease, not your distress" (2:185). Many variations on these principles occur in hadiths: "This religion is ease [*yusr*]," that is, free of

[48] Cf. especially Zurqānī's commentary to the *Muwaṭṭa'* (Cairo, A.H. 1279-1280), III, 184.

[49] The literature of this branch of Islamic jurisprudence has been dealt with in fullest detail by Friedrich Kern, *ZDMG*, LV (1901), 61ff., and in the introduction to his edition of Ṭabarī, *Ikhtilāf al-fuqahā'* (Cairo, 1902), pp. 4-8. Of the various synoptical works on the differences among the schools, the one most commonly used is the great *Kitāb al-mīzān* (The Balance) by the Egyptian mystic 'Abd al-Wahhāb al-Sha'rānī (d. 973/1565). There is a partial French translation by Nicolas Perron, *Balance de la loi musulmane ou Esprit de la législation islamique et divergences de ses quatre rites jurisprudentiels* (Algiers, 1898; published by the Gouvernement général de l'Algérie).

troublesome burdens. "In the eyes of God the best of religion is *al-ḥanīfīya al-samḥa*," the liberal *ḥanīfīya*.[50] "We have come to lighten things, not to aggravate them."[51] 'Abdallāh b. Mas'ūd (d. 32/635), who was of the first Islamic generation, and is one of the authoritative figures of early Islamic tradition, states the following as the guiding principle for the development of the law: "He who forbids that which is permitted is to be judged as he who declares the forbidden permissible."[52]

The doctors of the law proved faithful to this principle. One of the most respected among them, Sufyān al-Thawrī (d. 161/778) states the following doctrine: "Knowledge means that you are able to grant a permission and base it on the authority of a reliable traditionist. Anyone can find a restriction easily enough."[53]

The wiser teachers of later times were also guided by such considerations. The following principle, regarding dietary regulations, is characteristic: "When it is uncertain whether a thing should be declared as forbidden or as permitted (*matā turuddida bayn al-ibāḥa wa'l-taḥrīm*), permission prevails, for it is the root," that is, in and of itself everything is permitted; prohibition is something superadded, and in case of doubt one should fall back on the primary condition.[54]

Guided by such a view, the jurists pressed their ingenuity into service to find means of evasion whenever the literal text of the Qur'ān would have led to an oppressive situation for the believers. Liberal interpretation of the text would often lighten a burden, or explain it away entirely. Hermeneutic rules were framed by means of which the jurists would simply annul the obligatory character (*wujūb*) of laws meant to enjoin or prohibit. An imperative expression—positive or negative—may be taken to convey no more than the desirable or commendable nature of an act, and failure, by omission or commission, to comply with a law couched in such an imperative is then no longer regarded as a serious infraction that must be punished.[55]

An eminent Muslim jurist of the first century, Ibrāhīm al-Nakha'ī (d.

[50] Bukhārī, *Imān* no. 28. This sentence has also been cited as a Qur'ān verse. Cf. Nöldeke, *Geschichte des Qorāns*, 2nd ed., I, 181.

[51] Bukhārī, *'Ilm* no. 12, "*Wuḍū'* " no. 61, *Adab* no. 79.

[52] Ibn Sa'd, VI, 126:3.

[53] Ibn 'Abd al-Barr al-Namarī, *Jāmi' bayān al-'ilm wa-faḍlihi* (abridged ed., Cairo, A.H. 1320), p. 115:9. This view may be compared with the Talmudic principle *ko*ᵃḥ *dᵉ-hattārā 'adīf*, "the power of permission is of greater worth," Bab. *Berākhōt* 60a, and frequently elsewhere.

[54] In Damīrī, *Ḥayāt al-ḥayawān al-kubrā* (Cairo, A.H. 1319), s.v. *sunjāb*, II, 41:21.

[55] Cf. also the hadith in Bukhārī, *I'tiṣām* no. 16.

96/714-715) followed the principle of never declaring anything to be absolutely enjoined or prohibited, but rather, of asserting only this much: they (the Companions) disapproved (*yatakarrahūna*) of this, they recommended (*yastaḥibbūna*) that.[56] A teacher of the next generation, ʻAbdallāh ibn Shubrama (d. 144/761-762) would not pronounce with certainty except on those matters that the law regarded as permissible (*ḥalāl*). In his opinion, it was impossible to determine what must be forbidden (*ḥarām*) (apart from those things forbidden in trustworthy traditions).[57]

We could cite many more instances of the prevalence of this view in Islamic jurisprudence. But a single example will have to do. It demonstrates how this point of view works in the methodology of the Muslim doctors of the law. We read in the Qur'ān (6:121), "Do not eat of anything over which the name of Allah has not been uttered, for it is a sin." Anyone who wishes to interpret this text objectively will be compelled to see in it a strict prohibition against eating the flesh of an animal slaughtered without a preceding ritual benediction.[58] The whole context of this prohibition bears witness that the "mention of God" (*dhikr Allāh*) refers to a specific ritual act, and not to some silent remembrance of God and God's beneficence. Earlier in the passage, it says, "Eat of that over which the name of God has been uttered . . .", "why do you not eat of that over which the name of God has been uttered, seeing that He has set forth in detail what He has forbidden you (to eat)?" The admonition is directed at people who, prompted by asceticism or an enduring attachment to pagan superstitions (for some dietary regulations were known to the pagan Arabs), practiced abstinences that Muhammad had declared obsolete and had abolished. But the Prophet did stipulate as an indispensable condition that a benediction including the name of Allah must be pronounced before one may eat of the flesh of any animal that may lawfully be used for food.[59] This is probably a borrowing of the Jewish custom of the obligatory *berākhā* before the animal is slaughtered and the meat eaten. Muhammad brands the omission of this blessing as *fisq*, sin,

[56] Dārimī, *Sunan* (Cawnpore, A.H. 1293), p. 36 [*Muqaddima* no. 21]. The report makes sense only if one reads, as I have, "that which is absolutely binding" (*wājib*) in the place of *ḥalāl*, "that which is permitted" in the text.

[57] Ibn Saʻd, VI, 244:20.

[58] According to Barhebraeus' *Nomocanon*, too, "the name of the living God must be pronounced as one slaughters an animal" (cf. the passages in Karl Böckenhoff, *Speisegesetze mosaischer Art in mittelalterlichen Kirchenrechtsquellen*, Münster, 1907, p. 49). For similar matters in the *Nomocanon*, see Siegmund Fraenkel in *Deutsche Literaturzeitung*, XXI (1900), 188.

[59] Cf. Ibn Saʻd, VI, 166:21.

thus affirming in no uncertain terms that the practice he has instituted is a compulsory one. What has not been properly blessed must not be eaten. Such is, indeed, the view of the strict interpreters of the law (among the four schools, especially of the school of Abū Ḥanīfa) as affects both theoretical exegesis and the application of the law in daily life, and such remains, to this day, the view of Muslims who insist upon living in strict conformity with the law. Even during a hunt (Sura 5:4) the name of God should be pronounced before falcon or hound is released. Only then is the quarry admissible as food.[60] But the business of daily life readily showed that the stringent observance of such a law and such a prohibition ran into difficulties. How could a Muslim be sure that the requirement had in fact been satisfied? It was not long before jurists of most schools of law reached the conclusion that the negative imperative in the text of the law is not to be taken at face value; rather, it is to be understood as expressive of a wish that it is commendable (*mustaḥabb*) for the Muslim to fulfill, but that should not be construed as a strict obligation, and does not entail the consequences of a binding law.[61] When an oversight or hindrance results in failure to observe the law—or wish, we ought to say—that failure does not render it unlawful to eat the food in question. Passing through degrees of mitigation, one could arrive at the principle, "the flesh of an animal slaughtered by a Muslim is in all circumstances admissible as food, whether he (audibly) pronounced the name of God over it or no," because "the Muslim is constantly mindful of God, whether or not he makes it obvious in so many words." Once such a conviction had arisen, it was not hard to devise one traditional confirmation for it or another, so that such principles received sanction in the form of hadiths traced back to the Prophet.

In such explications of the text, the doctors of the law had grammar on their side. It was certainly true that failure to comply with Qur'ānic sentences that employed the imperative could not in each case be considered a grave sin. We read, for example, in Sura 4, vs. 3: "So marry those of the women who please you." The theologians argue that one cannot conclude from this verse that a person must marry, but only that a person may marry if he wishes. It should not be left unmentioned, however, that among the many acute interpreters of revelation there was also no lack of those who deduced from the imperative grammar of the verse that to

[60] *Muwaṭṭa'*, II, 356. See my article "Bismillāh" in James Hastings, *Encyclopaedia of Religion and Ethics* (New York, 1908-1927), II, 667b [= *Gesammelte Schriften*, V, 168].

[61] Cf. Subkī, *Mu'īd al-ni'am*, p. 203:10.

marry was in fact a duty of every Muslim, and that celibacy was forbidden. In their view, "marry!" means "you must marry," not merely "you may marry."

9. The most illuminating example of the freedom of the schools of scriptural exegesis in contrast with the self-abnegation of slavish legalism is their position toward a law customarily regarded as one of the laws that give everyday Muslim life its characteristic stamp. I have in mind the prohibition of wine.[62]

In the Qur'ān, drinking wine is branded an abomination. It is well known, however, that this divine prohibition met, at the beginning of Islamic history, with powerful resistance in a society that was not ready to renounce the freedom of the pagan Arabs in favor of legal barriers.[63] We will only mention in passing that the wine songs of the Islamic world,[64] and the role that extravagant drinking and drunkenness played in the diversions of caliphs—princes of the faith—and of prominent members of society are unlikely reflections of a society whose religious law stigmatizes the drinking of wine as the "mother of all vile things." All this could come under the category of libertinism, and be seen as frivolous infraction of a religious law that society at large acknowledged as binding.

On this issue, antinomian tendencies made their appearance very early. Already some of the Prophet's Companions in Syria (the most eminent among them being Abū Jandal), who did not let the Qur'ān interfere with their drinking, justified their transgression with the following Qur'ān verse (5:93): "Those who believe and do good works are not regarded as sinful on account of what they eat as long as they place their trust in God, believe, and do good works."[65] No wonder that 'Umar, a strict caliph, had them flogged for this liberal interpretation.

A different methodological direction is represented by the Eastern

[62] This topic has now been thoroughly treated by Caetani, *Annali dell'Islam*, III, 448-78: Il vino presso gli Arabi antichi e nei primi tempi dell'Islam.

[63] *Muhammedanische Studien*, I, 21ff. [= *Muslim Studies*, I, 28ff.]. Now compare also Lammens, *Mo'āwia*, p. 411 (*MFO*, III, 275).

[64] The poets of the Umayyad period occasionally say in so many words that the wine they are speaking of is *ḥalāl*, permitted by law. Cf. Jamīl al-'Udhrī (Iṣbahānī, *Kitāb al-aghānī*, Cairo, A.H. 1285, VII, 79:15), and Ibn Qays al-Ruqayyāt (*Dīwān*, edited by N. Rhodokanakis, Vienna, 1902, no. 57, 5: *aḥallahu Allāhu lanā* [edited by Muḥammad Yūsuf Najm (Beirut, 1378/1958), p. 144]. It is not likely that there is any reference in these verses to distinctions made by theologians (Baghdādī, *Khizānat al-adab*, Cairo, A.H. 1299, IV, 201).

[65] Ibn al-Athīr, *Usd al-ghāba*, V, 161; Suhaylī, Notes to Ibn Hishām's *Sīrat Rasūl Allāh* (edited by Ferdinand Wüstenfeld, Göttingen, 1858-1860), II, 175.

theologians' exercise of their exegetical ingenuity in order to limit the scope of the prohibition as it applies to other kinds of strong drink—drinks that a stringent and consistent interpretation of the law would have to subsume under the prohibition of wine. Some jurists endeavored to establish the conclusion that, with the exception of wine made of grapes, it is not strong drink in itself that is forbidden, but only intoxication.[66] Hadiths were even invented to support this conclusion. One of them reports, on the authority of 'Ā'isha, that the Prophet said,[67] "You may drink, but do not get drunk." On the assurance of such documents, even devout people no longer restricted themselves to drinking water, and those who held rigorous views were at pains to prove that "whatever causes intoxication when consumed in large quantities is prohibited even in the slightest amount." There was also a widespread school of theology that followed the letter of the law, and held that only *khamr*, wine made from grapes, was forbidden. Other fermented beverages are simply *sharāb* (drink) or *nabīdh*,[68] but not wine. On this view, apple wine, date wine, and so on, could be declared licit, and by lexical means one could open before the believers a wide door to many a concession to thirst.[69] Naturally, the condition remains in force that pleasure must not rise to the pitch of drunkenness. Even such a pious caliph as 'Umar II is reported to have declared that *nabīdh* was permitted.[70] An 'Abbāsid caliph, wishing to avoid conflict with the law, urgently sought his *qāḍī*'s opinion regarding *nabīdh*.[71] And since the requirements of sociability prevented people from relinquishing such beverages, the legal debate on the issue of wine was of interest to cultured society, particularly because it was often linked to philological or literary matters.

At the literary gatherings that the caliph al-Mu'taṣim held at court, and at which the flower of society gathered, among the favorite topics of dis-

[66] Subkī, *Mu'īd al-ni'am*, p. 147.

[67] Nasā'ī, *Sunan* (Shāhdara, A.H. 1282), II, 263–69 [see *Ashriba* no. 48].

[68] *Nabīdh* is also the name of a drink the Prophet himself used to take. Ibn Sa'd, II, i, 131:5, 9.

[69] That some people did have a bad conscience about their drinking appears from the following anecdote. The caliph Ma'mūn used to have the *qāḍī* Yaḥyā ibn Aktham present at meals. At these occasions he consumed *nabīdh* liberally himself, but never offered a drink to the *qāḍī*. "I cannot tolerate that a *qāḍī* should drink *nabīdh*." Ibn Abī Ṭāhir Ṭayfūr, *Kitāb Baghdād*, p. 258:8ff. Ma'mūn speaks in the same vein to the *qāḍī* of Damascus, who refuses the date wine offered him. *Aghānī*, X, 124:12.

[70] Ibn Sa'd, V, 276:16.

[71] Yāqūt, *Irshād al-arīb*, edited by D. S. Margoliouth (Leiden and London, 1907–1926), II, 261:2.

cussion were the classical Arabic synonyms for wine and the varying application to them of the prohibition of wine.[72] Chances are that it was not the rigorous view that prevailed in the deliberations of the esthetes of Baghdad. On such occasions expression was even given to views of the most radical opposition to religious restrictions, and those who held such views went to the point of making fun of the devout who upheld those restrictions. They recited a verse, attributed to Dhū 'l-Rumma, in which it is said of the devout that "they are thieves, who are called Qur'ān readers" (*humu 'l-luṣūṣu wa-hum yud'awna qurrā'ā*).[73] Or the words of another poet: "Who can prohibit the water of the rainclouds when the water of the grape has mingled with it? I detest the severities imposed on us by the transmitters of the law. I like Ibn Mas'ūd's opinion."[74]

Already in the second century, the ingenuity of the theologians of Kufa yielded a theory in line with Ibn Mas'ūd's opinion. Although outright permission of the "water of the grape" was out of the question, they furnished the legal conscience of the believers with diverse means of relief, and of these means even well-intentioned people widely availed themselves.[75]

In biographical works, pieces of information like the following are not infrequent: Wakī' b. al-Jarrāḥ, one of the most famous theologians of Iraq, celebrated for his ascetic ways (d. 197/813) "showed great endurance in drinking the *nabīdh* of the Kufans," shutting his eyes to the fact that, basically, what he was drinking was also wine.[76] Khalaf b. Hishām, a famous Kufan Qur'ān reader (d. 229/844) drank *sharāb* ("beverage," for one does not call the devil by his name) "on the strength of Qur'ānic exegesis (*'alā 'l-ta'wīl*)." His biographer does, to be sure, add that as he neared the end of his life, Khalaf repeated all the prayers he had said during his forty years' failure to give up wine; for the prayers of a wine drinker were invalid, and he had to make up for them.[77] Sharīk, the *qāḍī* of Kufa at the

[72] Mas'ūdī, *Murūj al-dhahab*, edited by Barbier de Meynard and Pavet de Courteille (Paris, 1861-1877), VIII, 105:4 [edited by Charles Pellat (Beirut, 1966-1974), V, 133].

[73] In Qālī, *Amālī*, II, 48:12.

[74] Ibn Qutayba, *'Uyūn al-akhbār*, III, 373:17 [I, 325]. Ibn Qutayba's essay about beverages, mentioned there, was formerly available only in excerpts in the *Al-'Iqd al-farīd*, but it has now been edited by A. Guy in the Arabic periodical *Al-Muqtabas* (Cairo), II (1325/1907), 234-48, 387-92, 529-35. [Cf. the more recent edition of the *Kitāb al-ashriba* by Muḥammad Kurd 'Alī (Damascus, 1366/1947)].

[75] Ibn Sa'd, VI, 67 penult., 175:20.

[76] Dhahabī, *Tadhkirat al-ḥuffāẓ*, I, 281 [I, 307f.].

[77] Ibn Khallikān, *Wafayāt al-a'yān*, edited by Ferdinand Wüstenfeld (Göttingen, 1835-1850), III, 15, no. 217 [edited by Iḥsān 'Abbās (Beirut, n.d.), II, 242f., no. 218].

time of the caliph al-Mahdī, used to relate sayings of the Prophet to people eager to hear hadiths; even as he did so one could smell *nabīdh* on his breath.[78] Or there is an example from a later period, which has to do with a famous preacher of the sixth Islamic century, Abū Manṣūr Quṭb al-Dīn al-Amīr, whom the caliph al-Muktafī sent as his ambassador to the Seljuq sultan, Sanjar ibn Malik-shāh. This pious man, who had the posthumous honor of being buried near the pious ascetic al-Junayd, composed a treatise on the permissibility of wine drinking.[79]

Naturally, in legal circles, the advocates of rigor were moved to zealous protest against this trend and its manifestations. In contrast to liberties that some people "introduced in contradiction to the *sunna*" (*aḥdathū*), they would drink, as long as they lived, nothing but "water, milk, and honey."[80] They managed to marshal against these mitigations of the law the Prophet's words of condemnation—as they managed to do against every liberal trend in the history of Islam. "My community" (as a hadith is made to proclaim), "will, in days to come, drink wine. They will not call it by its proper name, and their princes (*umarā'uhum*) will support them in what they do."[81] Such people are threatened that God will turn them into apes and hogs, like the transgressors of bygone nations.[82]

In any case, the manner in which the question of wine was treated by a widely acknowledged school, that of Kufa, shows that with the growth of legal ingenuity in the interpretation of the religious law, various means were contrived to mitigate the literal rigor of the text.

The differences of opinion about the admissibility of such hermeneutic methods, and about the proper extent and manner of their application, comprise a large portion of the doctrines that set apart the legal rites into which the Muslim world is divided. Let it suffice for us, as historians of Islam, to observe that the great majority of the schools of law have in many cases availed themselves of the free exercise of such hermeneutics, to the end that life in the spirit of the law might be brought into line with the actual ways of society, and that the narrow law of Mecca and Medina might be adapted to larger circumstances; for as foreign lands were conquered and radically different ways of life encountered, requirements arose that the letter of the law could not easily accommodate.

This is the sole reason why the soul-destroying pedantry of the jurists

[78] *Ibid.*, III, 114, no. 290 [II, 465, no. 291]. [79] *Ibid.*, VIII, 108, no. 733 [V, 212, no. 723].
[80] Ibn Sa'd, VI, 64:3, 7. [81] Ibn al-Athīr, *Usd al-ghāba*, V, 12:1.
[82] Bukhārī, *Ashriba* no. 6.

of Islam must claim the interest of the historian of religions and civilizations. It was for this reason that I felt justified in giving some indications on matters that are so dreary from the point of view of religious ethics. In addition, they also prepare us for what I shall have to say in my last chapter about adaptation in Islam to modern circumstances.

10. Before concluding our discussion of the law, we must deal with two harmful consequences that came about as the theological spirit was trained to such quibbling discriminations. One was the overall spiritual orientation brought about by such tendencies; the other an appraisal of religious life that proved detrimental to the inwardness of religion.

Let us take up the first. Owing to the dominance gained by the tendencies I have described, the spirit of casuistry and the pedantic juggling of words came to hold sway, especially in Iraq.[83] The task of interpreting God's word and of regulating life in conformity to God's word became lost in absurd sophistry and dreary exegetical trifling: in thinking up contingencies that will never arise and debating riddling questions in which extreme sophistry and hair-splitting are joined with the boldest and most reckless flights of fancy. People debate far-fetched legal cases, casuistic constructs quite independent of the real world. For example: under the laws of inheritance, what share of the estate may be claimed by a male ascendant at the fifth degree of removal from the deceased if the latter died childless?[84] This, as it happens, is a relatively tame instance. The law of inheritance, with its varied possibilities, early became a popular and suitable arena for the mental gymnastics of casuistry.[85]

Popular superstition, too, furnishes the jurists with material for such exercises. Since in popular belief the metamorphosis of man into beast is within the range of natural occurrences, the jurists inquire in all seriousness into the legal status of enchanted persons and their responsibilities under the law.[86] Since, on the other hand, demons frequently assume human shape, the jurists assess the consequences of such transformations for religious law; serious arguments and counterarguments are urged, for

[83] "In Iraq scant attention is paid to *tawḥīd* (questions of belief); *fiqh* predominates." 'Aṭṭār, *Tadhkirat al-awliyā'*, II, 175 top.

[84] Ibn Khallikān, X, 22, no. 803 [VI, 148, no. 793].

[85] Cf. Juynboll's article "Akdarīya" in *EI*[1], I, 229f. The problem of a grandfather's status under the law of inheritance was from early times a subject of the jurists' casuistry (Ibn Sa'd, II, ii, 100:9) and of differences of opinion (cf. Damīrī, I, 351, under *ḥayya*). Cf. *Al-Imāma wa'l-siyāsa* (Cairo, 1904), II, 76. The information concerning this particular problem of inheritance, gathered in Muttaqī, *Kanz al-'ummāl*, VI, 14-18, is extremely instructive about the genesis of legal rules in early Islam.

[86] Damīrī, II, 289f., under the entry *qird*.

example, whether such beings can be numbered among the participants necessary for the Friday service.[87] Another problematic case that the divine law must clarify: how is one to deal with progeny from a marriage between a human being and a demon in human form (a further eventuality admitted in popular belief)?[88] What are the consequences in family law of such marriages? Indeed, the problem of *munākaḥat al-jinn* (marriages with the *jinn*) is treated in such circles with the same seriousness as any important point of the religious law.[89]

Advocates of the legality of such mixed marriages (Ḥasan al-Baṣrī is one) cite cases in which the human party's fidelity to the *sunna* is not in question. Damīrī, the author of an extremely important zoological lexicon, who incorporates such facts into his article on *jinn*, speaks of his per-

[87] *Ibid.*, I, 265, under the entry *jinn*.

[88] Sexual relations between human beings and demons (cf. the Akkadian *ardat lilī*) are the theme of a type of fable that spread indirectly from Babylonian fancy into Arabic folktale and thence into Islamic superstition. We are given the names of people who, in Arab antiquity or in the history of non-Arabs, sprang from such mixed unions. Cf. Jāḥiẓ, *Ḥayawān*, I, 85ff. [I, 185ff.], where such fables are vigorously repudiated. Jāḥiẓ calls people who consider them possible "deplorable scholars" (*'ulamā' al-saw'*) and stresses explicitly that he is only reporting what others have said. (Cf. also Damīrī, II, 25-27, under the entry *si'lāt.*) For examples from Islamic popular belief, see R. Campbell Thompson, "The Folklore of Mossoul," *Proceedings of the Society of Biblical Archaeology*, XXVIII (1906), 83, and A. H. Sayce, "Cairene Folklore," *Folklore*, XI (1900), 388. That such relations do in fact occur has also been inferred from Qur'ān 17:64, 55:56, 74. Cf. Damīrī, II, 27:19. In religious law, the fact that the partners to the marriage are different in kind (*ikhtilāf al-jins*) is considered by many jurists an *impedimentum dirimens* to the admissibility of such marriages; they base this view on Qur'ān 16:72: "Allah has given you wives from among yourselves, *min anfusikum*." But it is not universally acknowledged as an impediment; cf. Subkī, *Ṭabaqāt*, V, 45:5 from bottom. That the legal inadmissibility of such marriages was not beyond dispute appears from the fact that Yaḥyā ibn Ma'īn and other orthodox authorities ascribed the sharp intelligence of certain scholars, mentioned by name, to the circumstance that one parent of each was a *jinnī* (Dhahabī, *Tadhkirat al-ḥuffāẓ*, II, 149 [II, 571]). Ibn Khallikān, IX, 44ff., no. 763 [V, 346ff., no. 753], mentions a person whose milk-brother was a demon. [There is no such information in this biography, which discusses the poet al-Mu'ayyad al-Ulūsī]. Cf. also my *Abhandlungen zur arabischen Philologie* (Leiden, 1896-1899), II, cviii; now also MacDonald, *The Religious Attitude and Life in Islam*, pp. 143f., 155. Alfred Bel relates that the people of Tlemcen used to believe of an inhabitant, recently dead (1908), of their city that he was married to a *jinnīya* besides his legitimate wife ("La Population musulmane de Tlemcen," *Revue des études ethnographiques et sociologiques*, I (1908), 206). The jurists also dealt with the question of whether angels and *jinn* are legally competent to acquire property (*milk*); Subkī, *Ṭabaqāt*, V, 179.

[89] Cf. my *Abhandlungen zur arabischen Philologie*, I, 109. In this respect we may consider Shāfi'ī an exception to the spirit prevalent among the theological jurists. His school transmits from him the principle that "if an otherwise irreproachable man were to assert that he had seen *jinn*, we would declare him unqualified to give testimony in a court of law"; see Subkī, *Ṭabaqāt*, I, 258:4 from bottom.

sonal acquaintance with a *shaykh* who was the wedded husband of four female demons.[g]

Moreover, legal ingenuity invents tricks (*ḥiyal*) that are of advantage in certain situations. These legal fictions constitute an integral part of *fiqh*. They often serve—as, for example, where vows are involved—to ease the conscience. Scholars of the law are consulted to find a "way out"—and this aspect of their activity can hardly be celebrated as good for the moral temper of social life. As a poet of the Umayyad era puts it, "There is no good in a vow if there is no way out of it."[90] Legal scholarship faced this need resolutely. The Ḥanafite school of law (with its cradle in Iraq) particularly distinguished itself in the investigation of such legal devices, although the other schools were not left far behind.[91] The master of the school blazed the trail. Fakhr al-Dīn al-Rāzī, great exegete and religious philosopher, devotes a long excursus in his giant Qur'ān commentary to the excellencies of the *imām* Abū Ḥanīfa, and most of the proofs he offers for Abū Ḥanīfa's legal profundity have to do with the solution of difficult problems in the law of vows.[92]

It must be recognized that it was not only piety that often mutinied against the conjunction, created by the dominant theology, of such matters with religion and the word of God. (The eleventh century A.D. will offer us the most forceful example of such rebellion, cf. Chapter IV.) Folk humor also exercised its sarcasm on the activities, and complacent arrogance, of these theologians and perverters of the law. Abū Yūsuf of Kufa (d. 182/795), student of Abū Ḥanīfa, and chief *qāḍī* of the caliphs al-Mahdī and Hārūn al-Rashīd, is the whipping boy of the anecdotes in which folk

[g] Damīrī, *Ḥayāt al-ḥayawān*, I, 260:4ff.

[90] Jarīr, *Dīwān* (Cairo, A.H. 1313), II, 128:13 [edited by Nu'mān Muḥammad Amīn Ṭaha (Cairo, 1969-1971), II, 993, v. 2]; *Naqā'iḍ Jarīr wa'l-Farazdaq*, edited by A. A. Bevan (Leiden, 1905-1912), II, 754:3.

[91] "Das Prinzip der *Taḳijja* im Islam," *ZDMG*, LX (1906), 223 [= *Gesammelte Schriften*, V, 69; partial French translation in *Arabica*, VII (1960), 134]. Abū Yūsuf (Ch. II, Sec. 10) already composed a tractate about such *ḥiyal*; cf. Jāḥiẓ, *Ḥayawān*, III, 4:2 [III, 11]. This becomes a constant subject of practical *fiqh*, especially in the Ḥanafite school. One of the earliest works of this sort, by Abū Bakr Aḥmad al-Khaṣṣāf (d. 261/874), court jurist to the caliph al-Muhtadī, is considered the fundamental work of this legal art. It is now available in a printed edition, *Kitāb al-Khaṣṣāf fi'l-ḥiyal* (Cairo, A.H. 1314). [The problem of the *ḥiyal*, legal devices or stratagems, first brought to the attention of modern scholarship by Goldziher in this and one or two other studies, was examined in detail by the late Joseph Schacht. For a general account, see his article "Ḥiyal" in *EI*², where further references are given.]

[92] Rāzī, *Mafātīḥ al-ghayb*, I, 411-13.

humor pokes fun at lawyers—a literature that also found its way into the Thousand and One Nights.

The second consequence was the harmful effect on the course of religious life. The predominance, in religious learning, of the tendency to search into the law, using the methods of casuistry, as I have said elsewhere, gradually resulted in impressing upon the teachings of Islam the stamp of a quibbling legalism. Under the influence of this tendency, religious life itself was seen from a legal point of view. This was not likely to strengthen true piety, the devotion of the heart. A faithful adherent of Islam is thus, even in his own consciousness, under the governance of man-made rules. Next to them the word of God, which is for the Muslim the source and means of moral improvement, orders only an exiguous part of the customs and observances of life, and indeed is forced into the background. Precisely those people are considered doctors of the faith who employ the methodology of jurisprudence to investigate the ways in which the law's demands are fulfilled, who subtly develop and manipulate the findings of these investigations, and carefully see to it that they are adhered to. It is understood that these people are meant in the saying ascribed to the Prophet: "The scholars (*'ulamā'*) of my community are as the prophets of the people of Israel"[93]—they, and not religious philosophers or moralists, not to mention the representatives of secular sciences.

I have mentioned that there was no lack of earnest men who raised their voices in strict condemnation of this perversion of the religious ideal, which manifested itself very early in the history of Islam, and who worked hard to rescue the inwardness of religion from the clutches of quibbling religious lawyers. We have seen that they have the support of excellent hadiths. Before making their acquaintance, we must turn our attention to the dogmatic developments in Islam.

[93] "Die Religion des Islams," p. 111:16ff.

III. *The Growth and Development of Dogmatic Theology*

1. Prophets are not theologians.[a] The message that springs from the spontaneous urgency of their conscience, the religous conceptions that they awaken, do not take the form of a deliberately planned system. Indeed, more often than not, their teachings defy all attempts at rigorous systematization. Only in later generations, after a closed community has been formed by the common cultivation of ideas that had kindled the first believers' spirit, is the stage set, both by developments within the community and influences on it from without, for those to play their part who feel called to interpret the prophetic revelations,[1] who fill in the gaps in the prophet's teaching and round it out, who expound it (often incongruously) and comment on it—which is to say, who read into it things that never entered the mind of its author. The theologian answers questions that lie outside the prophet's sphere of interest; he reconciles contradictions the prophet would have been at ease with; he devises inflexible formulas, and erects rows upon rows of argument into ramparts, in the hope of securing those formulas against assault from within and without. He then derives all his systematically ordered tenets from the prophet's words, not infrequently from their most literal sense. He proclaims that those tenets are what the prophet had intended to teach from the outset. Theologian disputes with theologian, each hurling the cunning arguments of an arrogant subtlety at anyone who, using the same means, draws different conclusions from the living words of the prophet.

Before such inclinations can be acted on, prophetic revelation must take the form of a holy writ, a canonically fixed and formally defined text. A tangle of dogmatic commentaries then springs up around scripture, removing the text from the spirit that pervades its true essence. The

[a] On the development of Islamic theology, see Louis Gardet and M. M. Anawati, *Introduction à la théologie Musulmane: essai de théologie comparée* (Paris, 1948); H.A.R. Gibb, "The Structure of Religious Thought in Islam," in his *Studies in the Civilization of Islam*, edited by S. J. Shaw and W. J. Polk (Boston, 1962), pp. 176-218; D. B. MacDonald, *The Religious Attitude and Life in Islam* (Chicago, 1909); and idem, *Aspects of Islam* (New York, 1911).

[1] This claim is expressed in Islam in the sentence *al-'ulamā' warathat al-anbiyā'*: "The scholars of religion are the heirs of the prophets."

commentaries are more intent on proof than on elucidation. They are the inexhaustible sources from which the speculations of systematic theology flow.

Shortly after its rise, Islam, like other religions, entered upon such a phase of theological development. Simultaneously with the events that were the subject of our second chapter, the beliefs of Islam also became objects of reflection. The growth of a dogmatic theology in Islam took place along with the growth of speculation about the religious law.

It would be an arduous task to derive from the Qur'ān itself a system of beliefs that is coherent, self-sufficient, and free of self-contradiction. Of the most important religious ideas we get only general impressions, which yield contradictory views on some particulars. The Prophet's beliefs were reflected in his soul in shades that varied with the moods that dominated him. In consequence, it was not long before a harmonizing theology had to assume the task of solving the theoretical problems such contradictions caused.

Now, search for inconsistencies in the revelation seems early to have made them, in Muhammad's case, a matter for reflection. Already during the Prophet's lifetime the revelations were exposed to critics who kept a watch for their shortcomings. The indecisive, contradictory character of his teachings was the butt of scornful remarks. Thus, despite the stress that the revelation was "a (clear) Arabic Qur'ān with no crookedness in it" (39:28, cf. 18:1, 41:3) the Qur'ānic text itself admits in a Medinese sura that the divine revelation consists "in part of solidly made verses, which form the core of the book, and in part of ambiguous ones. Those with an evil inclination in their heart seek after what is unclear in it, wishing to trouble people's minds and wishing to interpret it. But no one but God knows its interpretation. Those who are firmly rooted in knowledge say: 'We believe in it; it is all from our Lord' " (3:7).

Such scrutiny of the Qur'ān was all the more pertinent in the next generation, when not only the enemies of Islam busied themselves with discovering its weaknesses, but among the believers as well the careful consideration of its contradictory statements had acquired urgency.

An example will soon show us how in the debate over a fundamental religious doctrine—the freedom of the will—arguments for both sides of the issue could be drawn from the Qur'ān.

The hadith unfolds before us a picture of this intellectual movement in the community, as of every other aspect of the internal history of Islam. In the hadith, naturally, it is projected back into the time of the Prophet, and the Prophet is associated also with settling problems. In fact, this intellectual trend does not antedate the period in which theological thought began to germinate. As the hadith would have it, believers had already harassed the Prophet by pointing out dogmatic contradictions in the Qur'ān. Such discussions (according to the hadith) stirred him to anger. "The Qur'ān," he says, "was not revealed with the purpose that you might seize on one part of it to strike at another, as the nations of the past did with the revelations of their prophets. Rather, in the Qur'ān one thing confirms another. You should act according to what you understand of it; you should accept on faith what is confusing to you."[2]

The artless believer's sentiment is put forward as the Prophet's own dictum. Such is the method of the hadith.

2. Political circumstances on the one hand, and the stimulus of contacts with the outside world on the other, imposed upon the early Muslims, who had not been much disposed to riddling over theological niceties, the need to take distinct positions on questions for which the Qur'ān had no definite and unequivocal answer.

That internal political circumstances stirred dogmatic controversy is readily shown. The Umayyad revolution presented the Muslims with a new political and constitutional situation. It also gave them the first opportunity in their history to try their hand at theological questions: to judge the new institutions in the light of religious demands.

Here we must once more turn our attention to a matter of early Islamic history that we touched on in the last chapter: the assessment of the Umayyad rulers' religious attitude.

The once current view of the Umayyads' relation to Islam may now be regarded as quite obsolete. Taking their cue from the Islamic historical tradition, students of Islam used to believe that the Umayyads stood in rigid and conscious opposition to the demands of Islam, and governed accordingly. The rulers of that dynasty, and their governors and administrators, were made out to be no less than the heirs of the enemies of nascent Islam, and it was thought that their attitude toward religion was a new guise in which the old Quraysh spirit of animosity—or at best indifference—to Islam had survived.

The Umayyads, it is true, were not holy-minded, and they affected no

[2] For hadiths disapproving of such inclinations, see Ibn Sa'd, IV, i, 141:15ff.; *ZDMG*, LVII (1903), 393f. Cf. also Bukhārī, *Tafsīr* no. 237 (concerning Sura 41), with a number of Qur'ān passages that were found contradictory and laid before Ibn 'Abbās for an explanation.

extravagant piety. Life at their court did not in all respects conform to the narrow, ascetic norms that the pious expected the heads of the Islamic state to follow, and whose particulars the pious put forward in their hadiths with the claim that they had been ordained by the Prophet. There are reports of the devout inclinations of certain Umayyads,[3] but there can be no question that they did not satisfy the pietists, for whom the ideal government was that of Abū Bakr and 'Umar in Medina.

The Umayyads were aware that as caliphs or *imāms* they stood at the head of an empire whose foundations had been laid by a religious upheaval: they were conscious of being true adherents of Islam. This cannot be denied them.[4] Nonetheless, a gulf stretched between their criteria in running the Islamic state and the pietistic expectations of the holy-minded, who watched with impotent fury the doings of their Umayyad rulers and whose party was in large measure responsible for the historical traditions preserved about those rulers. The Umayyads' view of the duty they owed Islam failed to conform to the notions and wishes of the "Qur'ān readers." The Umayyads knew that they were steering Islam onto new paths. One of their most powerful servants, the bitterly maligned Ḥajjāj ibn Yūsuf, presumably spoke as the Umayyads thought

[3] Ibn Sa'd, V, 174:13. Before his succession to the throne, 'Abd al-Malik led a pious ascetic life (*'ābid, nāsik*); see Julius Wellhausen, *Das arabische Reich und sein Sturz* (Berlin, 1902), p. 134 [translated as *The Arab Kingdom and Its Fall* (Calcutta, 1927), p. 215]. The *Kitāb al-imāma wa'l-siyāsa* (Cairo, 1904)—a book wrongly ascribed to Ibn Qutayba (cf., concerning this, M. J. de Goeje in *RSO*, I, 1907, 415ff.)—willingly offers information about the piety of the Umayyads. When people came to offer the caliphate to 'Abd al-Malik's father, Marwān I, they found him busy reading the Qur'ān by the light of a small lamp (II, 22 bottom). It is also reported that Marwān, even as caliph, was zealous in his efforts to have the religious laws laid down in established form (Ibn Sa'd, II, ii, 117:8). 'Abd al-Malik himself calls on people to "revive Qur'ān and *sunna*. . . . There can be no difference of opinion about his piety" (*Al-Imāma wa'l-siyāsa*, II, 25:9). Even in Ḥajjāj, so odious to the pious, the sources report some traits of devotion (72:3, 74:10; cf. Ṭabarī, II, 1186, orders for days of penitence and prayer in the mosques. Particularly noteworthy is Jāḥiẓ, *Ḥayawān*, V, 63:5 from bottom [V, 195], where it is reported of Ḥajjāj that he harbored a deep religious reverence for the Qur'ān—*yadīnu 'alā 'l-Qur'ān* [Hārūn emends to *yudnī 'alā 'l-Qur'ān,* a somewhat different sense]—in contrast with the partiality to poetry and genealogy prevalent among the Umayyads and their courtiers). Very important evidence is furnished by the poetry in which poets wishing to please caliphs and statesmen celebrate them as religious heroes; e.g., Jarīr, *Dīwān*, I, 168:8 [I, 296, vs. 24]; II, 97:5 from bottom [I, 275, vs. 17] (Marwān, the grandfather of 'Umar II, is called *dhū'l-nūr* and is mentioned in order to add to the glory of the pious caliph). In *Naqā'iḍ Jarīr wa'l-Farazdaq*, I, 104, vs. 19, Jarīr calls the caliph *imām al-hudā*, "the *Imām* of right (religious) guidance." See also 'Ajjāj, *Dīwān*, edited by Wilhelm Ahlwardt in *Sammlungen alter arabischer Dichter*, II (Berlin, 1903), Appendix p. 22:15. Cf. *Muhammedanische Studien*, II, 381 [= *Muslim Studies*, II, 345].

[4] C. H. Becker, *Papyri Schott-Reinhardt I* (Heidelberg, 1906), p. 35.

when, at the sickbed of 'Umar's son, he dropped an ironic remark about the old regime.[5]

No doubt the Umayyads' rise to power inaugurated a new system. Their idea of Islam, honestly held, was political: "Islam had united the Arabs and led them to rule a world empire."[6] The satisfaction that religion afforded them was in no small measure due to the fact that Islam "had brought glory and high rank, and had taken possession of the heritage of nations."[7] To maintain and extend the political might of Islam internally and externally was, as they saw it, their task as rulers. In doing so they believed themselves to be serving the cause of religion. Those who crossed them were treated as mutineers against Islam, somewhat as Ahab, king of Israel, had treated the zealous Elijah as *'okher Yisrael*, "he that troubleth Israel" (1 Kings 18:17). When they battled rebels who claimed a religious ground for their resistance, the Umayyads acted in the conviction that they drew the punitive sword against the enemies of Islam in the course of duty, that Islam might endure and flourish.[8] They marched on holy places, they trained their mangonels on the Ka'ba (for centuries their pious enemies would charge them with this grave crime of sacrilege), but they believed, whenever the needs of state demanded their action, that they were acting in behalf of Islam: punishing its enemies, and menacing the seat of rebellion against the unity and internal strength of the Islamic state.[9] In their view, all those were enemies of Islam who, on whatever pretext, subverted the unity of the state that the shrewdness of Umayyad policy had consolidated. Despite all favors shown the family of the Prophet—a fact for which the evidence was first collected in Lammens' recent work on Mu'āwiya[10]—they fought the 'Alid pretenders who threatened their state. They did not flinch from the battle at Karbalā', whose bloody outcome has remained to this day the subject of the martyrologies of the Shī'īs, who heap maledictions upon them. There

[5] Ibn Sa'd, IV, i, 137:5, 20. Ḥusayn and his partisans are fought as "renegades from the *dīn* who set themselves against the *Imām* (Yazīd, the son of Mu'āwiya)"; Ṭabarī, II, 342:16.

[6] So characterized by Wellhausen, *Die religiös-politischen Oppositionsparteien im alten Islam* (Berlin, 1901; Abhandlungen der Königlichen Gesellschaft der Wissenschaften zu Göttingen, Philologisch-Historische Klasse, V, no. 2), p. 7 [translated as *The Religio-political Factions in Early Islam* (Amsterdam, 1975), p. 8].

[7] Ṭabarī, I, 2909:16.

[8] Jarīr, (*Dīwān*, I, 62:13 [II, 744, vs. 30]) celebrates the suppression of such rebels as a victory over the *mubtadi'ūn fī'l-dīn*, innovators in religion.

[9] G. van Vloten, *Recherches sur la domination arabe, le chiitisme et les croyances messianiques sous le khalifat des Omayades* (Amsterdam, 1894), p. 36.

[10] Lammens, *Mo'āwia*, pp. 154ff. (*MFO*, II, 46ff.).

was no severing the interests of Islam from the interests of the state. Accession to power had been, in the dynasty's view, a religious success. Their loyal supporters understood that the Umayyads' actions were faithful to Islam; their panegyrists forever praised them as its protectors. It even appears that among their loyal subjects, some groups held the Umayyads in religious veneration, as defenders of the rights of the Prophet's house held the 'Alid pretenders whose aura of holiness stemmed from their bloodline.[11]

The change that came with the Umayyads was seen in a different light by those pious people who dreamt of a kingdom that was not of this world, and who fostered, on various pretexts, an antipathy to the dynasty and to the spirit in which it governed. In the judgment of most of them, the power of this congenitally tainted dynasty had been conceived in sin. In the eyes of the dreamers, the new government was illegitimate and irreligious. It did not accord with their theocratic ideal, and seemed to hinder the effective realization of their aspiration: a state that would be to God's pleasure. In its origin it had already encroached on the right of the Prophet's holy family, and its political acts had shown it to be wholly without regard for the sanctuaries of Islam. Moreover, the representatives of the ruling system were seen to be men who, even in their personal conduct, did not show sufficient diligence in observing the laws of Islam as the pious dreamed them. This is the opinion put in the mouth of the Prophet's grandson Ḥusayn, the first 'Alid pretender: "They practice obedience to Satan and forsake obedience to God, display corruption, obstruct divine statutes, arrogate to themselves unlawful portions of the spoils of war,[12] and allow what God has forbidden and forbid what God has allowed."[13] They abandon the sacred *sunna* and promulgate arbitrary decrees that run counter to religious views.[14]

[11] This follows from Ibn Sa'd, V, 68:23ff. [The veneration of the Umayyads in some Muslim circles, to which Goldziher first drew attention (see further his *Muhammedanische Studien*, II, 46–47, 97; = *Muslim Studies*, II, 54, 96–97) was further discussed by Henri Lammens in his *Le Califat de Yazīd Ier* (Beirut, 1910-1921), p. 14, and forms the subject of an important study by Charles Pellat, "Le Culte de Mu'āwiya au IIIe siècle de l'hégire," *Studia Islamica*, VI (1956), 53–66, where other studies are also mentioned.]

[12] In tendentious reports this (*yasta'thirūna bi'l-fay'*) is dwelt upon as one of their offenses; Ibn Sa'd, IV, i, 166:11; Abū Dāwūd, *Sunan*, II, 183 [*Sunna* no. 27; see Wensinck, *Concordance*, I, 13:2f.].

[13] Ṭabarī, II, 300:9ff.

[14] For their *bid'as*, Kumayt, *Al-Hāshimīyāt*, edited by Josef Horovitz (Leiden, 1904), p. 123:7ff., is very important.

Now it should have been strictly demanded by intransigent advocates of religion that such people be resisted to the utmost, that at the very least one must passively refrain from according their rule any sign of recognition. As a theory this was easy to propose, but it would have been hard to carry into execution. The good of the state, the interests of the religious community, must prevail over all other considerations. This meant that violent shocks must be avoided and the actual government necessarily tolerated. The appeal to divine judgment, expressed in pious maledictions,[15] proved an ineffectual weapon. Man, it was felt, should offer no resistance to what God tolerated. The object of man's hope should be that God would one day fill with righteousness the world that was now full of iniquity. Such unspoken hopes gave birth to the idea of the *mahdī*; the real and the ideal were reconciled by a firm belief in the future coming of the divinely guided theocratic ruler. We shall have further occasion to speak of this subject (Ch. V, Sec. 12).

One of the public manifestations of the Islamic ruler's authority, and one that issued from the theocratic character of his rule, was that he or his representative exercised the office of leading the public religious service as *imām*, conductor of the liturgy. No matter how much it vexed the pious to see these embodiments of godlessness act in that sacred role—it was thought that they did not shrink even from performing it while drunk—they became reconciled to this as well. In the interest of maintaining tranquillity in the state, one may "perform the *ṣalāt* behind a pious man or behind a malefactor." Such was the formula for the toleration practiced by the pious.

But not all found a resting place in such a passive attitude. The matter also needed to be settled in principle. The experiences of daily life and the intransigent advocacy of religious demands brought into the foreground the question: is it at all correct to exclude from the faith, in principle, the transgressors against the law, and to regard one's position in relation to them as very nearly one of resigned submission to force? After all, the transgressors *are* Muslims, their lips acknowledge God and His prophets, and their hearts may well do the same. To be sure, they render themselves guilty of violations of the law—the terms for these were disobedience and revolt—nonetheless, they are believers. There was a large party that decided this question in a manner that suited the exigencies of reality

[15] For example, Sa'īd ibn al-Musayyab, who in every prayer cursed the Banū Marwān; cf. Ibn Sa'd, V, 95:5.

even better than the common view of resigned submission. The men of this party laid down the principle that what mattered was the formal avowal of faith. Where there is faith, practice and behavior can do no harm; where faith is lacking, no number of lawful works can do any good. *Fiat applicatio*. Thus the Umayyads were vindicated as true and good Muslims. SInce they were of the *ahl al-qibla*, those who prayed facing in the direction of the Ka'ba and so avowed their membership in the community of believers, they had to be regarded as believers. The pious scruples about them were quite groundless.

The party whose adherents theoretically elaborated this doctrine of toleration called itself *Murji'a*.[16] The word means "those who defer," and the sense of it is that they do not presume to ascertain the ultimate fate of their fellow men but leave it to God to sit in judgment over them, and to make His decision.[17] In one's relation to others in this world, one must be satisfied with their formal avowal of belonging to the community of true believers in Islam.[18]

For this stand there is a precedent in the moderation displayed amid the dissensions of an earlier age by those who wanted no part in the stormy dispute over 'Alī and 'Uthmān: which of the two was to be regarded as a true believer, and which a sinner and so unworthy of the caliphate. The moderate party left it to God to settle this question, which opposing camps of Muslims had made their shibboleth.[19]

Such moderation was naturally not to the taste of those pious groups who saw nothing but ungodliness and apostasy in the policies that had predominated in the state, and in the men who stood for them. To begin with, the leniency of the Murji'a stood in direct opposition to the views of those who supported 'Alid claims and nurtured the idea of a theocratic state built on divine justice and governed by the family of the Prophet. Hence the sharp antagonism between Murji'ites and the partisans of the

[16] The doctrine did not exclude the possibility that even a Murji'ite might rebel against Ḥajjāj's cruelties (Ibn Sa'd, VI, 205:12); by such resistance one was not pronouncing judgment on the Umayyad caliphate.

[17] Regarding linguistic usage, cf. Nawawī, *Tahdhīb al-asmā'*, p. 108:7 from bottom: Ibn Sīrīn was *arja' al-nās li-hādhihi'l-umma,* meaning that he was most forbearing in judging his fellow men, but stringent toward himself. [This is one of several explanations of the term *murji'a* offered by Muslim and Western scholars. For a discussion, see the article "Murdji'a" in *EI*[1] (by A. J. Wensinck).]

[18] According to some Murji'ites, the pious caliph 'Umar II, with whom they had discussed these questions, embraced their view; Ibn Sa'd, VI, 218:20.

[19] Ibn Sa'd, VI, 214:19: *al-murji'at al-ūlā*. The opinion of Burayda ibn al-Ḥuṣayb (*ibid.*, IV, i, 179:11ff.) is an example of this trend.

'Alids.[20] The contrast is even sharper between the Murji'a and another rebellious movement. As Umayyad successes accrued and the conflicts between opposing parties grew ever more bitter, those who had adopted the Murji'ite position found cause to sharpen their principal concepts, to take another step in formulating their view, and to reject explicitly the notion of denouncing the existing government as one of unbelievers. They were pushed to this step because the most inveterate enemies of the existing political order, the Khārijites (of whom we shall have further occasion to speak, cf. Ch. V, Sec. 2) spread disquiet by their slogan that faith in a general way was not sufficient, that grave sins irreparably barred the sinner from the community of believers. What then was to be the fate of the unhappy Umayyads, who were, in the Khārijite view, of all transgressors the worst?[21]

Thus the seedbed of this controversy, which reaches back into the earliest history of Islam (it cannot be dated with more precision), lay in the nature of the political developments in the state and in the various attitudes toward them that different strata of the Muslim population assumed. It was not a theological need that gave the first impulse to discussions of the proper role of *'amal* (works, praxis) in determining what makes a Muslim a Muslim.[22]

The time came when live political issues were no longer in the foreground of the debate over this question. It then became a topic for discussions of a more or less academic interest, with a few other dogmatic niceties and subtleties joined to it. If *'amal* is not an absolutely necessary element in the definition of who is a true believer, then—as the opposition says—an ingenious Murji'ite could conclude that a person cannot be

[20] For Murji'ites against the partisans of 'Alī, see *Muhammedanische Studien*, II, 91 n. 5 [= *Muslim Studies*, II, 92 n. 2]. Cf. *Sabā'ī*, fanatic Shī'ī (a follower of 'Abdallāh ibn Sabā') in contrast to *murji'* (Ibn Sa'd, VI, 192:17). This opposition survived into the time when the profession of Murji'ite views no longer had any but theoretical significance. Jāḥiẓ, *Al-Bayān wa'l-tabyīn* (Cairo, A.H. 1311-1313), II, 149 bottom [edited by 'Abd al-Salām Muḥammad Hārūn (Cairo, 1367-1370/1948-1950), III, 350], cites the following epigram by a Shī'ī: "If it gives you pleasure to see a Murji'ite die of his disease in advance of his death, / Keep praising 'Alī in his presence, and pronounce prayerful blessings on the Prophet and those of his house (*ahl baytihi*)."

[21] The condemnation of the Umayyad rulers by these pious fanatics is thrown into clear relief in *Aghānī*, XX, 106. In Ibn Sa'd, V, 182:15ff., Khārijites most cruelly kill a man spreading a hadith in which the Prophet warns against rebellion and teaches passivity and patient endurance.

[22] This does not conflict with the information that van Vloten collected about *irjā'*; *ZDMG*, XLV (1891), 161ff.

branded a *kāfir* because he bows down to the sun; his act is only a sign of unbelief, and does not in itself constitute unbelief (*kufr*).[23]

Murji'ite ideas gave rise, in particular, to one basic question on which theological parties stood divided and Muslim theologians forever sharpened their wits: in faith can one distinguish degrees of more and less? Such a position is inadmissible in the view of those who do not consider works an integral part of the definition of a Muslim. For them the question of degree cannot arise. The extent of faith cannot be measured in feet and inches, or weighed in pounds and ounces. But those who see works as necessary, over and above the confession of faith, for the definition of a true Muslim admit the possibility of a quantitative view of the extent of faith. After all, the Qur'ān itself speaks of increase in faith (3:173, 8:2, 9:124, etc.) and in guidance (47:17). An increase or decrease in works entails an analogous change in the extent of faith. The orthodox theologians of Islam are not in full theoretical agreement on this point. Besides those who will not hear of increments and diminutions in faith, there are also theologians who uphold the formula that "faith consists in confession and works; it can grow and lessen."[24] All depends on the school of thought one follows within orthodoxy. It was in such subtle discriminations that a politically prompted controversy finally spent itself.[25]

3. At almost the same time, however, another problem brought forth the first germ of a truly theological interest.[b] This was a different matter from general quibbles over whether or not one person or another could be regarded as a true believer. It had to do with a religious idea of pro-

[23] Ibn Khallikān, II, 10, no. 114 [I, 277, no. 115].

[24] For differences of opinion within orthodoxy (Ash'arites and Ḥanafites) on this question, see Friedrich Kern, *MSOS*, XI (1908), ii, 267. It is characteristic of hadith that a Companion is represented as already discussing the theory of the increase and decrease of faith; Ibn Sa'd, IV, ii, 92:15ff.

[25] At length it became possible, it appears, to use the label *murji'a* for Muslim communities of a Deist sort, in which the principle of monotheism was maintained but ritual observations were dropped. True, the distinguishing feature of the Murji'a had been their low estimation of *'amal*. Muqaddasī (wrote 375/985) applies the name Murji'a to nominal Muslims he has observed in the region of Mt. Demavand. He reports about them that there are no mosques in their region and the population neglects the practices required by Islam. They consider it enough that they are *muwaḥḥidūn* and pay their taxes to the Islamic state (*Aḥsan al-taqāsīm*, edited by M. J. de Goeje in *BGA* III, 2nd ed., Leiden, 1906, 398 bottom).

[b] On the question of free will and predestination in Islamic theology, raised by Goldziher in this and the following section, there is an extensive literature by modern scholars. For recent discussions, see W. Montgomery Watt, *Free Will and Predestination in Early Islam* (London, 1948); Josef van Ess, *Zwischen Ḥadīṯ und Theologie, Studien zum Entstehen prädestinatianischer Überlieferung* (Berlin, 1975).

found urgency, on which definite positions were taken relative to a traditional, uncomplicated, unreflecting popular belief.

In Islam, the first violent shock to naive belief did not come with the intrusion of scientific speculation, as a sort of consequence of it. It was not the effect of an emerging intellectualism. Rather, we may assume that it grew out of a deepening of the Muslims' religious ideas: out of piety, not freethinking.

The idea of absolute dependence had generated the crudest conceptions of God. Allah is a potentate with unbounded power: "He cannot be questioned about His acts" (21:23). Human beings are playthings in His hands, utterly without will. One must hold the conviction that God's will cannot be measured by the yardstick of human will, which is encompassed with limitations of all kinds, that human capacity shrivels to nothing next to the limitless will and absolute might of Allah. Allah's might also includes the determination of human will. A human being can perform an act of will only as God directs his will. Such is the case also in man's moral conduct: the volition in making a moral choice is determined by God's omnipotence and eternal decree.

But the believer must be equally assured that God does not wreak arbitrary violence on man. The idea must not arise that God's government is that of a *ẓālim*, an unjust ruler, or tyrant—a conception that would certainly mar the image of a human ruler, too. Precisely in connection with rewards and punishments, the Qur'ān repeatedly reassures man that Allah does injustice to no one, not even "the size of the filament on a date-stone" (4:49) or "the groove in a date-stone" (4:124). "We lay on no soul a burden that it cannot bear; we have a book that speaks the truth, and no injustice shall come upon them" (23:62). "And Allah created the heavens and the earth with truth, so that each soul might be recompensed according to what it has earned, with no one wronged" (45:22). But the question must have arisen in the pious mind: can a greater injustice be envisioned than that God rewards or punishes actions determined by a will outside of human capacity? That God deprives man of all freedom and self-determination in his acts, that He determines human conduct down to the minutest particulars, that He takes from the sinner the very possibility of doing what is good, that "He has sealed up their hearts, and spread a heavy cover over their eyes and ears" (2:7), and will nevertheless punish man for his disobedience and deliver him to eternal damnation?

Many pious Muslims, in humble devotion to Allah, may have entertained a general conception of God as such an arbitrary being. For such an exaggeration of the sense of dependence the holy book offers numerous instances of excellent support. The Qur'ān has many parallels to the notion of God's hardening Pharaoh's heart, and has a large number of general statements variously expressing the thought that God makes capacious enough for Islam the breasts of those He wishes to lead aright, but constricts the breasts of those He wishes to lead astray, as if they were trying to scale heaven (6:125). No soul is free to believe except with God's permission (10:100).

There is probably no other point of doctrine on which equally contradictory teachings can be derived from the Qur'ān as on this one. There are many deterministic statements, but one can set against them revelations in which it is not Allah who leads men astray but Satan, the evil Adversary and deceitful whisperer in men's ears (22:4, 35:5-6, 41:36, 43:37, 58:19), ever since the time of Adam (2:36, 38:82 ff.). Moreover, those who wished to advocate the total freedom of man's will, unthreatened even by the influence of Satan, could find a whole arsenal of arguments in the same Qur'ān, from whose unequivocal statements the precise opposite of the *servum arbitrium* could also be concluded. Man's good and evil deeds are referred to, characteristically, as his "acquisition," which is to say they are actions of his own effort (for example, 3:25, and frequently elsewhere). "The (evil) they have acquired covers their hearts like rust" (83:14). Even the notion of the sealing up of hearts can be quite well accommodated with saying that "they follow their own inclinations [*ittaba'ū ahwā'ahum*] (47:14, 16). Man's own desires lead him astray (38:26). It is not God who puts obduracy into sinners' hearts; rather, they grow hard (by their own wickedness), they are "like a rock, or harder" (2:74). Satan himself rejects the imputation that he leads men astray; man (on his own account) is far gone in error (50:27). Historical examples also lend this conception validity. God says, for example, that He gave right guidance to the impious people of Thamūd, but "they preferred blindness to guidance. Then they were overtaken by the thunderbolt of punishment, of humiliation, for what they had acquired for themselves. But we saved those who believed and were godfearing" (41:17). In other words: God gave them guidance and they would not follow; of their own free will they committed evil against God's decree; of their own free choice they made that evil their own. God guides man on the right path, but it depends on man whether he gratefully submits to that guidance or stubbornly rejects it (76:3). "Each acts in his own way" (17:84). "The truth is from your Lord. Let him who will, believe; let him who will, disbelieve" (18:29). "This (revelation) is a reminder; whoever wishes, will take the road to God" (76:29). To be sure, God does not stand in the way of the wicked either; He gives them the power and capacity to do evil, just as He gives to the good the capacity to do good, and smoothes their way to it (*fa-sa-nuyassiruhu li'l-yusrā . . . fa-sa-nuyassiruhu li'l-'usrā*, 92:7, 10). In this connection, I want to make an observation that is of some importance for understanding the problem of the freedom of the will in the Qur'ān. A large part of those Qur'ānic statements commonly used to draw the conclusion that God himself brings about man's sinfulness and leads man astray will be seen in a different light if we understand more precisely the word customarily taken to mean "to lead astray." In a good many Qur'ān verses we read "Allah guides whomsoever He will and lets stray whomsoever He will," but such statements do not mean that God directly leads the latter into error. The decisive verb (*aḍalla*) is not, in this context, to be understood as "lead astray," but rather as "allow to go astray," that is, not to care about someone, not to show him the way out of his predicament. "We let them (*nadharuhum*) stray in their disobedience" (6:110). We must imagine a solitary traveler in the desert: that image stands behind the Qur'ān's manner of speaking about guidance and error. The traveler wanders, drifts in limitless space, on the watch for the true direction to his goal. Such a traveler is man on the journey of life. Those whom belief and good works have proved worthy of God's benevolence, God rewards with His guidance, but the evildoers He allows to stray; He leaves them to their fate, withdraws His favor from them, extends no hand to guide them. But it is not as though He had led them outright into error. For the same reason, blindness and groping are favorite metaphors for the state of sinners. They cannot see; they must stray without plan or goal. With no guide to help them, they go irretrievably to their ruin. "Enlightenment [*baṣā'ir*] has come from your God; he who sees does so to his own good, he who is blind is so to his own harm" (6:104). Why did he fail to make use of the light that was lit for him? "We have revealed to you the book with the truth for mankind. He who lets himself be guided (by it) does so to his own good; he who goes astray (*ḍalla*) does so to his own harm" (39:41).

This state of being left to one's own devices, uncared for by God, is a notion much applied in the Qur'ān to people whose past conduct has rendered them unworthy of God's grace. It is the premise of God's action, when it is said that God forgets the wicked because the wicked have forgotten Him (7:51, 9:67, 45:34). God forgets the sinner; that is to say, He does not care about him. Guidance is the recompense of the good. "Allah does not guide the wicked" (9:109); He allows them to stray aimlessly. Unbelief is not the consequence but the cause of straying (47:8, and especially 61:5). To be sure, "he whom God allows to stray cannot find the right road" (42:46) and "he whom He allows to stray has no guide" (40:33) and goes to his ruin (7:178). In every instance, what happens is a withdrawal, by way of punishment, of the grace of guidance; these are not cases of leading into error and causing ungodliness. The early Muslims, who were close to the original ideas of Islam, sensed and understood this. It is related in a hadith: if someone, out of disesteem (*tahāwunan*), misses three Friday assemblies, God seals up his heart.[26] The "sealing up of the heart" was understood to mean a condition into which man falls only through his neglect of religious obligations. An old prayer that the Prophet teaches Ḥuṣayn, a new convert to Islam, runs: "O Allah, teach me to walk rightly guided and guard me from the evil in my own soul,"[27] which is to say, do not abandon me to myself but extend to me a guiding hand. There is no question, however, of leading into error. On the other hand, the feeling that to be abandoned to oneself is the severest form of divine punishment is given expression in an old Islamic oath formula: "If I do not speak the truth (in assertory oaths) or if I fail to keep my vow (in promissory oaths), may God exclude me from his might and power (*ḥawl wa-qūwa*) and abandon me to my own might and power,"[28] which is to say, may He withdraw His hand from me, so that I must see how I manage without His guidance and help. This is the sense in which "allowing to go astray"—and not "leading astray"—must be understood.[29]

4. We have seen that the Qur'ān can be used to document the most contradictory views on one of the fundamental questions of religious ethics. Hubert Grimme, who devoted profound study to analyzing the

[26] Ibn Ḥanbal, *Musnad* (Jābir), cited in Ibn Qayyim al-Jawzīya, *Kitāb al-ṣalāt wa-aḥkām tārikihā* (Cairo, A.H. 1313), p. 46 [see Wensinck, *Concordance*, VII, 112:22ff.].

[27] Tirmidhī, II, 261 bottom [*Da'awāt* no. 69]. A favorite devotional formula begins: *Allāhumma lā takilnā ilā anfusinā fa-nu'jiza*, "O God, do not entrust us to ourselves, lest we be wanting in strength"; cf. Bahā' al-Dīn al-'Āmilī, *Al-Mikhlāt* (Cairo, A.H. 1317), p. 129:2, where a large number of old devotional formulas are assembled.

[28] Such oath formulas (*barā'a*) can be found in Mas'ūdī, *Murūj al-dhahab*, VI, 297 [IV, 201]; Ya'qūbī, *Ta'rīkh*, II, 505, 509; Ibn al-Ṭiqṭaqā, *Al-Fakhrī*, edited by Wilhelm Ahlwardt (Gotha, 1860), p. 232 [edited by Hartwig Derenbourg (Paris, 1895), pp. 266f.].

[29] I now see that in this view I agree with Carra de Vaux, *La Doctrine de l'Islam* (Paris, 1909), p. 60 (published after the writing of the section above).

theology of the Qur'ān, reached an enlightening point of view that may help us work free of this confusion. He found that Muhammad's contradictory statements about the freedom of the will and predestination belong to different periods in his activity and correspond to the different impressions that changing circumstances produced in him. In the first, Meccan, period he took the position of total freedom of the will and total responsibility; in Medina he sank closer and closer to the doctrine of unfreedom and *servum arbitrium*. The most striking doctrines on this score come from his last years.[30] If such a periodization could be established with certainty, it might provide a guiding thread for those ready to take a historical view. We cannot expect to find such readiness among the old Muslims who had to wind their way through contradictory doctrines, decide in favor of one or another, and by some manner of harmonization come to terms with passages that clashed with the position they adopted. The sense of dependency that prevails in all aspects of Muslim consciousness no doubt tipped the scales in favor of denying the freedom of the will. Virtue and vice, reward and punishment are, in this view, fully dependent on God's predestination. Human will has no role to play.

But already at an early stage—we can trace the trend back to the end of the seventh century—this tyrannical view began to perturb pious minds that could not be at ease with the unrighteous God that the dominant popular conception implied. Outside influences also contributed to the germination and gradual deepening of pious scruple. The earliest protest against unlimited predestination appeared in Syrian Islam. The emergence of that protest is best explained by Kremer's view[31] that the early Muslim doctors' impulse to doubt unlimited predestination came from their Christian theological environment, for, as it happened, in the Eastern Church the debate over this point of doctrine occupied theologians' minds. Damascus, the intellectual focus of Islam during the Umayyad age, was the center of speculation about *qadar*, the fixing of fate; from Damascus that speculation rapidly spread far and wide.

Pious scruples led to the conviction that man in his ethical and legal conduct cannot be the slave of an unalterable predestination, but rather, man creates his own acts and so becomes the cause of his own bliss or damnation. The doctrine of those who adopted this view came in time to

[30] Hubert Grimme, *Mohammed* (Münster, 1892-1895), II, 105ff.

[31] Alfred von Kremer, *Culturgeschichtliche Streifzüge auf dem Gebiete des Islams* (Leipzig, 1873), pp. 7ff. [translated in S. Khuda Bukhsh's *Contributions to the History of Islamic Civilization* (Calcutta, 1929-1930), I, 64ff.].

be called *khalq al-af'āl*, "the creation of acts." Its upholders, because they restricted *qadar*, were curiously referred to—*lucus a non lucendo*—as the Qadarīya. They liked to call their opponents the *Jabrīya*, the people of blind compulsion (*jabr*). This was the earliest theological dispute in Islam.

While the Qur'ān could furnish both parties with arguments in equal measure, there was a mythological tradition favorable to the determinists. It may have evolved as a kind of *haggada* very early in Islam; it may have emerged only in the course of these disputations—who could set precise dates of origin in such matters? According to this tradition, immediately after creating Adam, God took his entire posterity, in the form of small swarms of ants, out of the substance of the first man's gigantic body, and already then determined the classes of the elect and the damned, incorporating them into the right and left sides of Adam's body. Each embryo has the fated course of its life outlined by an angel especially appointed to that end. According to an idea borrowed from India, it is "written on the forehead."[32] Among other things, the angel records whether the person is fated to bliss or damnation. Correspondingly, the eschatological tradition also takes a determinist course. God rather arbitrarily sends the unhappy sinner to hell. The only moderating element is the prophets' acknowledged right of intercession (*shafā'a*).

The conceptions underlying deterministic views were much too deeply rooted in the popular mind; the contrary doctrine of the Qadarīya, stressing self-determination and full accountability, could not find a large body of supporters. The Qadarites had to put up a stiff defense against the attacks and objections of their opponents, who battled them with the received interpretation of the sacred scriptures and with popular fables like those above. For the history of Islam, the Qadarite movement is of great importance as the first step toward liberation from the dominance of traditional notions, a step prompted not by freethinking but by the demands of pious thought. The Qadarites did not lift their voice in a protest of reason against ossified dogma; theirs was the voice of religious conscience against an unworthy conception of God and of God's relation to His servants' religious instincts.

A hoard of hadiths, invented for the denigration of the Qadarite doctrine, bear witness to the opposition into which such tendencies ran, and to the scant sympathy that Qadarite thinking met with. As in other cases,

[32] Cf. *ZDMG*, LVII (1903), 398.

the Prophet himself is made to express the general orthodox sentiment. The Qadarites are said to be the Magians of the Islamic community. For as the followers of Zoroaster set against the creator of the Good a principle that is the cause of Evil, so the Qadarites take man's evil acts out of the province of God's creation. Disobedience is created not by God but by the autonomous will of man. Hadiths, furthermore, represent Muhammad and 'Alī as sharply condemning the Qadarites' efforts to justify their doctrines through disputation, and as heaping every possible scorn and insult on Qadarite heads (see n. 32).

Yet another remarkable phenomenon has to do with the problem of *qadar*. The rulers in Damascus, people who did not, as a rule, show much of a taste for points of theology, were also uncomfortable with the Qadarite movement gaining ground in Syrian Islam.[c] At times they took a position of unqualified hostility towards the advocates of free will.[33]

These expressions of the ruling circles' disposition did not spring from an aversion to theological squabbles, harbored by men engaged in the great labor of consolidating a new state. Certainly, men whose energies were spent in laying the broad foundations of the state and in battling dynastic enemies on every front may have found it repugnant that the masses should have their minds stirred up with pedantic perplexities over the freedom of the will and self-determination. Strong-minded people in positions of power usually do not rejoice to see the masses adopt an argumentative habit of mind. But there was a more profound reason for the Umayyads' particular sense of danger on seeing the dogma of predestination weaken. The danger was not religious; it was political.

They were well aware that their dynasty was a thorn in the flesh of the pious, of the very people whose holy living commanded the heart of the common man. They could hardly fail to know that in the view of many

[c] On the political implications of the struggle between predestination and free will, see J. Obermann, "Political Theology in Early Islam: Ḥasan al-Baṣrī's Treatise on Qadar," *JAOS*, LV (1955), 138–62; and the article on Ḥasan al-Baṣrī in *EI*² (by H. Ritter). For a comprehensive survey of the exponents of free will in early Islam, see the article "Ḳadariyya" in *EI*² (by J. van Ess), where further references to sources and modern literature will be found.

[33] Wellhausen, *Das arabische Reich*, pp. 217, 235 [= *The Arab Kingdom*, pp. 347, 377]. Wellhausen stresses in the second of these passages that political, not theological, considerations led them to take such a position. Advocates of the freedom of the will cite letters, reputed to have been written by Ḥasan al-Baṣrī to the caliph 'Abd al-Malik and to Ḥajjāj. In these letters this pious man tries to convince the rulers of the absurdity of persisting, as they do, in the belief that acts of will are predetermined. Cf. Ibn al-Murtaḍā, *Kitāb al-milal wa'l-niḥal*, edited by T. W. Arnold (Leipzig, 1902), pp. 12ff. [= *Ṭabaqāt al-mu'tazila*, edited by Susanna Diwald-Wilzer (Wiesbaden, 1961), pp. 17ff.].

of their subjects they were usurpers who had come to power by violent and injurious means, enemies of the family of the Prophet, murderers of sacred persons, profaners of holy places. To curb the masses, to keep them from riot against the dynasty or its representatives, no form of belief was better suited than the belief in predestination. It is God's eternal decree that these men must rule; all their actions are inevitable and destined by God. It was opportune that doctrines such as this should spread among the people. The Umayyads listened with pleasure to their court panegyrists' laudatory epithets, in which their rule was recognized as the will of God, a *decretum divinum.* A believer could not very well rebel against that. And indeed, poets glorified the Umayyad caliphs as men "whose rule was predestined in God's eternal decree."[34]

Just as this idea was to serve the general legitimation of the dynasty, it was readily applied to calm the people when they inclined to see injustice and tyranny in the acts of their rulers. The dutiful subject must regard "the *amīr al-mu'minīn* and the wounds he inflicts as fate; let no one find fault with his doings."[35] These words come from a poem written as a kind of echo to an act of cruelty by an Umayyad ruler. The belief, it was intended, should strike root that whatever they did had to happen, that it had been destined by God, and no human will could avert it. "These kings," as some early Qadarites say, "shed the blood of the believers, unlawfully seize property that is not theirs, and say: 'Our actions are the consequence of *qadar.*' "[36] After the Umayyad caliph 'Abd al-Malik, who had to engage in a fierce struggle to secure his power, had lured one of his rivals to his palace, and there, with the approval of his confidential jurisconsult, had him murdered, he had the head thrown to the crowd of the victim's followers in front of the palace, who awaited his return. Then the caliph had it announced to them, "The Commander of the Faithful has killed your leader, as it was foreordained in God's inalterable decree. . . ." So it is related. Naturally, one could not resist God's decree, whose mere instrument the caliph was. The followers quieted down and paid obeisance to the murderer of the man who had a day earlier commanded their loyalty. While the historical accuracy of this narrative is not beyond question, it does furnish valid evidence for the connection people saw between the government's actions and the inevitability of fate. I ought not, it is true, neglect to mention that the appeal to divine foreordainment was

[34] *ZDMG*, LVII (1903), 394. Consider Farazdaq's fatalistic verse in Joseph Hell, "Al-Farazdaḳ's Lieder auf die Muhallabiten," *ZDMG*, LX (1906), 25.

[35] *Aghānī*, X, 99:10.

[36] Ibn Qutayba, *Ma'ārif*, p. 225 [441].

accompanied by a quantity of dirhems, meant to palliate the horrible sight of the head of 'Amr ibn Sa'īd flung to the crowd.[37]

The Qadarite movement in the age of the Umayyad dynasty was thus the first step in the undermining of simple Islamic orthodoxy. That is its great, if unintended, historical achievement, whose significance justifies my devoting such a large part of this essay to it. The breach that had been made in naive popular belief was soon to be made wider by endeavors which, in the measure as intellectual horizons broadened, extended the critique of the traditional forms of belief.

5. In the meantime, the Islamic world had become familiar with Aristotelian philosophy, and many of the educated were affected by it in their religious thinking. From this an incalculable danger to Islam arose, notwithstanding all efforts to reconcile the traditions of religion with the newly acquired truths of philosophy. On certain issues it seemed nearly impossible to erect a bridge between Aristotle—even in his Neoplatonic disguise—and the assumptions of Islamic belief. The beliefs in the world's creation in time, in the attention of providence to individuals, in miracles, could not live with Aristotle.

A new speculative system was needed to maintain Islam and Islamic tradition among rational thinkers. In the history of philosophy, this system is known as *kalām*, and its practitioners as the *mutakallimūn*. Originally, the word *mutakallim* (literally: "speaker") denoted, in a theological context, one who made a dogma or a controversial theological problem into a topic for dialectical discussion and argument, offering speculative proofs for the positions he urged. Thus the word *mutakallim* had originally as its grammatical complement the particular question on which the theologians' speculation centered. It is said, for instance, that a certain person is *min al-mutakallimīna fī'l-irjā'*, one of those who discuss the problem raised by the Murji'a.[38] The term soon came to be more broadly used, and was applied to those who "take doctrines, accepted in religious belief as truths above discussion, and turn them into subjects of debate, talk and argue about them, and state them in formulas meant to make them acceptable to thinking heads." Speculative activity to that end then received the name *kalām* (speech, oral discussion). In accordance with its purpose to give support to religious doctrines, the *kalām* started from

[37] *Al-Imāma wa'l-siyāsa*, II, 41.

[38] Ibn Sa'd, VI, 236:19. According to some, Muḥammad ibn al-Ḥanafīya was the first to expound the theory of the Murji'a; *ibid.*, V, 67:16. For the definition given here, see also "Die islamische und die jüdische Philosophie," *Allgemeine Geschichte der Philosophie* (Berlin and Leipzig, 1909; Part I, Section v, of Paul Hinneberg's *Die Kultur der Gegenwart*), p. 64.

anti-Aristotelian postulates, and was, in the true sense of the phrase, a philosophy of religion. Its earliest fosterers are known as the Mu'tazilites.[d]

The word means "those who separate themselves." I shall not repeat the tale commonly told to account for the name, and I assume that the correct explanation of it is that this group too had its germ in pious impulses, that pious and in part ascetic people—*mu'tazila*, "those who withdraw" (ascetics)[39]—gave the first impetus to the movement which, as it was joined by rationalist groups, came to stand in ever-sharper opposition to dominant conceptions of belief.

It is only in their ultimate development that the Mu'tazilites justify the appellation "freethinkers of Islam" under which Heinrich Steiner, a professor in Zurich, introduced them in the first monograph (1865) devoted to this school.[40] Their emergence was prompted by religious motives, like that of their predecessors. Nothing could have been farther from the early Mu'tazila than a tendency to throw off chafing shackles, to the detriment of the rigorously orthodox view of life. One of the first questions pondered and resolved by the Mu'tazila was whether, in contrast to the Murji'ite position, a grave sin attaches to a person the quality of being a *kāfir*, and thus brings him to eternal punishment in hell, just as unbelief

[d] In this and the following sections, Goldziher discusses the Mu'tazila, the first major theological school in Islam, and the pioneers of speculative dogmatics. At one time it was customary among scholars to describe the Mu'tazilites as rationalists or even as freethinkers. These descriptions, no doubt intended as compliments by nineteenth-century European writers, derived from the hostile and derogatory descriptions of the orthodox polemicists who until comparatively recently were our only source of information about Mu'tazilite doctrines. The recovery of some works of Mu'tazilite inspiration required a reassessment of their genuine role and, more particularly, of their political significance in early 'Abbāsid times. The beginnings of this reassessment can be seen in Goldziher's presentation. An entirely new theory of the nature and significance of the Mu'tazila movement was given by the Swedish scholar, H. S. Nyberg, in his article on the Mu'tazila in EI[1] (s.v.). For later discussions, see H.A.R. Gibb, *Mohammedanism, an Historical Survey*, pp. 112-18; Henri Laoust, *Les Schismes dans l'Islam; Introduction à une étude de la religion musulmane* (Paris, 1965), pp. 101ff.; W. Montgomery Watt, *Islamic Philosophy and Theology* (Edinburgh, 1962), pp. 58-71; J. van Ess, *Anfänge muslimischer Theologie* (Beirut, 1974).

[39] For this sense of the designation Mu'tazila, see my "Materialien zur Kenntniss der Almohadenbewegung in Nordafrika," *ZDMG*, XLI (1887), 35 n. 4 [= *Gesammelte Schriften*, II, 196 n. 4]. Cf. Ibn Sa'd, V, 225:4, where *mu'tazil* is used as a synonym of *'ābid* and *zāhid* to mean an ascetic. In an old (1233) Arabic translation of the New Testament, of Nestorian origin, *pharisee* (one who sets himself apart) is rendered by the same word; Yūsuf Sarkīs, "Tarjama 'arabīya qadīma min al-Anjīl al-Ṭāhir," *Al-Mashriq*, XI (1908), 905 penultimate.

[40] [*Die Mu'taziliten; oder, die Freidenker im Islam; ein Beitrag zur allgemeinen Culturgeschichte* (Leipzig, 1865).] There is a more recent monograph by Henri Galland, *Essai sur les Mo'tazélites: les rationalistes de l'Islam* (Geneva, 1906).

does. The topic does not indicate an upsurge of liberated thinking. Moreover, the Mu'tazila introduces into theology the concept of a middle state between those of believer and unbeliever—an unusual speculation for philosophical minds.

The man whom the Muslim historians of theology call the founder of the Mu'tazila, Wāṣil ibn 'Aṭā', is described by the biographers as an ascetic, and in a poem lamenting his death he is praised as "having touched neither dirhem nor dinar."[41] His companion, 'Amr ibn 'Ubayd, is also described as a *zāhid* (ascetic) who prayed through entire nights, performed the pilgrimage to Mecca on foot forty times, and always made an impression as somber "as if he had come direct from his parents' funeral." A pious, ascetic sermon of admonition that he addressed to the caliph al-Manṣūr has been preserved—in stylized form, it is true—and it shows no sign of rationalist proclivities.[42] If we look through the biographical dictionaries of the Mu'tazilites, we find that even in later times[43] an ascetic way of life takes pride of place among the celebrated characteristics of many of them.

Nonetheless, the religious ideas their teaching particularly stressed (the reduction of the arbitrary power of God in favor of the idea of justice) contained many a seed of opposition to current orthodoxy, many an element that might easily lure a skeptic to join them. Connection with the *kalām* soon gave their thinking a rationalist tinge and compelled them more and more to set themselves rationalist goals. Cultivation of these goals brought the Mu'tazila into an ever keener conflict with standard orthodox opinion.

When we sum up our consideration of the Mu'tazila, we shall have to tax them with a number of unattractive traits. But they will retain one undiminished merit. They were the first to expand the sources of religious cognition in Islam so as to include a valuable but previously—in such connection—rigorously avoided element: reason (*'aql*). Some of their most highly respected representatives went so far as to say that "the first, necessary condition of knowledge is doubt,"[44] or "fifty doubts are

[41] Cf. the biography in Ibn al-Murtaḍā, *Al-Milal wa'l-niḥal*, p. 18:12 [= *Ṭabaqāt al-mu'tazila*, p. 29].

[42] In Bayhaqī, *Al-Maḥāsin wa'l-masāwī*, p. 364 penultimate line ff. For the ascetic portrait, Ibn al-Murtaḍā, *Al-Milal wa'l-niḥal*, p. 22:5ff. [= *Ṭabaqāt al-mu'tazila*, p. 36].

[43] In the fourth century: *shaykh min zuhhād al-mu'tazila*, "a shaykh from among the Mu'tazilite ascetics"; Yāqūt, *Irshād al-arīb*, II, 309:11.

[44] Alfred von Kremer, *Culturgeschichte des Orients unter den Chalifen* (Vienna, 1875-1877), II, 267.

better than one certainty,"[45] and more of the kind. It was possible to say of them that, to their way of thinking, there was a sixth sense besides the usual five, namely, *'aql*, reason.[46] They raised reason to a touchstone in matters of belief. One of their early representatives, Bishr ibn al-Mu'tamir of Baghdad, wrote a veritable paean to reason, as part of a didactic poem of natural history. It is preserved and commented on by al-Jāḥiẓ who was of the same school of thought:

> How excellent is reason as a pilot and companion in good fortune and evil,
> As a judge who can pass judgment over the invisible as if he saw it with his own eyes.
> . . . one of its actions is that it distinguishes good and evil,
> Through a possessor of powers whom God has singled out with utter sanctification and purity.[47]

Some of them, in extreme skepticism, assigned to the evidence of the senses the lowest possible position among the criteria of knowledge.[48] At any rate, they were the first in Islamic theology to assert the rights of reason. In doing so, they had gone far from their point of departure. At its apex, the Mu'tazilite school engaged in relentless criticism of certain elements of popular belief that had long been viewed as essential components of the orthodox creed. They called into doubt the inimitability of the literary style of the Qur'ān. They questioned the authenticity of the hadith, in which the documentation of popular belief had taken shape.

[45] In Jāḥiẓ, *Ḥayawān*, III, 18 [III, 60]; cf. *Ḥayawān*, VI, 11 [VI, 35ff.] about skeptics. Such principles had an effect even on Ghazālī, remote as his position was from the Mu'tazilites. Cf. his saying: "whoever does not doubt, cannot consider matters rationally," in Hebrew translation *mī she-lō y^esappēq lo y^e'ayyēn* (*Mōznē ṣedeq*, Hebrew edition by Jacob Goldenthal, p. 235). The Arabic original of Ghazālī's saying is cited in Ibn Ṭufayl, *Ḥayy ibn Yaqẓān*, edited by Léon Gauthier (Algiers, 1900), p. 13:4 from bottom [2nd ed. (Beirut, 1936), p. 16:8f., giving as his source Ghazālī's *Mīzān al-'amal*; for this quotation, see the edition of the *Mīzān al-'amal* by Sulaymān Dunyā, Cairo, 1964, p. 409].

[46] Māturīdī, Commentary on *Al-Fiqh al-akbar* (Haydarabad, A.H. 1321; of improbable authenticity), p. 19.

[47] Jāḥiẓ, *Ḥayawān*, VI, 95 [VI, 292, vss. 12-15. Goldziher left a lacuna for a word in the printed text—and in the Vienna manuscript of the *Kitāb al-ḥayawān*—which he considered corrupt. For a full text of these lines and alternate translations, see the note by Oscar Rescher in *Der Islam*, XVI (1927), 156.] This free exercise of reason is contrasted (96:6 [294, vs. 38]) with the passive acceptance of received opinion (*taqlīd*) characteristic of mediocre minds.

[48] Cf. Maimonides, *Dalālat al-ḥā'irīn*, I, Ch. 73, Proposition XII. About the skepticism of the *mutakallimūn*, see my "Zur Geschichte der ḥanbalitischen Bewegungen," p. 2 [= *Gesammelte Schriften*, V, 136; partial French translation in *Arabica*, VII (1960), 135].

Their criticism of popular belief was directed chiefly at the mythological elements of eschatology. They eliminated from the body of obligatory belief, and gave allegorical explanations of, the bridge Ṣirāṭ which one must cross before entering the next world, thin as a hair and sharp as the edge of a sword, over which the elect glide quick as lightning into Paradise, while those destined for damnation teeter and plummet into the bottomless pit gaping beneath them. They also eliminated the scales in which the acts of man are weighed, and many similar conceptions. The chief guiding thought of their philosophy of religion was to purge the monotheistic concept of God from those elements of traditional popular belief that had clouded and deformed it. This purgation was to take two principal courses: the ethical and the metaphysical. The idea of God must be cleansed of all conceptions that prejudice belief in his justice, and of all that might obscure his absolute unity, uniqueness, and immutability. At the same time they upheld the idea of a God who creates, acts, and provides, and objected vehemently to the Aristotelian version of the idea of God. The Aristotelians' doctrine of the eternity of the world, their belief that the laws of nature are inviolable, their negation of a providence that takes account of individuals—these were walls that divided the rationalist theologians of Islam, for all their freedom of speculation, from the followers of Aristotle. The inadequate proofs they worked with brought upon them the scorn and sarcastic criticism of the philosophers who did not recognize them as opponents of equal standing, or their methods of thought as worthy of consideration.[49] Their way of going about their business justified the charge that philosophical independence and unprejudiced thought were wholly alien to them, for they were tied to a clearly defined religion, and their purpose in working with the tools of reason was to purify that religion.

As I have already stressed, this work of purification was aimed particularly at two points of doctrine: the justice and unity of God. Every Mu'tazilite textbook consists of two parts: one contains the "Chapters on Justice" (*abwāb al-'adl*) and the other the "Chapters on the Profession of Faith in Unity" (*abwāb al-tawḥīd*). This division into two parts determines the plan of all Mu'tazilite theological works. Because of this orientation of their religio-philosophical efforts, they assumed the name *ahl al-'adl wa'l-tawḥīd*, "the people of justice and of the profession of faith in

[49] Baḥya ibn Paquda, *Kitāb ma'ānī al-nafs,* edited by Ignaz Goldziher (Berlin, 1907; Abhandlungen der Königlichen Gesellschaft der Wissenschaften zu Göttingen, Philologisch-Historische Klasse, New Series, IX, 1), n. to 4, 5ff.

unity." A relative chronology can be established for these considerations: the questions concerning justice were asked first. They are linked directly to Qadarite doctrines whose implications the Mu'tazilites follow up and make explicit. They start from the assumption that man has unlimited freedom of volition in his acts, that he is himself the creator of those acts. Were the case otherwise, it would be unjust of God to hold man responsible for what he does.

In the conclusions that the Mu'tazilites drew from this fundamental idea, advanced with the certainty of axiom, however, they went several steps beyond the Qadarite position. Having inscribed upon their banner the doctrine of man's self-determination, and rejected the notion of God's arbitrary rule, they found that this rejection implied something further for their concept of God: God must necessarily be just; the concept of justice cannot be separated from the concept of God; it is impossible to conceive of an act of will on the part of God that fails to meet the stipulations of justice. Divine omnipotence is limited by the requirements of justice, which it can neither ignore nor waive.

In taking this position, they introduced into the conception of divinity an element quite alien to the early Muslims' conception of it: the element of necessity (*wujūb*). There are things that, with reference to God, may be called necessary. *God must.* From the point of view of early Islam, such a phrase could only be regarded as flagrantly absurd, even as blasphemous. Since God created man with the intention of bringing about his eternal felicity, He had to send prophets to teach them the means of, and the ways to, felicity. That He did so was not the result of His sovereign will; it was not a gift from God that God's wholly autonomous will might have withheld. It was, rather, an act of divine benevolence that God was obliged to perform (*luṭf wājib*). Had He granted mankind no guidance, He could not be thought of as a being whose deeds are good. He was obliged to reveal himself through His prophets. God himself admits this necessity, in the Qur'ān. "It is incumbent upon Allah (He owes it, *wa-'alā'llāhi*) to give right guidance." Such is their interpretation of Sura 16:9.[50]

Besides the concept of the necessary *luṭf*, the Mu'tazilites introduced a second, closely related, concept into the notion of God: the concept of the salutary, *al-aṣlaḥ*. God's decrees intend, again by necessity, man's ultimate felicity. A person is free to follow, or to reject, the teachings re-

[50] Rāzī, *Mafātīḥ al-ghayb*, V, 432.

vealed for the benefit of mankind. But a just God must, by necessity, reward the good and punish the wicked. God's arbitrary power that, according to orthodox tastes, capriciously peoples paradise and hell is abolished, and the incongruity that the just man's virtue and obedience do not guarantee a reward in the next world is adjusted by an equitability that by necessity governs God's acts.

They went a step further in this sphere of ideas. They laid down the law of compensation, *al-'iwaḍ*: yet another limitation to the arbitrary power of God as it is implied in the orthodox conception. For undeserved pain and suffering that the just endure here on earth because God finds it *aṣlaḥ*, expedient and salutary, for them that they should do so, they must receive compensation in the next world. This would not in itself be a peculiar view; indeed, with the dubious word *must* toned down, it would agree with a postulate of orthodox sensibility. But a large part of the Mu'tazila postulates such compensation not only for true believers or innocent children who underwent unmerited pain and suffering here on earth, but also for animals. An animal must receive compensation in another life for the suffering that the selfishness and cruelty of mankind has inflicted on it in this world. Otherwise God would not be just. A transcendental protection of animals, as it were.

We can see how consistently these Mu'tazilites worked out their doctrine of divine justice, and how in the end they set a free man over against a relatively unfree God.

These views are related to one more essential ethical position.

From the viewpoint of religious ethics, what is good and what is evil? Or, as the theological terminology has it, what is pleasing (*ḥasan*) and what is abhorrent (*qabīḥ*)? Orthodoxy answers: good-and-pleasing is what God commands; evil-and-abhorrent is what God forbids. The divine will, which cannot be held accountable, and its dictates are the yardstick for good and evil. Nothing is good or evil because reason makes it so. Murder is reprehensible because God has forbidden it; had the divine law not branded murder as wicked, it would not be wicked. The Mu'tazilite disagrees. In his view, there is absolute good and absolute evil, and reason is the instrument for ethical value judgments. Reason is the *prius*, not the divine will. A thing is good not because God has commanded it, but God has commanded it because it is good. Is this not tantamount to saying—if we translate into modern terms these definitions of the theologians of Basra and Baghdad—that God, in decreeing His laws, is bound by the categorical imperative?

6. We have looked at a series of ideas and principles which show that the conflict between Mu'tazilite thought and the simple religious conceptions of the orthodox did not turn on metaphysical issues alone. The Mu'tazilites' conclusions were of radical importance for fundamental ethical views, and specifically within Islam they were relevant to the conception of divine legislation.

But their contribution was even greater in the other area in which their rationalist philosophy of religion was engaged: in the area of the monotheistic idea. To begin with, they had to clear away a heap of debris that had come to engulf this idea and debase its purity. Their foremost concern was to wipe out the anthropomorphic conceptions of traditional orthodoxy, which they saw as incompatible with a dignified conception of God. Orthodoxy would not agree to any but a literal understanding of the anthropomorphic and anthropopathic expressions in the Qur'ān and the traditional texts. God sees, hears, is moved to anger; He smiles, sits and stands; He even has hands, feet, ears. Such matters, to which there are frequent references in the Qur'ān and other texts, must be understood according to the letter. The Ḥanbalite school in particular fought for this crude conception of God, which they considered *sunna*. At best these most conservative believers were willing to admit that while they demanded a literal understanding of the words of the text, they could not precisely say how one was to envision the reality to which such conceptions corresponded. They demanded unquestioning belief in the literal meaning of the text, *bilā kayfa*, "without *how*." (This position was therefore called *balkafa*.) A closer definition of that *how*, they argued, passes human understanding, and man ought not meddle with things that have not been rendered subject to his thought. Known by name are the old exegetes who considered it correct to say that God was "flesh and blood," with limbs, so long as one added that these may not at all be thought of as resembling those of man, following the Qur'ān verse "Nothing is like Him; He is the one who hears and sees" (42:11). But, in their view, one could not think of anything as really existing that was not substance. The conception of God as a purely spiritual being was for these people tantamount to atheism.

Muslim anthropomorphists on occasion set forth their view in an unbelievably crude manner. I am intentionally adducing facts from a later period, to suggest the free course such ideas must have enjoyed at a time when no spiritualist opposition had yet exercised its moderating influence. The example of an Andalusian theologian may demonstrate the excesses possible in this area. A very famous theologian from Mallorca who died in Baghdad around the year 524/1130, Muḥammad ibn Sa'dūn, known by the name Abū 'Āmir al-Qurashī, went to the lengths of making the following statement: "The heretics cite in evidence the Qur'ān verse 'Nothing is like Him,' but the meaning of that verse is only that nothing can be compared to God in His divinity. In form, however, God is like you or me." The case would seem to be as with the verse in which God addresses the wives of the Prophet: "O women of the Prophet, you are not like any other woman" (33:32), that is, other women are of a lower order of merit, but in appearance the Prophet's wives are just like them. It must be said that there is more than a little blasphemy in orthodox hermeneutics of this kind. Its proponent did not flinch from the most extreme consequences. He once read verse 68:42, in which the following is said of the Last Judgment: "On the day when the thigh is bared, and they are summoned to prostrate themselves. . . ." To refuse a figurative explanation as forcibly as possible, Abū 'Āmir struck his own thigh and said: "A real thigh, just like the one here."[51] A similar example is reported from two hundred years later. In the course of a lecture in Damascus, the famous Ḥanbalite shaykh Taqī al-Dīn ibn Taymīya (d. 728/1328) cited one of those passages in which God's "descent" is mentioned. To exclude any ambiguity and to illustrate concretely his conception of God's descent, the shaykh descended a few steps from the pulpit and said "Exactly as I am descending now" (*ka-nuzūlī hādhā*).

These are offshoots of the old anthropomorphic trend against which the Mu'tazilites waged the first religious campaign when, to assure the purity and dignity of the Islamic concept of God, they gave metaphorical interpretation and spiritual sense to every anthropomorphic expression in the sacred writings. Out of such endeavors a new method of Qur'ānic exegesis arose, which was called by the old term *ta'wīl* (in the sense of figurative interpretation), and against which, in all periods of Islamic history, the Ḥanbalites protested.[52]

[51] Ibn 'Asākir, *Ta'rīkh Dimashq*, fasc. 340 (Ms. Landberg, now in the Yale University Library [cf. Leon Nemoy, *Arabic Manuscripts in the Yale University Library* (New Haven, 1956), p. 127, no. 1182].

[52] The Ḥanbalite theologian Muwaffaq al-Dīn 'Abdallāh ibn Qudāma (d. 620/1233) wrote a *Dhamm al-ta'wīl*, "Reprobation of *ta'wīl*." Two manuscript copies have recently been acquired by the Library of the Asiatic Society of Bengal (*List of Arabic and Persian Mss. Acquired . . . 1903-1907*, nos. 405 and 795; these should be entered in *GAL*, I, 398 [cf. *GAL*, SI, 689, no. 19]). Ibn Taymīya (more about him in Chapter VI) wrote repeated polemics against the *ta'wīl* of the *mutakallimūn* and established limits for the traditionally acceptable

In the case of the hadith, another method was also available to the Mu'tazilites: they could reject as inauthentic those texts that reflected, or were conducive to, an excessively crude anthropomorphism. Thus they sought to rid Islam of all the debris of foolish fables that, favored by story-loving popular belief, had piled up especially in the area of eschatology, and had found religious accreditation in the form of hadiths. No conception is more stressed in orthodox theology than the one based on the words of verse 75:23, that the righteous will see God bodily in the next world. The Mu'tazilites could not accept this, and were not particularly impressed by the more exact definition of that vision in hadiths that reject outright any form of *ta'wīl*: "As you see the moon shining in the sky."[53] Thus the material vision of God, which the Mu'tazilites removed from its immediate literal sense by a spiritual interpretation of the text, remained a point of sharpest contention between their party, joined by other theologians infected with Mu'tazilite scruples, and the party of conservative orthodoxy, joined, in these matters, by people who held an intermediate position of rationalist compromise—about whom we shall hear more.

7. In the questions under the category of *tawḥīd*, the profession of faith in God's unity, the Mu'tazilites rose to an even higher general viewpoint by posing the question of divine attributes in a comprehensive fashion. Is it at all possible to ascribe attributes to God without tarnishing belief in God's indivisible, immutable unity?

Attempts to answer this question occasioned a great display of hairsplitting dialectics, both on the side of the various Mu'tazilite schools of thought—for in the various definitions of their doctrines the Mu'tazilites present no united front—and on the side of those who attempted to mediate between the Mu'tazilite and the orthodox positions. For already here we must anticipate something to which we shall soon return: from the beginning of the tenth century there arose mediating tendencies that allowed drops of rationalism to trickle into the oil of orthodoxy, in order to defend the old formulas against unrestrained rationalist doubts. These elaborations of doctrine in which orthodox dogma is diluted by a few rationalistic flourishes, and which essentially represent a return to traditional orthodoxy, are associated with the names of Abū 'l-Ḥasan al-

---

kind of *ta'wīl*, such as *Tafsīr sūrat al-ikhlāṣ* (Cairo, A.H. 1323), pp. 71ff.; "Risālat al-iklīl fī'l-mutashābih wa'l-ta'wīl," in *Rasā'il*, II, 2ff.

[53] Ṭabarī, *Tafsīr*, commentary to Sura 45, vss. 27-28 (Cairo, A.H. 1323-1329, XXV, 85 bottom).

Ash'arī (d. 324/935 in Baghdad) and Abū Manṣūr al-Māturīdī (d. 333/944 in Samarkand). Al-Ash'arī's system came to prevail in the central provinces of the Islamic world; al-Māturīdī's found acceptance farther east, in Central Asia.[e] There are no essential differences between the two schools. Such as there are hinge mostly on petty disputes, of whose scope we may form a reasonable idea by looking, for example, at the following controversy: may a Muslim use the phrase "I am a Muslim, if God wills"? The students of al-Ash'arī and of al-Māturīdī give conflicting answers to this question, supporting their views with dozens of subtle theological arguments. On the whole, the position of the Māturīdites is more liberal than that of their Ash'arite colleagues. They are a shade closer to the Mu'tazilites than the Ash'arites are. I will cite as a single example the different answers to the question: what is the basis for man's obligation to know God?

The Mu'tazilites answer: reason. The Ash'arites: it is written that we must know God. The Māturīdites: the obligation to know God is based on the divine commandment, but that commandment is grasped by reason. In this view, reason is not the source but the instrument of the knowledge of God.

This example illustrates the scholastic methodology, in general, of theological disputes in Islam. When we immerse ourselves in the ingeniously contrived definitions relating to the problem of divine attributes, we are prompted to recall the battles Byzantine theologians fought over single words, indeed letters, about *homoousia* and *homoiousia*. Can we ascribe attributes to God? To do so would, after all, introduce multiplicity into His one and indivisible being. And even if we think of these attributes (as, given the nature of God, we must) as being in no way distinct from God's essence, as being inherent in His essence from all eternity and not superadded to it—even then the mere positing of such existents, eternal even though inseparably joined to God's essence, would imply the admission of eternal entities besides the one eternal God. But that is *shirk*, "association." *Tawḥīd*, the pure belief in God's unity, therefore demands that one reject the supposition that God has attributes, whether eternal and inherent, or additional to his essence. This consideration had to lead to the denial of divine attributes; to the view that God is all-knowing but not by a knowledge, all-powerful but not by a power, living but not by a

[e] On the theological schools of al-Ash'arī and al-Māturīdī, see the article "Ash'ariyya" in *EI*² (by W. Montgomery Watt); L. Gardet and M. M. Anawati, *Introduction à la théologie musulmane*, and the general works by Gibb and Laoust, cited above.

life. There is no distinct knowledge, power, and life in God; all those things that strike us as attributes are indivisibly one, and not distinct from God Himself. To say that God is knowing is no different from saying "God is powerful" or "God is living." Were we to multiply such statements to infinity, we would still not be saying anything but "God is."

There can be no doubt that these considerations served the cause of letting the monotheistic idea in Islam shine forth in greater purity than in the tarnished conceptions of literal-minded popular belief. But to the orthodox this purification must have appeared as *ta'ṭīl*, stripping the concept of God of its contents; as pure *kenôsis*. "What the talk of these people amounts to is that there is in heaven no God at all."[54] This is how, at the beginning of the dogmatic controversy, a traditional orthodox writer in complete naiveté characterizes the doctrines of his rationalist opponents. The Absolute cannot be approached; it cannot be cognized. Were God identical with His attributes comprehended in a unity, could one not pray "O knowledge have mercy on me!"? Moreover, the denial of attributes clashes at every step with clear Qur'ānic statements in which mention is made of God's knowledge, power, and so on. Therefore these attributes may—indeed must—be predicated of Him. To deny them is evident error, unbelief, and heresy.

It was the task of the mediators to reconcile, by means of acceptable formulas, the rigid negation of the rationalists with the traditional concept of the divine attributes. Those who took al-Ash'arī's intermediate position devised to this end the following formula: God knows by a knowledge that is not distinct from His essence. The additional clause is intended to effect a theological rescue of the possibility of attributes. But with this we are far from done with hair-splitting formulas. The Māturīdites, too, strove to mediate, to erect a bridge between orthodoxy and the Mu'tazila. In general they were content with the agnostic statement that God has attributes (for they are stated in the Qur'ān), but one cannot say either that the attributes are identical with God or that they are distinct from His essence. To some of them, the Ash'arite statement of the divine attributes seemed unworthy of the godhead. God, according to that statement, is knowing *by* an eternal knowledge. By (*bi*). Does the grammatical construction not suggest an instrument? Are then the workings of God's knowledge, might, will—all those divine powers that form the

[54] Abū Ma'mar al-Hudhalī (d. 236/850 in Baghdad), in Dhahabī, *Tadhkirat al-ḥuffāẓ*, II, 56 [II, 472].

infinite plenitude of His being—not immediate? Is the conception of immediacy not destroyed by that short syllable *bi*, which has the grammatical function of indicating an instrument? Dreading that such grammar might be derogatory to God's majesty, the shaykhs of Samarkand found the ingenious expedient of stating the mediating formula in the following manner: He is knowing and has knowledge that is attributed to Him in an eternal sense, and so on.

It was not for nothing, we see, that the Muslim theologians in Syria and Mesopotamia lived next to the dialecticians of the conquered nations.

8. One of the weightiest subjects of dogmatic debate was the concept of the divine word. How is one to understand the attribution of speech to God? How is one to explain the operation of this attribute in the act of revelation embodied in the holy scriptures?

Although these questions belong in the context of the theory of attributes, they were treated as distinct and independent subjects of theological speculation. They also came early to form the subject of a controversy independent from that context.

Orthodoxy answers these questions so: speech is an eternal attribute of God, which as such is without beginning or intermission, exactly like His knowledge, His might, and other characteristics of His infinite being. Consequently revelation, the acknowledged manifestation of the speaking God—the Qur'ān being the revelation that claims the Muslim's chief interest—did not originate in time, by a specific act of God's creative will, but has existed from all eternity. The Qur'ān is uncreated. That to this day is the orthodox dogma.[f]

After the foregoing it will cause no surprise that in this notion too the Mu'tazilites saw a breach of pure monotheism. To ascribe to God the anthropomorphistic attribute of speech, to admit an eternal entity besides God, was in their view nothing less than to destroy the unity of the godhead. In this instance, their opposition could be grasped by the man in the street, for it did not hinge on mere abstractions, as the general debate about attributes had. For once, a perfectly concrete thing was in the foreground of speculation. Once the question of the divine word had been separated from the controversy about attributes, in which it had had its first roots, the focus of the issue was: is the Qur'ān created or un-

[f] The burning problem of the preexistence or createdness of the Qur'ān has been discussed in a number of studies. See, for example, W. Madelung, "The Origins of the Controversy Concerning the Creation of the Koran," *Orientalia Hispanica*, edited by J. M. Barral (Leiden, 1974), I, i, 504-25.

created? So formulated, the question was bound to attract the interest of the simplest Muslim, even if the answer to the question hinged on a series of considerations to which he remained wholly indifferent.

To explain the notion of "the speaking God," the Muʿtazilites devised a singular mechanical theory, and in doing so exchanged one bundle of troubles for another. It cannot be the voice of God, they argued, that manifests itself to a prophet when he feels the divine revelation acting upon him through his sense of hearing. The sound is created. When God wishes to manifest Himself audibly, He causes, by a specific creative act, speech to occur in a material substratum. That is the speech which the prophet hears. It is not the immediate speech of God, but rather a speech created by God, manifested indirectly, and corresponding in its contents to the will of God. This theory offered a form into which they could fit their doctrine of the created Qur'ān, which they set against the orthodox dogma of the eternal and uncreated word of God.

No other Muʿtazilite innovation sparked such violent controversy, reaching beyond scholastic circles and making itself felt in public life. The caliph al-Ma'mūn took up the cause, and acting as a kind of high priest of the state, ordered his subjects, under pain of severe punishments, to adopt the belief in the created Qur'ān. His successor, al-Muʿtaṣim, followed in his footsteps. Orthodox theologians and those who refused to make open declaration of their position were subjected to harassment, imprisonment, and torture. Docile *qāḍīs* and other religious authorities were ready to assume the office of inquisitors, in order to vex and persecute the stiff-necked supporters of the orthodox view, and also those who were not sufficiently unambivalent in declaring themselves for belief in the created Qur'ān, the sole belief in which salvation lay.

An American scholar, Walter M. Patton, published in 1897 an excellent work in which he illustrated the course of this rationalist inquisition by examining the case of one of its most eminent victims. This thoroughly documented study presents the vicissitudes of the *imām* Aḥmad b. Ḥanbal, the man whose name was to become in Islam the watchword of uncompromising belief.[55] I have said elsewhere, and may repeat here, that "the inquisitors of liberalism were, if possible, even more terrible than their literal-minded colleagues. In any case their fanaticism is more repugnant than that of their imprisoned and mistreated victims."[56]

It was only in the reign of the caliph al-Mutawakkil—an unappealing

[55] *Aḥmed ibn Ḥanbal and the Miḥna* (Leiden, 1897). Cf. *ZDMG* LII (1898), pp. 155ff.

[56] *Muhammedanische Studien*, II, 59 [= *Muslim Studies*, II, 65].

bigot who had no trouble combining theological orthodoxy with a life of drunkenness and the patronage of obscene literature—that adherents of the old dogma could again raise their heads in freedom. The persecuted now became persecutors, and they knew very well how to put into practice, to the greater glory of Allah, the old adage *vae victis*. This was also a time of political decline—and at such times obscurantists flourish. The range of the concept of the uncreated Qur'ān widened more and more. A general and elastically unclear formulation of the dogma that the Qur'ān is eternal and uncreated was no longer found adequate. What is the uncreated Qur'ān? God's thought, God's will expressed in this book? Is it the particular text that God revealed to the Prophet "in clear Arabic with nothing crooked in it"? As time passed, orthodoxy grew insatiable: "What is between the two covers of the book is the word of God." Thus the concept of being uncreated includes the written copy of the Qur'ān, with its letters written in ink and put on paper. Nor is that which is "read in the prayer niches," that is, the daily Qur'ān recitation as it emerges from the throats of the believers, distinct from God's eternal, uncreated word. The mediators, Ash'arites and Māturīdites, made some concessions that reason suggested. Concerning the principal issue, al-Ash'arī advanced the doctrine that God's speech (*kalām*) is eternal, but that this means only spiritual speech (*kalām nafsī*) which is an eternal attribute of God, without beginning or interruption. On the other hand, revelations received by prophets, and other manifestations of the divine word, are in each case exponents of the eternal, unceasing speech of God.[57] Al-Ash'arī then applied this conception to every material manifestation of revelation.

Let us listen to what al-Māturīdī has to say about the mediating position: "When the question is raised: 'What is it that is written in copies of the Qur'ān?' we say: 'It is the word of God, and so too what is recited in the niches of the mosques and produced in the throats (speech organs), is the speech of God, but the (written) letters and the sounds, melodies, and voices are created things.' Such is the definition established by the shaykhs of Samarkand. The Ash'arites say: 'What is written in a copy of the Qur'ān is not the word of God but only a communication of the word of God, a relation of what the word of God is.' Therefore they consider it permissible to burn a fragment of a written copy of the Qur'ān (for it is not in itself the word of God). To justify this view they argue

[57] Shahrastānī, *Kitāb al-milal wa'l-niḥal*, edited by William Cureton (London, 1842-1846), p. 68.

that the word of God is His attribute, that His attribute is not manifested separately from God; therefore, what appears in separate form, such as the contents of an inscribed sheet of paper, cannot be regarded as the speech of God. But we (the Māturīdites) say to this: 'This assertion of the Ash'arites has even less validity than the opinion of the Mu'tazila.' "

We see that those who sought an intermediate position could not agree among themselves. The orthodox proceeded all the more consistently to extend, out of all measure, the range of their concept of the uncreated Qur'ān. The formula *lafẓī bi'l-qur'ān makhlūq*, "my uttering of the Qur'ān is created" was in their view archheretical. A pious man like al-Bukhārī, whose collection of hadith is, next to the Qur'ān, the most sacred book known to orthodox Muslims, was exposed to harassment because he considered such formulas admissible.[58]

Al-Ash'arī's followers, as we have just seen, are said to have left themselves somewhat more freedom of maneuver in defining the word of God, but al-Ash'arī himself did not hold out for his rationalist formula. In the final, definitive, statement of his theological views he declares: "The Qur'ān is on the preserved (heavenly) tablet; it is in the heart of those who have been given knowledge; it is read by the tongue; it is written down in books in reality; it is recited by our tongues in reality; it is heard by us in reality, as it is written: 'If a polytheist seeks your protection, grant it to him so that he may hear the speech of Allah' (9:6)—thus what you say to him is Allah's own speech. This is to say: all of these are essentially identical with the uncreated divine word, which has been on the heavenly tablet from all eternity, in reality (*fī 'l-ḥaqīqa*), and not in some figurative sense, not in the sense that all these are copies, citations, or communications of a heavenly original. No; all these are identical with the heavenly original; what is true of the original is true of those spatial and temporal manifestations that ostensibly come into being through a human agency."[59]

9. All that we have learned so far about the nature of the Mu'tazilite movement confers on these religious philosophers the right to lay claim to the name of rationalists. I shall not dispute their right to the name. It is their merit to have raised reason to a source of religious knowledge for the first time in Islam, and furthermore, to have candidly admitted the usefulness of doubt as the first impulse to knowledge.

[58] "Zur Geschichte der ḥanbalitischen Bewegungen," p. 7 [= *Gesammelte Schriften*, V, 141].

[59] *Kitāb al-ibāna 'an uṣūl al-diyāna* (Haydarabad, A.H. 1321), p. 41.

But is that enough for calling them liberal? That title we must certainly refuse them. They are in fact, with the formulas they directed against orthodox conceptions, the very founders of theological dogmatism in Islam. Those who wished to be saved must, in the Mu'tazilite view, put their belief in these, and no other, rigid formulas. With their definitions, it is true, they meant to bring reason and religion into harmony. But to a conservative traditionalism unencumbered with definitions they opposed rigid and narrow formulas, and engaged in endless disputations to maintain them. Moreover, they were intolerant in the extreme.[g] A tendency to intolerance lies in the nature of the endeavor to frame religious belief in dogma. During the reign of three 'Abbāsid caliphs, when the Mu'tazilites were fortunate enough to have their doctrines recognized as state dogma, those doctrines were urged by means of inquisition, imprisonment, and terror until, before long, a counterreformation once again allowed those Muslims to breathe freely for whom religion was the sum of pious traditions, and not the result of dubious ratiocination.

A few Mu'tazilite statements will bear witness to the intolerant spirit that ruled the theologians of the movement. One of their doctors declares quite clearly: "Whoever is not a Mu'tazilite should not be called a believer." This is only one of the conclusions drawn from their more general doctrine that no one may be called a believer who does not seek to know God "in the way of speculation." The common people of simple, unreasoning belief did not, in this view, belong to the community of Muslims at all. There could be no belief without the exercise of reason. The issue of *takfīr al-'awāmm*, "proclaiming the masses as unbelievers," was ever alive for the Mu'tazilite science of religion. Therefore there was no lack of those who averred that one could not perform valid prayers

[g] In this passage Goldziher makes an important point concerning the Mu'tazila. While still willing to grant them the title of rationalists and even, to some extent, of freethinkers, he refuses to join earlier European writers on the subject in calling them liberals, and draws attention to their persecution, once they had achieved power, of those other theologians who refused to accept their doctrines. The notion of "liberal" as understood in Goldziher's day was incompatible with intolerance or repression. The Mu'tazila were innovators in two respects: first, in trying to formulate Islam in the form of a system of dogmas, and second, in trying to impose that system by force as a state-sponsored, official orthodoxy. They were largely unsuccessful in the first, and totally unsuccessful in the second. Though Mu'tazilite dogmas were finally rejected, and left virtually no trace on the intellectual history of Sunnī Islam, the practice of formulating dogmas remained and gave rise to a rich development of dogmatic theology. The notion of a state-imposed orthodoxy, however, remained alien to the spirit of Islam. There have been few attempts in Islamic history to formulate and impose such a doctrine, and all of them have failed.

behind a simple, unreasoning believer; to do so would be no better than having an impious believer for one's prayer leader. A famous representative of this school, Mu'ammar b. 'Abbād, regarded as unbelievers all who did not share his opinion on the attributes and the freedom of the will. Another devout Mu'tazilite, Abū Mūsā al-Murdār—whom we might mention as an example for the pietistic beginnings of this movement—assumed the same attitude, and proclaimed his own doctrines as the sole means of salvation, so that it could be argued against him that, from his exclusionary standpoint, only he himself and at most three of his students would be able to enter the Paradise of true believers.[60]

It was truly a piece of good fortune for Islam that state patronage of this mentality was limited to the time of those three caliphs. How far would the Mu'tazilites have gone if the instruments and power of the state had been longer at the disposal of their intellectual faith! How some of them envisioned matters appears, for instance, from the teaching of Hishām al-Fuwaṭī, one of the most radical opponents of the admissibility of divine attributes and predestination. "He considered it permissible to assassinate those who rejected his doctrines, and to lay hands on their property in violence or in secrecy; for they were unbelievers and their lives and goods were free for all to take."[61] These are naturally only theories from a schoolroom, but they were followed out to the conclusion that territories in which the Mu'tazilite beliefs did not prevail were to be regarded as *dār al-ḥarb*, "lands of war." Islamic geography divides the world into seven climatic zones, but there is a more trenchant division: the land of Islam and the land of war.[62] The second category includes all regions among whose inhabitants unbelief still rules although the summons (*da'wa*) to embrace Islam has been carried to them. It is the duty of the head of the Islamic state to levy war on such territories. That is *jihād*, the holy war ordered in the Qur'ān, one of the surest paths to martyrdom.[h] It was with these ideas in mind that some Mu'tazilites wished to proclaim as lands of war all regions in which Mu'tazilite

[60] For the relevant passages and further discussion, see *ZDMG*, LII (1898), 158n., and the introduction to *Le Livre de Mohammed ibn Toumert* (Algiers, 1903), pp. 61–63, 71–74.

[61] Shahrastānī, *Al-milal wa'l-niḥal*, p. 51 bottom line.

[62] Māwardī, *Al-Aḥkām al-sulṭānīya*, edited by Maximilian Enger (Bonn, 1853), pp. 61ff. Imam Shāfi'ī does not distinguish between the two zones, *dār al-islām* and *dār al-ḥarb*. This produces, in secondary issues, differences from the other schools. Cf. Abū Zayd al-Dabbūsī, *Ta'sīs al-naẓar* (Cairo, n.d.), p. 58.

[h] For a brief account of Muslim teachings concerning the holy war, see the article "Djihād" in *EI*[2] (by E. Tyan).

dogma did not have the ascendancy. Against these one must draw the sword, as against unbelievers and idolaters.[63]

This was no doubt an extremely vigorous rationalism. But those whose teachings were the starting point and seedbed of such fanaticism cannot be celebrated as men of liberal and tolerant views.[i] Unfortunately this is not always kept in mind when historical assessments of the Muʿtazila are made. Authors of sophistic fantasies about hypothetical developments in Islam at times draw pictures of how salutary it would have been to the evolution of Islam if the Muʿtazila had successfully risen to spiritual dominance. In view of the foregoing, it is difficult to credit such suggestions. We cannot deny the Muʿtazilites one salutary consequence of their work: they were the ones who brought *ʿaql*, reason, to bear upon questions of belief. That is their indisputable and far-reaching merit, which assures them an important place in the history of Islam and Islamic civilization. Moreover, in consequence of the battles they had fought, and despite all obstacles and refusals, the rights of reason were in larger or smaller measure also recognized in orthodox Islam. Reason could no longer be lightly dismissed.

10. We have mentioned repeatedly the names of the two *imāms*, Abū 'l-Ḥasan al-Ashʿarī and Abū Manṣūr al-Māturīdī, the one active in the center of the caliphate and the other in Central Asia, who smoothed the controversies of theology by mediating formulas that came to be recognized as tenets of orthodox Islamic belief. It would be profitless to study in detail the minuscule differences between their two closely related systems. Historical significance was attained by the first. Its founder had himself been a disciple of the Muʿtazilites, who suddenly deserted that school—in the legend, the Prophet moved him to the change, appearing

[63] Ibn al-Murtaḍā, *Al-Milal wa'l-niḥal*, pp. 44:12, 57:5 [= *Ṭabaqāt al-muʿtazila*, pp. 77, 96].

[i] Goldziher is here arguing against the somewhat idealized picture of the Muʿtazila and their role in Islam first set forth by Heinrich Steiner in his book *Die Muʿtaziliten, oder die Freidenker im Islam* (Leipzig, 1865) and adopted by some other late nineteenth-century and early twentieth-century writers. These views are now generally abandoned (with the exception of a few romantic and apologetic popularizers). Steiner and his successors believed that the Muʿtazila were rationalists, freethinkers, and liberals, and that their continued success would have been more beneficial to Islam (that is, more congenial to nineteenth-century European liberal tastes) than the traditionalists who replaced them. Goldziher, while recognizing the achievement and importance of the Muʿtazila, was the first to attempt some correction of this romanticized picture of them, and to draw attention to some other features of their doctrines and of their methods of propagating them. The discovery and study after Goldziher's time of authentic Muʿtazilite sources enabled scholars for the first time to see them in their own terms and not those of hostile polemicists. This new evidence has in the main confirmed and, indeed, strengthened Goldziher's arguments.

in a dream—and made a public declaration of his return to the pale of orthodoxy. He, and even more his students, furnished orthodoxy with mediating formulas of a more or less orthodox character. Nonetheless, they too failed to suit the taste of the traditional conservatives. For a long time the Ash'arites could not venture to teach their theology in public. It was not taught as a formally acknowledged part of the system of orthodox theology until the middle of the eleventh century, when the famous vizier of the Seljuqs, Niẓām al-Mulk, established in the great schools he had founded in Nishapur and Baghdad positions for the public teaching of the new theological ideas. The most famous representatives of the new theology occupied professorships at these institutions. These institutions are associated with the victory of the Ash'arite school over the Mu'tazila on the one side, and intransigent orthodoxy on the other. The work of these institutions marks, therefore, an important turning point not only in the history of Muslim education, but also in Islamic theology. We must now examine the Ash'arite movement more closely.

It is one thing to call al-Ash'arī a mediator, but quite another to assume indiscriminately that his theological orientation produced a mediatory position on all points of doctrine about which the struggle of conflicting opinions raged in the eighth and ninth centuries. He did, it is true, devise mediating formulas even in such matters as the freedom of the will and the nature of the Qur'ān. Nevertheless, what must be regarded as most characteristic of his theological attitude is the position he took on an issue more relevant than any other to the religious conceptions of the masses: his definition of how the anthropomorphic descriptions of God are to be understood.

His position on this issue cannot be called conciliatory. A compendium of theology has survived, luckily, from the pen of this greatest theological authority in orthodox Islam. In it he both presents his own doctrines in positive form and refutes polemically the contrasting views of the Mu'tazilites—not, we may add, without a fanatic fury. Until recently, this treatise[64] had been given up for lost, and was known only fragmentarily from quotations, but a few years ago it became accessible in a complete edition published in Hyderabad. It is one of the basic texts for anyone who wishes to work, in whatever fashion, on the history of Islamic theology. Even in the introduction, al-Ash'arī's attitude toward rationalism is rendered suspect by the following declaration: "The position

[64] The *Ibāna*, see n. 59 above.

we take and the religious views we profess are: to hold fast to the Book of our Lord and to the *sunna* of our Prophet and to what has been related on the authority of the Companions and the Followers and the *imāms* of hadith. In these we find our firm support. Moreover we profess what Abū 'Abdallāh Aḥmad ibn Muḥammad ibn Ḥanbal taught—may God cause his face to be radiant, elevate his rank, and make his reward abundant—and we contradict all who contradict his teachings; for he is the most excellent *imām* and the perfect chief, through whom God has brought to light truth and abolished error, made distinct the right path and conquered the fallacious innovations of the heretics . . . and the doubt of the doubters. May God have mercy on him; he is the *imām* of highest standing and the honored and admired friend."

Thus at the outset of his creed al-Ash'arī proclaims himself a Ḥanbalite. That does not augur a conciliatory position. Indeed, when he comes to speak of the anthropomorphist question, he heaps all his scorn on the rationalists who seek figurative explanations for the concrete terms of the holy scriptures. Not satisfied with the rigor of the orthodox theologian, he also shows himself a grammarian. God Himself says, after all, that He revealed the Qur'ān in "clear Arabic"; it follows that the Qur'ān can only be understood in the light of correct Arabic usage. But when in the world had any Arab ever used the word "hand" to mean "benevolence," and so on? What Arab has ever employed all those tricks of language that rationalist interpreters want to read into the clear text in order to despoil the idea of God of all content? "Abū 'l-Ḥasan 'Alī b. Ismā'īl al-Ash'arī says: We seek right guidance from God, in Him is our sufficiency, and there is no might and no power except in God and He is the one upon whom we call for assistance. Now then: When we are asked: 'Do you say that God has a face?' we answer: 'That is what we say, in contradiction of the heretics, for it is written: *the face of your Lord endures, in glory and honor* (55:27).' When we are asked 'Do you say that God has hands?' we answer 'That is what we say, for it is written *His hand is above their hands* (48:10), and also *what I created with my two hands* (38:75). Moreover it is related that the Prophet said: *God passed His hand over Adam's back and extracted his progeny from it*, and that he said *Allah created Adam with His hand and created the garden of Eden with His hand, and planted the tree Ṭūbā in it with His hand, and wrote the Torah with His hand.* And it is written *His two hands are stretched forth* (5:64); and it says in the hadith *both His hands are right hands.* Literally so, and not otherwise.' "

To escape crass anthropomorphism, he does, to be sure, insert into his creed the clause that by face, hand, foot, and so on, we are not to understand members of a human body, that all this is to be understood *bilā kayfa*, without asking how (Sec. 6 above). But to add this clause is not to mediate; for traditional orthodoxy had held the same view. This was no mediation between Ibn Ḥanbal and the Muʿtazila; this was—as we could see from al-Ashʿarī's prefatory declaration—the Muʿtazilite renegade's unconditional surrender to the standpoint of the traditionalists' inflexible *imām* and his followers. By his far-reaching concessions to popular belief, al-Ashʿarī caused the loss to the Muslims of important Muʿtazilite achievements.[65] His position left intact the belief in magic and witchcraft, not to speak of the miracles of saints. The Muʿtazilites had done away with all these.

11. The mediation that did play an important part in the history of Islamic theology, and the essentials of which may be regarded as a theological guideline sanctioned by consensus (*ijmāʿ*), must be associated not with the name of al-Ashʿarī himself but with the school that bears his name.

To begin with, it was now no longer possible, even while steering an orthodox course, to depose *ʿaql*, reason, as a source of religious knowledge. We have just seen the passage in al-Ashʿarī's creed in which he makes solemn declaration of his sources of religious knowledge. No mention is made of the right of reason, not even as a subsidiary means to ascertaining the truth. With his school, the case is different. If not as intransigently as the Muʿtazilites, they too affirmed that *naẓar*, the speculative cognition of God, was every person's duty, and condemned *taqlīd*, unthinking acquiescence in received opinion. Besides making this general demand, the principal leaders of the Ashʿarite school followed in several particulars the Muʿtazilite road, and remained faithful to a method which, as I have just showed, their *imām* attacked and persecuted with all the weapons in his dogmatic and philological arsenal. The Ashʿarite theologians paid no attention at all to their master's protest, but continued to make abundant use of the method of *ta'wīl* (Sec. 6 above). They could not otherwise have avoided *tajsīm*, anthropomorphism. The insistence that "Ashʿarite" and "Ḥanbalite" must be identical concepts simply could not match the facts. But what would al-Ashʿarī have said of the method that now came to prevail in the orthodox application of *ta'wīl*? All the tricks of artificial hermeneutics were mustered to conjure

[65] Martin Schreiner, "Zur Geschichte des Asʿaritenthums," *Actes du huitième Congrès International des Orientalistes* (Leiden, 1892-1893), II, Sec. 1A, 105.

away—that is the only way to put it—the anthropomorphic expressions from Qur'ān and hadith.

In the case of the Qur'ān, the Mu'tazilites had already accomplished the work, on the whole satisfactorily. About the hadith they cared less. The problem could always be solved by conveniently declaring the hadiths with objectionable statements to be inauthentic, so one did not need to bother one's head for an interpretation in harmony with reason. In this the orthodox theologians could not go along with the Mu'tazila. Thus their exegetical art now came to be focused on hadith texts; as well it might, for anthropomorphism had gained vast ground in the boundlessly expanding sphere of the hadith. Let us take an example from the hadith collection (*Musnad*) of Aḥmad ibn Ḥanbal. "One morning the Prophet appeared among his companions in a cheerful mood, with a beaming face. When asked the reason, he said: 'Why should I not be cheerful? Last night, the Lord appeared to me in the most beautiful form and called to me and asked: 'What do you think the heavenly company are discussing just now?'[66] I said: 'Lord, I do not know.' (This exchange is repeated twice more.) He laid both His hands on my shoulders so I felt their coolness even in my breast, and there was revealed to me all that is in heaven and earth.' " There follow various pieces of information about the theological conversations of the heavenly company.[67]

It would have been vain endeavor to counteract such flagrant anthropomorphisms through exegesis; nor did the rationally inclined theologians feel obliged to do so when faced with a text that, like the one just cited, had not been included in the canonical collections. They had a graver responsibility when faced with texts that had a place in the canonical corpus and were therefore recognized as normative by the entire community of believers. On such texts they practiced their arts. We read, for example, in the highly esteemed collection of Mālik b. Anas: "Our Lord descends every night to the lowest heaven (there are seven) when one-third of the night is still left, and says: 'Who has a prayer to address to me, that I may grant it? Who has a wish that I may fulfill it? Who asks my pardon for his sins that I may pardon him?' "[68] In this case the an-

[66] In rabbinic haggada, too, the opinion is expressed that questions of law are discussed in heaven as they are in the schools: Bab. *Pesaḥim*, 50a top; *Ḥagīgā*, 15b bottom; *Giṭṭin*, 6b bottom. God Himself ponders the divergent opinions of the scholars of the law; He Himself studies and investigates the law. This last idea is frequently expressed in the *Sēder Eliyyāhū Rabbā* (edited by Meir Friedmann, Vienna, 1900), e.g., p. 61 last line but one.

[67] Ibn Ḥanbal, *Musnad*, IV, 66.

[68] *Muwaṭṭa'*, I, 385; Bukhārī, *Tawḥīd* no. 35. For other examples on which *ta'wīl* was prac-

thropomorphism was removed by means of a grammatical trick, made available by the nature of the old Arabic script, which does not contain any graphic expression of the vowels. Instead of *yanzilu*,[69] "he descends," they read the factitive form *yunzilu*, "he causes to descend," namely, the angels. Thus the text's statement about God's change of place vanishes; it is not God who descends, but He causes angels to descend, who sound these calls in God's name. Another example. From Genesis 1:27, Muslim tradition took the hadith "God created Adam in His form." But God has no form. The possessive *his* must refer to Adam: God created Adam in the form which he (Adam) received.[70] These examples demonstrate the very frequently applied method of using grammatical alterations to obviate theological difficulty.

Recourse was had quite as often to lexical stratagems, where the multiple meanings of Arabic words proved most serviceable. Here is an example. "Hell will not be full until the All-Powerful sets His foot on it (on hell); then it will say 'enough, enough.' "[71] This text was troublesome for a refined conception of God. Such versatility of ingenious thought went into its interpretation that it represents a complete sampler of the hermeneutical arts cherished by the Ash'arite school. First of all, they thought to find a purely external remedy in replacing in the text of the hadith the subject of the phrase "sets his foot" with a pronoun: "Hell will not be full until he sets his foot on it." Who *he* is is left obscure; but at least the concrete predicate is not linked to a subject that means "God" in the language. This is, of course, self-deception, and nothing is gained by it. Others hoped to remedy the situation by retaining the subject *al-jabbār*, the All-Powerful, as it stands in the text, but not referring the word to God. From the language of Qur'ān and hadith, they could easily prove that the word also means a stiff-necked, rebellious character. Thus

---

ticed, see *Die Ẓāhiriten*, p. 168 [= *The Ẓāhirīs*, pp. 154f.]. In Damascus, Ḥasan ibn 'Alī al-Ahwāzī (d. 446/1055) compiled a collection of hadiths to give support to the crudest anthropomorphism. Cf. Yāqūt, *Irshād al-arīb*, III, 153.

[69] A version in Ibn Sa'd, VI, 37:23, has *yahbiṭu* and ends: "until, at break of day, he ascends (*irtafa'a*)."

[70] Other interpretations were also attempted to explain away the anthropomorphism of this saying. They are listed in Abū Muḥammad ibn al-Sīd al-Baṭalyawsī, *Al-Inṣāf fī'l-tanbīh*, edited by Aḥmad 'Umar al-Maḥmaṣānī (Cairo, A.H. 1319), pp. 120f. This book is of great importance for the study of the questions discussed here. See also Muḥammad al-'Abdarī, *Kitāb madkhal al-shar' al-sharīf* (Alexandria, A.H. 1293), II 25ff., and further, Subkī, *Ṭabaqāt*, II, 135:13.

[71] Bukhārī, *Tafsīr* no. 264 (to Sura 50, vs. 30), *Tawḥīd* no. 7; cf. also Ibn al-Athīr, *Al-Nihāya fī gharīb al-ḥadīth* (Cairo, A.H. 1322), I, 142; *Lisān al-'arab*, V, 182, s.v. *jbr*.

it could be argued that the *jabbār* who would set his foot on hell was not God but some violent person, a man sent to hell, whose violent intervention would put an end to the peopling of hell. On serious scrutiny, however, this way out of the difficulty proved quite as slippery as the first, for the meaning of the hadith is put beyond doubt by a series of parallel versions. In the place of *jabbār*, many parallel texts explicitly say *Allah* or *Lord of majesty* (*Rabb al-ʿizza*). We have not escaped the difficulty; the subject must be God. But what will the theological exegete not attempt in his desperate ingenuity? His arts have foundered on the subject; he tries his luck with the object. He (the meaning is now unquestionably God) sets His foot, *qadamahu*. Must this word be understood to mean, of all things, "foot"? It is a homonym that means a variety of things. Among them, *qadam* can mean "a group of people who have been sent ahead," in our case to hell. It is these people and not His foot that God sets upon hell. But once again an authentic parallel is found which, unhappily, substitutes a synonym (*rijlahu*) for *qadamahu*, and *rijlahu* undoubtedly means "his foot." Not so; the Arabic lexicon knows no *undoubtedly*; one word can have so many meanings. *Rijl* can also mean *jamāʿa*, "an assembly." It is such an assembly—of sinners, of course—that God sets down at the gate of hell, whereupon hell shrieks "enough, enough, enough!"

Thus it was not excessive on my part to call the efforts brought to bear on this short saying a sampler of exegetical violence. The theologians who made these efforts were not Muʿtazilites, however, but Ashʿarites of the purest water. One can imagine the philological wrath the founder himself would have poured out on the heads of his followers.

12. If this rationalist activity of the Ashʿarite school was welcomed as a way out of *tajsīm*, which all parties held in abhorrence, it was bound to arouse definite discomfort in all orthodox believers genuinely faithful to tradition. The matter is linked to a further circumstance. The Ashʿarites' method gave offence to conservative theologians because of a doctrine that they shared with the Muʿtazila, and that is an essential principle of all *kalām*: that "a demonstration built on traditional elements furnishes no certain knowledge." In this view, knowledge supported only by traditional sources is uncertain, depending on components that can be of no more than relative value for ascertaining the facts: for instance, on interpretation that is at the discretion of individual judgment, or on the significance assigned to rhetorical peculiarities (tropes, metaphors, and so on). Such sources of knowledge can be assigned an absolute value only in questions of legal practice, and even there they leave room for differences

of opinion about the conclusions to be drawn. In questions of dogma they have only a subsidiary value. One must base oneself on rational proof; it alone furnishes certain knowledge.[72] Not long ago, the recently deceased Egyptian *muftī* Muḥammad 'Abduh (d. 1905)[j] could still, in the same spirit, declare it as a principle of orthodox Islam that "when reason and tradition are in contradiction, the right of decision rests with reason." "This is a principle," he says, "which very few people oppose, and only people who are of no account."[73]

Although as a rule the Ash'arites employed their rational proofs in support of orthodox dogma, and, faithful to their master's principle, guarded against letting their syllogisms lead them to statements that deviated from the path of sound orthodoxy, it was unavoidable that their assertion of the preeminence of reason over tradition in theological proof should be an abomination in the eyes of the intransigent old school. And how much more of one in the eyes of the anthropomorphists, those slaves to the letter who would not hear of metaphors, tropes, and other rhetorical-exegetical dodges in connection with the scriptural attributes of God!

Consequently, for the adherents of the old traditionalist school, there was nothing to choose between Mu'tazilite and Ash'arite. The *kalām* itself, the very principle of it, was the enemy, and it was immaterial whether it led to orthodox or heretical results.[74] "Flee from *kalām*, no matter what form it takes, as you would flee from a lion," is their motto. Their sentiments are expressed in the wrathful words they ascribed to al-Shāfi'ī: "My verdict on the people of *kalām* is that they should be beaten with whips and the soles of sandals, and then paraded through all

[72] Cf. the peremptory formulation of this principle in Fakhr al-Dīn al-Rāzī, *Ma'ālim uṣūl al-dīn*, Ch. II, 10 (Cairo, A.H. 1323, on the margin of the same author's *Muḥaṣṣal*, p. 9). After enumerating the subjective elements in any demonstration by means of tradition, he writes: "It follows from this that traditional proofs are productive only of suppositions (*ẓannīya*), while rational proofs are apodictic (*qaṭ'īya*), and suppositions cannot be set against apodictic knowledge." The basic principle of the *kalām* is always: *al-dalā'il al-naqlīya lā tufīd al-yaqīn*, "traditional proofs do not furnish certainty"; al-Ījī, *Al-Mawāqif fī 'ilm al-kalām*, with the Commentary of Jurjānī (Istanbul, A.H. 1239), p. 79.

[j] On Muḥammad 'Abduh, a major figure among modernist Muslim theologians, see the article devoted to him in *EI*[1] (by J. Schacht), and H.A.R. Gibb, *Modern Trends in Islam* (Chicago, 1947). A number of more recent studies on Muḥammad 'Abduh have been concerned primarily with his political and legal doctrines.

[73] *Al-Islām wa'l-naṣrānīya ma'a'l-'ilm wa'l-madanīya* (Cairo, n.d., posthumously printed), p. 56.

[74] Cf. Martin Schreiner, *Beiträge zur Geschichte der theologischen Bewegungen im Islam* (Leipzig, 1899), pp. 64-75 = *ZDMG*, LII (1898), 528-39.

tribes and encampments while it is proclaimed of them, 'Such is the reward of those who forsake the Qur'ān and *sunna* and give themselves up to the *kalām*.' "[75] In their opinion, *kalām* was a science that reaped no divine reward when it led its practitioner to sound views, but which could easily lead to error, and so to unbelief.[76] The true Muslim should not bend his knee to *'aql*, reason. Reason is not required for the grasping of religious truth; that truth is comprised in Qur'ān and *sunna*.[77] There was, in this view, no difference between *kalām* and Aristotelian philosophy; both led to unbelief. They had no use for anything like *fides quaerens intellectum*. Belief is bound to the letter of the received texts, solely and exclusively. Reason should not be caught trespassing in this area.

Thus it may be said of the mediating theology of the Ash'arites that it fell between two stools. Such is the reward of those who vacillate between two sides and have a wink for each. Philosophers and Mu'tazilites turned up their noses at the Ash'arites, whom they considered obscurantists, muddled thinkers, superficial dilettantes, with whom it was impossible even to engage in earnest disputation. But such censure did not save the Ash'arites from the fanatical curses of the partisans of tradition. They got little thanks for the battles they fought in behalf of religion against Aristotelian philosophy.

13. Besides their theology proper, the Ash'arites' natural philosophy also deserves particular attention.[k] It may be called the prevalent conception of the physical world in orthodox Islam.

The philosophy of the *kalām* cannot be regarded as a closed system, but in general it may be said that its philosophical world view mainly follows the paths of the pre-Aristotelian philosophers of nature,[78] and in particular those of the atomists among them. From the first, even before the rise

[75] In Ibn Taymīya's "Al-'Aqīda al-ḥamawīya al-kubrā," *Rasā'il*, I, 468 bottom.

[76] Subkī, *Ṭabaqāt*, I, 241:5.

[77] A famous traditionist, Abū Sulaymān al-Khaṭṭābī al-Bustī (d. 388/998), wrote a book under the title *Al-Ghunya* (not *al-ghayba* as in Abū'l-Maḥāsin ibn Taghrī Birdī, *Al-Nujūm al-zāhira*, edited by William Popper, Berkeley, 1909, II, 84:15) *'an al-kalām wa-ahlihi*, "The Dispensability of Kalām and of Those Who Practice It"; Subkī, *Ṭabaqāt*, II, 218:15.

[k] On this whole question see the important study by S. Pines, *Beiträge zur islamischen Atomenlehre* (Berlin, 1936), especially pp. 94ff., where further literature is cited. On later attempts to refute this doctrine, see Majid Fakhry, *Islamic Occasionalism and Its Critique by Averroes and Aquinas* (London, 1958).

[78] On the sources of Mu'tazilite metaphysics and natural philosophy we should now note S. Horovitz's studies: *Über den Einfluss der griechischen Philosophie auf die Entwicklung des Kalām* (Breslau, 1909), and the review by M. Horten in *OLZ*, XII (1909), 391ff. On the philosophy of the *kalām* now see also M. Horten, *Die philosophischen Probleme der spekulativen Theologie im Islam* (Bonn, 1910; Renaissance und Philosophie, III).

of the Ash'arite school, the philosophers of *kalām* were reproached for not admitting that phenomena could be constant and subject to laws. Al-Jāḥiẓ mentions the Aristotelians' objection, urged against his fellow-Mu'tazilites, that their method for proving the unity of God (*tawḥīd*) could be maintained only at the cost of denying all the truths of nature.[79] Al-Naẓẓām, one of the boldest representatives of the school, could be reproached—by opponents ignorant of the deeper sense and coherence of his philosophical theories—with having denied the law of the impenetrability of bodies.[80] Such an opinion of his has in fact been related, and is demonstrably a consequence of his dependence on Stoic views of the physical world.[81]

Even though the Mu'tazila were at war with peripatetic philosophy, an occasional Mu'tazilite would clothe himself in an Aristotelian cloak, and attempt to make his theories more acceptable by decking them in philosophical flourishes—which, to be sure, did not much affect the philosophers' view of them. The philosophers looked with contempt upon the methods of the *kalām*, and did not consider the *mutakallimūn* opponents of equal rank, worthy of being engaged in disputation. They declared that they had no common ground with the *mutakallimūn*, and so a serious discussion with them was impossible. "The *mutakallimūn* allege that reason is the noblest source of knowledge. But what they call by that name is not in reality reason at all, and their methods of thought do not, in any philosophical sense, conform to the rules of reason. That which they call reason, and with which they pretend to operate rationally, is a mere web of fancies."

This judgment applies even more conclusively to the Ash'arites. The statements of the Aristotelians and Neoplatonists of the tenth to thirteenth centuries branding the natural philosophy of the *kalām* phantasmagorical and contrary to reason[82] are most pertinent to the case of the Ash'arites who, in the interest of their theological assumptions, resisted all views premised on the operation of laws in the physical world. They agreed with the Pyrrhonians in denying the reliability of sense perception, and left the widest room possible for the assumption that the senses deceive. They denied the law of causality, the "fountainhead and guiding star of all rational science" (Th. Gomperz). They held that nothing in the

[79] *Ḥayawān*, II, 48 [II, 134f.].

[80] Ījī, *Mawāqif*, p. 448.

[81] Cf. S. Horovitz, *Griechische Philosophie*, p. 12; M. Horten, "Die Lehre vom Kumūn bei Naẓẓām," *ZDMG*, LXIII (1909), 784ff.

[82] See notes 48 and 49 above.

world occurs according to inalterable laws, by real necessity: the event that precedes is not the cause of the event that follows. They harbored such fear of the concept of causality that they were reluctant to call God the "first cause," preferring the name of Maker (*fāʿil*) of nature and its phenomena.[83] Consequently they admitted the possibility of occurrences contrary to nature. It might be possible to see things not within the observer's field of vision. It could be said of them sarcastically that they admitted the possibility of a blind man in China seeing a midge in Andalus.[84] They replaced the laws of nature with the concept of habit.

It is no law, but only a habit God has established in nature (*ijrā' al-ʿāda*) that certain events follow other events; they do not follow by necessity. It is not necessary for the lack of food and drink to cause hunger and thirst, but it habitually does. Hunger and thirst arise when the accident of being hungry and thirsty becomes attached to a substance. If this accident does not occur (and God can prevent it), hunger and thirst do not occur. The Nile rises and ebbs from habit, not as a result of the operation of cause and effect in nature. If the accident of rising fails to obtain, the water level will not budge an inch. The hypothesis that what seems to us a law of nature is but a habit in nature was used to explain anything and everything. God has established in nature the habit that certain constellations of stars correspond to the ensuing of certain events. Thus the astrologers may be right; but they express themselves fallaciously.[85] Each event that happens or fails to happen is the result of a particular creative act on God's part. God mostly allows natural events to take their habitual course, but not without exception. When God suspends the habit of natural phenomena, there occurs what we call a miracle, and what the Ashʿarites called a breach of habit, *kharq al-ʿāda*. The continuation of a habit corresponds to ever-renewed acts of creation. We are accustomed to say that a shadow is attributable to the absence of sunlight from a certain place. Wrong! A shadow is not the consequence of the absence of sunlight; it is created and is something positive. This permits the *mutakallimūn* to explain the hadith that in Paradise there is a tree under whose shadow one can ride a hundred years and not come out of the shade. How is this conceivable, seeing that before the entry of the believers into Paradise the sun was already folded up (81:1)? After all, no sun, no

[83] Maimonides, *Dalālat al-ḥā'irīn*, I, Ch. 69, beginning.
[84] Jurjānī on *Mawāqif*, p. 512:3 from bottom.
[85] Ibn Ḥajar al-Haytamī, *Al-Fatāwā al-ḥadīthīya*, p. 35.

shadow. Very well; shadow has nothing to do with sun; God creates the shadow, in a simple breach of natural habit.[86]

This view of nature pervades the Ash'arite theologians' whole conception of the world. Al-Ash'arī himself applied it widely. The doctrine is ascribed to him, for example, that it was by mere habit of nature that a person could not use his sense of vision to perceive smells and tastes. God could endow our sense of vision with a capacity for perceiving smells; but that is not the habit of nature.[87]

Thus orthodox Islamic theology, built on Ash'arite foundations, demands the rejection of the concept of causality, in any form whatever. The theologians not only denied that inalterable and eternal laws of nature caused all natural occurrences, but rejected formulations of causality that came nearer the standpoint of the *kalām*, as, for example, the suggestion that "causality is not eternal but originated in time, and God created in causes the power always to bring about the same consequences."[88]

This world view excluded the concept of an accidental event because it held that a determining intention is a necessary condition of an event. The exclusion of accident does not mean that an event was regarded as the inevitable consequence of a causality observable in the conformity of events to laws. Within this view of nature, all demands of dogmatic theology could be comfortably accommodated. We have seen with what ease a formula for miracles was found. Nor was it more difficult to accept all instances of the supernatural in which dogma requires a Muslim to believe. Since there is no law and no causality, there is also nothing miraculous and supernatural. When rotting bones are endowed with the accident of life, the Resurrection arrives. It is the result of a particular act, as indeed all natural events are the results of particular acts and not of constant laws.

In this fashion the *kalām*, accepted in its Ash'arite form by Islamic orthodoxy, opposed to Aristotelianism a method of thought well suited to

[86] In Zabīdī, *Itḥāf al-sāda al-muttaqīn* (Cairo, A.H. 1311), X, 53.

[87] Ījī, *Mawāqif*, p. 506.

[88] The formulations, which are to be rejected, of the concept of causality are assembled by Sanūsī (end of fifteenth century), *Les Prolégomènes théologiques*, edited and translated by J. D. Luciani (Algiers, 1908), pp. 108-12. Sanūsī, whose compendia are considered fundamental works of orthodox theology, devoted a further dogmatic statement to the refutation of causality. In this book, listed among his works in Abū'l-Qāsim al-Ḥafnāwī, *Ta'rīf al-khalaf bi-rijāl al-salaf* (Algiers, 1325/1907), I, 185, "he refutes, with compelling proofs, the operation of enduring causes."

support theological doctrines. Since the twelfth century it has been the dominant religious philosophy in Islam.

But these subtleties, too, were to have their sovereign value reduced by a counterpoise, by the intervention of a further element of religious history. We shall take it up in our next chapter.

IV. *Asceticism and Sufism*

1. The thought of rejecting this world, coupled with a sense of absolute dependency, had dominated the beginnings of Islam.[a]

It was, as we have seen, the vision of the end of the world and the Day of Judgment that awakened Muhammad to prophethood. That vision bred an ascetic mood among those who followed him. Contempt for earthly things was the watchword.

Muhammad never ceased to proclaim that the aim of the believer's life was felicity in the next world. There was no deliberate shift of attention in Medina, but as circumstances changed and Muhammad's military activities proceeded, an abundance of secular considerations mingled, before long, with the other matters that occupied his thought.

It was precisely the prospect of tangible gain that made it possible to attract and hold the greater part of the Arab masses that joined him. Not all figures in early Islamic history were *qurrā'* (men of prayer) and *bakkā'ūn* (weepers, penitents). A share in the spoils of war must have been among the preeminent inducements that enabled Islam to draw people to its banners. The Qur'ān itself recognized this when it sought to heighten the fighters' zeal with Allah's promise of much booty, *maghānim kathīra* (48:19). When one reads the ancient narratives about the *maghāzī* (military expeditions) of the Prophet, one is truly astonished at the reports of magnificent distributions of plunder, which inevitably, as by a law of nature, follow the accounts of the various pious wars.

The Prophet, to be sure, did not disavow the higher goals to which these plundering expeditions were to lead. The Qur'ān continued to speak against exclusive attention to the ambitions of this world, the

[a] Since Goldziher's day, Sufism, along with other forms of Oriental mysticism, has attracted considerable attention in the Western world and given rise to an extensive literature of very uneven quality. Scholarly accounts include the following: A. J. Arberry, *Introduction to the History of Sufism* (London, 1942); *idem*, *Sufism: An Account of the Mystics of Islam* (London, 1950); *idem*, *Revelation and Reason in Islam* (London, 1957); R. A. Nicholson, *The Mystics of Islam* (London, 1914); *idem*, *Studies in Islamic Mysticism* (Cambridge, 1921); *idem*, *The Idea of Personality in Sufism* (Cambridge, 1923); G. C. Anawati and Louis Gardet, *Mystique musulmane* (Paris, 1961); Henry Corbin, *L'Homme de lumière dans le soufisme Iranien* (Paris, 1971); Helmut Ritter, *Das Meer der Seele* (Leiden, 1955). For a good general introduction, see Fritz Meier's chapter on Sufism in *Islam and the Arab World*, edited by B. Lewis (New York, 1976), pp. 117-28.

dunyā: "Allah has many *maghānim*" (4:94). "You want the frail goods of this world, but the will of Allah is for the other world" (8:67). The ascetic tone of the first Meccan revelations survived as a didactic element within the Medinese realism. But reality steered the spirit of the young Islamic community onto an entirely different course from the one that the Prophet had followed at the beginning of his work and that he had bidden his faithful to follow.

Even before, but especially soon after his death, the old watchword yielded to a new. The idea of rejecting the world was supplanted by that of conquering it. Faith was to lead the believers to success: "Say: 'there is no God but God,' and you shall prosper, by it you will rule the Arabs and subjugate the non-Arabs (*'ajam*), and if you believe, you will be kings in Paradise."[1] And in the event, this conquest of the world was not confined to spiritual goals. The treasures of Ctesiphon, Damascus, and Alexandria were not calculated to stiffen ascetic proclivities. One cannot fail to be astonished when one reads lists, from as early as the third Islamic decade, of the great riches gathered by the pious warriors and men of prayer, of the vast pieces of land they called their own, of the well-appointed houses they furnished at home and in the conquered territories, of the luxury with which they surrounded themselves.

Documentary information is available about the possessions of certain people adorned by the highest degree of Muslim piety. We can, for example, look at the estate left by al-Zubayr ibn al-'Awwām, of the tribe of Quraysh, a man of such piety that he is considered one of the ten people to whom the Prophet could grant during their lifetime the happy assurance that their services to Islam would guarantee their entrance into Paradise. The Prophet called him his apostle (*ḥawārī*). This Zubayr left landed property that after payment of all debts brought a net price variously estimated in the reports between 35,200,000 and 52,000,000 dirhams.[b] He was, to be sure, celebrated for his generous works of char-

[1] Ibn Sa'd, I, i, 145:13.

[b] *Dirham*, from the Greek drachma, was used to designate a unit of silver currency inherited from Sasanid Persia and current in the medieval caliphate, more especially in the earlier provinces. The standard weight of a dirham varied in the neighbourhood of 2.97 grams.

The *qinṭār* or quintal is a measure of weight, consisting of 100 *raṭls*. The *raṭl* varies greatly with time, place, and the material weighed. The *raṭl* used in Mecca in early Islamic times is estimated at 1.5 kg.

The *mithqāl* was a unit of weight, used more particularly for precious metals, based on the Byzantine *solidus*, and weighing 4.233 grams, with some minor variations in different times and places.

On weights and measures, see Walther Hinz, *Islamische Masse und Gewichte (Leiden, 1955:*

ity, but he certainly was a Croesus, and no contempt for this world is reflected in the inventory of the real estate he could call his own in various parts of the recently conquered lands: eleven houses in Medina alone, and others in Basra, Kufa, Fusṭāṭ, and Alexandria.[2] Another one of the ten pious men whom the Prophet assured of Paradise, Ṭalḥa ibn 'Ubayd Allāh, owned land in the value of roughly 30,000,000 dirhams. At the time of his death, his treasurer had at his disposal a further 2,200,000 dirhams in cash. In another account his liquid funds are estimated as follows: he left one hundred leather bags, each of which contained three *qinṭārs* of gold.[3] A heavy load for Paradise! At roughly the same time (37/657), there died in Kufa a pious man named Khabbāb, who had started life in great penury, and who had been in his youth a craftsman in Mecca, a profession that according to the Arab ideas of the time did little honor to a freeborn gentleman.[4] He became a Muslim, and as a result had to suffer greatly at the hands of his pagan fellow-Meccans. They tortured him with hot irons and mistreated him in other ways, but he persevered. He also took zealous part in the Prophet's military expeditions. When this man, so ardent in his religion, lay on his deathbed in Kufa, he pointed to a chest in which he had amassed 40,000—presumably meaning dirhams—and expressed the fear that in accumulating such wealth he had perhaps accepted in advance full compensation for his perseverance in the faith.[5]

Rich shares of plunder, and in peacetime generous stipends, offered the warriors an excellent opportunity for the accumulation of such worldly goods. After a military campaign in North Africa, led by 'Abdallāh ibn Abī Sarḥ during the reign of the caliph 'Uthmān, each rider received from the spoils 3,000 *mithqāls* of gold. People like Ḥākim ibn Ḥizām, who refused to accept the stipends offered him by Abū Bakr and 'Umar, must have been exceedingly rare.[6]

Handbuch der Orientalistik, Ergänzungsband 1, Heft 1. See also Eliyahu Ashtor, *Histoire des prix et des salaires dans l'Orient médiéval* (Paris, 1969).

[2] *Ibn Sa'd*, III, i, 77.

[3] *Ibid.*, III, i, 158.

[4] See "Die Handwerke bei den Arabern," *Globus*, LXVI (1894), 203ff. [= *Gesammelte Schriften*, III, 316ff.].

[5] Ibn Sa'd, III, i, 117.

[6] Nawawī, *Tahdhīb al-asmā'*, p. 217:4; also Sa'īd ibn al-Musayyab, *ibid.*, p. 284:4 from bottom. Cf. Ibn Sa'd, V, 305:4ff. Characteristic for this state of affairs are other examples, chosen from a different point of view, in Lammens, *Mo'āwia*, pp. 148, 152 n. 5, 165ff., 177, 233ff. (*MFO*, II, 40, 44, 57ff., 69, 125ff.). Cf. also Mas'ūdī, *Murūj al-dhahab*, IV, 254f. [III, 77].

As Leone Caetani clearly demonstrates in various parts of his work on Islam, the Arabs' drive to conquest sprang chiefly from material want and cupidity,[7] which is easily explained by the economic circumstances of Arabia. Want and cupidity fired the enthusiasm to emigrate from a land that had declined and to occupy more fertile areas. The new faith was a welcome motive for this migration, which economic necessity promoted.[8] This is not to say that rapacity alone set the goals for the religious wars of early Islam. Besides those warriors who *yuqātilūna 'alā ṭama' al-dunyā*, "fight out of a desire for the things of this world," there were men impassioned by faith, who *yuqātilūna 'alā 'l-ākhira* "fight for the sake of the next world."[9] But it was certainly not this last strain that gave the mood of the fighting masses its true character.[c]

Thus the material good fortune of Islam early caused the ascetic idea, dominant in the beginning, to be forced into the background. Zealous participation in extending Muhammad's religion could on occasion suit secular considerations and fulfill worldly desires. In the generation after Muhammad one could already say that each pious act must now be reckoned twice, for "the next world is no longer our care, as it used to be, but instead the things of this world, *al-dunyā*, sway us."[10]

2. The gradual retreat of the ascetic disposition was not halted as the Umayyads rose to power, and in the political arena as well the theocratic spirit had the worst of it. The spirit of the society took its bearings from the mentality of men who were no saints. According to a saying of the Prophet that mirrors the thinking of the pious, "there will be no more Caesar in Syria and no more Chosroes in Iraq. By God, you will spend

[7] Caetani, *Annali dell'Islam*, II, 399, 405, 543. [8] *Ibid.*, II, 1080ff.

[9] Ibn Sa'd, V, 50:27. Concerning the twofold motivation for the waging of war, see also Nöldeke's review of Caetani in *WZKM*, XXI (1907), 305.

[c] The economic aspects of the Islamic expansion were examined by the German scholar Carl Heinrich Becker, who took up and developed the studies of Caetani on this theme. His views may be found in his contribution to the first edition of the *Cambridge Medieval History* and in a number of other studies, all of them reprinted in his *Islamstudien*, I (Leipzig, 1924); for a sociological discussion, see G. H. Bousquet, "Observations sur la nature et les causes de la conquête Arabe," *Studia Islamica*, VI (1956), 37-52. On climatic and other factors, see K. W. Butzer, "Der Umweltfaktor in der grossen arabischen Expansion," *Saeculum*, VIII (1957), 359-71; *idem*, "Late Glacial and Post Glacial Climatic Variations in the Near East," *Erdkunde*, II (1957), 21-35. A Russian orthodox Marxist view was given by E. A. Belyaev in his book *Arabs, Islam and the Arab Caliphate in the Early Middle Ages*, translated by Adolphe Gourevitch (New York and London, 1969). Among recent general histories of medieval Islam, one giving special importance to economic matters is Claude Cahen, *L'Islam des origines au debut de l'empire Ottoman* (Paris, 1970).

[10] Nawawī, *Tahdhīb al-asmā'*, p. 362:6.

their treasures in the way of God." This spending of the plundered treasures "in the way of God" and for the benefit of the poor and the needy was intended by such pious hadiths to counterbalance the materialistic strand in the successful conquests.[11] But this view was not to the taste of the people who determined the uses to which the acquired goods should be put. In their opinion, the treasure amassed through conquest and augmented by wise domestic management was not there simply to be spent "in the way of God," that is, for pious purposes. The classes into whose hands such worldly goods had fallen wanted to use them to enjoy the world. People were not satisfied to "accumulate treasures for heaven." An old tradition relates that Mu'āwiya, the governor of Syria during the reign of the caliph 'Uthmān, and the later founder of the Umayyad dynasty of caliphs, quarreled with the pious Abū Dharr al-Ghifārī[d] about what was meant in Sura 9 verse 34, "As for those who hoard silver and gold and do not spend it in the way of God, announce to them a painful punishment." The secular-minded statesman advanced the view that this warning had no reference to the contemporary circumstances of the Islamic state, but only to the rapacious leaders of the other religions, of whom the immediately preceding portion of the text speaks. His pious opponent argued that "the warning was meant for them and for us." This was not in line with Mu'āwiya's thinking, and he found Abū Dharr's interpretation dangerous enough to appeal to the caliph against it. The caliph summoned Abū Dharr to Medina, and banished him to a small locality nearby, to make sure that his doctrines, so hostile to this world, could not influence public opinion against the prevalent spirit.[12]

This is a reflection of the ruling mentality, to which the interpreters of religious doctrines also had to bow. It saw only eccentricity in people who represented the original Islamic ideal, who like Abū Dharr taught on the Prophet's authority that "if a person collects silver and gold, they

[11] *Ibid.*, p. 519:8. Very important is the hadith in Bukhārī, *Jihād* no. 36, where the Prophet voices his apprehension about the "good things of the earth and the delights of the world" that will after his death accrue to the believers. His fears are alleviated by the hope that the treasure to be gained will be turned to pious account.

[d] Abū Dharr al-Ghifārī (also mentioned above, Ch. I, Sec. 8 and Ch. II, Sec. 4) was a Companion of the Prophet who died in the year 31 or 32 of the Hijra (651–652). Long noted for his humility and asceticism, he has in modern times become the subject of a new cult as the remote ancestor of Arab socialism. See Werner Ende, *Arabische Nation und islamische Geschichte: die Umayyaden im Urteil arabischer Autoren des 20 Jahrhunderts* (Beirut, 1977), pp. 210-21.

[12] Ibn Sa'd, IV, i, 166.

are like hot coals in his hands until he uses them for pious purposes," who like Abū Dharr refused to acknowledge as their brother any man, faithful Muslim though he might be, who built great houses or owned fields and herds.[13] Indeed, in the texts that document religious thinking, we meet signs of undisguised disapproval directed at all asceticism in excess of the measure established by religious law—asceticism that would no doubt have enjoyed the unconditional approval of the Prophet during the first decade of his vocation. The temper of the times had now changed completely. In the form of hadith we have documentary evidence of the new spirit.

Aspiration to otherwordly values could naturally not be expunged from Islam, but it was now to rule jointly with a sense for man's interests in this world. A didactic statement was devised in which the Prophet teaches, in the spirit of the Aristotelian just middle, that "the best among you is not the one who neglects the next world for the sake of this world, nor the one who does the reverse. The best among you is he who takes from both" (*man akhadha min hādhihi wa-hādhihi*).[14]

In traditional sources examples of excessive asceticism are often related in such a way that the Prophet's disapproval follows immediately upon the tale.

This is most characteristically shown by the reports about the ascetic inclinations of 'Abdallāh the son of 'Amr ibn al-'Āṣ, the famous general of early Islamic history. In the tradition 'Abdallāh appears, in contrast to his father, as one of the foremost religious disciples of the Prophet and one of those who pondered the Prophet's law with the greatest diligence.[15] The Prophet hears of his inclination to impose continuous fasts on himself, and to go without sleep in order to spend the nights reciting the Qur'ān. He earnestly admonishes 'Abdallāh to keep these ascetic habits within reasonable limits. "Your body has a claim on you; your wife has a claim on you; your guest has a claim on you."[16] "He who

[13] *Ibid.*, p. 169:8, 24. Abū'l-Dardā' said: "He who has two dirhams will face a closer reckoning on the Day of Resurrection than he who has but one" (Ibn Sa'd, VI, 200:15).

[14] Ibn Qutayba, *'Uyūn al-akhbār*, III, 375:10 [I, 327].

[15] Cf. Ibn Sa'd, II, ii, 125:10ff.

[16] *Ibid.*, IV, ii, 9ff., in different versions. The person to whom this precept of the Prophet is addressed varies from story to story. For example, in Ibn Sa'd, III, i, 287:21, it is 'Uthmān ibn Maẓ'ūn; in another place (cf. *Muhammedanische Studien*, II, 396 n. 1 [= *Muslim Studies*, II, 358 n. 9; the note cites Bukhārī, *Adab* no. 83]) it is 'Abdallāh ibn 'Amr. The stories about the son of 'Umar presuppose an already assembled Qur'ān: 'Abdallāh wants to recite it all every day; the Prophet finds it sufficient if he works his way monthly through the holy book, or at most in ten or six days. (For examples of pious men praised for their recitation

undertakes a continuous fast has in reality not performed the duty of fasting," that is, it is not credited to him as a work of religious merit.[17]

The Prophet is represented as reproving people who give themselves up to uninterrupted devotions at the cost of neglecting their daily business. Some men once praised a traveling companion of theirs who did nothing but recite invocations and supplications while riding, and perform *ṣalāt*-prayers while stopping. "But," the Prophet asked, "who made sure of the fodder for his mount, and who prepared his food?" "We all saw to his needs." "Then each of you is better than he."[18] A great many traditional narratives about extravagant penitential vows, the mortification and torture of the flesh—whose prototype is a certain Abū Isrā'īl[19]—show an unmistakable tendency to declare such efforts to be of little or no religious worth. "If the monk (*rāhib*) Jurayj (the diminutive of Gregorius) had truly been a man of religious learning he would have known that to fulfill his mother's wish was of greater worth than to give himself up to his devotions."[20]

Celibacy in particular draws the Prophet's most rigorous censure. He rebukes a certain 'Akkāf ibn Wadā al-Hilālī, who had resolved upon an unmarried life: "So you have made up your mind to be one of the brethren of Satan! If you want to be a Christian monk, join them openly. If you are one of us, you must follow our *sunna*; and our *sunna* is married life."[21] Similar statements are ascribed to the Prophet with regard to

---

of the whole Qur'ān in five, six, and seven days, see Ibn Sa'd, VI, 49:6, 58:12, 60:24. Even more is done during Ramaḍān when the custom is to read through the whole book every two nights.) The report (*ibid.*, IV, ii, 11 bottom) that 'Abdallāh could read Syriac perhaps indicates a Christian influence on his ascetic inclinations.

[17] Ibn Ḥanbal, *Musnad*, II, 64: *lā ṣāma man ṣāma al-abada*.

[18] Māwardī, *A'lām al-nubūwa* (Cairo, A.H. 1319), p. 153.

[19] *Muhammedanische Studien*, II, 395 [= *Muslim Studies*, II, 358].

[20] Ibn al-Athīr, *Usd al-ghāba*, V, 132:7; cf. Ibn Sa'd, IV, ii, 17:13. On the occasion and context of this saying, see the hadiths in Josef Horovitz, *Spuren griechischer Mimen im Orient* (Berlin, 1905), pp. 78-79.

[21] It is always the *sunna* that is brought to bear when married life is recommended. Celibacy is contrary to the *sunna*. Monastic life, *rahbānīya*, is regarded as *bid'a* (innovation in religion, cf. Chapter VI), Ibn Sa'd, V, 70:6; *al-rahbānīya al-mubtada'a* (Ibn Qutayba, *'Uyūn al-akhbār*, III, 375:12 [I, 327]; cf. *Muhammedanische Studien*, II, 23 n. 6 [= *Muslim Studies*, II, 34 n. 7]). A celibate ascetic is censured, despite his piety and observance of the laws in other respects, as *tārik al-sunna*, "one who has forsaken the *sunna*"; cf. Yāfi'ī, *Rawḍ al-rayāḥīn* (Cairo, A.H. 1297), p. 28:8. It is all the more striking that 'Abdallāh ibn 'Umar, in all else an ideal of loyalty to the *sunna*, had originally intended to lead a celibate life (Ibn Sa'd, IV, i, 125:19). Ibn al-Jawzī quotes—although doubting its authenticity—the following saying by the Companion Abū Birza (I have lost the reference, unfortunately [cf. Ibn Ḥanbal, *Musnad*, V, 163]): Were I a day from the end of my life, I would still want to be a married man when

those who wish to part with their possessions and spend all on works of piety, at a disadvantage to their own families.[22]

These teachings of the Prophet, linked to specific cases, are in keeping with the general didactic maxims attributed to him. "There is no monasticism (*rahbānīya*) in Islam; the monasticism of this community is the Holy War."[23] This sentence is all the more remarkable for its contrast between the pious contemplative life in the lonely cell of the cloister and the active life of the warrior—the life that, as we have just mentioned, had caused the ascetic tendencies of earliest Islam to vanish.

In considering the Prophet's utterances against *rahbānīya*, we cannot overlook that they usually appear as direct polemics against the ascetic life in Christianity. In many maxims the Prophet is represented as opposing extravagant fasting, fasting in excess of what the law prescribes: "For every bite that a believer puts into his mouth he receives a reward from God." "God loves the Muslim who keeps up the strength of his body more than He loves the weakling." "He who eats and is thankful (to God) is as worthy as he who practices renunciation and fasting."[24] It is no act of virtue to divest oneself of one's property and become a beggar. Alms are to be given only by those who live in plenty, and even they must think first of their kin.[25] In all these maxims the idea seems to rule that the law has prescribed a measure for the renunciation of worldly goods and that no form of mortification is desired in excess of the law.

It is not without importance for our inquiry to stress once more that it

---

I meet Allah, for I heard the Prophet say, "The worst among you are the unmarried ones among you" (*shirārukum 'uzzābukum*). People have in mind such hadiths—which hadith criticism did not as a rule formally recognize as authentic, but whose content met with approval—when they consider celibate men unworthy of functioning as leaders (*imāms*) in the canonical prayer service (E. Michaux-Bellaire, "La Maison d'Ouezzan," *RMM*, V (1909), 32:9 from bottom). We must note that rejection of marriage found no place among the component ideas of Islamic asceticism. Cf. the information gathered in Lammens, *Mo'āwia*, p. 165 (= *MFO*, II, 57 n. 8), and the examples from legends of saints in C. Trumelet, *L'Algérie légendaire* (Algiers, 1892), pp. 436, 442. Very characteristic is the prayer said at the Ka'ba by a man known as an ascetic (*zāhid*), in Subkī, *Ṭabaqāt*, III, 289:18. Compare also the interesting information in E. Doutté, *Les Marabouts* (Paris, 1900), pp. 84ff., and E. Montet, *Le Culte des saints musulmans dans l'Afrique du Nord et plus spécialement au Maroc* (Geneva, 1909; Mémoires publiés à l'occasion du Jubilé de l'Université de Genève), pp. 39, 66.

[22] Examples quoted in my article "De l'ascétisme aux premiers temps de l'Islam," *RHR*, XXXVII (1898), 314ff. [= *Gesammelte Schriften*, IV, 159ff.].

[23] *Muhammedanische Studien*, II, 394 [= *Muslim Studies*, II, 357].

[24] W. Pertsch, *Die arabischen Handschriften der Herzoglichen Bibliothek zu Gotha* (Gotha, 1877-1892), II, 255ff., no. 1001, folio 93.

[25] Ibn Sa'd, IV, i, 19:15ff., a very characteristic report.

is scarcely likely that Muhammad himself uttered any one of the statements cited here as attributed to him. Despite all his regard for the exigencies of the world, despite all the indulgences that, as it appears from various passages of the Qur'ān, he claimed for himself,[26] he had the highest respect for true ascetics: penitents, men of prayer, men of fasting. Celibacy was perhaps the one exception. There can be no doubt that those sayings are closer to his thought in which *zuhd*, self-abnegation from all worldly things, is recommended as a lofty virtue, by the practice of which man obtains God's love.[27] It is all the more important to learn how the antiascetic view of life, called forth by the material circumstances of Islam, came to expression in sayings and judgments that—as described in our second chapter—were shored up by the Prophet's authority.

The same tendency is manifest in another area of the traditional literature: in reports about the life of the Prophet and of the Companions.

The dominance of the antiascetic spirit can best be seen from the small, intimate traits that tradition almost unintentionally allows to creep into characterizations of those who represent the holiest aspirations. The Prophet's own biography is full of such traits.

On the whole, we may regard Muhammad's steadily increasing sensuality as attested fact.[e] Nonetheless, the phenomenon that meets us in the prophetology of Islam is unique in the religious literature of all times and peoples. No other founder of a religion has been described from his human, indeed, all-too-human side without detriment to the idealized picture that people painted of him (Ch. I, Sec. 9). Muhammad is so described in Muslim tradition.[28] The explicit relation of such character

[26] Cf. *RHR*, XXVIII (1893), 381.

[27] Such is the Prophet's teaching in the thirty-first of the "Forty Traditions" of Nawawī. A man came to the Prophet and said: "O Prophet of God! Instruct me how to act so God will love me and people will love me!" He said: "Renounce the world and God will love you; renounce people's possessions and people will love you." The hadith is not included in the more rigorous collections, and is attested only in that of Ibn Māja [*Zuhd* no. 1], which is evidence that in the third century it was not in all quarters acknowledged as an authentic saying of the Prophet.

[e] The sensuality attributed to the Prophet has long been a subject of controversy. It was used extensively by medieval Christian polemicists to discredit the founder of a rival faith, and has continued to interest some modern scholars, who treat it either in a spirit of derision, like Gibbon, or as a weapon against Islam, like Henri Lammens. It has correspondingly called forth a series of refutations and denials by defenders of Islam, both Muslims and others. For a discussion, see Norman Daniel, *Islam and the West; the Making of an Image* (Edinburgh, 1958), pp. 96ff.

[28] Jāḥiẓ, *Al-Tarbī' wa'l-tadwīr*, edited by G. van Vloten in *Tria Opuscula* (Leiden, 1903),

traits would surely have been suppressed or softened in an environment that regarded asceticism as a perfect way of life. Rather, these traits were reported practically as a commentary to the Qur'ān's words "I am but flesh like you" (18:110). There is no trace of an attempt to divest him of human appetites and passions. On the contrary, there is an evident effort to bring him close, as a human being, to all future believers. The open admission is put in his mouth: "Of your world (*dunyā*), women and perfumes have become dear to me"—with the addition, "and my heart's delight is prayer." There were many opportunities, to be sure, for decking the Prophet in attributes wholly alien and contrary to ascetic inclinations. Tradition, sincerely enough, even represents his antagonists as accusing him of giving himself up to the company of women, which in their view was hardly in keeping with the character of a prophet.[29]

We find the same kind of information in the intimate biographical notices transmitted to us about the pious Companions. We are now in a better position than before to examine this aspect of the Muslim biographical tradition. The ongoing edition of Ibn Sa'd's great *Kitāb al-Ṭabaqāt* has made available a source in which attention is paid to biographical data neglected elsewhere, and which includes the minutest features of the private lives of the earliest heroes of Islam.[f] It is characteristic that these biographies, as a rule, furnish detailed traditional information about the habits of these holy-minded persons in perfuming themselves, in dyeing their beards and hair, in embellishing and adorning their clothes.[30]

---

pp. 132ff. (= *Rasā'il*, Cairo, A.H. 1324, p. 125 [edited by Charles Pellat, Damascus, 1955, pp. 68ff.]), emphasizes that the Prophet was not of a surly, morose temperament, and indeed that his sense of humor never failed him. Zubayr ibn Bakkār (d. 256/870) composed a monograph on the jokes of the Prophet (Nadīm, *Al-Fihrist*, edited by Gustav Flügel, Leipzig, 1871, p. 110:6 [edited by Riḍā Tajaddud, Tehran, 1391/1971, p. 123]); the quotation in Qasṭallānī's commentary on Bukhārī (Cairo, A.H. 1285), IX, 500:8, is probably taken from this book.

[29] Cf. Nöldeke, *Geschichte des Qorāns*, 2nd ed., I, 170 n. Very interesting information is furnished in Ibn Qayyim al-Jawzīya, *Al-Jawāb al-kāfī li-man sa'ala 'an al-dawā' al-shāfī* (Cairo, n.d.), p. 171.

[f] The edition of Ibn Sa'd was completed in 1918; the indices were published in three parts between 1921 and 1940. On Ibn Sa'd and his works, see the article in *EI*², *s.v.* (by J. W. Fück).

[30] It is not without tendentious intent that in the section devoted to information about Abū Bakr, Ibn Sa'd (III, i, 133:25 to 136:5) devotes three full pages to the documentation of the utterly trivial fact that the devout caliph was in the habit of applying cosmetics to his beard. (This particular feature is abundantly dealt with in the biographies of other Companions as well.) The tendentious character of such reports becomes evident when we read (*ibid.*, p. 150:21) that "some foolish Qur'ān-readers (that is, pietists) aver that dyeing one's beard is forbidden." Traditions of the former type are therefore accumulated to serve as

The use of perfume, in particular, is stressed—a practice that the pietists, sworn enemies of the cosmetic arts, zealously condemned. For example, 'Uthmān ibn 'Ubayd Allāh relates, as a memory from his schooldays, that the children could smell the fragrance of perfume when four men, mentioned by name, passed in front of the schoolhouse. One of them was Abū Hurayra, one of the most important authorities in the transmission of hadith.[31]

Traditions also dwell on the luxury that exemplary people, known for their piety, displayed in their clothing. We not infrequently read that they dressed in velvet. Such luxury is usually justified by a maxim attributed to the Prophet, to the effect that when God favors a person with prosperity, He likes the person to show it. The Prophet propounded this doctrine to rebuke men of property who came into his presence in wretched attire.[32] Such is not the manner of a religious tradition that finds its ideal in contempt for all worldly concerns.[g]

From the many examples available for characterizing the temper and life of the circles that cultivated this kind of hadith, I would like to mention one small detail. It illustrates, in naive form, the matter at hand.

It concerns the person of Muḥammad ibn al-Ḥanafīya, the son of 'Alī, whom a large group of religious zealots celebrated as the *Mahdī*, the divinely chosen savior of Islam, and as the sustainer of the theocratic idea under the first Umayyads who were denounced as godless usurpers.[h] Before the child's birth his father, 'Alī, had received from the Prophet the privilege of giving his son the Prophet's own name; and like the Prophet, the son was known by the name Muḥammad Abū 'l-Qāsim. On him hung the belief in the continued bodily existence and future *parousia* of

---

overwhelming arguments against such pietists. Naturally, examples of the pietist attitude were also faithfully set down, e.g., VI, 201:12, 231:13, and so on.

[31] Ibn Sa'd, III, ii, 103.

[32] *Ibid.*, IV, ii, 29:10; VI, 17:17, and frequently elsewhere.

[g] On these and similar texts reflecting the greater wealth, changed attitudes, and new interests of the early centuries of the Islamic empire, see S. D. Goitein, *Studies in Islamic History and Institutions,* chapter 11, "The Rise of the Middle-Eastern Bourgeoisie in Early Islamic Times," pp. 217-41. A story told in a Shī'ite work about Imam Ja'far al-Ṣādiq vividly illustrates the change. The *Imām*, it is said, was reproached by one of his disciples for wearing fine apparel although his ancestors had worn simple garments. Ja'far al-Ṣādiq is quoted as replying that his ancestors had lived in a time of scarcity, while he lived in a time of plenty, and that it was proper to wear the clothing of one's own time (Abū 'Amr Muḥammad al-Kashshī, *Ma'rifat akhbār al-rijāl*, Bombay, A.H. 1317, p. 249). Cf. Max Weber, *The Sociology of Religion*, translated by E. Fischoff (London, 1965), p. 263.

[h] On the role of Muḥammad ibn al-Ḥanafīya as the predecessor of the 'Abbāsid dynasty, see *EI*², articles " 'Abbāsids" and "Hāshimiyya" (by B. Lewis).

the divinely chosen person recognized as *Mahdī*—a belief that we shall learn more about in the next chapter. Thus he was the object of the pious hopes of the devout, and of the paeans of partisan poets. About this sacred person the biographical traditions furnish the following detail. Abū Idrīs reports: "I saw Muḥammad ibn al-Ḥanafīya using henna and *katam* (a hair dye). I asked him if 'Alī had used such cosmetics, and he said no. 'What are you doing it for then?' I asked. He said: 'To court the women.' "[33] It would be useless to look for such admissions in the literature of the Syrian or Ethiopic hagiology. It is true that if we examine the character of this *Mahdī* in the light of historical reality, we see a man who was, to all appearances, of worldly disposition, not at all disinclined to enjoy the pleasures and benefits of the earth.[34] Nevertheless, in Islamic tradition he is an embodiment of concern with holy things. People saw no contradiction between such a religious character and the incongruous admission that, perhaps not without humorous intent, is put in his mouth. One could accumulate from the early period of Islam many biographical reports such as this. They set in sharp relief the attitude we have just seen reflected in didactic sayings attributed to the Prophet.

3. Such maxims and doctrines would not, however, have been voiced if at the time of their origin there had not been in the Islamic community a strong undercurrent that favored and continued to favor the ascetic spirit, seeing in it the true and genuine manifestation of religiosity. We have just mentioned that there were pietists[35] to whom the embellish-

[33] Ibn Sa'd, V, 85:5.

[34] Cf. Hubert Banning's dissertation, *Muḥammad ibn al-Ḥanafīja* (Erlangen, 1909), p. 73 top; also p. 68 about his avarice, in the satisfaction of which he sought compensation for the claims he had renounced.

[35] They are usually referred to as *qurrā'*, literally, "(Qur'ān-)readers." Mention is made of such *qurrā'* in the Prophet's entourage; they are further described as people who by day "drew water (*yasta'dhibūna*) and gathered wood for the Prophet (cf. Joshua 9:21, 23, 27) and at night stood before the columns (see " 'Säulenmänner' im Arabischen," *ZDMG*, LV, 1901, 505 [= *Gesammelte Schriften*, IV, 311; partial French translation in *Arabica*, VII (1960), 252]) and prayed"; Ibn Sa'd, III, i, 36 last line, also 38:8, 14. The term is commonly applied to people who, out of contempt for all worldly concerns, give themselves up to devotional exercises and lead a contemplative ascetic life. Cf., for example, Ibn Sa'd, VI, 255:18: Dāwūd al-Ṭā'ī did not (in his clothing) resemble the *qurrā'* (ascetics in general are discussed). Freethinkers, or people of a worldly disposition, applied the word in a bad sense to those who hypocritically affected piety (Ch. II, Sec. 9). *Taqarra'a*, the fifth form of the verb *qara'a*, is synonymous with *tanassaka*, to devote oneself to the ascetic life (Qālī, *Amālī*, III, 47 penultimate line). When the great philologist Abū 'Amr ibn al-'Alā' devoted himself to asceticism (*lammā taqarra'a*), he threw in the fire his vast collection of philological materials (Jāḥiẓ in my *Abhandlungen zur arabischen Philologie*, I, 139:9 [citing an MS. passage corresponding to *Bayān*, I, 321]). Similarly, the above-mentioned Dāwūd al-Ṭā'ī, when he be-

ment of a person's exterior was a breach with the Islamic ideal of life. It goes almost without saying that Abū Isrā'īl (Sec. 2 above) is found among these. He said of 'Abd al-Raḥmān ibn al-Aswad, a respected member of the community who appeared in clothes that were anything but penitential: "When I see this man I think I have before me an Arab turned into a Persian landowner—that is how he dresses, how he perfumes himself, how he rides out."[36]

This undercurrent appears to have found many representatives especially in Iraq, soon after the conquest and in the early Umayyad period. They are commonly called *'ubbād* (sing. *'ābid*), people who dedicate themselves to the devout service of God. Among them was Mi'ḍad ibn Yazīd, of the tribe of 'Ijl, who fought in the Azerbaijan campaign in the reign of 'Uthmān. With a number of companions, he withdrew to a cemetery that he might "serve God" there.[37] Al-Rabī' ibn Khuthaym of Kufa is the perfect illustration of such a person, in his style of life as much as in his views. Of the things of this world, nothing could rouse his interest except such questions as "how many mosques are there in the territory of the tribe of Taym." He would not permit his small daughter the most innocent of children's games; he himself was of course wholeheartedly averse to the entertainments imported from Persia. He scorned his share of the spoils of war.[38] It must be particularly stressed that, as both these examples show, the asceticism of these people did not include withdrawal from the business of war which, after all, served the expansion of the faith. In this early period of Islam, ascetic traits were also exhibited by people whose participation in the wars is narrated in detail. Thus to Muhammad's dictum rejecting monasticism, the clause was attached: "the *rahbānīya* of my community is the *jihād* (religious war)."

The more society gave itself up to material interests and pleasures, the

---

came an *'ābid* (*ta'abbada*), would have nothing more to do with any of the studies (including hadith) in which he had formerly excelled (Ibn Sa'd, VI, 255:10). [For other views on the significance of the *qurrā'*, see Martin Hinds, "Kufan Political Alignments and Their Background in the Mid-Seventh Century A.D.," *IJMES*, II (1971), 346-67, especially pp. 358 ff.; also, G.H.A. Juynboll, "The *qurrā'* in Early Islamic History," *JESHO*, XVI (1973), 113-29. The latter accepts, with some modifications, the theory advanced by M. A. Shaban in his *Islamic History A.D. 600-750 (A.H. 132): A New Interpretation* (Cambridge, 1971), pp. 23, 50-51.]

[36] Ibn Sa'd, VI, 202:18. Cf. the same Abū Isrā'īl in connection with a saying about the avoidance at prayer of superfluous ornament in dress; *ibid.*, p. 231:15.

[37] *Ibid.*, p. 111:6.

[38] *Ibid.*, pp. 127:22, 131:14, 133:11, 18, 25. Characteristic too is the religious motivation of his aversion to poetry (cf. also p. 53:17). Ibn Sa'd's entry on this man is very instructive about the ways in which the ascetic tendency manifested itself in those days.

more reason had those who sought the Islamic ideal in the age of its origins to protest against the growing worldliness. This they did by demonstrating in their own persons the rejection of all worldly concerns. Representatives of this tendency also introduced ascetic traits into the biographies of the earliest believers in Islam, and thus even into those of the heroes of war, in order that the models for all believers might protest against worldliness and appear as examples of an ascetic world view.[39] We have, in fact, data to support the assumption that the ascetic bent was coupled with opposition to secular authority. During the reign of the caliph 'Uthmān an inquiry was set on foot against a man who was reputed to abuse the *imāms*, did not participate in the public Friday ceremonies (presumably in protest against the acknowledged government), kept a vegetarian diet, and lived in celibacy.[40] Faced with a state of public affairs that they could not in their heart condone, some people entrenched themselves in a withdrawn life of renunciation, inscribing upon their banner the motto *al-firār min al-dunyā*, "flight from the world."

A very important external factor also played a part. We have just seen that some of the antiascetic sayings show an undisguised polemical thrust against the ascetic tendencies in Christianity. The reason for this polemic was that Christian asceticism offered at the beginning of Islam the immediate model for the realization of the ascetic world view, and that those people within Islam who nurtured an inward inclination to reject this world received their first stimulus from, and were influenced by, the

[39] Compare the biographies in the Sufi *Ṭabaqāt* of the early caliphs and Companions. Among them 'Alī in particular is a model of the ascetic life, not only in character sketches composed on such tendentious lines, but also in the popular memory (cf. especially Qālī, *Amālī*, II, 149:9ff.). Even outside of tendentious contexts, the biographies are not infrequently adorned with ascetic features. We may mention, for example, the description of the last hour of the Companion Mu'ādh ibn Jabal, a man to whom Muhammad had entrusted the Islamicization of the Yemen and who had accompanied the Prophet in many a battle. The pestilence raging in Syria carried off many members of his family, and at last himself. In the last moments of his life he is reputed to have spoken of the love of God. He is represented as having said on the point of death: "Welcome, O Death, welcome dear visitor, you who find me here in poverty. My God, you know that I have ever feared you, but today you are the one to whom my hopes reach out. Such love as I had for the world and for being long in it was not for digging canals and planting trees, but for going thirsty in the midday heat, for enduring (difficult) hours, and for the throng of *'ulamā'* assembling for *dhikr*" (Nawawī, *Tahdhīb al-asmā'*, p. 561). Biographies with a pious tendency often complement the bravery and heroic spirit of the Muslim warriors with the features of ascetic piety. This is still true of the ascetic literature of late periods. Even Nūr al-Dīn and Saladin occupy the highest positions in the hierarchy of saints (Yāfi'ī, *Rawḍ al-rayāḥīn*, p. 285 top). 'Alī's earlier title to sanctity and theirs are, at bottom, of a kind.

[40] Ibn al-Athīr, *Usd al-ghāba*, III, 88, under the entry 'Āmir ibn 'Abd al-Qays.

example of Christian wandering monks and penitents. Indeed, even before Muhammad's time, such penitents—mentioned in the old Arabic poems—had represented in Arab eyes the ascetic way of life. In many passages of pagan Arab poetry Christian monks and nuns, their customs, and their manner of clothing, serve as second terms of comparison for a variety of completely heterogeneous things.[41] They were the ones who inspired the use in the Qur'ān (9:112, 66:5) of the appellations *sā'iḥūn, sā'iḥāt* (wandering men or women) for the devout ascetic members of Muhammad's community. He had before his mind's eye the wandering monks of whom he must have seen many during his comings and goings before his prophetic call.[42] A variant of the hadith directed against *rahbānīya* is precisely "the institution of wandering monks does not exist (*lā siyāḥata*) in Islam." The two words are completely synonymous.[43]

With the expansion of Islam, particularly in Syria, Iraq, and Egypt, the ascetically minded gained a much broader scope for observing such models. The experiences they gained from their contacts with Christianity became a very school of asceticism in Islam. Ascetic inclinations now manifested themselves in a heightened degree, and conquered ever-growing groups of Muslims. Representatives of this tendency also supplemented their doctrinal material from the New Testament, borrowing from it parables and maxims, and using them in recommendation of their world view. As Professor D. S. Margoliouth recently demonstrated, the oldest literary work of this genre is replete with disguised borrowings from the New Testament.[44] This ascetic mood, making itself more and more felt in life and doctrine, seemed strange to the common run of believers. This appears, for example, from the story of the lady

[41] See my "Der Dīwān des Ǧarwal b. Aus Al-Ḥuṭej'a," p. 218 (to no. 79, vs. 7) [= *ZDMG*, XLII (1893), 174ff.; also *Gesammelte Schriften*, III, 267ff.]. To the examples given there add the verses cited by Jāḥiẓ, *Ḥayawān*, V, 145:3 [V, 494:6], and VI, 121 penultimate line [VI, 367:4]. L. Cheikho deals with the same subject in his journal *Al-Mashriq*, XI (1908).

[42] Cf. the various references in *RHR*, XXVIII (1893), 381.

[43] For an example, see L. Cheikho, " 'Uhūd Nabī al-Islām wa'l-khulafā' al-rāshidīn li'l-naṣārā," *Al-Mashriq*, XII (1909), 611:7 from bottom. Cf. also Munk's translation of Maimonides, *Le Guide des égarés* (Paris, 1856-66), II, 304, no. 2. *Athwāb al-siyāḥa* means a monk's habit as opposed to secular dress in Damīrī, *Ḥayāt al-ḥayawān*, II, 165:1, under the entry *'aqrab*. Consequently, it is figuratively said that the crow—a bird that signifies mourning, inhabits ruins, and has black plumage—practices *siyāḥa*. See D. C. Phillott and R. F. Azoo, "The Birds' Complaint before Solomon," *Journal of the Asiatic Society of Bengal*, New Series, III (1907), 176:7 from bottom.

[44] "Notice of the Writings of Abū 'Abdallah al-Ḥārith b. Asad al-Muḥāsibī, the First Ṣūfī Author," *Transactions of the Third International Congress for the History of Religions* (Oxford, 1908), I, 292f.

who once saw a company of young people showing great circumspection in their walk and deliberation in their speech—no doubt in noticeable contrast to the Arab liveliness in speech and movement. On asking who these curious people were, she was told they were *nussāk*, "ascetics." She could not refrain from the remark: " 'Umar, by God, made himself heard when he spoke, hurried along when he walked, and caused pain when he struck—he was the truly pious man (*nāsik*)."[45] One will see from a glance at Sura 31 verse 18 that the manner of these young *nussāk* would have met with Muhammad's approval.

It is easily understandable that such people manifested their asceticism above all in their eating habits. It goes almost without saying that they did a great deal of fasting; the polemical hadiths and stories against excessive fasting must have been aimed at them.[46] We encounter, further, cases of abstinence from meat, a form of asceticism for which examples are quoted already from the period of the Companions.[47] A certain Ziyād ibn Abī Ziyād, a client of the tribe Makhzūm, is described as a man of ascetic self-abnegation who constantly engaged in devout exercises, clothed himself in coarse wool (*ṣūf*), and refrained from eating meat. In the time of 'Umar II, this man was presumably only one representative of an entire class.[48] The saying ascribed to the Prophet is directed against them: "If anyone spends forty days without eating meat, his character is corrupted."[49]

Besides these negative elements in the conduct of daily life, positive features also developed in cult and world view. They did not in themselves stand in opposition to Qur'ānic teachings; they merely exaggerated particular elements of the religious and ethical doctrines of the Qur'ān. But while in the Qur'ān these elements were links of equal value with others in the chain of Islamic doctrines, they were accorded a central significance by the people to whom Islamic asceticism owed its formation. Among these people all other elements of religious life were relegated to the background. Such one-sided excess was the seedbed of the

[45] Ibn Sa'd, III, i, 208:26.

[46] It is reported about 'Abdallāh ibn Mas'ūd, one of the Prophet's most pious Companions, that he refrained from supererogatory fasting on the ground that he considered prayer more important, and fasting, by enfeebling the body too much, could be detrimental to prayer; Ibn Sa'd, III, i, 109:25. The same 'Abdallāh forbade Mi'ḍad and his companions (Ch. IV, Sec. 3) to engage in ascetic exercises in the cemetery. Ibn Sa'd, VI, 111:6.

[47] Ṭabarī, I, 2924:9; Ibn al-Athīr, *Usd al-ghāba*, V, 286.

[48] Ibn Sa'd, V, 225:4.

[49] Ṭabarsī, *Makārim al-akhlāq* (Cairo, A.H. 1303), p. 66.

conflict that was later to break into the open between these ascetic tendencies and the orthodox Islamic system of doctrine.[50]

4. Two elements in particular appeared in the earliest stage of Islamic asceticism as objects of such excess: one was liturgical, one ethical. The liturgical element is connoted by the term *dhikr*, "mention," which has retained its position throughout the evolution of Islamic mysticism. Official Islam limits liturgical prayer to specified times of day and night. The ascetic attitude broke through such limits and bounds by making the Qur'ānic admonition "to remember God often" (33:21) central to the practice of religion, and by raising the devotional exercises that it called *dhikr* to preeminence in practical religion. Next to *dhikr*, other religious practices suffered a great devaluation, and shrank to trivial and secondary things. To this day such mystical litanies form the backbone of the brotherhoods that are the old ascetics' heirs.

The ethical trait that appears in sharp relief in the asceticism of this early period is the exaggerated form of trust in God (*tawakkul*), which these Muslim ascetics carried to the utmost degree of passive quietism. It meant a total indifference to one's personal interests and the rejection of all initiative to secure them. Those who professed it abandoned themselves completely to God's care and to the fate that God had fixed for them. They were in God's hands as a corpse in the hands of its washer:[51] indifferent and wholly without volition. In this sense they called themselves *mutawakkilūn*, "those who trust in God." From such circles a number of statements of principle have been transmitted from which it is clear that they disdained lifting a hand to secure the necessities of life. To make an effort would violate one's trust in God. They did not concern

[50] These matters are discussed in greater detail in my article (used here), "Materialien zur Entwicklungsgeschichte des Ṣūfismus," *WZKM*, XIII (1899), 35ff. [= *Gesammelte Schriften*, IV, 173ff.; partial French translation in *Arabica*, VIII (1961), 240ff.]

[51] This simile is used in two ways: first, as it is applied in the text (Subkī, *Mu'īd al-ni'am*, p. 224:4; Yāfi'ī, *Rawḍ al-rayāḥīn*, p. 315 last line, from Sahl al-Tustarī); second, in the sense that the adept in his relation to his master is as a corpse in the hands of the one washing it, that is, he allows his will to be wholly absorbed in the will of the *shaykh*, for example, 'Abd al-Karīm al-Rāzī (Ghazālī's student) in Subkī, *Ṭabaqāt*, IV, 258 last line. The unlikely assumption that the analogous expression in the *Constitutions* of the Jesuit order (*perinde ac cadaver*) is a borrowing from the Sufi brotherhoods has recently been voiced again in G. Bonet-Maury, "Les Confréries religieuses dans l'Islamisme et les ordres militaires dans le Catholicisme," *Transactions of the Third International Congress for the History of Religions*, II, 344. D. B. MacDonald, *The Religious Attitude and Life in Islam*, p. 219, also regards the Sufi derivation of the Jesuit rule as a proven fact. The possibility of an influence exerted by Islamic Sufism on Christian mysticism has recently been admitted also by Carra de Vaux, and rendered more likely by the evidence of synchronisms (*La Doctrine de l'Islam*, pp. 247f.).

themselves with the means of livelihood, but left their needs directly to God. They called their trusting inactivity the noblest mode of sustaining oneself, as opposed to the toil of the merchant, the humiliation of the artisan, and the self-abasement of the beggar. "They contemplate the Glorious One and take their sustenance from His hand without looking to the means." It is mentioned as a particular virtue of these people that they "do not number tomorrow among the days":[52] that the future, and care about future needs, are wholly excluded from their thought. A hadith (a highly suspect one, to be sure) is related:[53] "Wisdom descends from heaven, but does not settle into the heart of any man who pays heed to the next day." He who trusts in God is "the son of the moment" (of the time, *ibn al-waqt*), "he looks neither backward at what is past nor forward at what is to come."[54]

It is to be expected that complete ἀκτημοσύνη, lack of possessions, and contempt for all material goods were among the predominant ideas of these people. He who belonged to them was a *faqīr*, "a poor man." Moreover, just as they were indifferent to hunger and all manner of material privation, they were indifferent to all other bodily things. To seek a physician's help to alleviate bodily suffering was unthinkable. They were unaffected by the judgments and opinions of mankind. "No man is firmly established in trust of God until the praise and censure of mankind are wholly indifferent to him." Coupled with this quietism was a complete indifference to the treatment one received at the hands of others: μὴ ἀντιστῆναι τῷ πονηρῷ (Matt. 5:39).

That such a view of life did not match with the notions current among Muslims—whose religion in the first century had already evolved to the stage of realism—is proved by a systematic series of hadiths and anecdotes that can be understood only when recognized as conscious polemics against the religious consequences of this extravagant form of trust in God. How could such quietism meet with approval in a religious commonwealth at the height of its march of conquest, among people who had only recently left the desert to settle comfortably in cities of ancient luxury and ease?

[52] Ghazālī, *Iḥyā' 'ulūm al-dīn* (Cairo, A.H. 1289), IV, 445.

[53] Muḥibbī, *Khulāṣat al-athar*, III, 148. Sufyān ibn 'Uyayna teaches: "Your concern about where your morning meal will come from is accounted against you as a sin," *fikruka fī rizqi ghadin yuktabu 'alayka khaṭī'atan* (Dhahabī, *Tadhkirat al-ḥuffāẓ*, III, 8 [III, 786]).

[54] Qushayrī, *Risāla fī 'ilm al-taṣawwuf* (Cairo, A.H. 1304), p. 243:10 from bottom; 'Abd al-Qādir al-Jīlānī, *Al-Ghunya li-ṭālib ṭarīqat al-ḥaqq* (Mecca, A.H. 1314), II, 151; Bahā' al-Dīn al-'Āmilī, *Al-Kashkūl* (Cairo, A.H. 1288), I, 94 last line, on Shiblī's authority.

5. Thus at this time two contrary tendencies opposed each other within Islam. They find expression in a conversation between two devout men, Mālik ibn Dīnār and Muḥammad ibn Wāsi', on the topic of the highest good. The former finds the source of the greatest happiness in owning a plot of land that enables one to obtain one's food without dependence on others. According to the latter the happy man is he who finds his breakfast without knowing what he will eat in the evening, and finds his supper without knowing what he will eat the next morning.[55] These elevated expressions of a quietist view of life bear witness to a pious reaction, mindful of the ascetic beginnings of Islam, against an increasingly prevalent worldliness.[56]

We have already mentioned that this attitude was nourished by the observation of Christian monasticism, with whose goals the principles cited above match almost to the word. It is most noteworthy that Matthew 6:25-34, and Luke 12:22-30—the New Testament passages, much used in ascetic sayings, about the birds of the air that neither sow nor reap nor gather grain into barns but are fed by the heavenly Father—are found, in a nearly literal rendition, at the center of these *tawakkul* theories.[57] Imitating the dress of Christian hermits or monks, these Muslims who renounced the world to turn penitents and ascetics were given to clothing themselves in rough wool (*ṣūf*).[58] This custom can be traced back at least as far as the time of the caliph 'Abd al-Malik (685-705). It gave rise to the name *ṣūfī*,[59] which the representatives of the ascetic tendency came to bear when their practical asceticism had evolved to a higher stage, and had become coupled with a particular philosophy that was to have a determining influence on their conception of religion. That stage was Sufism.

[55] Dhahabī, *Tadhkirat al-ḥuffāẓ*, IV, 39 [IV, 1241].

[56] One of the oldest descriptions of the ascetic ideal is contained in a long apocryphal exhortation (*waṣīya*) by the Prophet to Usāma ibn Zayd. Two versions of it are in Suyūṭī, *Al-La'ālī al-maṣnū'a fī'l-aḥādīth al-mawḍū'a*, a revision of a similar work by Ibn al-Jawzī (Cairo, A.H. 1317), II, 166f. One of the versions is also related by the Ikhwān al-Ṣafā', *Rasā'il* (Bombay, A.H. 1305-1306), I, ii, 98.

[57] Jean Besse, "Les Diverses Sortes de moines en Orient avant le Concile de Chalcédoine (451)," *RHR*, XL (1899), 177.

[58] *Ṣūf* is worn by the poor as well as the penitent (Ibn Qutayba, *'Uyūn al-akhbār*, III, 317 penultimate line [I, 269], 352:6 [I, 302]); convicts too were dressed in *ṣūf* (Ibn Sa'd, VIII, 348:21; *Aghānī*, V, 18:20). Abū Mūsā al-Ash'arī says to his son: "Had you seen us in our Prophet's company when we were caught in the rain, you would have noticed the smell of sheep coming from our (moist) *ṣūf* clothes." The point of the story is to show the ascetic conduct of those around the Prophet (Ibn Sa'd, IV, i, 80:18).

[59] See Theodor Nöldeke, "Ṣūfī," *ZDMG*, XLVIII (1894), 47.

6. The intrusion of Neoplatonic speculation into the intellectual sphere of Islam was in this respect of decisive importance. This philosophical trend, whose profound effects on the development of Islam will later claim our attention, offered a theoretical theological background to the practical ascetic tendencies we have just described. Those who were imbued with contempt for the things of this earth and turned their souls to the divine that alone endured could find strength for this "supraterrestrial, divine life and conduct" in Plotinus's theory of emanations with its dynamic pantheism. They could sense the radiation of divine power through the whole universe. They learned that the things of this world are like a mirror in which the divine finds its reflection. But these mirror images are mere appearance, and have a relative reality only inasmuch as they reflect the one real existence. Accordingly man must strive, by examining his soul and stripping away material veils, to experience the action upon him of the eternal beauty and goodness of the divine; he must lift his soul toward the divine in order to divest himself of the appearance of individual existence and to achieve the absorption of his personality in the one real divine existence.

> In the beginning my soul and yours were but one; my manifestation and yours, my vanishing and yours. . . . It would be false to speak of *mine* and *yours*; *I* and *you* have ceased to exist between us.[60]

> I am not I, you are not you, nor are you I. I am at once I and you, you are at once you and I. In my relation to you, O beauty of Khotan, I am perplexed whether you are I or I am you.[61]

The boundaries of personality are the veil that conceals the divine from man. Somewhat extravagantly, the following words are put in the mouth of the Prophet himself—whom, indeed, the Sufis represent as the herald of their theories: "Your existence is a sin no other sin compares with."[62] What is meant is the active experience of existing, one's assent to one's life as a sovereign individual. Through contemplative absorption in one's soul, through devotional practices and the ascetic mortification

[60] From the quatrains of Jalāl al-Dīn Rūmī. The verses cited here are taken from Prof. Alexander Kégl's Hungarian version (Budapest, 1907; Abhandlungen der Ungarischen Akademie der Wissenschaften, I. Kl., vol. XIX, no. 10) based on *Rubā'īyāt ḥaḍrat-i Mawlānā* (Istanbul, A.H. 1312, published by the Persian journal *Akhtar*).

[61] *Ibid.*

[62] *Wujūduka dhanbun lā yuqāsu bihi dhanbun ākharu*, in 'Abd al-Qādir al-Jīlānī, *Sirr al-asrār* (on the margin of the *Ghunya*), I, 105.

of the flesh which call forth ecstatic states of intoxication with the divine,[63] the personality, the ego, the duality of man and God are cancelled, and man achieves a complete insensibility to bodily states, an existence "without anxiety, without a thought to the useful and the harmful." As Jalāl al-Dīn Rūmī, the greatest interpreter of this world-view describes it:

> Cleanse yourself of all attributes of self
> So you may look upon your radiant essence.[64]

Then even space and time vanish from consciousness as categories of existence:

> My place is placeless; my track trackless.[65]

For the Sufi who encompasses the truth of heaven and earth there is no above and below, no before and behind, no right and left.[66]

"He who does not step outside the palace of natural being," says Ḥāfiẓ, "cannot reach the village of truth."[67] For the Sufi the image of drunkenness expresses the stripping away of all modalities (*ṣifāt*) that are called into being because the individual is affected by external impressions; it expresses the suppression of all workings of will and emotion; it expresses the frame of mind designated, in contrast to the psychological state differentiated by affects, by the word *jam'* (concentration, the Hindu *samadhi*).[68] The Sufi is drunk with the stupefying beauty of the divine light that irradiates his soul, fills it to the brim and robs him of his corporeal senses.

The highest goal of the Sufi life, the dissolution of the individual in the sole reality of divine existence, is also conceived through the image of love. This love (*maḥabba*) seized al-Ḥallāj, whom the orthodox put to death in Baghdad (309/921) because of his claim to complete union with the godhead; it was of this love that he spoke to his followers before de-

[63] Duncan B. MacDonald gives a psychological analysis of the Sufi states in the sixth and seventh lectures ("Saints and the Ascetic-Ecstatic Life in Islam") in *The Religious Attitude and Life in Islam*, pp. 156-219.

[64] *Masnavī-i Ma'navī, the Spiritual Couplets of Maulāna Jalalu-'d-Dīn Muḥammad-i Rūmī*, translated by E. H. Whinfield (London, 1887), p. 52.

[65] *Selected Poems from the Dīvāni Shamsi Tabriz*, edited and translated by R. A. Nicholson (Cambridge, 1898), p. 124.

[66] 'Aṭṭār, *Tadhkirat al-awliyā'*, II, 216:8.

[67] *Der Diwan des grossen lyrischen Dichters Hafis*, edited and translated by Vincenz, ritter v. Rosenzweig-Schwannau (Vienna, 1858-1864), I, 324 (*ghazal*s in *dāl*, no. 11).

[68] Cf. Paul Oltramare, *L'Histoire des idées théosophiques dans l'Inde* (Paris, 1906-1923; Annales du Musée Guimet, Bibliothèque d'études, XXIII), I, 211 n. 2.

livering himself into the hands of the executioner.[i] The most famous among Sufi poets who wrote in Arabic, 'Umar ibn al-Fāriḍ (d. in Cairo, 632/1235)—one of whose mystical poems Hammer-Purgstall introduced into German literature under the title *Das arabische Hohe Lied der Liebe* (Vienna 1854)[j]—received from posterity, because of his chief poetic motif, the epithet *sulṭān al-'āshiqīn*, "prince of lovers."

The intoxicating drink itself the Sufis frequently call *sharāb al-maḥabba*, "the love potion."[69]

"Love is the extinction of will and the burning away of all corporeal qualities and desires."[70]

> Love came and freed me of all else. It graciously lifted me up after it had flung me to the ground. The Lord be thanked that He has dissolved me like sugar in the water of His union (*wiṣāl*).
>
> I went to the physician and said to him: "O, man of discernment, what (medication) do you prescribe for the lovesick? You prescribe the dissolution of qualities and the extinction of my existence." That means: Step outside all that is.
>
> As long as you remain sober, you will not attain the delight of intoxication; as long as you do not give up your body, you will not attain the divine service that is of the soul; as long as you do not annihilate your self in the love of the Friend, as water annihilates fire, you will not attain existence.

This love vindicates the Sufi on the day of judgment:

> Tomorrow when man and woman go into the assembly of judgment, faces will be yellow for fear of the reckoning. I will step in front of you, holding my love in my hand, and say: "Let my account be drawn up from this."[71]

Thus love of God is the formula for the concentrated effort of the soul to dissolve apparent personal existence in the truth of all-encompassing,

[i] Al-Ḥallāj is the subject of a famous treatise by the French orientalist Louis Massignon, *La Passion d'al-Hosayn-ibn-Mansour al-Hallaj, martyr mystique d'Islam* (Paris, 1922; new edition, Paris, 1975); translated by Herbert Mason as *The Passion of al-Hallāj*. Princeton, 1981.

[j] Hammer's translation is of little value. On Ibn al-Fāriḍ, see *EI²*, s.v. (by R. A. Nicholson, revised by J. Pedersen), where references to texts, translations, and studies are given.

[69] Cf. Shādhilī's explanation in Yāfi'ī, *Rawḍ al-rayāḥīn*, p. 289 (different stages of divine intoxication).

[70] Ghazālī, *Iḥyā' 'ulūm al-dīn*, IV, 348:3; 'Aṭṭār, *Tadhkirat al-awliyā'*, II, 156:9.

[71] From Rūmī's quatrains (after Kégl; cf. n. 60 above).

divine being. It is a thought that produced, in all languages of the civilized nations of Islam, a poetry that is among the jewels of world literature.

This world view was suited to serve as the theoretical foundation for the quietism and *dhikr* cult of the practical ascetics. By meditating and practicing *dhikr* they strove to attain the ecstatic states in which their divine intoxication and divine love found manifestation. This was an entirely different path from the one taken by orthodox Islam, which also aspired to love God, as inculcated by Qur'ān and hadith.[72]

Thus in setting up the objective for the perfecting of the human soul, in defining the highest good, the Sufis went a step beyond the ideal of the philosophers. Ibn Sab'īn of Murcia (d. 668/1269 in Mecca),[k] philosopher and Sufi, to whom the "Sicilian questions" of the Hohenstaufen ruler Frederic II were presented for an answer, found the following formula to express this: for the old philosophers the highest goal was to come to resemble God (Ch. I, n. 23), but the Sufi wishes to attain dissolution in God by means of his capacity for being irradiated by the graces of God, for blotting out the impressions of the senses, and for purifying the impressions of the spirit.[73]

7. The Sufis, insofar as they saw any value in taking their stand on Islamic ground, or at least in being acknowledged as standing on such ground, read their world view into the Qur'ān and the sacred traditions, and cited passages of sacred texts in proof of their theories. This is a process the historian of religions can parallel from other times and places. In proceeding so, the Sufis became the Islamic inheritors of Philo, and in their scriptural interpretation displayed a conviction that beneath the ostensibly indifferent literal sense of the sacred texts profound philosophical truths lay hidden which an allegorical interpretation could bring to light. An example is the parable related in the Qur'ān (36:13ff.) "of the people of the town when the messengers came to them; when We sent to them two and they called them liars, so We reinforced them with a third

[72] The idea of the love of God as the supreme goal of Muslim life is described, from the orthodox point of view, by the Ḥanbalite Ibn Qayyim al-Jawzīya in his ethical tractate *Kitāb al-jawāb al-kāfī*, pp. 141-47, 168-70. This work is certainly not without a polemic intent toward Sufism, which its author found repugnant.

[k] Ibn Sab'īn was also studied, though in less detail, by Louis Massignon. For a short account, see *EI*², s.v. (by A. Faure).

[73] M.A.F. Mehren, "Correspondance du philosophe Soufi Ibn Sab'īn Abd Oul-Haqq avec l'empereur Frédéric II de Hohenstaufen," *JA*, 7th Series, XIV (1879), 377ff., 451.

and they said: 'We have been sent to you.' The people said: 'You are but flesh like us. God has sent nothing down; you are only lying.' They said: 'Our Lord knows that we have been sent to you.' " Surely these words of God cannot refer to such a commonplace occurrence as the literal meaning would imply! No; the city is no other than the body; the three messengers are the spirit, the heart, and reason. On this basis, an allegorical interpretation is offered for the whole story: the rejection of the first two messengers, the subsequent arrival of the third, the behavior of the inhabitants of the city and their punishment.

Thus Sufi exegesis has its own allegorical *ta'wīl* (Ch. III, Sec. 6). It is an esoteric interpretation of scripture that produced an extensive literature[74] and informs all Sufi works. In order to secure a legitimate and traditional Islamic point of departure for this esotericism, they borrowed from Shī'ism (see further Chapter V) the doctrine asserting that Muhammad entrusted to his mandatary, 'Alī, the secret meaning of the revelations. These teachings, transmitted only among the elect, are the kabbalah of Sufism. 'Umar ibn al-Fāriḍ, the Sufi poet whose name has just been mentioned, expresses this view, firmly held in Sufi circles, in the following words: "By means of *ta'wīl* 'Alī made clear what had been obscure, by means of a knowledge that he had obtained (from the Prophet) as a legacy (*waṣīya*)."[75]

'Alī was for them the patriarch of Islamic mysticism. From the orthodox viewpoint of the *sunna*, this notion had to be decisively re-

[74] One of the earliest works in this genre is the exegetical book *Ḥaqā'iq al-tafsīr* ("Truths of Scriptural Interpretation") by Abū 'Abd al-Raḥmān al-Sulamī of Nishapur (d. 412/1021; see *GAL*, I, 201, no. 1 [also *GAL*, SI, 361f.]). "In it he conveyed," an orthodox historian writes, "calamitous ideas and the allegorical explications of the Bāṭinīya" (Dhahabī, *Tadhkirat al-ḥuffāẓ*, III, 249 [III, 1046]). This Sulamī also fabricated hadiths on Sufi lines; see "Neuplatonische und gnostische Elemente im Ḥadīṯ," *ZA*, XXII (1909), 318 [= *Gesammelte Schriften*, V, 108; partial French translation in *Arabica*, VII (1960), 8]. A book of his with the title *Sunan al-ṣūfīya* is mentioned by Suyūṭī (*Al-La'ālī al-maṣnū'a*, II, 178); it is presumably the work in which Sulamī's contributions to Sufi hadith can be found. A famous Sufi commentary on the Qur'ān, and the most instructive one about the spirit and intent of such exegesis, is the *Tafsīr* of Muḥyī al-Dīn ibn 'Arabī of Murcia (d. 638/1240 in Damascus). There are several printed editions; the first is Būlāq, A.H. 1283, in 2 vols. Muslim authors frequently refer to another book that follows this tendency, the *Ta'wīlāt al-Qur'ān* by 'Abd al-Razzāq al-Kāshī, or al-Kāshānī, of Samarqand (d. 887/1482). It is extant in several manuscripts (*GAL*, II, 205, no. 3 [also *GAL*, SI, 280, no. 4]). In our text the allegory of the sinful city and the three divine messengers is taken from this book.

[75] Verse 626 of his *Tā'īya* (poem rhyming in *tā'*), famous in Sufi circles; *Jalā' al-ghāmiḍ fī sharḥ dīwān al-Fāriḍ* (Beirut, 1894), p. 120:8.

pudiated; for according to the orthodox view the Prophet kept nothing from the generality of his community and communicated no secret knowledge to anyone.[76]

These ideas are connected with a further phenomenon. In many Sufi circles, the cult of 'Alī was manifested in fanatic form. Occasionally even the Sufi mystical doctrines were pervaded by this cult. Moreover, in proportion as they were removed from orthodoxy, several branches of the fictive chain of Sufi tradition were traced through the line of 'Alid *Imāms*. The Bektashi order—about whose cult of 'Alī and the *Imāms* we may learn from G. Jacob's recent work—is an example of the Sufi tendency to venerate 'Alī.[1]

8. The English scholars who have recently devoted profound study to Sufism, its origin, and its development—in particular E. H. Whinfield, E. G. Browne, and R. A. Nicholson—have thrown into clear relief the Neoplatonic character of Sufism.[77] This does not, however, exclude recognition of other influences that provided the evolving religio-philosophical system of Sufism with building blocks quite as essential for the forms it was to take. A comprehensive historical view of Sufism cannot deny that these influences were determinant. I have in mind Indian influences, which made themselves felt as the eastward expansion of Islam to the Chinese border put Indian thought more and more within

[76] *Muhammedanische Studien*, II, 14 [= *Muslim Studies*, II, 26f.]. However, in the Sunnī tradition as well there are reports of certain Companions whom the Prophet favored with instruction kept from the others. Ḥudhayfa ibn al-Yamān in particular enjoyed such a privilege; he is accordingly known by the title *ṣāḥib al-sirr* or *ṣāḥib sirr al-nabī*, "possessor of the Prophet's secret"; cf. Bukhārī, *Isti'dhān* no. 38, *Faḍā'il al-aṣḥāb* no. 27. This report can only mean that Ḥudhayfa received esoteric teachings from the Prophet, but—and this is of interest—the theologians interpreted it to mean that the Prophet revealed to Ḥudhayfa the names of the *munāfiqūn*, those of ambivalent disposition toward Islam. Cf. Nawawī, *Tahdhīb al-asmā'*, p. 200:5. In fact, we encounter Ḥudhayfa as the authority for many eschatological and apocalyptic hadiths. In Muslim's collection (V, 165 [*Faḍā'il al-ṣaḥāba* no. 68]), in the section "The Excellencies of 'Abdallāh ibn Ja'far," we find the following report by this man: "One day the Prophet made me sit behind him on his mount and secretly whispered to me (*asarra lī* [actually *fa-asarra ilayya*], corresponding to Hebrew *laḥash, lᵉḥīshā*, in similar contexts) hadith that I would never tell anyone." Bukhārī did not include this hadith in his collection. Note that this 'Abdallāh ibn Ja'far was only ten years old when the Prophet died.

[1] See below, n. 100. Georg Jacob is the author of several works on the Bektashi order; the most important are noted by Goldziher in this chapter. The most comprehensive account of the subject is J. K. Birge, *The Bektashi Order of Dervishes* (London and Hartford, Conn., 1937).

[77] The Spanish scholar Miguel Asín Palacios examines the Neoplatonic elements in the Sufi system of Muḥyī al-Dīn ibn 'Arabī, in "La psicologia según Mohidin Abenarabi," *Actes du XIVe Congrès International des Orientalistes* (Paris, 1908), III, i, 79-150.

the horizons of Islam. Indian influence is evidenced by some literary works, and it is manifested by the admission of Hindu elements into the gamut of Muslim religious ideas.

In the second Islamic century, when the vigorous activity of translators expanded the range of intellectual resources at the Arab reader's disposal, some specifically Buddhist works were also translated into Arabic. We find an Arabic version of *Bilawhar wa-Būdhāsaf* (Barlaam and Josaphat),[m] and also a *Kitāb al-Budd.*[78] From the cultured gatherings at which adherents of the most diverse religious views met for the free exchange of ideas, followers of the *sumanīya*, the Buddhist world view, were not absent.[79] I wish to mention only in passing that *zuhd* (asceticism)—a religious attitude that emerged in contrast to legalist Islam, and that is not the same thing as Sufism—shows considerable traces of the intrusion of Hindu ideals of life. One of the foremost poetic representatives of the conception of *zuhd*, Abū 'l-'Atāhiya, presents as the model of the venerable man:

> The king in beggar's clothes; he is the one who is greatly reverenced among mankind. . . .

Is this not the Buddha?[80]

To take an example from a later period, we may recall Alfred v. Kremer's work, pointing out the Indian elements in the religious and social

[m] On this book, see *EI*², article "Bilawhar wa-yūdāsaf" (by D. M. Lang), where the history and diffusion of this book in Arabic and other languages are studied. Goldziher's assumptions concerning Buddhist and other Indian influence on Islamic mysticism were long shared by other scholars, but have since been questioned. See, for example, A. J. Arberry's *Introduction to the History of Sufism*, pp. 38-39, 45. For a comparative study, see R. C. Zaehner, *Hindu and Muslim Mysticism* (London, 1960).

[78] *Fihrist*, pp. 118, 119, 136 [? These works are, in fact, mentioned on pp. 119, 163, 305; Tehran ed., pp. 132, 186, 364. The *Kitāb al-Bilawhar wa-Būdhāsaf* has most recently been edited by Daniel Gimaret (Beirut, 1972), and translated with a useful introduction in his *Le Livre de Bilawhar et Būḏāsf selon la version arabe ismaélienne* (Geneva and Paris, 1971)]. About such texts, cf. Fritz Hommel, "Die älteste arabische Barlaam-Version," *Verhandlungen des VII. Orientalisten-Congresses*, Semitic Section (Vienna, 1888), pp. 115ff. The intellectual curiosity of the educated is drawn to the phenomenon of the Buddha (Jāḥiẓ, *Al-Tarbī' wa'l-tadwīr*, p. 137:10 [76]).

[79] *Aghānī*, III, 24. [On the Sumanīya, see E. E. Calverley, "Sumaniyyah," *Muslim World*, LIV (1964), 200-202. For a broader treatment of the subject, see Maqbul Ahmad, *Indo-Arab Relations, An Account of India's Relations with the Arab World from Ancient up to Modern Times* (New Delhi, 1969).]

[80] "Ṣāliḥ b. 'Abd-al-Ḳuddūs und das Zindīḳthum während der Regierung des Chalifen al-Mahdī," *Transactions of the Ninth International Congress of Orientalists* (London, 1893), I, 114 [= *Gesammelte Schriften*, III, 11].

world view reflected in Abū 'l-'Alā al-Ma'arrī's principles of personal conduct and in his philosophical poems.[81]

We have evidence that Indian ideas entered the Muslims' intellectual field of vision not merely in the form of theories. In the early 'Abbāsid period, in Iraq itself, Muslims could already have direct and palpable experience of Indian wandering monks, just as the Christian *sā'iḥūn* could in earlier times be seen in Syria (Sec. 3 above). Al-Jāḥiẓ (d. 255/868) unfolds before us a vivid picture of wandering monks who certainly did not belong to either Christianity or Islam. He calls them *zindīq* monks (*ruhbān al-zanādiqa*). *Zindīq* is a vague designation, but this case, among others, shows that its reference cannot be limited to Manicheans. His informant relates to al-Jāḥiẓ that such monks always travel in pairs; if you see one of them, you must only look a little more closely and you will find his companion nearby. Their rule consists in never sleeping in the same place twice. They combine their migratory life with four qualities: saintliness, purity, veracity, and poverty. An anecdote from these monks' mendicant life, narrated in detail, leads up to the point that a monk took upon himself the suspicion of theft, and submitted to cruel mistreatment, rather than betray a thieving bird. He did not wish to cause the killing of a living thing.[82] If these people were not Indian sadhus or Buddhist monks, at the very least they aspired to be like them, and copied their view and manner of life.

Such encounters and experiences must have exercised an early influence on Sufism which in any case, by virtue of its original tendencies, shows extensive kinship with Indian ideas. We may, for example, see a sign of Buddhist influence in the predilection of Muslim ascetic literature for the figure of the powerful monarch who forsakes his earthly realm and devotes himself to a life of detachment from the world.[83] The motif is presented, it is true, in a singularly unimpressive manner, falling far short of the overwhelming grandeur of the figure of the Buddha. A mighty king once notices two gray hairs in his beard; he plucks them out; they keep reappearing. This prompts him to reflect that they are two messengers from God sent to admonish him to abandon the world and

[81] *Über die philosophischen Gedichte des Abū-l-'Alā al-Ma'arry*, Sitzungsberichte der Philosophisch-historischen Classe der Kaiserlichen Akademie der Wissenschaften zu Wien, CXVII, no. 6 (Vienna, 1888), 30ff.

[82] Jāḥiẓ, *Ḥayawān*, IV, 147 [IV, 457ff.]; Rosen, *Zapiski Peterskogo Universiteta*, VI, 336-40.

[83] For example, the stories in Yāfi'ī, *Rawḍ al-rayāḥīn*, pp. 208-11. From the same sphere of ideas comes the tale of the "Turkish King and his Son-in-law," the great ascetic, in Ibn 'Arabshāh, *Fākihat al-khulafā'*, edited by Georg Freytag (Bonn, 1832), I, 48-53.

give himself up to God. He obeys: abruptly leaves his realm, wanders through forests and deserts, and devotes himself to the service of God to the end of his days.[84] There is a large group of ascetic stories that hinge on this motif of weariness of power.

It is plainly decisive of our question that the legend of one of the most eminent patriarchs of Sufism has the lineaments of the biography of the Buddha. I have in mind the legend of the holy Ibrāhīm ibn Adham (d. ca. 160/162 = 776/778). Various legends propose various immediate motives for his flight from the world, but all versions serve a single theme: Ibrāhīm, the son of a king from Balkh—summoned, according to some reports, by a divine voice; prompted, according to others, by contemplating the modest and carefree life of a poor man he observes from his palace window—casts aside his princely cloak and exchanges it for beggar's clothes, leaves his palace, severs all ties to this world—even to wife and child—goes to the desert, and there leads a wanderer's life.

Among the various motives for the prince's flight from the world, yet another deserves particular attention. It is told by Jalāl al-Dīn Rūmī. Ibrāhīm ibn Adham's palace guards one night hear a noise from the roof of the palace. When they investigate, they lay hands on some men who allege that they are looking for their runaway camels. The intruders are brought into the prince's presence. He asks them who has ever sought camels on a rooftop, and they answer: "We are doing no more than follow your example, who are aspiring to union with God while you continue to sit on your throne. Who has ever come near God in a place like that?" On this, it is said, the prince fled from his palace, never to be seen again.[85]

9. Indian influence led, in a variety of ways, to the sharpening of Sufi concepts. The pantheistic idea passed beyond its Neoplatonic conception. But it was especially the idea of the absorption of the personality that rose to the heights of the *atman*-concept, although it did not quite attain to its Indian counterpart. The Sufis call the state of absorption *fanā'* (annihilation),[86] *maḥw* (extinction), *istihlāk* (destruction)—an almost in-

[84] Qurṭubī's *Tadhkira*, condensed by Sha'rānī as *Mukhtaṣar al-tadhkira* (Cairo, A.H. 1310), p. 15 bottom.

[85] *Masnavī* (Whinfield), p. 182. For a pictorial representation of the miraculous episodes legend relates about Ibrāhīm ibn Adham, found in the Delhi Archaeological Museum, see H. Beveridge, "Ibrāhīm b. Adham," *JRAS* (1909), pp. 751f., and now also Vincent A. Smith, "Ibrahim b. Adham," *JRAS* (1910), p. 167.

[86] In distinction to physical death, the great *fanā'* (*al-fanā' al-akbar*), they call this state the lesser *fanā'* (*al-fanā' al-aṣghar*). About the relation between the concept of *fanā'* and nirvana,

definable goal. They assert that its essence is incapable of a self-consistent definition. It manifests itself in the form of intuitive knowledge and is not amenable to logical cognition. "When the temporal associates with the eternal, it has no existence left. You hear and see nothing but Allah when you have reached the conviction that nothing besides Allah exists; when you recognize that you yourself are He, that you are identical with Him; there is nothing that exists except Him." Annihilation of the existence of self is the condition of union with God.

> Let me become nonexistent, for nonexistence summons me in organ tones "to Him we return."[87]

Individual existence is entirely dissolved in the all-being of the godhead. Neither space nor time, nor the modalities of existence limit the disappearance of boundaries; man rises to complete identity with the ground of all being, the intellectual grasp of which is beyond all cognition.

As the Buddhist in his gradual ascent to the highest stage of the annihilation of individuality follows an eightfold way—the "noble path"—so Sufism has its *ṭarīqa*, its way, with diverse stages of perfection and various stations. Those who walk in that way are "the wayfarers" (*al-sālikūn*, *ahl al-sulūk*). While the Buddhist and Sufi ways vary in matters of detail, they agree in principle. For instance, meditation[88] (*murāqaba* in Sufism, *dhyānā* in Buddhism) plays a significant part in both as a stage preparatory to perfection, "when the one who meditates and the object meditated become entirely united."

That is the goal of the Sufis' *tawḥīd*, the intuition of unity. It is radically different from the standard Islamic monotheistic belief in God. A Sufi could go so far as to say that it was *shirk* (Ch. II, Sec. 4) to assert "I know God," for that proposition admits the duality of cognizing subject and cognized object. This too is Indian theosophy.[89]

10. In practical life Sufism is embodied, as an institution, in various Sufi societies and orders whose members foster the Sufi views on world

---

see the apposite remark by Count E. v. Mülinen in G. Jacob's *Türkische Bibliothek*, XI (Berlin, 1909), 70.

[87] *Masnavī* (Whinfield), p. 159.

[88] Ibrāhīm ibn Adham is the author of the saying, "meditation is the pilgrimage of the mind" (*ḥajj al-'aql*).

[89] 'Aṭṭār, *Tadhkirat al-awliyā'*, II, 184:8. Cf. Oltramare, *Histoire*, I, 116: "Connaître intellectuellement Brahman, c'est un propos absurde; car toute connaissance suppose une dualité, puisque, dans toute connaissance, il y a le sujet qui connaît, el l'objet qui est connu."

and religion. As early as about 150/770, people began to gather in special houses—convents—where, far from the world's bustle, they would live for their spiritual goals and communally practice the exercises that would lead to them. Once again the development of this conventual life shows unmistakable Indian influences, just as the mendicant life of the Sufis outside the convent-communities reflects the manner of the Indian mendicant monks (*sadhu*). Neoplatonic influences alone do not suffice for an explanation of this practical manifestation of Sufi asceticism. The admission of adepts into the Sufi community is accomplished by the bestowing of the *khirqa*, that is, the piece of clothing that symbolizes the Sufi's poverty and his flight from the world. In its fashion, Sufi legend traces the origin of the *khirqa* back to the Prophet himself;[90] but we cannot fail to recognize that this symbol of admission resembles admission to the community of *bhikshus* by "receipt of the clothes and the rules."[91] Some forms of the religious *dhikr*-exercises of the Sufi communities, as well as the means used to attain divestiture of self and a state of ecstasy (such as the discipline of holding one's breath)[92] have been examined in the light of their Indian models, and their dependence on those models has been proved, by Kremer.

One of these means of devotion soon spread outside Sufi circles: the rosary. For its use in Islam—where it is undoubtedly of Indian origin—there is evidence from as early as the ninth century, first from eastern Islam, the home of Indian influence on Sufi fraternities. As with everything new (see *bid'a* in Chapter VI), this foreign custom was long resisted by those who fought each and every religious intrusion. In the fifteenth century al-Suyūṭī still had to write an apologetic work in defense of the use of the rosary that has enjoyed such favor ever since.[93]

[90] As a part of the Sufi effort to find support in earliest Islam for the legitimacy of Sufi views and institutions, the following legend was fabricated: when Muhammad proclaimed to the poor (*fuqarā'*) that they would enter Paradise before the rich (*Muhammedanische Studien*, II, 385 top [= *Muslim Studies*, II, 348f.]), they fell into ecstasy and ripped their clothes (an expression of the ecstatic state; see "Einige arabische Ausrufe und Formeln," *WZKM*, XVI (1902), 139 n. 5 [= *Gesammelte Schriften*, IV, 353 n. 5]). Then the angel Gabriel descended from heaven and told Muhammad that God demanded His share of the rags. He then took one of the torn pieces and hung it on God's throne. This is said to be the prototype of the Sufi dress (*khirqa*); Ibn Taymīya, *Rasā'il*, II, 282.

[91] *The Satapatha-Brāhmana*, translated by Julius Eggeling (Oxford, 1882; The Sacred Books of the East, XII), pp. 85, 95.

[92] Kremer, *Culturgeschichtliche Streifzüge*, pp. 50ff. [= *Islamic Civilization*, I, 117ff.]. For the Indian elements, cf. Rama Prasad, *The Science of Breath and the Philosophy of the Tatwas* (London, 1890).

[93] Cf. my article "Le Rosaire dans l'Islam," *RHR*, XXI (1890), 295ff. [= *Gesammelte Schriften*, II, 374ff.].

Thus in a historical assessment of Sufism, one must constantly take into account the Indian contribution to the evolution of this religious system whose first growth was out of Neoplatonism. Snouck Hurgronje was right when in his inaugural address at Leiden he included among the proofs of the Indian origins of East Indian Islam the phenomenon that in that part of the world Sufi ideas form the core and the foundation even of popular religion.[94]

11. In our description of the Sufi view of the world we have so far stressed the ideas common to all Sufis, and we have presented them as they appear at the height of the evolution of Sufism. These ideas were produced by an historical development that we have not attempted to describe here, but such a description is expected soon from the pen of Reynold A. Nicholson, a proven scholar of the history of Sufism.[n] Moreover, Sufism does not present a homogeneous, closed system either in its theories or in its practice. There is no precise agreement even on the definition of general aims; and there is more variation yet in details of thought. Various ramifications and differences in the theoretical evolution of the system were caused, not only by internal developments, but also by reactions to the outside, and by the historical influences dominant in the different Sufi environments.[95]

This diversity appears even in the ideas of what Sufism means. In a survey of the development of Sufism, Nicholson managed to collect from literary sources up to the fifth Islamic century seventy-eight different definitions of the Sufi way of thought (*taṣawwuf*).[96] They do not exhaust the list of definitions. Abū Manṣūr ʿAbd al-Qāhir al-Baghdādī, a scholar from Nishapur who taught in Baghdad (d. 429/1037), and whose writings deal chiefly with theological divergences within Islam, collected from the writings of Sufi authorities, and presented in alphabetical order, close to one thousand definitions of the concepts *ṣūfī* and *taṣawwuf*.[97]

[94] C. Snouck Hurgronje, *Arabië en Oost Indië* (Leiden, 1907), p. 16 [and the French version, "L'Arabie et les Indes Neerlandaises"]; *RHR*, LVII (1908), 71 [= *Verspreide Geschriften*, IV, ii, 107f.]. On this branch of Sufism, see now the Leiden dissertation by D. A. Rinkes, *Abdoerraoef van Singkel; Bijdrage tot de kennis van de mystiek op Sumatra en Java* (Heerenveen, 1909).

[n] Goldziher is presumably referring to R. A. Nicholson, *The Mystics of Islam* (London, 1914).

[95] Cf. now also R. A. Nicholson's important article, "The Oldest Persian Manual of Sufism," *Transactions of the Third International Congress for the History of Religions*, I, 293ff.

[96] "A Historical Enquiry Concerning the Origin and Development of Sufism," *JRAS* (1906), pp. 303ff.

[97] Subkī, *Ṭabaqāt*, III, 239 last line.

Naturally differences of detail correspond to such diversity of opinion about the fundamental concept.[98]

In the various branches of Sufism—the orders—diverse and divergent theories have appeared, varying according the doctrines of the founders whom the orders celebrate as their teachers. The ascetic exercises and customs that form the practical side of Sufi life also exhibit numerous formal differences. The organization of the various Sufi brotherhoods that have spread over the entire area of Islam rests upon diverse and divergent rules.

A fundamental cleavage appears in Sufi attitudes toward the Islam of the law. The first patriarchs of the Sufi conception of religion had indeed assigned a higher value to the "works of the heart" than to the formal observance of Islamic law—"the works of the limbs" as they put it—but they did not declare the latter to be worthless, or even superfluous. They did believe that the works of the limbs acquired their value and meaning only in the presence of, and in concert with, the works of the heart. Hearts (*al-qulūb*), not limbs (*al-jawāriḥ*), are to be recognized as the organs of religious life. A nomist tendency of this kind persisted in Sufism throughout its history. It required the Sufi to remain in harmony with formal Islam and its laws, but to find in a spiritual experience of the formal observances the entelechy of living by the law.[99] Then there were others who saw the formalities of the law as symbolic, as metaphors and allegories, but did not deny that these formalities had a relative value. Others made a complete break with the formal system of Islamic law, asserting that the shackles of the law do not bind those who have attained knowledge. Not only individual adepts but whole orders of dervishes (one thinks of the Bektashis, for example) were notorious for a complete absence of scruple about the legal norms of Islam.[100] There was also no

[98] A mystic from the fourth Islamic century, Abū Sa'īd ibn al-A'rābī of Basra (d. 340/951), states the following concerning this: "They (the Sufis) use the expression *jam'* (concentration), although each of them has a different conception of it. The same is true of *fanā'*. They all use the same word but understand it variously. For the meaning of these words is unlimited. They refer to intuitive knowledge, but intuitive knowledge cannot be delimited"; Dhahabī, *Tadhkirat al-ḥuffāẓ*, III, 70 [III, 853].

[99] For an exposition of this principle by one of its oldest representatives, al-Ḥārith al-Muḥāsibī (d. 243/857, in Baghdad), see Subkī, *Ṭabaqāt*, II, 41 penultimate line. *Qulūb* (hearts) play the preeminent role in the ethical theories of Muslim ascetics. The very titles of their writings demonstrate this. Cf. *REJ*, XLIX (1904), 157.

[100] See especially Georg Jacob, *Beiträge zur Kenntnis des Derwisch-Ordens der Bektaschis* (Berlin, 1908; Türkische Bibliothek IX), and the same author's recent *Die Bektaschijje in ihrem Verhältnis zu verwandten Erscheinungen* (Munich, 1909; Abhandlungen der

lack of those who not only proclaimed their freedom from the ritual laws, but also affirmed that all rules of conventional morality and social custom were abolished for the Sufi, and felt "beyond good and evil."[101] In this they had prototypes among the Indian yogis and the Christian gnostics.[102] There are analogical developments in Western mysticism, as for instance among the Amalricans[o] with their libertine principles, which they derived, quite as the Muslim Sufis, from a pantheistic world view. Since in the eyes of these Sufis the phenomenal world had no reality, they met all attributes of this illusory existence with the most rigid negation. The requirements of this insubstantial life were to them wholly indifferent.

According to their relation to the law, it was possible to group the Sufis in two classes: nomists ("with law") and anomists ("without law"). This dualism may put us in mind of a cleavage that Clement of Alexandria reports of the gnostic Hermetics of antiquity. In their relation to the law the Hermetics exhibited two different views. Some of them taught that one must live free of and indifferent to the law (ἀδιαφόρως ζῆν); others exaggerated abnegation and proclaimed a life of renunciation (ἐγκράτειαν καταγγέλουσι).[103] The same is true of the differences among Sufi systems.

12. The word dervish means a person who shares the Sufi way of life.[p]

Philosophisch-philologischen Klasse der Königlich Bayerischen Akademie der Wissenschaften, XXIV, pt. iii, no. 2), especially p. 43 about gnostic parallels.

[101] Oltramare, *Histoire*, I, 214: "A partir du moment où la connaissance s'est éveillée en moi, où je me suis uni à Brahman, il n'y a plus pour moi d'actes ni d'obligations; il n'y a plus ni Véda, ni pluralité, ni monde empirique, ni *saṁsāra*." *Ibid*., p. 356: "Tout alors lui (le yogin) devient indifférent. Dans le monde physique, d'abord: 'Il n'y a plus pour lui d'aliments prohibés ou prescrits; tous les sucs sont pour lui sans suc' . . . Dans le monde moral aussi: 'La méditation du yogin libère de tous les péchés, quand même le péché s'étendrait sur de nombreux *yojana*.' "

[102] As according to the Gnostic Epiphanes, the son of Karpokrates. Contemplation of the Highest renders all external acts indifferent and meaningless. This leads to the rejection of all legality and moral order. Even the Ten Commandments are scorned. The γνῶσις μοναδική, the union of the spirit with the highest unity, elevates it above all confining forms of religion. See August Neander, *Genetische Entwicklung der vornehmsten gnostischen Systeme* (Berlin, 1818), pp. 358f.

[o] The reference is to the followers of Amalric of Bena, a French theologian who died at the beginning of the thirteenth century.

[103] *Stromata*, III:v [edited by Otto Stählin, 2nd ed. (Berlin, 1960-1970), I, 214:11-13].

[p] The word dervish is of uncertain etymology. An explanation commonly offered, though open to doubt, is that it is of Persian origin and means "one who seeks doors"—that is, a mendicant. It is used both in the general sense of a member of a Sufi fraternity and, especially in Persian and Turkish, in the more restricted sense of a mendicant religious.

But distinctions must be made. There are the earnest adepts of divine love and ecstatic enthusiasm, people who strive to perfect their souls in a life of renunciation and meditation. Then there are wandering dervishes who lead a life of unrestrained and dissolute beggary and make of Sufism a pretext for their idleness and a means to deceive the masses. There are also those inhabitants of Sufi monasteries who, averse to work, misuse the outward forms of the Sufi life to secure a carefree existence and an independent livelihood.[104] From their mouths too we hear the phrases of divine love; they too pretend that they "walk in the way." But serious Sufis cannot very well consider themselves of a kind with such people.

> The dervish who bestows [on humanity] the mysteries of the world makes, every minute, a gift outright of a whole empire. Not he who begs for bread is a dervish, but he who delivers up his soul.[105]

The true dervish is not the traveling beggar and parasite. Nonetheless this vagabondage also manifests certain ethical views that may be of interest to the historian of religions. As an example we shall mention just one group among these free dervishes: the ones known as *malāmatīya*, literally, "people of censure."

The appellation is claimed not only by wandering dervishes. It is also used to designate earnest and sedentary Sufis, on account of their peculiar mode of life. The essential thing about these people, who have rightly been compared to the Cynics of antiquity, is their extreme indifference to outward show. Indeed, they attach value to arousing wrath by their conduct and to drawing on themselves the disapproval of other people.[106] They commit the most shameless acts, merely to carry into execution their principle of contemning the contempt that others have for them, *spernere sperni*. They wish to be regarded as transgressors of the law even when in fact they are not. They are intent on arousing the contempt of mankind so they may prove their indifference to its judgment. In doing so they carry to an extreme a universal Sufi rule that Jalāl al-Dīn Rūmī expresses in the following maxim:

[104] Cf. Subkī, *Mu'īd al-ni'am*, pp. 178f.

[105] From Jalāl al-Dīn's quatrains. Within the Sufis' own writings the complaint is constantly reiterated that many unworthy people manage to be numbered among them, who misuse their Sufi affiliation for profane purposes.

[106] Cf. an early example in Aloys Sprenger, *Das Leben und die Lehre des Moḥammad* (Berlin, 1869), p. clxxix note (Shiblī). The Malāmatīs must not, however, be confused with the Malāmī brotherhood, widespread in Turkey. About the latter, M. Hartmann has recently furnished important information, *Der islamische Orient* (Berlin, 1905-1910), III, index s.v.

Leave your sect and make yourself an object of contempt. Cast aside honor and good name, and seek disfavor.[107]

They have spread through the entire territory of Islam. Al-Kattānī, author of a monograph about the holy men of Fez[108] stresses the *malāmatī* character of many of his heroes. Central Asian Islam has created the supreme figure of the *malāmatī* dervish in the legend of Shekh Meshreb, "the wise fool and pious unbeliever."[109] In these people there endures a characteristic attribute of ancient monasticism, which—as Reitzenstein has recently shown—goes back to the Cynics. According to it, "shamelessness (ἀναισχυντία) is a requirement of religion."[110]

13. Sufism struck deep roots very early in the theological literature of Islam. Its popular forms embraced vast numbers of Muslims. Quietly active, it proved itself a powerful movement, destined to exercise a lasting influence on the concept and orientation of Muslim religiosity. Sufism came to play a role of the highest importance in the definitive formation of the religious views and ideas of Islam.

Let us, however, first examine the relation of Sufism to the prevailing modes of thought within Islam, whose representatives fought to keep them unchanged.

Sufism appears, first of all, as an important spiritual liberation, an expansion of the constricted religious horizon, over against the legal and doctrinal system of official Islam as developed by the jurists and *mutakallimūn*. Painstaking, blind obedience is replaced by self-education through asceticism; the ingenious scholastic syllogisms are supplanted by a mystical immersion in the essence of the soul and by its liberation from the dross of materiality. Into the foreground moves the theme of the love of God as the mainspring of asceticism, of detachment from the self, of knowledge. The divine service is regarded as a service of hearts, and is contrasted, in full awareness of an opposition, to the service of limbs. So too the bookish knowledge of the theologians is supplanted by the knowledge of the heart; speculation is replaced by intuition. To the Sufi, the law (*sharī'a*) is propaedeutic: a point of departure for the way. It leads to the lofty path (*ṭarīqa*) that the Sufi must then follow, whose stringen-

[107] *Masnavī* (Whinfield), p. 91.

[108] The work is analyzed by René Basset, "Recherches bibliographiques sur les sources de la Salouat el-Anfâs," *Recueil de mémoires et de textes publié en l'honneur du XIVe Congrès des Orientalistes* (Algiers, 1905), pp. 1ff.

[109] Hartmann, *Der islamische Orient*, I, 156ff.

[110] Richard Reitzenstein, *Hellenistische Wundererzählungen* (Leipzig, 1906), pp. 65ff.

cies are rewarded by the attainment of truth (*ḥaqīqa*), and whose ultimate goal is not fully reached even when knowledge (*ma'rifa*) has been attained. For all this merely prepares the traveler to aspire to certainty, *'ilm al-yaqīn*. Only by concentrating his spiritual intuition upon the sole real existence can the Sufi rise to a direct grasp of real certainty (*'ayn al-yaqīn*). At this stage the knower's dependence on tradition and instruction has entirely ceased. While the contents of the knowledge proper to the previous stage (*'ilm al-yaqīn*) are conveyed to mankind by the prophets, the divine knowledge of the highest stage of perfection irradiates, without any mediation,[111] the soul of the beholder. Yet above this is the highest stage of all: *ḥaqq al-yaqīn*, "the truth of certainty," which no longer lies on the path of Sufi self-education.

Essentially, this path of development leads to the recognition that confessional differences are of no consequence in relation to the holy truth to which one must aspire.[q]

I am neither Christian, nor Jew, nor Muslim.[112]

The diversity of churches, creeds, and religious practices loses all meaning for the soul of those who seek union with the godhead. Indeed, for them everything is but a veil that hides the essential. He who grasps the truth peels away the veil when he reaches knowledge of the sole true reality. Despite protestations of their highest respect for the Islam of the law, most of them share a tendency to erase the boundaries between creeds. All religions have the same relative value with respect to the high goal to be reached, and the same lack of value if they fail to call forth the love of God. This alone can be a uniform standard of value in the assessment of religions. Voices are raised to proclaim that recognition of the unity of God serves to bring mankind together, while laws cause division.[113]

Jalāl al-Dīn Rūmī makes God say to Moses in a revelation:

[111] 'Aṭṭār, *Tadhkirat al-awliyā'*, II, 177:11ff. It is against this that the polemic of Ibn Taymīya, the Sufis' adversary, seems directed, charging the adepts of Sufism with arrogance: *innahu ya'khudhu min ḥaythu ya'khudhu al-malak alladhī ya'tī al-rasūla*, "he would derive his knowledge from the same source as the angel that comes to a Prophet," that is, from direct divine communication (*Rasā'il*, I, 20).

[q] On this line of thought in Sufism, see R. A. Nicholson, *The Mystics of Islam*, pp. 87ff.

[112] *Dīvāni Shamsi Tabriz*, p. 124.

[113] 'Aṭṭār, *Tadhkirat al-awliyā'*, II, 159:12. Ibn Taymīya (*Rasā'il*, I, 148 top) mentions Sufis who harbor a veritable hatred for Prophets, and especially for Muhammad, because he "established a division among mankind and punished all who would not accept it."

> The lovers of ritual are one group, and those whose hearts and souls are aglow with love are another.[114]

Muḥyī 'l-Dīn ibn 'Arabī writes:

> There was a time when I took it amiss in my companion if his religion was not near to mine;
> But now my heart takes on every form: it is a pasture for gazelles, a monastery for monks,
> A temple of idols and a Ka'ba for pilgrims, the tables of the Torah and the holy book of the Qur'ān.
> Love is my religion, and whichever way its riding beasts turn, that way lies my religion and belief.[115]

And again Jalāl al-Dīn:

> If the image of our beloved is in the temple of idols, it is an absolute error to go round the Ka'ba; if the Ka'ba lacks his fragrance, it is a synagogue. And if we sense in the synagogue the fragrance of union with him, it is our Ka'ba.[116]

Islam, as we see, is not exempt from this indifference to creeds. To al-Tilimsānī, a student of Ibn 'Arabī's, is ascribed the following bold sentence: "The Qur'ān is *shirk* (Ch. II, Sec. 4) pure and simple. The profession of unity is only in what we (the Sufis) say."[117]

In some of these declarations that confessional particulars are insignificant when set against the one goal to which religion must lead, expression is given not only to a tendency toward the highest tolerance ("There are as many roads to God as people have souls")[118] but also to the recognition that it is the nature of denominations to disturb and retard. They are not sources of truth; truth is not to be ascertained through the strife of different creeds. "Do not reproach the seventy-two sects for their squabbling; Not seeing the truth, they knocked at the door of fables" (Ḥāfiẓ).[119]

[114] *Masnavī* (Whinfield), p. 83.

[115] See the text in *Die Ẓāhiriten*, p. 132 [= *The Ẓāhirīs*, p. 124 n. 3. Goldziher cites the Arabic text of this poem as a "curiosity" from his travel notes. He reserves judgment on the authenticity of the poem.] Cf. also Jacob, *Beiträge zur Kenntnis des Derwisch-Ordens der Bektaschis*, p. 23.

[116] From Jalāl al-Dīn's quatrains.

[117] In Ibn Taymīya, *Rasā'il*, I, 145: *al-Qur'ān kulluhu shirk wa-innamā al-tawḥīd fī kalāminā*.

[118] Edward G. Browne, *A Literary History of Persia* (London, 1902-1924), II, 268.

[119] *Dīwān*, I, 584 (*Dāl* no. 108).

The statement is not unique in which the mystic Abū Sa'īd Abū 'l-Khayr, friend of the philosopher Avicenna, expresses his conviction:

> Until mosque and *madrasa* are quite effaced, the work of the *qalandars* (= dervishes) will not be accomplished;
> Until belief and unbelief are quite alike, no man will be a true Muslim.[120]

In thoughts of this kind, the Sufis were at one with the freethinkers of Islam whom different considerations had led to the same results.[121]

If the law as an end in itself is distasteful to the true Sufi—even though it may retain some value as a means of asceticism—even more so is the dogmatic theology of the *kalām*: the demand that man's knowledge of God should be based on speculation. The Sufi's knowledge is not erudition; it is not derived from books and reached by study. Jalāl al-Dīn finds in the Qur'ān's words (Sura 102) his support for the following counsel:

> Notice in your heart the Prophet's knowledge, without book, without teacher, without instructor.[122]

The theologian's customary booklearning is alien to them. They feel aversion to the *'ulamā'* and the scholars of hadith; such people, they say, merely spread confusion in our time.[123]

For grasping the truth what use are proofs, so obligatory in the theologians' view? Proofs whose knowledge some even consider a necessary condition of belief? "There is no relying," Ibn 'Arabī says, "on the faith of those who believe on the strength of proofs, for their belief is based on speculation and is therefore exposed to objections. Not so the intuitive belief that dwells in the heart and cannot be refuted. No knowledge that rests on reflection and speculation is safe from being shaken by doubt and confusion."[124] "In the assembly of lovers another procedure prevails; the

[120] In Hermann Ethé, *Die Rubā'is des Abū Sa'īd Abulkhair* (Munich, 1875; Sitzungsberichte der Bayerischen Akademie der Wissenschaften, Philosophisch-philologische Classe, II), p. 157.

[121] Cf. Friedrich Rosen, *Die Sinnsprüche Omars des Zeltmachers* (Stuttgart and Leipzig, 1909), especially the poems translated on pp. 118ff.

[122] *Masnavī* (Whinfield), p. 53.

[123] Dhahabī, *Tadhkirat al-ḥuffāẓ*, IV, 15 [IV, 1216]: *yushawwishūna 'alaynā awqātanā*.

[124] Nicholson, "The Lives of . . . Ibnu'l-'Arabi," p. 819 [= Ibn al-'Imād, *Shadharāt al-dhahab*, V, 198]. Cf. the chapter that develops this line of thought in Ghazālī, *Iḥyā' 'ulūm al-dīn*, III, 13ff. The mystic Muḥyī al-Dīn ibn 'Arabī addressed a letter to his younger contemporary, the theologian Fakhr al-Dīn al-Rāzī, in which he demonstrates the deficiency of Fakhr al-Dīn's science. Perfect knowledge is had directly from God, not from tradition and

wine of love causes a different intoxication. One thing is the knowledge that is acquired in the *madrasa*, and another thing is love."[125] The *ṭarīqa* does not lead along the "dizzying mountain paths of dialectics," or through the defiles of syllogisms. The *yaqīn* is not to be reached by way of the subtle deductions of the *mutakallimūn*. Knowledge is drawn from the depths of the heart, and the soul's contemplation of itself leads to it. "The Sufis," Qushayrī writes, "are people of union with God (*al-wiṣāl*), not people of demonstration by proof (*al-istidlāl*) like the ordinary theologians."[126] An earlier mystic had already gone to the length of declaring that "when the truth becomes manifest, reason (*'aql*) retreats. Reason is the instrument for the fulfillment of man's relation of dependence on God (*'ubūdīya*), but not the instrument for grasping the true essence of God's Lordship (*rubūbīya*).[127]

This is a downright denial of the theory of knowledge maintained by the *mutakallimūn*, a rejection of their apotheosis of reason.[128] Splitting hairs over degrees of freedom of the will must indeed have been distasteful to people who lived in the infinite, and to whom a single volition seemed a drop in the ocean of the world, a mote in the radiance of God's absolute will. A person who surrenders his self and gives up all initiative will not bear with talk about will and autonomous choice. It was mere waste of breath, so they saw it, to squabble over the positive attributes of

---

teachers. The Sufi Abū Yazīd al-Bisṭāmī (d. 261/875) is reputed to have similarly addressed the *'ulamā'* of his time: "You receive dead knowledge from dead people; we receive our knowledge from the Living One who does not die" (quoted from 'Abd al-Wahhāb al-Sha'rānī in Ḥasan al-'Adawī's commentary on the *Burda*, Cairo, A.H. 1297, II, 76). The full text of the letter is published in Bahā' al-Dīn al-'Āmilī, *Kashkūl*, pp. 341f., but in this text the reference to Abū Yazīd al-Bisṭāmī's saying is missing. Ibn Taymīya (*Rasā'il*, I, 52 bottom) presents Ibn 'Arabī's controversy with al-Rāzī (and one of his companions) in the form of an oral debate.

[125] From Jalāl al-Dīn's quatrains.

[126] *Risāla fī 'ilm al-taṣawwuf,* end.

[127] 'Aṭṭār, *Tadhkirat al-awliyā'*, II, 274.

[128] These thoughts too may be found in Indian theosophy, and ultimately, through various intermediaries, they may derive from it. Cf. the passages quoted by Oltramare, *Histoire*, illustrating relevant doctrines. I, 120: "Ce n'est pas par l'enseignement que l'ātman peut être perçu; ce n'est pas non plus par l'entendement, ni par la connaissance des Écritures; seul, celui qu'il choisit, le comprend; l'ātman leur révèle son existence" (from the Kāthaka Upanishad). P. 115: "C'est pourquoi le brahmane doit se débarrasser de l'érudition et demeurer comme un enfant." P. 210: "Cette connaissance n'est pas le fruit de quelque activité intellectuelle ou dialectique. C'est le savoir profane qui a besoin de preuves et de raisonnements, mais l'Être se révèle par sa propre lumière; qu'est-il besoin de la démonstrer?" In Neoplatonism the same idea is expressed: spiritual contemplation, not logic and syllogism, enable one to grasp the intelligible world. See *Kitāb uthūlūjiyā Arisṭāṭālīs (Die sogenannte Theologie des Aristoteles)*, edited by F. Dieterici (Leipzig, 1882), p. 163:3 [edited by 'Abd al-Raḥmān Badawī in *Aflūṭīn 'inda'l-'arab* (Cairo, 1955), p. 156:13].

the being they could only grasp, if at all, by means of negations! Consequently we at times meet the great mystics in theological camps where (owing to nonmystical considerations, naturally) *kalām* is rigorously rejected. ʻAbd al-Qādir al-Jīlānī and Abū Ismāʻīl al-Harawi (author of a Sufi manual, d. 481/1088) are found among the Ḥanbalites; Ruwaym and Ibn ʻArabī among the related Ẓāhirites.[129]

The ideals of life that Sufism set before the Muslim were also different from those that the establishment found agreeable. Through these ideals the Sufis had an effect on the masses. People turned from the vigorous figures of the champions of the faith (all the ancient martyrs were warriors) to the paler forms of hermits, penitents, and monastery-dwellers. Even the ideal figures of earlier times had to be invested with the attributes of the new heroes; their sword, so to speak, was unbuckled and they were dressed in a Sufi's habit.[130]

14. It will surprise no one that the theologians' fraternity was none too favorably disposed to the Sufis. Many are the ironic remarks of theologians against the coarse woolen clothes (*ṣūf*) to whose use the Sufis owe their name.[131] The philologist al-Aṣmaʻī (d. 216/831) speaks of a contemporary of his, a theologian, in whose presence someone spoke of people who walked about in coarse penitential garments. "I never knew until now," noted the theologian, "that filth is a part of religion."[132] Their doctrines, and perhaps too their religious attitudes, their indifference to the explicit laws of Islam—indifference that frequently reached the point of rejecting all observances[133]—drew upon them severe attacks from the representatives of established theology. This was in the nature of things. They gave the scholastic theologians just cause to regard them as *zindīq*s—a name the theologians applied indifferently to all kinds of freethinking people who did not follow the beaten path of scholasticism. These Sufis spoke a language that must have struck the ordinary theologians as quite alien. Abū Saʻīd al-Kharrāz was charged with unbelief because of the following sentence in one of his books: "The man who re-

[129] See "Zur Geschichte der ḥanbalitischen Bewegungen," p. 11 [= *Gesammelte Schriften*, V, 145; partial French translation in *Arabica*, VII (1960), 137].

[130] Cf. note 39 above.

[131] Awzāʻī's judgment perhaps belongs here: "To dress in *ṣūf* while traveling is according to the *sunna*, but to do so when settled is *bidʻa*" (Dhahabī, *Tadhkirat al-ḥuffāẓ*, III, 232 [III, 1028]).

[132] Ibn Qutayba, *ʻUyūn al-akhbār*, III, 355:5 [I, 305].

[133] See " ʻAlī b. Mejmūn al-Maġribī und sein Sittenspiegel des östlichen Islam," *ZDMG*, XXVIII (1874), 326 [= *Gesammelte Schriften*, VI, 34; partial French translation in *Arabica*, VIII (1961), 247f.]; cf. Ch. III, Sec. 6.

turns to God holds fast to Him (clings to Him), dwells in the proximity of God, forgets himself and all that is not God; if you ask him from where he has come and where he means to go he can answer you with nothing but 'Allah.' "[134] If such a statement seemed suspect, how much more cause had the strict theologians to frown at talk of *fanā'* and *baqā'*, annihilation of the self and union with the godhead, of divine drunkenness, of the worthlessness of the law, and the like. How much more yet at Sufi practices, which at an early period already included the mystical dance! Toward the end of the ninth century, as the dark spirit of orthodoxy came to power in Baghdad, several famous Sufis were subjected to cruel inquisition.[135] Characteristic of the spirit of the times was the saying of al-Junayd (d. 297/909), one of the most celebrated Sufis of the ancient school: "No man has reached the stage of truth until a thousand friends have declared him an unbeliever."[136] And once in a while, if a Sufi drew too sharply the conclusions from his union with the divine, he might, like al-Ḥallāj and al-Shalmaghānī, make the executioner's acquaintance.[r]

15. If we examine the relation between Sufism and official Islam, two phenomena in particular claim our attention. Each represents a mediation of the salient contradictions, one from the Sufi and one from the orthodox side.

The first shows that even on the Sufi side the need was felt to smooth over (if only outwardly) the conflict with Islamic law, to avoid the appearance that Sufism was an outright negation of Islam. In some less radical Sufi circles, too, the antinomian tendency dominant within Sufism caused a profound discomfort. Such Sufis gravely lamented the contempt for, and actual setting aside of, Islamic law, and declared that such circumstances meant a corruption of Sufism.[137] In their view, the law, the

[134] 'Aṭṭār, *Tadhkirat al-awliyā'*, II, 40:19.

[135] Nicholson, "Historical Inquiry . . . ," p. 323.

[136] 'Aṭṭār, *Tadhkirat al-awliyā'*, II, 48, 74 bottom.

[r] Ḥallāj and Shalmaghānī were both executed in Baghdad on charges of blasphemy, the former in 309/922, the latter in 322/934. On the repression of dissent, see further Ch. Five, especially Sec. 8, below.

[137] Even after Qushayrī, such complaints were not, naturally, without substance. A series of statements are collected in *Al-Futūḥāt al-ilāhīya*, a commentary by Aḥmad ibn Muḥammad al-Shādhilī of Fez on *Al-Mabāḥith al-aṣlīya* by Abū'l-'Abbās Aḥmad ibn Muḥammad ibn al-Bannā al-Tujībī, a Sufi author originally from Zaragoza (Cairo, 1324/1906), I, 21ff. In Maghribi Sufism, the nihilistic attitude toward the law never found such striking expression as in the East; the warnings against it made the strongest impression in western Islam.

sharī'a, was a prerequisite for *ṭarīqa* and *ḥaqīqa* (Sec. 13 above). Without the law, to speak of the Sufi way was meaningless; for the law was the gate that led to the way. "Enter houses through their doors" (2:189).

Our most important evidence for this reaction within Sufism is the "Epistle" (*risāla*) that the great Sufi shaykh 'Abd al-Karīm ibn Hawāzin al-Qushayrī dispatched in the year 437/1045 to the Sufi communities in all Muslim lands. We must not think of this work as a kind of pastoral letter. The *Epistle* is a sizable book; it runs to no fewer than 244 closely printed pages in the Cairo (A.H. 1304) edition. It consists of a characterization of the most famous Sufi authorities, a selection of their sayings, and an adjoining compendium of the most important Sufi doctrines. All of the work reflects the intention to show the harmony of Sufism and law, and to prove that the real Sufi masters had reprobated all opposition to standard Islam, and that therefore a true Sufi must be a true Muslim in the traditional sense. The need for such a work is the best illustration of the open cleavage that had developed in the eleventh century between the two trends.

"You must know," Qushayrī addresses his companions, "that those of our company with discernment of the truth have most of them gone from this world; and in our time only their traces remain. A paralysis has struck our way; worse, it has been truly obliterated. Gone are the shaykhs who had furnished guidance; small is the number of the young who wish to copy their example. Self-abnegation has ceased; its rug is rolled up; worldly lusts have gained the upper hand. Veneration for the religious law has departed from men's hearts. They have come to consider that scant attention to religious prescriptions is the most reliable means to their end. They cast aside the distinction between the permissible and the forbidden . . . they take lightly the performance of the obligations of worship, they despise fasting and prayer, they gallop along the racecourse of negligence. . . . Then, not content with all this evil, they point to the highest truths and spiritual states, and pretend that they have been liberated from the shackles (of the law) and have attained to the truths of union (with God) (Sec. 6 above). . . . that they have unveiled the secrets of Oneness . . . and therefore the laws governing flesh and blood no longer apply to them."

Cf. also the Maghribi critique of eastern Sufism, *ZDMG*, XXVIII (1874), 325ff. [= *Gesammelte Schriften*, VI, 33ff.; partial French translation in *Arabica*, VIII (1961), 247f.].

To put a check to this state of affairs, Qushayrī wrote his book. It had a great impact on the Sufi world and helped repair the nearly broken bridges between orthodoxy and Sufism.

16. The second phenomenon we must mention is one of the most epoch-making facts in the history of Islamic religious thought. It made its appearance not long after Qushayrī, and represents the obverse of Qushayrī's efforts. Qushayrī had promoted a reaction in favor of the law, and against the nihilism of the mystics. Now we have to speak of the infusion of mystical ideas into legalist Islam. It is linked to the name of one of the greatest Muslim doctors, Abū Ḥāmid Muḥammad al-Ghazālī (d. 505/1111), the Abuhamet or Algazel of the medieval scholastics. This remarkable man had a powerful impact on the religious system into which Islam had evolved by his time. The Islamic idea of religion was overgrown and smothered by the casuistry of its lawyers and the scholastic ingenuities of its theologians. Al-Ghazālī was himself a famous teacher of, and writer on, both theology and law; indeed, he was one of the ornaments of the recently founded Niẓāmīya university in Baghdad (Ch. III, Sec. 10). His writings in the field of jurisprudence are among the fundamental works of the Shāfi'ite school. In the year 1095 he had the crisis of his spiritual life. To solve it, he renounced all scholarly success and personal respect that his illustrious professorial position had secured him, and retired to a life of contemplation. From secluded cells in the mosques of Damascus and Jerusalem, from a meditative solitude, he cast a critical eye on the dominant currents of religious thought from which, by his flight from the world, he had now also outwardly withdrawn. He wrote systematic works in which, abandoning the beaten paths of the complacent theologians, he presented in clearly articulated form the method he considered requisite for the reconstruction of the religious sciences of Islam; he wrote shorter treatises in which he gave powerful expression to particular points in his religious thinking. These were products of his turning away from trends whose dangers to the religious goals of study and of life he had recognized.

He saw these dangers embodied in two particular aspects of theological activity, which, he was convinced, were the archenemies of inward religiosity. These two were the subtleties of dogmatic dialectics and the ingenious casuistries of religious law. They had inundated the religious sciences and laid waste the religious spirit of the community. Ghazālī, who had once walked in the ways of the philosophers, and could never quite conceal their effect on the formation of his theological thought,[138] had written a *Destruction of the Philosophers*, well known in the medieval philosophical literature, in which he had declared merciless war upon Avicenna's peripatetic philosophy and pointed a finger at its weaknesses and contradictions. Now he was writing to show that the hairsplitting of the dogmatics of the *kalām* was a fruitless expense of spirit that, far from serving the purity and directness of religious thought and feeling, was cumbersome and detrimental, especially if it spread beyond the schoolroom, as the *mutakallimūn* demanded, and was planted in the heads of common folk, where it could only cause confusion.

More violent yet was his assault on the *fuqahā'* and their legal casuistry. Here too he could rely on personal experience. He had, after all, fled to the seclusion of a hermit's cell from the celebrated position of a professor of jurisprudence at the most brilliant university of Islam, and his writings had brought him fame and esteem in the discipline against which he now marshaled his arguments. He admitted that such studies were a legitimate concern of secular life, but protested most emphatically against mixing legal casuistry with matters of religion. Nothing could be more mundane, or more closely bound to temporal exigencies than this field of study, whose haughty practitioners put it about that it was a most holy thing. Salvation was not promoted by investigations into the civil law according to the *sharī'a*, into bills of sale and the disposition of inherited property, with all the subtleties that had over the centuries clung to these topics. On the contrary, such speculations proved, amid the religious dignity in which they had been decked, that they were instruments of the moral corruption of those who considered them the most important elements of theological learning, whose hollow vanity and worldly ambition such speculations furthered. Ghazālī was especially sharp in condemnation of trivial researches into, and disputations about, the ritual differences among the *madhāhib* (Ch. II, Sec. 7), which he considered a profitless business, noxious to the religious spirit.[139] Rejecting the dialec-

[138] To characterize the relation in which Ghazālī stood to the philosophy he combatted, we may cite the words of Abū Bakr ibn al-'Arabī (*qāḍī* in Seville, d. 546/1151): "Our *shaykh* Abū Ḥāmid penetrated into the body of philosophy; then he wanted to come out of it but could not" (quoted in 'Alī ibn Sulṭān al-Qārī's commentary to Qāḍī 'Iyāḍ's *Al-Shifā'*, Istanbul, A.H. 1299, II, 509).

[139] In this theological field, the later Sufi al-Sha'rānī was particularly interested in assessing the divergent doctrines on ritual (Ch. II, n. 49). He developed a special theory about their relation to one another, according to which the rules that vary from school to school

tics and the casuistry with which theologians and ritualists approached religion, Ghazālī demanded that religion be fostered as each individual's intimate experience. He found the focus of religious life in its training the believer to the intuitive life of the soul, to an awareness of man's dependency. In this, love of God must be the prime mover. Just as he undertook, with great mastery, a general analysis of moral sentiments, he included in his system a profound treatise on this motive and goal of religion, and marked out the way one must follow in aspiring to it.

By means of these doctrines, Ghazālī brought Sufism out of its isolation from the dominant conception of religion and established it as a standard element in the Muslim believer's life. Advancing ideas akin to Sufi mysticism, he wished to breathe spirit into the ossified formalism of the prevailing theology. That is why his work falls within the purview of this section. Indeed, Ghazālī had himself gone among the Sufis and practiced the Sufi way of life. What separated him from the Sufis was his rejection of their pantheistic goals and their contempt for the law. He did not forsake the ground of established Islam. His sole purpose was to ennoble the spirit in which doctrine was understood and law was practiced in Muslim life, to make these more heartfelt, to bring them nearer to the goals he had set for the religious life. "That which strives toward God, to

---

have only a relative significance. A single religious law has two aspects: severity (*tashdīd*, "making harder") and leniency (*takhfīf*, "making lighter"). The former is for people of greater perfection, of whom God demands renunciation; the latter is for those who are weaker, for whom the same law grants means of relief. The different schools of law represent, when they are at variance regarding the same law, each a different gradation of the religious law, all gradations being of the same value and the differences among them being only relative. Because of this argument, Sha'rānī calls the work in which he advances it most fully *The Balance of the Law*. Cf. "Zur Literatur des Ichtilāf al-maḏāhib," p. 676 [= *Gesammelte Schriften*, II, 144]. We mention this theory—which Sha'rānī celebrates in several of his works, stressing that the merit of discovering it is his very own—to emphasize that it was advanced more than five centuries before Sha'rānī in the *Qūt al-qulūb* (Cairo, A.H. 1310), II, 20 middle, by Abū Ṭālib al-Makkī (d. 386/996), a classical Sufi author praised as *shaykh al-sharī'a wa'l-ḥaqīqa*, "Master of the law and of mystical truth" (Damīrī, *Ḥayāt al-ḥayawān*, II, 120, under the entry *ṭayr*), and to whose works even Ghazālī acknowledges his great debt. The germs of this distinction may be traced as far back as the second Islamic century; the ascetic traditionist 'Abdallāh ibn al-Mubārak (d. 181/797, about him see M. Hartmann, "Die arabisch-islamischen Handschriften der Universitäts-Bibliothek zu Leipzig und der Sammlungen Hartmann und Haupt," *ZA*, XXIII (1909), 241) concludes about two contradictory hadiths that the rule stated in the one is meant for the elite of mankind (*al-khawāṣṣ*), and the rule stated in the other is meant for the generality of mankind (*al-'awāmm*); quoted in Zabīdī, *Itḥāf al-sāda al-muttaqīn* (Cairo, A.H. 1311), VII, 572.

obtain His nearness, is the heart and not the body. By heart I do not mean the palpable flesh. The heart is a divine secret, imperceptible to the senses."[140] It was in this spirit that he dealt with the observance of the law in his great systematic work. Convinced that the book was an act of reformation destined to instill new life into the dry bones of the prevailing Islamic theology, he gave it the proud title "The Revivification of Religious Sciences," *Iḥyā' 'ulūm al-dīn*.

Like many a reformer, he refused to entertain the idea that he was initiating a new order of things. He was, as he would have it, a mere restorer who had returned to the old doctrine that corruption had obscured. His gaze was fixed in nostalgia upon the immediacy of religious experience in the early period of Islam. He commonly reinforced his protest by examples from the early age of the Companions. By doing so he kept his teachings in touch with the *sunna*. In the religious atmosphere of the Companions, religiosity had not been nurtured on scholastic wisdom and legal lucubrations. His intention was to free the people from the tawdry and injurious trappings laid over the religious spirit, and to insure that the law, whose goal had been misunderstood, play its proper role in the moral education of man.

Before Ghazālī, only Sufis caught up in God, and their devoted disciples, far from the beaten track of orthodoxy, had fostered a silent and powerless opposition to rigid formalism and dogmatism. Now from Ghazālī's mouth the Muslims could hear the loud protest of a respected doctor of orthodoxy against the corruption Islam had suffered at the hands of its authorities in *fiqh* and *kalām*. The esteem that Ghazālī as an orthodox teacher enjoyed among all Muslims contributed to the success of his enterprise. Only scattered opposition was voiced against what the universally respected doctor had done, and that by people who were gravely threatened in their lofty religious dignity. In Spain, it is true, the *Iḥyā'* was publicly burnt at the behest of a group of *faqīhs* who could not bear its disparagement of them. This was a temporary, and in the long run ineffectual, resistance, and even within Spain it did not find universal approval.[141] Such desperate attempts at self-defense could not prevent the *ijmā'* of Islamic orthodoxy from inscribing Ghazālī's doctrine upon its banner. Ghazālī's person was surrounded with the halo of sanctity. An appreciative posterity bestowed on him the title of "Reviver of the

[140] *Iḥyā' 'ulūm al-dīn*, I, 54:17.

[141] "Die Šu'ūbijja unter den Muhammedanern in Spanien," *ZDMG*, LIII (1899), 619 n. 2 [= *Gesammelte Schriften*, IV, 222 n. 2].

Faith," *muḥyī 'l-dīn*, or "Renewer" (*mujaddid*),[142] whom Allah had sent to put a check to the decay of Islam, at the turn of the fifth and sixth centuries of its existence. The *Revivification* was acknowledged to be the most excellent book in the Islamic science of religion; it was seen as including all religious knowledge and was venerated "almost like a Qur'ān."[143] Orthodox Islam regards Ghazālī as the final authority. His name has been a watchword in the struggle against tendencies hostile to the *ijmā'*. His work is one of the most significant landmarks in the history of the development of Islam.[144]

17. We may agree, then, with the Muslims in regarding Ghazālī as a regenerator of Islam. Having presented the general religious views he advanced and by means of which he promoted Sufi ideas to constituent parts in Muslim religious life, we now wish to underscore his achievement in a particular area of religious thought.

The wise teachings of many of the greatest authorities in early Islam oppose, unambiguously and resolutely, the passion for declaring people to be unbelievers. They persistently stress that one must guard against denouncing as an unbeliever (*kāfir*) a person whose opinions differ from one's own, but who belongs to the *ahl al-ṣalāt* (those who participate in the Islamic prayer service)[145] or *ahl al-qibla* (those who face the *qibla* when they pray and so acknowledge their membership in the community).[146] We possess instructive information on the subject thanks to the work of al-Muqaddasī (ca. 985),[147] a geographer who, in his study of the Islamic world, was extremely interested in matters of religion.

There is no parallel between dogma in Islam and dogma in the religious system of any Christian church. In Islam there are no councils and

[142] And many other exorbitant epithets of praise, a whole series of which may be read, for example, in the inscription on a pen case in the Arab Museum in Cairo. This box was reputedly given as a gift to Ghazālī, but its authenticity is most doubtful. Cf. Aly bey Bahgat, "Note sur deux bronzes du Musée Arabe," *Bulletin de l'Institut Égyptien*, 4th Series, VII (1906), 57, where it is assumed that this exhibit is authentic.

[143] See the passages in A. S. Yahuda, *Prolegomena zu . . . Kitāb al-hidāja ilā farā'iḍ al-qulūb* (Darmstadt, 1904), p. 14 n. 2.

[144] This characterization of Ghazālī contains some material from my article in *Die Kultur der Gegenwart*, pp. 114f.

[145] The *faqīh* Ḥarb ibn Ismā'īl al-Kirmānī (d. 288/901), a contemporary of Aḥmad ibn Ḥanbal, was blamed for having, in his book *Kitāb al-sunna wa'l-jamā'a*, vilified those groups of the *ahl al-ṣalāt* that differed from his position; Yāqūt, *Mu'jam al-buldān*, edited by Ferdinand Wüstenfeld (Leipzig, 1866-1873), III, 213 last line.

[146] Cf. my introduction to *Le Livre de Mohammed ibn Toumert*, pp. 58-60.

[147] Muqaddasī, pp. 365f.

synods that, after vigorous debate, fix the formulas that henceforth must be regarded as sound belief. There is no ecclesiastic office that provides a standard of orthodoxy. There is no exclusively authorized exegesis of the sacred texts, upon which the doctrines of a church, and the manner of their inculcation, might be based. The consensus is the highest authority in all questions of religious theory and practice, but it is a vague authority, and its judgment can scarcely be precisely determined. Its very concept is variously defined. In theological questions it is especially difficult to reach unanimity about what is to be accepted without dispute, as the verdict of consensus. Where one party sees consensus, another may be far from seeing anything of the sort.

Were we to approach various great scholars within Muslim orthodoxy—all of whom are revered as authoritative doctors of Islam unless they are narrow-minded and intolerant party-men—and ask them what makes a person an unbelieving heretic and what we are to understand by the term *kāfir*, we would receive the most contradictory answers. And even those answers would be given with an awareness of their merely theoretical validity. For it would indeed be terrible, in life and in death, to be included in one of these definitions. "A real *kāfir* is cast out of the community; it is forbidden to associate with him in any manner; one may not eat with him; a marriage concluded with him is invalid; he must be shunned and despised; one may not pray with him if he acts as prayer leader; his testimony cannot be accepted in court; he cannot act as the guardian of a woman entering into marriage; when he dies, the prayer for the dead is not said over his body. If he is seized, one must first make three attempts to convert him, as one would with an apostate, and if they fail, he is to be put to death."[148]

These are severe words. In practice, however, few people—a disappearing minority of Ḥanbalite zealots, perhaps—are likely to have thought seriously of carrying such a theory into execution.[149] With reference to one particular theological heresy—the heresy that asserts the

[148] Introduction to *Ibn Toumert*, p. 57.

[149] Cf. the article "Zur Geschichte der ḥanbalitischen Bewegungen," p. 5 [= *Gesammelte Schriften*, V, 139; partial French translation in *Arabica*, VII (1960), 135ff.] and *passim*. Abū Maʿmar al-Hudhalī (cf. Ch. III, n. 54 above) plainly says: "Whoever says that God does not speak, hear, and see, that He is not benevolent and not angry (attributes which the Muʿtazilites subjected to *taʾwīl*) is a *kāfir*." But at the time of the inquisition (*miḥna*) he proved weak, and made concessions to the Muʿtazilite authority that saved him from further persecution. He could then airily say: *kafarnā wa-kharajnā*, "we became *kāfir*s and left (free)." See Dhahabī, *Tadhkirat al-ḥuffāẓ*, II, 56 [II, 471].

freedom of the will and consequently holds that man himself, rather than God, is the author of his acts—the hadith does ascribe to Muhammad the statement, "those who profess it are the Magians (dualists) of Islam," and accordingly, the attitude prescribed toward them is that of the most rigorous repudiation. Nor do the theological books hesitate to hurl the censure of *kāfir* and *fāsiq* (miscreant) upon men whose theological opinions have led them off the high road of common doctrine. But in the time of early orthodoxy, such people could live socially unmolested, and could even be active as highly regarded teachers of the law and faith.[150] They were scarcely bothered on account of their opinions, unless we regard the contemptuously shrugged shoulder of high orthodoxy as serious molestation, or mistake scattered excesses by the orthodox for evidence of the overall situation.

Only doctrines hostile to the state were taken seriously.[151] For example, in the Shīʿī schism, as we shall see, there were points on which constitutional law and dogmatic theory overlapped. But in the area of theology, the free development of doctrine was not much limited. This explains the remarkable phenomenon that in the history of Islamic theology a consciousness of being obliged to no one and answerable to no one is often glaringly apparent; that among the divergent theological opinions such odd views were not infrequently ventured as suggest that their authors were poking fun at gravely proffered subtleties, trying to reduce *ad absurdum* the exaggeration of dogmatic distinctions, and were certainly not contributing seriously to a scholastic disputation that had been pushed to an extreme.

Only rarely, in cases that seemed particularly dangerous, was there a serious wish really to deal with the authors of heterodox opinions in the manner that theory prescribed for dealing with a *kāfir*.

[150] See *ZDMG*, LVII (1903), 395. Ibn Saʿd, VI, 191: 7ff., cites a number of statements and judgments by the strict Kufan theologian Ibrāhīm al-Nakhaʿī, a contemporary of Ḥajjāj (d. 96/714), about the Murji'a. He states his dissatisfaction with their doctrine, warns people about its evil consequences, and thinks it best that one should not be too much in their company. He calls their doctrine *ra'y muḥdath*, "a newly devised opinion" or *bidʿa* (cf. Chapter VI); but he does not utter the words *kufr* or *kāfir*. Already in the middle of the second Islamic century, the beginnings of fanaticism appear: Sufyān al-Thawrī and a colleague of the same stamp refuse to attend the funerals of Murji'ites, although one of the dead men in particular was celebrated for the piety of his conduct (Ibn Saʿd, VI, 252:4, 254:1). Even so, their refusal did not carry the imputation that the Murji'ites were *kāfirs*. It is indicative of the prevailing opinion that Sufyān's conduct is mentioned as something extraordinary.

[151] Here too we may occasionally find milder views; for example, the opinion about the Qarmaṭīs' status as believers in Yāqūt, *Irshād al-arīb*, I, 86 bottom.

18. But the spirit of tolerance prevailed only in the early period, when differences of opinion no doubt existed in abundance but the clash of contrary opinions had not yet kindled partisan passions. The evil spirit of intolerance first appeared on both sides—the orthodox and the rationalist—as a result of the cultivation of scholastic dogmatic theology.[152]

It is related, among other things, in one of the reports about al-Ash'arī's last hours that he asked Abū 'Alī al-Sarakhsī (in whose house in Baghdad he died) to step up to his bed, and with ebbing strength he whispered to him the following declaration: "I bear witness that I regard no one among the *ahl al-qibla* as a *kāfir*, for they all direct their hearts to the same object of worship. Their disagreements are only a matter of different modes of expression." There is, it is true, another report that his last words were an anathema hurled at the Mu'tazilites. I am inclined to consider this latter report more reliable. The spirit of that time, agitated by dogmatic controversies, was more favorable to the fury of excommunication than to conciliatory tolerance. Not for nothing does the old saying charge that "the devotions of the *mutakallimūn* consist in sniffing out heresy."[153] In Chapter III we have seen the Mu'tazilites at work. The dogmatic literature proved faithful to the method of such masters. "*Kāfir*" and "heretic" are flung left and right, whenever opinions are ventured that differ from the author's own.

Amid this hairsplitting struggle over formulas and definitions, Sufism alone harbored a tolerant spirit. We have seen that Sufism even rose to the rejection of confessional distinctions. Al-Ghazālī did not go so far. Nevertheless, his writings are inexhaustible in their depreciation of all dogmatic formula making and quibbling which claim to be the sole means of salvation and therefore sacred. His dry scholastic language rises to the heights of ardent eloquence when he takes the field against such pretensions. He devoted a specific work to the idea of tolerance, entitled *Criterion for Distinguishing between Islam and Heresy.*[s] In it he proclaims to the Muslim world the doctrine that agreement on the most important fundamentals of religion is sufficient ground for acknowledging a person to be a believer, and that differences of opinion on points of dogmatic

[152] The theologians' opinions on this point are assembled in concise form in Sanūsī, *Muqaddima*, pp. 96-112.

[153] Jāḥiẓ, *Ḥayawān*, I, 80:14 [I, 174]; cf. 103:8 [I, 219].

[s] For a study of this book, with a translation of selected passages, see Hans-Joachim Runge, *Über Gazālī's Faisal-al-tafriqa baina-l-Islām wa-l-zandaqa: Untersuchung über die Unterscheidung von Islam und Ketzerei* (Kiel, 1938).

and ritual detail—and these include even the rejection of the caliphate as recognized by Sunnī Islam, that is, the Shīʿī schism—do not justify branding a person a *kāfir*. "You must curb your tongue about people who turn toward the *qibla*."

His greatest merit in the history of Islam is that he put his coreligionists once again in mind of this old doctrine, took it seriously, and gained a following for it.[154]

We have seen that in so doing he advanced no new idea, but taught Muslims to return to the better spirit of an earlier age. It was his achievement to have reawakened that spirit after people had grown unfaithful to it, and to have enriched it with ideas that his Sufism had inspired. From the divisive squabbles of theologians and the complacency of scholastic wisdom he turned—and strove to turn the souls of his fellow Muslims—to the inwardness of faith that brings people together, to the worship whose sanctuary is in the heart. This was the greatest effect of Sufism on the religious life in Islam.

[154] It is characteristic of the general direction followed by orthodoxy after Ghazālī that even a man like the Ḥanbalite zealot Taqī al-Dīn ibn Taymīya ("Zur Geschichte der ḥanbalitischen Bewegungen," p. 25 [= *Gesammelte Schriften*, V, 159; Partial French translation in *Arabica*, VII (1960), 139])—a theologian with a ready inclination to fanaticism and exclusivity—stands, on this issue, closer than many a rationalist to Ghazālī, whom he had combatted. In his commentary on Sura 112, *Sūrat al-Ikhlāṣ*, pp. 112f., he devotes a special excursus to the matter, with the conclusion that Muʿtazilites, Khārijites, Murji'ites, and moderate Shīʿites (*al-tashayyuʿ al-mutawassiṭ*) are not to be regarded as unbelievers. They stand on the ground of Qur'ān and *sunna* and go astray only in the interpretation of these sources. Nor do they in any way question the binding nature of the law. Excluded are the Jahmīya because of their intransigent rejection of all divine names and attributes (*nafy al-asmā' maʿa nafy al-ṣifāt*), and particularly the Ismāʿīlīs because of their abrogation of the validity of the ritual law. In this moderate opinion advanced by a bellicose Ḥanbalite, we may see an influence of the view that is in harmony with the early, tolerant *sunna*. From two radically opposed points of view, Ghazālī and his principal adversary, Ibn Taymīya, repudiated the influence that the dogmatic definitions of the scholastics had exerted on the essential nature of Islam.

V. *The Sects*

1. There is a tendency to attribute to sectarian divisions within Islam a much greater diversity than is warranted by the facts.[a]

Islamic theology is itself largely responsible for this. There was a tradition that declared, in praise of Islam, that Islam had seventy-three virtues, as against the seventy-one of Judaism and the seventy-two of Christianity. The tradition was misunderstood, and the virtues were turned into seventy-three branches. This error prepared the ground for the enumeration of seventy-three sects, each of them bound for Hell except the one "group that will escape" (*al-firqa al-nājiya*), the only one that leads to salvation—which is to say the one that conforms to the requirements of the *sunna*.[1] In circles more disposed to toleration—from which Ghazālī's name cannot, of course, be missing—this statement was given a correspondingly tolerant cast: "All (the branches) will enter Paradise; only one—the *zindīqs*—will enter Hell."[b]

Western views, too, were occasionally influenced by this misunderstanding of the Muslim tradition of the seventy-three virtues and by their transformation into "branches." People speak not only of the rites (such as Ḥanafite, Mālikite, and so on) as "sects" of Islam, but also regard theological differences, deviations from the common orthodox view, as instances of sectarian division. But such differences of opinion could never have given rise to the formation of a dissident church. It is, for example, a complete misunderstanding of the internal history of Islam to speak of a Muʿtazilite sect. True enough, the theologians on all sides were

[a] Two general works may be consulted on the history of sects in Islam: Henri Laoust, *Les schismes dans l'Islam: introduction à une étude de la religion musulmane* (Paris, 1965), and A. J. Arberry (general editor), *Religion in the Middle East, Three Religions in Concord and Conflict* (Cambridge, 1969), volume 2 of which is devoted entirely to Islam.

[1] About this old misunderstanding see my *Beiträge zur Literaturgeschichte der Schīʿa und der sunnitischen Polemik* (Vienna, 1874), p. 9 (Sitzungsberichte der Philosophisch-historischen Classe der Kaiserlichen Akademie der Wissenschaften zu Wien, LXXVIII, 445 [= *Gesammelte Schriften*, I, 267]); and "Le Dénombrement des sectes mohamétanes," *RHR*, XXVI (1892), 129ff. [= *Gesammelte Schriften*, II, 406ff.]. Cf. "Die dogmatische Partie der Sālimijja," *ZDMG*, LXI (1907), 73ff. [= *Gesammelte Schriften*, V, 76ff.].

[b] Since Goldziher's day, a good deal of sectarian literature has come to light, making it possible to study the beliefs of the various groups, particularly the little-known extremist groups, on the basis of better evidence than the polemics of their Sunnī opponents.

often ready to throw the epithet *kāfir*, "unbeliever," at those who rejected their theses. On occasion they would seriously dispute each other's membership in the Islamic community, each attempting to draw down on the other the practical consequences of "unbelief" (Ch. IV, Sec. 17). According to one story, an orthodox son refused his share of the estate left by his father who had professed, with the Mu'tazilites, the doctrine of free will, because according to Islamic law a difference in religious affiliation, *disparitas cultus*, is an obstacle to inheritance.[2] But such fanatic extravagance is not in keeping with the prevalent temper of the Islamic community. As it happens, this particular application of the law of inheritance is said in so many words to be the act of a madman.[3]

We may regard as real sects in Islam only those groups whose members depart from the *sunna*, the historically sanctioned form of Islam, on essential issues of fundamental importance for all Islam, and who on such issues contradict the *ijmā'*.

Divisions of this kind, still in effect in the present organization of Islam, go back to its earliest age.

In the foreground are not questions of religion but, it appears, questions of the constitution of the state. In a community based on religion, religious considerations will, however, inevitably pervade political questions, and political questions will take on the form of religious issues that give their own coloring to political strife.

The significance of the earliest dissenting movements consists precisely in this: within the warlike religion that was early Islam, the dissenting movements fostered religious considerations that, further enriched by elements imported into Islam, soon gave political cleavage a religious character.

At the beginning of the schism, however, political questions were uppermost. The religious issue was blended in with them, by way of leaven. Very soon it was to become a decisive element in perpetuating the schism.

[2] "Zur Geschichte der ḥanbalitischen Bewegungen," p. 5 n.2 [= *Gesammelte Schriften*, V, 139 n. 2, citing ibn Taymīya, *Rasā'il*, I, 438]. Qushayrī, *Risāla fī 'ilm al-taṣawwuf*, p. 15:5, reports the practical application of this idea by al-Ḥārith al-Muḥāsibī (d. 243/857 in Baghdad). This is all the more striking as Ḥārith belonged to the ascetic school that attached little importance to dogmatic subtleties. According to other reports (Qazwīnī, *Āthār al-bilād*, edited by F. Wüstenfeld, Göttingen, 1848, p. 215:16; Subkī, *Ṭabaqāt*, II, 38:12), the father was a Rāfiḍite (Shī'ī), which would be a more proper reason for the *disparitas cultus*.

[3] Ibn al-Faqīh al-Hamadānī, *Kitāb al-buldān*, edited by M. J. de Goeje (Leiden, 1885), p. 44:18.

2. After the death of Muhammad—about whose wishes concerning succession to the leadership of the community nothing is authentically known[c]—the gravest matter before the Muslim community was the decision to whom, at any time, the office of caliph should fall. Assurance that the Prophet's work would be carried on lay in the felicitous choice of a caliph (*khalīfa*, "successor"). From the very beginning there was a party of highly respected Muslims who were dissatisfied with the manner in which, in disregard of degrees of kinship to the Prophet's family, the caliphate had been bestowed on Abū Bakr, 'Umar, and 'Uthmān, the first three men to hold it. Accordingly, they would have preferred to elevate 'Alī to the caliphate. He was the Prophet's cousin and his closest blood relation; moreover, he had married the Prophet's daughter Fāṭima. This party was first prompted to an open declaration of its views when in the person of 'Uthmān, the third caliph, a member of the Umayyad family succeeded at the head of the Muslim community. This was the very family whose chief and whose members had offered stubborn resistance to nascent Islam, even if in Muhammad's lifetime they had yielded to success and joined the faith. While a member of it reigned, this family gained a preponderant influence on government, and thus a preponderant share in the material benefits yielded by the state. This led to mutiny among the discontented and the dispossessed, and at length to the murder of 'Uthmān. Open war followed between the party of 'Alī and the supporters of the assassinated caliph. In Arab fashion, these latter now claimed the role of avengers of the blood of 'Uthmān, and recognized the Umayyad Mu'āwiya, the governor of Syria, as their pretender to the throne.

One could not justly say that 'Uthmān was not a devout Muslim,[4] for all that he belonged to a family less than fanatic in religious matters. Among the charges brought against him, that of religious laxity was not in the foreground. Death came to him while he was busy reading the Holy Book, the definitive redaction of which, regarded to this day as the established Qur'ān text, had been an object of his labors. His opponents, it is true, seem to have cast suspicion even on this pious concern with the holy scripture of Islam.

[c] Goldziher is here implicitly rejecting the Shī'ite claim that Muhammad, during his lifetime, appointed his kinsman and son-in-law 'Alī as successor. On this question, see *EI*², articles "Imāma" (by W. Madelung) and "Ghadīr Khumm" (by L. Veccia Vaglieri). For a general discussion, see W. Montgomery Watt, *Islamic Political Thought; The Basic Concepts* (Edinburgh, 1968), chapter 3, pp. 31ff.

[4] *Der Islam im Morgen- und Abendlande* (Berlin, 1885-1887), I, 283.

Despite the religious disposition of the old caliph, during his reign a movement of religious agitation arose along with that of the political malcontents. At first it was feeble enough. It saw in ʿAlī, and only in him, the embodiment of the divine right to the institution of the caliphate. But it was not this group that made it possible for ʿAlī to become, and for a short while to rule as, the fourth in the line of caliphs, without having secured general recognition of his right to the office. He had to win the caliphate in war against the avengers of ʿUthmān and their chief, the Umayyad Muʿāwiya. By a cunning trick that August Müller called "one of the most undignified farces in world history,"[d] the party of Muʿāwiya contrived, in the midst of a battle that might easily have gone against them, to push through a call for arbitration. ʿAlī was a weak enough politician to agree to this ostensibly peaceful solution of the conflict. In the course of events it became clear that he had been fooled in every respect. His adversary gained the upper hand. No great acumen is needed to see that ʿAlī's ultimate defeat would inevitably have followed even if an assassin's dagger had not put an end to his struggles.

Ali's consent to the convocation of a court of arbitration was the first cause of sectarian division within Islam. In the caliph's camp there were zealots who made up their minds that the resolution of a conflict over succession to the Prophet's legacy must not be put in human hands, that the bloody ordeal of war must be seen through to the end. Sovereignty came from God, and a decision about it could not be entrusted to human discretion. With this slogan they withdrew from the ranks of ʿAlī's supporters. Because of this separation they are known to Islamic history as Khārijites, "those who go out." They rejected both of the pretenders as being in contempt of the law, for they had become convinced that in conducting the war each was animated by a worldly desire for power and dominion, and that neither had the triumph of "divine right" as his goal.[5] The caliphate must be conferred on the worthiest candidate by the free choice of the community. Drawing the logical conclusion from this requirement of free choice, and departing from the practice of former

[d] August Müller's somewhat simplistic presentation of these events is now accepted by few scholars. The discovery of new evidence and, in particular, of pro-Shīʿite and pro-Khārijite sources has made possible a reexamination of the traditional accounts and a reassessment of the events they describe. For a comprehensive study, see Erling Ladewig Petersen, *ʿAlī and Muʿāwiya in Early Arabic Tradition* (Odense, 1974). See also the *EI*² article, " ʿAlī ibn Abī Ṭālib" (by L. Veccia Vaglieri), where sources and literature are cited.

[5] See especially J. Wellhausen's *Die religiös-politischen Oppositionsparteien im alten Islam* [*The Religio-political Factions in Early Islam*].

nominations to the caliphate, they did not limit eligibility to certain eminent clans, nor even to the tribe of Quraysh from which the Prophet had come. "An Ethiopian slave" might be just as qualified for the caliphate as a son of the noblest clans.[e] On the other hand, they demanded of the head of the Muslim community the most rigorous submission to God and compliance with the religious law. If his conduct failed to answer these requirements, he was to be deposed by the community. On the conduct of the common man, as well, they were prepared to pass a more stringent judgment than the generally prevalent view demanded. In this they stood in the sharpest opposition to the view of the Murji'ites (Ch. III, Sec. 2). In contrast to the Murji'ites, the Khārijites regarded works as an integral element in the definition of faith—so much so that in their view anyone guilty of a grave sin was not only a sinner but an unbeliever.[6] Because of the austere aspects of their religious ethics they have been called, not without justice, the puritans of Islam.[7]

We may mention, as a characteristic feature of their ethical position, that they strove to weave moral imperatives into the fabric of strict legality much more than the orthodoxy of the time was in the habit of doing. The following detail will serve as illustration. Islamic law clearly lists the circumstances that invalidate the state of ritual purity required for the performance of prayer. These are without exception physical in nature. Khārijite law accepts all these rules, but adds certain further stipulations, which I quote from a recently printed Khārijite religious text:[8] "In the same way, the state of purity is invalidated by what issues from the mouth by way of falsehood and slander that may be to the hurt of one's fellow, or by way of things one would shrink from mentioning in the presence of one's fellow. It is invalidated by spreading scandal that plants

[e] Goldziher is here alluding to a hadith handed down in slightly variant forms, according to which the Prophet said: "Obey whoever is put in authority over you, even if he be a crop-nosed Ethiopian slave" (Wensinck, *Concordance*, I, 327). He was, however, mistaken in regarding this tradition as an expression of Khārijite egalitarianism. The message it conveys is not equality but obedience—the quietist doctrine of submission to authority in whatever form it comes. The combination of qualities described in the tradition is clearly intended to emphasize the duty of obedience by demanding it even for the ultimate improbability in physical, social, and racial terms. See S. D. Goitein, *Studies in Islamic History and Institutions*, pp. 203-204; further, B. Lewis, *Race and Color in Islam*, p. 20.

[6] For a classical description of Khārijite views as against the views of the rest of the Muslims, see *Aghānī*, XX, 105ff.

[7] Kremer, *Geschichte der herrschenden Ideen des Islams* (Leipzig, 1868), p. 360.

[8] Darwīsh al-Maḥrūqī, *Kitāb al-dalā'il fī'l-lawāzim wa'l-wasā'il* (Cairo, A.H. 1320), p. 20. For the same idea in ethical maxims, see Ibn Qutayba, *'Uyūn al-akhbār*, IV, 419:18ff. [II, 29].

hatred and enmity among people. Anyone who has without just cause abused, cursed, or spoken evil of people or animals has ceased being in a state of purity, and before he may pray, he must perform the ritual washing." In sum: untruthful, unseemly, and wicked words—ethical flaws—invalidate the state of personal purity no less than do physical impurities. Thus moral purity is required as preparatory to prayer.[9]

The principles that characterize the Khārijites' special position concern the organization of the state, theology, and ethics. On these grounds they continued, after the victory of the Umayyads, to fight against the dynasty they condemned as sinful, lawless, and ungodly. They carried rebellion against the Umayyads into the farthest corners of the vast empire. They did not form a fixed and united community; they did not flock together around a single caliphate. Rather, Khārijite bands that followed different military leaders, scattered throughout the empire, troubled the possessors of power. To deal with them required all the energy of the great generals to whose ability and good luck in war the Umayyads owed the consolidation of their caliphate. The disinherited classes of society readily joined the Khārijites, whose democratic tendencies and whose protest against the rulers' injustice were to their liking. The Khārijite revolt could easily serve as a framework for every antidynastic riot. It served as a cover and a form for the insurrection of the North African Berbers, lovers of liberty, against the Umayyad governor. Muslim historians could not understand the stubborn national resistance of the Berbers except as a Khārijite movement.[10] It was also in North Africa that Khārijism, espoused by compact groups, persisted longest.

After their revolts had been suppressed, the Khārijites were limited to the theoretical cultivation of their special doctrines in constitutional law, ethics, and theology. After they had been compelled to stop fighting sword in hand the state of affairs prevailing in the empire, they produced a very considerable theological literature. The study of Islam recently (1907) lost the scholar most familiar with that literature: Motylinski, director of the Medersa of Constantine (Algeria).[f]

[9] F. A. Klein, *The Religion of Islam* (London, 1906), p. 132.

[10] Cf. "Materialien zur Kenntnis der Almohadenbewegung in Nordafrika," pp. 31ff. [= *Gesammelte Schriften*, II, 192ff.].

[f] The work of Motylinski on the Khārijites of North Africa was continued by a number of other scholars, notably T. Lewicki (details of his various articles will be found in the *Index Islamicus*). Khārijite material on earlier history has been studied by L. Veccia Vaglieri and Roberto Rubinacci. For a general account, see the article "Khāridjites" in *EI*[2] (by G. Levi Della Vida).

As the Khārijites, at the time of their wars, had banded into scattered groups, so the religious doctrines that evolved in those groups varied in points of detail. Such differences would mostly be traced back to their original leaders. It is striking that in some of the chief theological issues they stood closest to the Mu'tazilites.[11]

Rationalist inclinations appeared in the thinking of the Khārijite theologians before their beliefs took the form of a fixed, positive system—while they were still in flux, with the main stress on those particulars that were contrary to orthodoxy. Within the Khārijite opposition to generally accepted doctrine there was a party that acknowledged only the Qur'ān as having legislative authority, and rejected everything else as without competence for the regulation of religious affairs.[12] One of their groups went so far as to impugn the reliability of the text of the Qur'ān. In their view, the Joseph sura did not belong in the Qur'ān; it was simply a story, with nothing sacred about it. It was unthinkable that this erotic tale was a part like other parts of a holy book revealed by God.[13] Devout Mu'tazilites voiced similar opinions about those parts of the Qur'ān in which the Prophet utters curses against his enemies (such as Abū Lahab). God could not have called such passages "a noble Qur'ān on a well-guarded tablet."[14]

Since the Khārijite community developed apart from the common Sunnī *ijmā'*, one may readily assume that it would occasionally vary from orthodoxy in its ritual and legal practice.[15] Because of their opposition to the consensus embodied in the four orthodox rites of the majority, the Khārijites were later characterized by the orthodox as *al-khawāmis*, "the Fivers," that is, separatists who stood outside the community of the four orthodox *madhāhib*.

There are to this day Muslim communities that profess to be Khārijites. Of the many subdivisions into which, as we have just seen, certain

[11] Cf. *RHR*, LII (1905), 232. A practical example is the way the Qur'ān verse 20:5 is dealt with in an Ibāḍī *khuṭba* in the third Islamic century, in Tahert; A. de C. Motylinski, "Chronique d'Ibn Ṣaghir sur les Imams Rostemides de Tahert," *Actes du XIVe Congrès International des Orientalistes* (Paris, 1908), III, ii, 126. This text is most illustrative of the spiritual life of the Ibāḍī groups of that period.

[12] Cf. "Kämpfe um die Stellung des Ḥadīṯ im Islam," p. 864 n. 5 [= *Gesammelte Schriften*, V, 90 n. 5].

[13] Shahrastānī, *Al-Milal wa'l-niḥal*, pp. 95:4 from bottom, 96:8 from bottom, concerning the Maymūnīya.

[14] Rāzī, *Mafātīḥ al-ghayb*, I, 268 (following al-Khaṭīb al-Baghdādī).

[15] For details, see Eduard Sachau, "Über die religiöse Anschauungen der Ibaditischen Muhammedaner in Oman und Ostafrika," *MSOS*, II (1899), ii, 47–82.

differences of doctrine had splintered the Khārijite movement, one system has survived, known after its founder as the Ibāḍīya. In North Africa the pronunciation *Abāḍīya* is preferred.[16] The Ibāḍites today live mainly in North Africa, in numerous communities:[17] in the Mzab region, in the district of the Jabal Nafūsa (Tripolitania)—whose inhabitants sent an Ibāḍite representative to the Chamber of Deputies in Istanbul—as well as in East Africa (Zanzibar). The East African Ibāḍites are originally from Oman in Arabia. In recent years one could observe that the Khārijites, as good as forgotten, living in remote backwaters secluded from the bustle of the world, have tried to bestir themselves to vigorous activity, and consciously to let the world know of their existence. Awakened perhaps by the European scholarly interest in their literature—an interest they have not failed to notice—they have had a number of their fundamental theological works printed in the last few years. They have also tried to pursue an aggressive propaganda by means of a journal of which, it seems, only a few issues have appeared.[18]

Thus the sect of the Khārijites is to be regarded as the oldest sectarian schism within Islam. Its vestiges survive to this day, as a group of Muslims distinct from the Sunnī-orthodox majority. Moreover, their history illustrates, in uncomplicated form, the characteristic formation of Islamic sects: the infusion of religious ideas into political strife.

3. A more significant role was played in the history of Islam by the sectarian movement set afoot by the opposition of the *Shī'īs.*[g]

It is stated even in the most elementary textbooks that Islam exists in two forms: the Sunnī and the Shī'ī. As we have seen, the origin of this cleavage was linked to the question of succession to the caliphate. Even

[16] Dr. S. M. Zwemer is mistaken when he speaks of the "Abadhi sect of Shiah origin," *The Mohammedan World of To-day* (New York, 1906), p. 102. [For a detailed account, see *EI*[2] article, "Ibāḍiyya" (by T. Lewicki).]

[17] According to Ibn Ḥazm (d. 456/1064) there were, in his time, Ibāḍīs also in Andalus; *Al-Faṣl fī'l-milal wa'l-ahwā' wa'l-niḥal* (Cairo, A.H. 1317-1321), IV, 179; cf. 191:8. They had presumably crossed over from North Africa, or perhaps were only transients in Spain, where Ibn Ḥazm met them.

[18] M. Hartmann, "Die École Supérieure des Lettres in Alger und die Medersas Algeriens auf dem XIV. Orientalistenkongress," *ZA*, XIX (1905), 355f.

[g] For more recent contributions to the early history of the Shī'a, see S. Moscati, "Per una storia dell'antica Šī'a," *RSO*, XXX (1955), 251-67; Marshall G. S. Hodgson, "How Did the Early Shī'a Become Sectarian?" *JAOS*, LXXV (1955), 1-13; and S.H.M. Jafri, *The Origins and Early Development of Shi'a Islam* (London, 1979). A collection of papers submitted at a symposium on Shī'ism was published under the title *Le Shî'isme imâmite* (Paris, 1972).

under the first three caliphs there had been a party that tacitly acknowledged the rights of the Prophet's family, though they did not go to war to maintain them. After its pretender's fall, this party continued its protest against the usurpation of power by later non-'Alid dynasties: first against the Umayyads, then against all successive dynasties that did not accord with their ideas of legitimacy. Against all these usurpations they urged the divine right of the Prophet's descendants through the line of 'Alī and Fāṭima. They condemned the three caliphs before 'Alī as wicked usurpers, and through all the centuries that followed they set themselves against the actual political order of the Islamic state, mentally or, as occasion allowed, in open war.

It lay in the nature of this protest that it should readily assume a form in which religious motives predominated. In the place of a caliph elevated to the throne by human investiture, the Shī'īs recognize as the sole legitimate secular and spiritual head of Islam the *Imām*, whose exclusive legitimacy derives from God's command and determination. It is by this title—more suitable than any other to a religious office—that they prefer to call the direct descendant of the Prophet whom at any given time they recognize as head of the community.

The first *Imām* is 'Alī. Among Sunnī Muslims, too, he is regarded, although without prejudice to his predecessors' right to rule, as a man of extraordinary virtues and knowledge. Ḥasan al-Baṣrī called him "the theologian of this community" (*rabbānī hādhihi 'l-umma*).[19] The Shī'īs raise him yet higher. In their belief, the Prophet entrusted him with knowledge that he had kept from most of his Companions, who were not worthy of it. This knowledge is passed down in the family by way of inheritance (Ch. IV, Sec. 7). The Prophet, by direct disposition, chose 'Alī for his successor as teacher and ruler, and explicitly named him as such. 'Alī is *waṣī*, one chosen by the Prophet's disposition. The denial that such a disposition, in favor of any person at all, ever existed is what fundamentally separates the orthodox Sunnīs from their Shī'ī opponents.[20] As the Shī'īs believe, the title of *amīr al-mu'minīn*, "commander

[19] Qālī, *Amālī*, III, 173:3, 198 penultimate line.

[20] *Muhammedanische Studien*, II, 117 [= *Muslim Studies*, II, 113f.]. There is, to be sure, no lack of tendentious Sunnī hadiths in which Muhammad makes known his will regarding the sequence of the men who are to lead the community after his death (cf. *ibid.*, II, 99 n. 1 [= *Muslim Studies*, II, 98 n. 5]). But these statements are not presented as absolutely decisive of the question of succession; they do not take the form of a solemn bill of investiture such as, the Shī'īs assert, was made in favor of 'Alī. In a tradition in Ibn Sa'd, III, i, 46:5ff., we

of the faithful," belongs to 'Alī alone.[21] This is a title that, beginning with the reign of 'Umar, all caliphs of all dynasties assumed; it is found in Western medieval literature in the distorted forms *miramolin*, *miramomelin*, *miramomelli*.[22] 'Alī's legitimate successors as *Imāms*, the heirs to his rule and to his special knowledge and spiritual qualities, are exclusively his direct descendants through his wife Fāṭima. Thus the first is the Prophet's grandson Ḥasan, then his brother Ḥusayn, and then, one after the other, the rest of the 'Alid *Imāms*. Each successor is the *waṣī* of his predecessor, consecrated as the legitimate holder of the divine office by his predecessor's explicit designation in conformity to God's decree.[23] The chain of succession has been eternally fixed by God, and imposed by Muhammad as a divine institution.[24] Shī'ī exegesis, the pinnacle of arbitrary and forced interpretation,[25] finds even Qur'ānic passages in which this order is set down.

The caliphate in any other form was seen, in a secular sense, as robbery, and in a spiritual sense, as suppression of the sole authoritative source of religious guidance for the community. For in every age the *Imām* alone is the community's teacher and leader in religious matters, empowered and qualified by divine right and by the miraculous quality of infallibility bestowed by God. Accordingly, it necessarily follows

---

find support for the assertion that the Prophet himself designated 'Uthmān as one of his caliphs. It is interesting that the original transmitter of this report is a *mawlā 'Uthmān*—which is a sure indication of its nature.

[21] Abū Ja'far Muḥammad al-Kulīnī (d. 328/939 in Baghdad), *Al-Uṣūl min al-jāmi' al-kāfī* (Bombay, A.H. 1302), p. 261.

[22] Max van Berchem, "Titres califiens d'Occident," *JA*, 10th Series, IX (1907), 297ff.; Max Grünbaum, *Gesammelte Aufsätze zur Sprach- und Sagenkunde* (Berlin, 1901), p. 226.

[23] See a critique of these assumptions by an 'Alid in Ibn Sa'd, V, 239:2ff.

[24] In a series of flagrantly counterfeit hadiths in which God Himself, or Khaḍir, or Muhammad state by name what the Twelvers' sequence of *Imāms* will be. A Jew of the tribe of Aaron knows them from the "Book of Hārūn" (about which see "Ueber Bibelcitate in muhammedanischen Schriften," *ZATW*, XIII (1893), 316 [= *Gesammelte Schriften*, III, 310]). These Shī'ī fables are collected in Kulīnī, *Uṣūl al-kāfī*, pp. 342–46. The proofs from the Old Testament for the theory of *Imāms* (which were advanced by Shī'īs just as Sunnī apologists demonstrated Muhammad's mission from Biblical books) have been collected in a booklet by a modern Shī'ī theologian. Cf. Sayyid 'Alī Muḥammad, *Zād qalīl*, published in a lithographic edition of the Ithnā'asharīya Press in Lucknow (1290/1873). [For a discussion of the descendants of 'Alī and of the changing nature of the claims advanced on their behalf, see *EI*[2] article " 'Alids" (by B. Lewis).]

[25] This kind of Qur'ānic exegesis may be illustrated by the following explication of the beginning of Sura 91. "The sun and its radiance"—that is Muhammad. "The moon when it follows it" is 'Alī. "The day when it discloses it" is Ḥasan and Ḥusayn. "The night when it covers it"—that is the Umayyads. This explanation appears in the form of hadith, as the Prophet's own interpretation of the revelation. See Suyūṭī, *Al-La'ālī al-maṣnū'a*, I, 184.

from God's justice that He does not deprive any generation of such guidance. The presence of an *Imām* is in every generation indispensable, for without such an illuminate person the goal of God's law and guidance could not be attained. The imamate is a necessary institution (*wājib*), inherited in uninterrupted succession by members of the legitimate branch of the Prophet's family.

Thus in Shīʿism the religious considerations soon outweighed the political ones. The immediate occasion for this shift was provided by the earliest object of Shīʿī protest: the Umayyad dynasty, whose conduct—quite apart from the question of legitimacy—was forever a scandal to pietists. These rulers, the pietists thought, had allowed worldly considerations to predominate in the government of the Islamic state that should have been a theocracy.

Soon after the Umayyads' rise to power, during the second reign of the dynasty, the partisans of the ʿAlid family found a most imprudently chosen occasion to plunge Ḥusayn, the Prophet's grandson, into bloody struggle against the Umayyad usurper. The battlefield of Karbalā' (680) furnished them with a large number of martyrs. Even today, mourning for them lends a sentimental feature to Shīʿī Islam. A second failure followed soon afterwards when the Shīʿīs, under the flag of al-Mukhtār, once more measured themselves against the might of the triumphant Umayyads. Al-Mukhtār had chosen for his ʿAlid pretender Muḥammad ibn al-Ḥanafīya, a son of ʿAlī born not of Fāṭima but of "the Ḥanafī woman." This was an early augury of the internal divisions of Shīʿism.

4. Even after suffering decisive defeats, the Shīʿīs continued their protest and struggle against the various forms of political order recognized by the *ijmāʿ* of the Islamic state. They rarely succeeded in raising openly the flag of their *Imām* and pretender; and when they did so their struggle, hopeless from the first, met with inevitable defeat. They had to be content with paying mental homage to the *Imām* of the age, facilitating and preparing his victory by secret propaganda, and yielding outwardly to the facts while hoping for the righteous change that God would bring in the political affairs of the community.

Consequently, secret organizations arose that, led by a chief of propaganda (*dāʿī*), diffused their ideas among the masses. Naturally, the authorities always kept them under surveillance and spied into their affairs. The persecution of ʿAlids was, for this reason, an unceasing concern of the rulers, to whom that secret revolutionary propaganda was not unknown, and who necessarily saw in it a danger to the tranquillity of the state. The 'Abbāsids knew this even better than the Umayyads, for it had been precisely the 'Alid propaganda against Umayyad rule that in the middle of the eighth century enabled the descendants of 'Abbās to accomplish the overthrow of the Umayyads—prepared by Shī'ī subversion—and to take advantage of their fall, on the pretext that the claims of the grandson of Muḥammad ibn al-Ḥanafīya had been legally ceded to the 'Abbāsid family. Having plucked for themselves the fruit of Shī'ī propaganda, the 'Abbāsids had all the more reason to be on their guard against continued subversion by those who would not regard them, any more than the Umayyads, as the rightful successors of the Prophet. They strove therefore to deflect people from the veneration of 'Alī. Al-Mutawakkil razed the tomb of Ḥusayn. People were not to recall at that sacred place that it was a son of 'Alī, and not a descendant of 'Abbās, who had shed his blood for the rights of the Prophet's house. Many of the most eminent 'Alids, including some who belonged to the chain of *Imāms*, suffered harsh persecution. During 'Abbāsid rule, some ended their lives in prison,[26] some on the scaffold, some by secretly administered poison. In the time of the caliph al-Mahdī, a Shī'ī who was steady in his 'Alid loyalties was compelled to spend years in hiding—they ended only with death—to escape the caliph's clutches. It was at the peril of his life that he would venture from his hiding place to attend the Friday service.[27] Such people had been instrumental in what the 'Abbāsids regarded as the true victory of the rights of the Prophet's family; they therefore seemed even more dangerous to 'Abbāsid dynastic claims than they had seemed in the previous age, whose rulers had on principle denied the dynastic rights of the "family." To the 'Abbāsids it must have seemed insupportable, in more ways than one, to be challenged on the ground of legitimacy.[28]

The "tribulations (*miḥan*) of the family of the Prophet" are an inexhaustible theme of Shī'ī literature. There are hadiths in which the Prophet is made to foretell them. The utterances tradition ascribes to 'Alī constantly speak of the evil destiny awaiting his descendants.[29] In one of these evident forgeries it is told that 'Alī refused to recognize certain vis-

[26] Ibn Sa'd, V, 234 bottom.

[27] *Ibid.*, VI, 261:9ff.

[28] From the point of view of a partisan of the 'Alids, the 'Abbāsid al-Manṣūr was, despite the 'Abbāsid claim to legitimacy, a *jā'ir* (usurper); the pious theologian Abū Dhu'ayb said so to his face (Nawawī, *Tahdhīb al-asmā'*, p. 112:6).

[29] About the *miḥan* of the Shī'īs, see a letter of Abū Bakr al-Khwārizmī to the Shī'ī community in Nishapur; *Rasā'il Abī Bakr al-Khuwarizmī* (Istanbul, A.H. 1297), pp. 130ff. For the hadith about the trials of the partisans of 'Alī, see Ya'qūbī, *Ta'rīkh*, II, 242.

itors as being of his party (*shīʿa*), although his doorkeeper Qanbar had so announced them, because he did not see on them the distinguishing features by which one recognizes true adherents of the Shīʿa: bodies attenuated by privations, lips parched with thirst, and eyes bleary from tireless weeping.[30] The true Shīʿī is persecuted and wretched, like the family whose rights he maintains and for whose cause he suffers. People soon regarded it as the vocation of the Prophet's family to endure hardship and persecution. The tradition was accepted that each true descendant of the Prophet's family must suffer tribulations, and that accordingly one might cast suspicion on the genealogy of anyone who had claimed such kinship but had spent an untroubled life.[31]

Ever since the black day of Karbalāʾ, the history of this family—as the Shīʿīs, not without an inclination to the tragic, represent it—has been a continuous series of sufferings and persecutions. These are narrated in poetry and prose, in a richly cultivated literature of martyrologies—a Shīʿī specialty—and form the theme of Shīʿī gatherings in the first third of the month of Muḥarram, whose tenth day (*ʿāshūrā*) is kept as the anniversary of the tragedy at Karbalāʾ.[32] Scenes of that tragedy are also presented on this day of commemoration in dramatic form (*taʿziya*). "Our feast days are our assemblies of mourning." So concludes a poem by a prince of Shīʿī disposition recalling the many *miḥan* of the Prophet's family.[33] Weeping and lamentation over the evils and persecutions suffered by the ʿAlid family, and mourning for its martyrs: these are things from which loyal supporters of the cause cannot cease. "More touching than the tears of the Shīʿīs" has even become an Arabic proverb.[34]

Modern, educated Shīʿīs (who condemn the Umayyads no less passionately than naive Shīʿīs do) have found in this mournful mood of their faith a great religious value. They find in it an element of noble sentiment, indeed of humanism, in contrast to the ossifying effect of the law

[30] Muttaqī, *Kanz al-ʿummāl*, VI, 81, no. 1271.

[31] Dhahabī, *Tadhkirat al-ḥuffāẓ*, IV, 11 [IV, 1211].

[32] Cf. E. G. Browne, *A Catalogue of the Persian Manuscripts in the Library of the University of Cambridge* (Cambridge, 1896), pp. 122–42 (with references). About the products of this literature, see "Spottnamen der ersten Chalifen bei den Schīʿiten," *WZKM*, XV (1901), 330f. [= *Gesammelte Schriften*, IV, 304f.]; recent ones are listed in R. Haupt, *Orientalischer Literaturbericht*, I (1908–1909), nos. 3080–81. The martyrologies are also called *maqātil*.

[33] Thaʿālibī, *Yatīmat al-dahr* (Damascus, A.H. 1304), I, 223 [edited by Muḥammad Muḥyī al-Dīn ʿAbd al-Ḥamīd (Cairo, A.H. 1375-1397), I, 309]; Ibn Khallikān, IX, 59 [V, 372], where instead of *maʾāthimunā* read *maʾātimunā*.

[34] Maydānī, *Majmaʿ al-amthāl* (Cairo, A.H. 1284), I, 179 [edited by Muḥammad Muḥyī al-Dīn ʿAbd al-Ḥamīd (Cairo, 1379/1959), I, 316, no. 1712]: *araqqu*.

and its practices. They regard it as the most precious and human thing proper to Islam.[35] "To weep for Ḥusayn," writes an Indian Shīʿī who has also written books in English about philosophy and mathematics, "is the glory of our lives and souls, or else we would be the most ungrateful of creatures. In Paradise we will still mourn for Ḥusayn. It is the condition of Muslim existence." "Mourning for Ḥusayn is the token of Islam. It is impossible for a Shīʿī not to weep. His heart is a living tomb, the true tomb for the head of the beheaded martyr."[36]

5. The nature of Shīʿī activity, described above, and the dangers that attended the dissemination of Shīʿī doctrines determined that a subversive rather than a fighting propaganda should characterize the Shīʿa. In view of the dangers that any disclosure of their holy secret might draw down on all sharers in it, prudence dictated a certain secretiveness, a stealthiness of step. According to a saying of a Shīʿī *Imām*, the two angels who constantly attend each human being in order to record his words and deeds withdraw immediately as two believers (that is to say, two partisans of the Shīʿa) meet to speak together. The *Imām* Jaʿfar, who taught this, was reminded of the contradiction between this maxim and the statement in the Qur'ān (50:18): "He (a human being) speaks no word without a ready observer beside him." Surely that listener is the guardian angel who hears what the man says! The *Imām* sighed from the depths of his heart, tears fell on his beard, and he said: "Yes, God has indeed commanded the angels, out of His respect for the believers, to leave them alone in their private conversations. Even if the angels do not write down what the believers say, God knows all that is hidden and veiled."[37]

In addition, the constant danger in which partisans of the Shīʿa found themselves bred and nurtured among them an ethical theory that is in large measure characteristic of their mentality, and that necessarily follows from their clandestine ways. This theory did not originate among the Shīʿīs. It is accepted as legitimate by other Muslims as well, on the authority of Qur'ān 3:28. It had served the same purpose among the Khārijites. But in the system of the Shīʿīs it was developed into a funda-

[35] A. F. Badshah Husain, *Ḥusain in the Philosophy of History* (Lucknow, 1905), p. 20.

[36] *Ibid.*, pp. 9, 18, 30. [The original English text was unavailable to the translators.]

[37] Kulīnī, *Uṣūl al-kāfī*, p. 466. The withdrawal of the two guardian angels is postulated for yet another case: they do not try to protect a man against what is destined for him by God's decree (*al-muqaddar*); they must leave free course to that which has been decreed. Ibn Saʿd, III, i, 22:13.

mental doctrine, and observance of it was made, for the good of the community, an essential duty of each member. It is summed up in the word *taqīya*, which means "caution." The Shī'ī not only *may* conceal his true faith; he *must* do so. In a region ruled by his enemies he must speak and act as though he were of their number in order not to draw down peril and persecution on his comrades.[38] It is easy to imagine what a school of ambiguity and dissimulation was created by this training in *taqīya*, which is an essential rule of Shī'ī discipline. But the lack of freedom to make open profession of one's true faith is also a school of suppressed fury against one's powerful adversary: a fury that gathers itself into unrestrained hatred and fanaticism. It prompts quite peculiar religious doctrines, of a kind totally incongruous with orthodox Islam. Someone once asked the *Imām* Ja'far al-Ṣādiq: "O grandson of the Prophet, I am unable to support your cause actively; all I can do is to dissociate myself mentally (*al-barā'a*) from your enemies and to curse them. What then is my worth?" The *Imām* replied: "My father told me in the name of his father, who had had it from his father who had heard it taught directly by the Prophet: 'Whoever is too weak to help us, the people of the Family, to victory, but in his chamber hurls curses at our enemies, is lauded (by the angels) as blessed . . . and they pray God in his behalf: "O God, have mercy on this your servant who does all he is capable of doing; could he do more he assuredly would." And a voice brings God's reply: "I have granted your prayer and extended my mercy to his soul, and will admit it among the souls of the elect and the righteous." ' "[39] This cursing of enemies is a Shī'ī religious law; to fail to practice it is a religious lapse.[40] This attitude of mind too left its characteristic mark on Shī'ī literature.

6. Thus the Shī'ī system hinges on its theory of the imamate and on the legitimate succession of men whom God has chosen from among the Prophet's descendants and designated for that office. The *Imām* of the age may present himself openly or, personally known only to a few, claim his rights by clandestine propaganda. In either case, to acknowledge him is quite as much an article of faith as to confess belief in the one God and the prophethood of Muhammad. It is required much more stringently

[38] About *taqīya*, cf. "Das Prinzip der *taḳijja* im Islam," pp. 213ff. [= *Gesammelte Schriften*, V, 59ff.; partial French translation in *Arabica*, VII (1960), 131ff.].

[39] Commentary by the *Imām* Ḥasan al-'Askarī to Sura 2, vs. 18 [cf. *GAL*, SI, p. 333].

[40] Kulīnī, *Uṣūl al-kāfī*, p. 105.

than any orthodox catechism requires acknowledgment of the historical caliphate.

According to Shīʿī theology, the acknowledgment of the *Imām* is not supplementary to a sound theological position but is an integral part of the profession of faith, inseparable from the highest truths of religion. I quote a Shīʿī theologian: "To know God means to recognize the truthfulness of God and His Prophet, to be attached [*muwālāh*] to ʿAlī, to submit to his authority and to that of the *Imāms* of guidance (after him), and to dissociate oneself from their adversaries. That is to know God." "No man is truly a Muslim unless he recognizes God and His Prophet and all the *Imāms* and the *Imām* of his age and surrenders his affairs into the hands of the *Imām* and devotes himself to the *Imām*'s cause."[41] In Shīʿī doctrine, to the five "pillars of Islam" (Ch. I, Sec. 7) a sixth is added: *al-wilāya*, attaching oneself to the *Imāms*, which also entails *al-barāʾa*, dissociation from their enemies.[42] In the Shīʿī creed, this duty is chief among religious duties. "Love for ʿAlī consumes all sins as fire consumes dry wood."[43] This mentality forms the core of the religious character of the Shīʿa. A Khārijite characterized it thus: "They hang their religion on an Arab clan and aver that attachment to that clan lets them dispense with good works and escape punishment for evil."[44]

7. To understand the Shīʿī doctrine of *Imāms* it is necessary to stress the conceptual difference between the theocratic sovereignty of the caliphs in Sunnī Islam and that of the legitimate *Imāms* in the Shīʿa.

For Sunnī Islam, the caliph is there to guarantee the carrying out of Islamic obligations, to represent and embody in his person the duties of the Islamic community. "At the head of the Muslims"—I quote verbatim from a Muslim theologian—"there must necessarily stand someone who sees to it that their laws are carried out, their statutes maintained, their borders defended, and their armies equipped, who makes sure that their obligatory taxes are collected, that men of violence, thieves, and highwaymen are suppressed, that services are held on Fridays and feast days, that minors (in need of a guardian) can be married, that the spoils of war are justly divided, and that similar legal obligations, which no single

[41] *Ibid*.

[42] For various maxims about this, see *ibid*., pp. 368ff., chapter "*Daʿāʾim al-islām*." This is why the faithful Shīʿī is a *mutawālī*, one who attaches himself (to the ʿAlid clan). The word is used as the special designation of a Syrian [and Lebanese] branch of the Shīʿī sect.

[43] Suyūṭī, *Al-Laʾālī al-maṣnūʿa*, I, 184. In this chapter (pp. 166ff.) there is an anthology of the tendentious hadiths fabricated by partisans of the Shīʿa in support of their position.

[44] *Aghānī*, XX, 107:19ff.

member of the community can take care of, are performed."[45] In short, he represents the state's judicial, administrative, and military power. As ruler he is nothing but the successor of the one who preceded him, having been designated as such by a human act (election, or nomination by the predecessor), and not entitled by the qualities inherent in his personality. Most importantly, the caliph of the Sunnīs has no authority to dispense spiritual instruction.

The *Imām* of the Shīʿīs, on the other hand, thanks to the personal qualities God has implanted in him, is the leader and spiritual instructor of Islam, the heir to the Prophet's office.[46] He rules and teaches in the name of God. Just as Moses could hear the voice from the thornbush say, "I am Allah, Lord of the Worlds" (Qur'ān 28:30), so too it is God's revelation that manifests itself through the *Imām* of the age.[47] The *Imām* represents divinely sanctioned sovereignty. But there is more: his superhuman qualities elevate him above the rest of mankind. He is superior to them not only by virtue of his hereditary and innate, rather than conferred, office, but also by virtue of his substance.

Since the creation of Adam, a divine, luminous substance has been passing from one chosen descendant of Adam into another. When it reached the loins of the common grandfather of Muhammad and ʿAlī, the divine light split in two; one part entered ʿAbdallāh, the father of the Prophet, and another his brother Abū Ṭālib, the father of ʿAlī. From him this divine light passed, from generation to generation, into the successive *Imāms*. The preexistent divine light is present in the substance of the *Imām*'s soul; it renders him *Imām* of his age and bestows on him extraor-

[45] ʿAlī al-Qārī, *Sharḥ al-fiqh al-akbar* (Cairo, A.H. 1323), p. 132 top.

[46] This is one respect in which the ʿAbbāsids did not stand back: they were fond of calling their caliphate "the legacy of prophethood," *mīrāth al-nubūwa* (*Aghānī*, X, 124:10; XVIII, 79:5; cf. Ibn Jubayr, *Riḥla*, 2nd ed. revised by M. J. de Goeje, Leiden and London, 1907, p. 92:2). Therefore one attribute of the ʿAbbāsid caliphate was *al-nabawī*, "going back to the Prophet." Cf. Ibn al-Qalānisī, *Dhayl ta'rīkh Dimashq*, p. 155:9, 5 from bottom, 165:5 from bottom, 193:11; Yāqūt, *Irshād al-arīb*, II, 54:12. But it was understood to be *nabawī* only in the sense that their rule had been legitimately inherited from the Prophet to whose family the ʿAbbāsids also belonged. Unlike the claims of the ʿAlid *Imāms* and the Fāṭimid caliphs, *nabawī* was not understood to mean that their descent endowed the ʿAbbāsid caliphs with an inborn competence and authority to instruct the Muslims in matters of religion. There is an isolated instance in the Umayyad age of calling the caliphate, out of flattery, the legacy of the Prophet. It occurs in a text the *kātib* ʿAbd al-Ḥamīd ibn Yaḥyā addressed to his caliph (if, indeed, it may be regarded as genuine); see Muḥammad Kurd ʿAlī, *Rasā'il al-bulaghā'*, p. 92:9. Here too the word legacy cannot have meant more than a claim to legitimacy.

[47] Quoted as a saying of the *Imām* Jaʿfar al-Ṣādiq on the authority of Suhrawardī, in ʿĀmilī, *Kashkūl*, p. 357:19.

dinary spiritual powers that far outstrip human standards. The substance of his soul is purer than that of the common mortal, "free of evil impulses and adorned with holy forms." This is roughly the way even moderate Shīʿism thinks of the nature of its *Imāms*. Extravagant forms of Shīʿism, as we shall see, followed a completely different course, and elevated ʿAlī and the *Imāms* into a near-divine or indeed divine sphere. This traducianist theory does not, it is true, appear in fixed and dogmatically homogeneous form, but it may be regarded as the generally accepted Shīʿī view of the character of the *Imāms*.

There is a variety of associated ideas. When God commanded the angels to prostrate themselves in adoration before Adam, their adoration was meant for the luminous substance of the *Imāms*, enclosed in Adam. After the angels' adoration, God bade Adam lift his glance to the top of the divine throne, and there he saw the reflections of those sacred luminous bodies "as a man's face is reflected in a clear mirror." Thus the celestial mirror-image of these holy bodies was raised to the very throne of God.[48] Popular superstition was not content even with such apotheoses. It extended the effect of the divine qualities inherent in the *Imāms*' bodies to the *Imāms*' temporal existence: the Shīʿī masses believe, for example, that the body of the *Imām* casts no shadow. No doubt such ideas took shape at a time when there was no longer an *Imām* visible in the flesh. The *Imām-Mahdī* (see below),[49] in particular, is invulnerable. Popular belief occasionally assumes the same about the Prophet,[50] as do legends about Muslim saints. Especially in North Africa, invulnerability is attributed to many *marabouts*.[51]

8. Not only popular belief but also theological theory strayed to exorbitant heights in forming its ideas of the nature of *Imāms*.

There are within Shīʿism extremist theories that regard ʿAlī and the *Imāms* outright as incarnations of the godhead: not only as sharers in divine attributes and in powers that raise them above the sphere of workaday humanity, but as forms in which the divine essence itself is manifested, and in which corporeality is but transitory and accidental. In the

[48] For details, see "Neuplatonische und gnostische Elemente im Ḥadīṯ," pp. 325ff. [= *Gesammelte Schriften*, V, 115ff.; partial French translation in *Arabica*, VII (1960), 9f.].

[49] Ibn Saʿd, V, 74:14.

[50] *Ibid.*, I, i, 113:8, based on Qur'ān 5:67: *wallāhu yaʿṣimuka min al-nās* (God protects you against people), which has been interpreted to mean the Prophet's bodily immunity. This is the subject of the eighth chapter of Māwardī's *Aʿlām al-nubūwa*, pp. 53-59.

[51] Montet, "Le Culte des saints musulmans," p. 32; cf. Achille Robert, "Fanatisme et légendes arabes," *Revue des traditions populaires*, XIX (1904), 110.

lists of Shī'ī sects furnished by Muslim polemicists and historians of religion (Ibn Ḥazm, Shahrastānī, and so on) we meet with the different varieties of this form of belief, whose representatives are still numerous today. One example is the group of sects known under the general name *'Alī-ilāhī*, that is, those who believe in 'Alī-the-God, a name that adequately describes the essential in their belief.[52] It combines the apotheosis of 'Alī with the elimination of essential parts of Islamic law. Unless divinity is extended also to Muhammad, the elevation of 'Alī often leads in such heresies to a lowering of the Prophet's rank to beneath that of the divine 'Alī. Some such sectaries concluded that it must have been by error that the angel Gabriel delivered God's message to Muhammad rather than to 'Alī, for whom it had been meant. Another sect, the *'Ulyānīya*, was also called the *Dhammīya*, "the rebukers," because they rebuked the Prophet for having usurped the dignity that belonged to 'Alī.[53] In the sect of the *Nuṣayrīs*, with whom we shall further concern ourselves near the end of this chapter, Muhammad is reduced, in relation to the divine 'Alī, to the subordinate function of "the veil" (*ḥijāb*).

The Shī'īs themselves call people who hold such beliefs *ghulāt*, "those who exceed the bounds." Their origins lie in early Islam. They appeared simultaneously with the political partisans of the 'Alid family. In very old hadiths, known also in Shī'ī circles, 'Alī and the 'Alids are themselves represented as objecting to such an overestimation of them, which can only result in breeding aversion to the family of 'Alī.[54]

There is yet a further aspect to these extravagant ideas. Heightened notions about 'Alī and his descendants were not their only consequence. They also brought about a grave change in the very concept of God; for the doctrine that the godhead was incarnate in persons of the holy 'Alid

[52] Such 'Alī-ilāhī believers may also be found, for example, among Turkoman peasants of the Kars (Ardahan) district, which after the war of 1877-1878 Turkey ceded to Russia. They were most recently studied by Devitzki. [On these doctrines, see *EI*[2] article "Ahl-i ḥaḳḳ" (by V. Minorsky).]

[53] Israel Friedländer, "The Heterodoxies of the Shiites in the Presentation of Ibn Ḥazm," *JAOS*, XXIX (1908), 102. Similar doctrines were proclaimed by al-Shalmaghānī, who had declared himself God and was executed in 322/934 in Baghdad. In his system of the progressive incarnations of divinity, Moses and Muhammad are considered impostors; the former because he acted treacherously in the mission entrusted to him by Hārūn, the latter because he did likewise in the mission entrusted to him by 'Alī. Yāqūt, ***Irshād al-arīb***, I, 302:13.

[54] M. J. de Goeje, "Al-Belādhorī's Ansāb al-aschrāf," *ZDMG*, XXXVIII (1884), 391; Ibn Sa'd, III, i, 26:10ff.; V, 158:18ff. Cf. I. Friedländer, " 'Abdallāh b. Sabā, der Begründer des Šī'a, und sein jüdischer Ursprung," *ZA*, XXIII (1909), 318 n. 3.

family paved the way to excessively materialistic ideas of divinity. In such extremist circles, completely mythological conceptions grew up, leaving those who professed them without a vestige of a right to contrast their faith to paganism.

It would take us too far afield to discuss in detail all those systems that burgeoned from the Shīʿī doctrine of incarnation. The sects bear the names of their founders: Bayyānīya, Mughīrīya, and so on. In translations of their descriptions by Muslim heresiographers, their doctrines are there for all to see.[55] To this literature I can refer those who wish more detailed proofs that Shīʿism was a particularly fecund soil for absurdities suited to undermine and wholly disintegrate the Islamic doctrine of God.

9. Amidst such extravagance—and the objective observer may regard even the moderate Shīʿī doctrine of the *Imāms* as extravagant—the doctrine of the sinlessness and infallibility of the *Imāms* took the form of strict dogma. It is one of the fundamental doctrines of Shīʿī Islam.

In orthodox Islam, as well, the questions are stressed: are prophets sinless by virtue of their prophethood, and, in particular, did the last and greatest of the prophets enjoy such immunity? An affirmative answer to these questions is certainly an obligatory dogma for every believing Muslim.[56] But the scope of the dogma is relative, as readily appears from the extreme variety of forms in which it has been stated, from an early period, by accepted doctrinal authorities. They are, for instance, not of one mind whether the quality of sinlessness extends to the time before the prophetic call, or only sets in when the person in question receives the divine message. Nor are the orthodox theologians of one mind whether the sinlessness granted to prophets extends only to grave sins, or includes all manner of lapses. Some, who admit a privilege of immunity only to grave sins, concede that prophets, no less than other mortals, are exposed to venial sins or at least "slips," *zalal*; that prophets also "occasionally choose the less excellent of two possible ways of action." Remarkably, an attempt was made to ascribe an exceptional position to John the Baptist (Yaḥyā ibn Zakarīyā in the Qur'ān): a hadith asserts that he never sinned or even thought of a misstep.[57] But this met with scant approval.

When the doctrine of sinlessness is applied to Muhammad himself,

[55] Friedländer, "Heterodoxies," *JAOS*, XXVIII (1907), 55ff.

[56] Klein, *The Religion of Islam*, p. 73. Even the philosopher Avicenna accepts it as indisputable that prophets are "in no way susceptible to error or forgetfulness." Cf. *Die Metaphysik Avicennas*, translation and commentary by Max Horten (Halle, 1907), p. 88:19.

[57] Nawawī, *Tahdhīb al-asmā'*, p. 624:3. Yaḥyā ibn Zakarīyā received special favors in other respects as well; cf. Ibn Sa'd, IV, ii, 76:11.

there is less diversity of opinion. Grave and trivial sins are equally barred from his conduct both before and after his calling. This is certainly contrary to the intention of the earliest Muslims, who put in the Prophet's mouth confessions of sinfulness and of a need for repentance: "Return to God (= repent), for I too return a hundred times a day."[58] "My heart is often veiled, and a hundred times a day I pray God for forgiveness."[59] These sentences are in harmony with the assumption behind the following prayer attributed to the Prophet: "My Lord, accept my penitence and hear my prayer and wash away my guilt (*ḥawbatī*) and establish my proof, guide my heart, strengthen my tongue and pluck all ill-will from my heart."[60] People convinced of the sinlessness of the Prophet would not have represented him as speaking and praying so. And had the Prophet himself been convinced of his sinlessness, he would not have received the revelation (Qur'ān 48:2) in the midst of his proud presentiment of approaching victory:[61] "That God may forgive you (the Prophet) all your sins, from the first to the last."[62]

For our present interest in the theological issue of immunity to sin this is the essential: in none of the diverse orthodox views, including Muhammad's own, on the sinlessness of the Prophet, is this ethical privilege anything but a gift of grace (*luṭf*) God conferred upon the Prophet. It was not a necessary attribute inherent from birth in his substance. Moreover, in Sunnī theology, this dogma has no bearing on the question of doctrinal infallibility. On the contrary, the human limitations of the Prophet are always so emphatically thrown into relief that any innate supernatural knowledge would appear wholly irreconcilable with the fundamental ideas held of the Prophet's character. Like his sinlessness, his knowledge in excess of the knowledge of others was not a general virtue inherent in his person. His knowledge was the result of instruction received, in specific instances, from God. People believe in the Prophet's veracity in order that they may acknowledge as God's revela-

[58] Ibn Sa'd, VI, 32:5.

[59] 'Alī al-Qārī, *Sharḥ al-fiqh al-akbar*, p. 51. There is a discussion of this hadith in Subkī, *Ṭabaqāt*, V, 123. The Prophet is represented as voicing anxiety over his fate in the next world: "I do not know what will happen to me." Ibn Sa'd, III, i, 289 last line.

[60] Qālī, *Amālī*, II, 267.

[61] Tradition (Ibn Sa'd, II, i, 76) connects this saying with the treaty of Ḥudaybiya (A.H. 6), which it regards, unfathomably, as a victory (*fatḥ*) although in reality it was a humiliation. This was also sensed by some Muslim historians: 'Umar, they say, would not have entered into such a treaty (*ibid.*, p. 74:5).

[62] For an explanation of the expression, cf. A. Fischer, "Zu Musil's zwei arabischen Inschriften aus Arabia Petraea," *ZDMG*, LXII (1908), 280.

tion all that he brought as such. His prophetic office was based on election to interpret the divine Will, not on his personal aptitude; he did not bring to his prophethood intellectual advantages that raised him above the level of human knowledge. In the Qur'ān, this is stated explicitly. Nor did the ideas that the theologians of early generations expressed in the form of hadiths go further. His adversaries wished to embarrass the Prophet with questions about things he did not know. "Why do they ask me about things I am ignorant of? I am but a man, and know only what God gives me to know."[63] In the orthodox view, the assumption that anyone besides God might know the hidden things is heresy and unbelief, a defiance of Qur'ān 27:65: "There is in heaven and earth no one but God who knows that which is hidden." This negation includes the Prophet himself.[64] How much more it applies to other people!

The Sunnī Muslims have great respect for the pious and learned among the Prophet's posterity—the very men who are the *Imāms* of the Shī'īs. But the Sunnīs do not ascribe different personal attributes to them than to other learned and pious Muslims. For example, in speaking of Muḥammad, surnamed al-Bāqir, the fifth-generation direct descendant of the Prophet, a Sunnī theologian acknowledges his profound learning—thanks to which he received the epithet *al-bāqir*, "the one who cuts through"—and praises his exemplary piety and submission to God. But to characterize him the theologian says only this: "He was an excellent man of the generation of Followers (*tābi'ī*, one of those who came after the generation of Companions) an outstanding *imām* (meaning scholar) on whose excellence agreement is unanimous. He is numbered among the *fuqahā'* (jurists) of the city of Medina."[65] The Shī'īs, who recognize him as their fifth *Imām*, were to characterize him very differently. For them he was no simple scholar of the law from Medina, but a sharer in the immaculate luminous substance of the Prophet's family. Even the Shī'ī writer I have already cited—modern, writing in English, imbued with rationalist ideas—describes Ḥusayn, for example, as the "primordial cause of existence" . . . "the essential connection between cause and effect" . . . "the golden link between God and man."[66]

The orthodox Sunnī position regarding the estimation of the Prophet and his holy descendants has not been invalidated by the childish and

[63] In Damīrī, *Ḥayāt al-ḥayawān*, II, 216:21, under the entry *ghirnīq*.

[64] 'Alī al-Qārī, *Sharḥ al-fiqh al-akbar*, p. 136 bottom.

[65] Nawawī, *Tahdhīb al-asmā'*, p. 113:7.

[66] Badshah Husain, *Ḥusain in the Philosophy of History*, p. 5.

fabulous notions with which fantasy has adorned the Prophet's figure. These have never become part of what a Muslim is obliged to believe. The mystic al-Sha'rānī collected enough of them to fill a whole chapter, in which the following excellencies, among others, are ascribed to the Prophet: "He could see not only forward but also backward; he possessed the gift of vision in the dark; when he walked by the side of a man who was by nature taller than he, his stature equaled the other man's; when he sat, his shoulder was above the shoulders of all who sat with him; his body never cast a shadow for he was all light."[67] But there can be no doubt that these notions show the influence of the exuberant theories that the Shī'īs had formed of their *Imāms*, to whom the Prophet could naturally not be inferior.[68] This is an additional proof of the previously mentioned Shī'ī connections of Sufism.

10. All these questions acquire an entirely different significance in Shī'ī Islam. The attributes ascribed to the souls of the *Imāms* elevate them above the measure of human nature: the *Imāms* are—as we have already seen—"free of evil impulses." Sin cannot come near them; the substance of divine light that lodges in them could not be reconciled with sinful inclinations. Moreover, it also confers on them the highest degree of certain knowledge, complete infallibility.[69] The Shī'īs teach that statements traced to the *Imāms* through reliable chains of transmission are to be accepted as more conclusive than the direct evidence of the senses. Such statements are, thanks to the infallibility of their authors, suited to offer absolute certainty, while the senses are susceptible to illusion and error.[70] Besides the religious knowledge available to all Muslims, the *Imāms* possess a secret knowledge they hand down each to the next: an apocalyptic tradition inherited by generation after generation of the holy family, that encompasses both the truths of religion and all that happens in the world. 'Alī knew not only the true meaning of the Qur'ān, which is hidden from the ordinary understanding, but also everything that would happen until the day of Resurrection. Every revolution that would "lead hundreds

[67] *Kashf al-ghumma 'an jamī' al-umma* (Cairo, A.H. 1281), II, 62-75, following Suyūṭī.

[68] All the qualities of the Prophet enumerated by Sha'rānī are also found in the picture that Shī'ī fantasy draws of him. See, for example, a popular presentation of Shī'ī doctrine, written in Turkish, by 'Abd al-Raḥīm Khō'ī (Istanbul, A.H. 1327), p. 10.

[69] Jāḥiẓ, *Al-tarbī' wa'l-tadwīr*, p. 137:17ff. (= *Rasā'il*, Cairo, A.H. 1324, p. 129 bottom) [76], mentions the Shī'ī view that the *Imāms* occupy a higher position than the prophets inasmuch as the prophets are susceptible to sin although not to error, but the *Imāms* neither sin nor err.

[70] Asad Allāh al-Kāẓimī, *Kashf al-qinā' 'an wujūb ḥujjīyat al-ijmā'* (Bombay, A.H. 1316), p. 209.

astray and bring hundreds to the right path" was known to him; he knew who would stir them up and who would lead them.[71] Belief in this secret prophetic knowledge of 'Alī prompted Shī'īs to compose odd literary products that reputedly contain his mysterious revelations.[72]

'Alī's knowledge passed, in the form of a secret tradition, to the *Imāms* who succeeded him. The *Imāms*, too, are inspired and can convey nothing but the truth. They therefore constitute the sole, unsurpassable, doctrinal authority, and thus they are the ones entitled to carry on the Prophet's office. Only their statements and decisions can demand unconditional belief and obedience. To have authentic validity, all religious doctrine must therefore go back to one of the *Imāms*. This form of verification of all doctrine is dominant in the Shī'ī religious literature. The source of a hadith is not the "Companion" who heard it from the Prophet's own mouth; it is the *Imām*, who alone has the authority to announce and interpret God's, and the Prophet's, will. To the *Imāms* are ascribed also the origins of the Qur'ānic exegesis peculiar to the Shī'a. In it, the most sublime and the most trivial are alike understood to have refer-

[71] Ya'qūbī, *Ta'rīkh*, II, 525 bottom. About a book by 'Alī in which the deeper sense of the Qur'ān is explained, see Ibn Sa'd, II, ii, 101:19. The Khārijites ridicule the secret knowledge attributed to the 'Alids; *Aghānī*, XX, 107:16ff.

[72] They allege possession of mysterious works ascribed to 'Alī (see previous note). These works are sometimes characterized as the sum of the Prophets' whole religious knowledge, sometimes as apocalyptic-prophetic writings in which are disclosed the great events of all time to come. The Prophet entrusted them to 'Alī, and they have been transmitted from generation to generation by the chain of *Imāms* who are, each in his own age, the bearers of the occult knowledge of the 'Alids. Of these books, the *Jafr* and the *Jāmi'a* are most frequently mentioned. The early Baghdad Mu'tazilite, Bishr ibn al-Mu'tamir (ninth century), in one of his didactic poems calls the Shī'īs people "deluded by the *Jafr*" (Jāḥiẓ, *Ḥayawān*, VI, 94:1 [VI, 289, vs. 46]). In Shī'ī literature even the outward appearance of these alleged secret books is described: the *Jāmi'a* is a scroll of seventy arm-lengths (measured by the Prophet's arm; see Kulīnī, *Uṣūl*, pp. 146–48; Kāẓimī, *Kashf al-qinā'*, p. 162). For the literature on this subject, see "Materialien zur Kenntnis der Almohadenbewegung in Nordafrika," pp. 123ff. [= *Gesammelte Schriften*, II, 284ff.]. Besides these two occult works, Kulīnī mentions a *Maṣḥaf Fāṭima* in the Imams' possession. The Prophet is said to have entrusted it before his death to his daughter, and it is said to be three times the size of the Qur'ān.

In time, occult prophetic books in general came to be called *Jafr*. This word seems to be disguised in the Maghribī *lenjefār* in E. Doutté, "Un Texte arabe en dialecte oranais," *Mémoires de la Société de Linguistique*, XII (1903), 347. The use and explanation of *jafr* books is one of the preeminent subjects of Islamic occultism. Cf., for example, *Fihrist al-kutub al-'arabīya al-maḥfūẓa bi'l-kutubkhāna al-khidīwīya al-miṣrīya* (Cairo, A.H. 1306–1309), VII, 83, 101. The famous mystic Muḥyī al-Dīn ibn 'Arabī took considerable part in this literary activity (*ibid.*, p. 552). About a *jafr* work by Abū Bakr al-Dimashqī (d. 1102/1690) preserved in the treasury of the Turkish sultans, see Murādī, *Silk al-durar* (Bulaq, A.H. 1291-1301), I, 51. [On these writings, see *EI*² article "Djafr" (by T. Fahd).]

ence to the theory of the *Imāms* and the other Shīʿī doctrines. Familiarity with this literature is indispensable for a comprehensive inquiry into the spirit of Shīʿism.[73]

It follows from all this that some of the principles that in Sunnī theology have a recognized role in the ascertainment of religious truth and propriety, in Shīʿī theology have a far lower value as sources of knowledge. The *ijmāʿ* itself is reduced to a mere formality. In theory, it is true, the influence of *ijmāʿ* on the resolution of religious questions is acknowledged. But Shīʿī theology sees the significance of consensus only in the fact that it cannot come into existence without the contribution of the *Imāms*. Only this integrating element can give meaning to the principle of *ijmāʿ*. Besides, in the Shīʿī view, history has hardly demonstrated that the *ijmāʿ* is a touchstone of truth. If the Sunnīs base their recognition of the historical caliphate on the consensus of believers, which after the Prophet's death gave form to, and sanctioned, the polity of Islam, the Shīʿīs see this very recognition as proof that mere *ijmāʿ* does not always match with truth and righteousness. Indeed, in resolving the question of the caliphate according to the Sunnī view, the *ijmāʿ* gave its sanction to injustice and violence. Thus this collective authority is diminished, or else interpreted to imply the agreement of the *Imāms*. Only the teaching and the will of the infallible *Imām*, or of his authorized deputy, carry a sure guarantee of truth and justice. Just as in any age the *Imām* alone is the legitimate political head of the Islamic community, so the *Imām* alone has the authority to decide questions that have not already been decided at the outset and for all time by the received law, and the *Imām* alone has the authority to interpret and apply the law.

Thus if we wish to characterize in brief the essential difference between Sunnī and Shīʿī Islam, we may say that the former is based on the *ijmāʿ*, and the latter on the authoritarian principle.[74]

11. We have indicated that even in the early period, when their theories were still in development, there was among Shīʿīs no unanimity on the persons of the *Imāms*. One of the earliest practical manifestations of the Shīʿī idea was linked, as we have seen (Sec. 3 above), to an *Imām* whose descent from ʿAlī was not through the Fāṭimid line. But even when

[73] See note 25 above.

[74] It is very much in the spirit of Shīʿism that the modern Shīʿī scholar Badshah Husain (*Ḥusain in the Philosophy of History*, p. 14) condemns the "pseudo-democratic form of government (in the time of the early caliphs) based on the consciousness of the general tendency of the people."

Fāṭimid descendants were chosen, different groups among the partisans of ʿAlī set up different chains of *Imāms*. The great diversity of branches within that family had furnished abundant occasion for this. After the death of the *Imām* Abū Muḥammad al-ʿAskarī, the Shīʿīs were already divided into fourteen varieties,[75] each preferring a different ʿAlid line for its sequence of Imāms.[76] The most widely accepted chain of *Imāms*, recognized among Shīʿīs to this day, is that of the sect of the so-called "Twelvers" (or *Imāmīs*). According to this group, the office of *Imām* passed from ʿAlī, through his direct descendants, down to an eleventh visible *Imām*, whose son and successor, Muḥammad Abū ʾl-Qāsim (b. Baghdad 872), was taken from earth while still a child not yet eight years old. He has lived since in occultation, invisible to mankind, and will appear at the end of time as the *Imām-Mahdī*, the savior of the world, to rid the world of all injustice and to establish the rule of peace and righteousness. This is the so-called "Hidden *Imām*," who has continued to live since his disappearance, and whose reappearance is daily awaited by the Shīʿī believer. Belief in a hidden *Imām* has spread among all branches of Shīʿism. Each Shīʿī group believes in the continued existence and future *parousia* of the *Imām* whom it regards as the last of its particular line of *Imāms*.

The various branches of the Shīʿa substantiate their belief in the continued life of the *Imām* they regard as the last, and as the one to reappear in the future, by means of authoritative statements invented to support this belief. We may gain an idea of the nature of such proofs from a saying ascribed to Mūsā al-Kāẓim (d. 183/799), the seventh *Imām* of the Twelvers, by the branch that regards him as the last link in the chain, the Hidden *Imām* who will one day return: "If anyone says about me that he

[75] The theologians of the various Shīʿī subsects developed a rich polemical literature against one another. It deals not only with differences about the imamate but also with other theological and legal issues on which the various Shīʿī groups came to hold divergent opinions. At the turn of the third and fourth Islamic centuries, the Imāmī theologian Ḥasan ibn Muḥammad al-Nawbakhtī, an experienced *mutakallim*, wrote a *Kitāb firaq al-shīʿa*, "Book on the Sects of the Shīʿa" [edited by Helmut Ritter, Bibliotheca Islamica IV (Leipzig, 1931)], and *Al-Radd ʿalā firaq al-shīʿa mā khalā al-imāmīya*, "Refutation of the Sects of the Shīʿa with the exception of the Imāmīya." Cf. Abūʾl-ʿAbbās Aḥmad al-Najāshī, *Kitāb al-rijāl* (Shīʿī biographical dictionary of scholars, Bombay, A.H. 1317), p. 46. Jāḥiẓ, who lived shortly after the emergence of the sects (d. 255/869), wrote a book about the Shīʿīs (*Kitāb al-rāfiḍa*) which unfortunately seems lost. He refers to it in a short essay "Fī bayān madhāhib al-shīʿa" (*Rasāʾil*, pp. 178–85; the citation is on p. 181:3 from bottom), which, however, delivers less than its title promises. [On these essays, cf. Charles Pellat, "Essai d'inventaire de l'oeuvre Ǧāḥiẓienne," *Arabica*, III (1956), 147ff., nos. 72, 153, 192.]

[76] Kāẓimī, *Kashf al-qināʿ*, p. 80.

tended me in my sickness, washed my corpse, embalmed it, wrapped it in shrouds, lowered it into the grave and then shook the dust of my grave from himself, you may denounce him as a liar. If (after my disappearance) people ask about me, the answer is 'He lives, thank God.' Cursed be the man who answers 'He is dead' when he is asked about me."[77]

The "return" (*al-raj'a*) is thus one of the decisive elements in the *imām*-theory of each branch of the Shī'a. Opinions differ only concerning the person of the hidden and awaited *Imām*, and the line to which he belongs.[78]

From the outset, those who hung their hopes on 'Alī and his descendants nurtured a solid confidence that the vanished *Imām* would one day return. At first this belief attached itself to 'Alī himself. A group of his followers, indoctrinated by 'Abdallāh ibn Sabā,[h] venerated 'Alī even during his lifetime as a superhuman being, refused (in the Docetist manner) to believe in his death, and were convinced that he had vanished and would some day return. This is the oldest manifestation of the extravagant cult of 'Alī, and the first manifestation in general of Shī'ī sectarianism.[79] The next object of the belief in an *Imām* who had vanished

[77] Najāshī, *Kitāb al-rijāl*, p. 237.

[78] About this belief, now see Friedländer, "Heterodoxies," *JAOS*, XXIX (1908), 23-30. This study is an important contribution to our knowledge of the internal sectarian development of the Shī'a.

[h] The role and, indeed, the identity of 'Abdallāh ibn Sabā have been questioned by subsequent scholarship. See the article on him in *EI*² (by M.G.S. Hodgson).

[79] About 'Abdallāh ibn Sabā and the doctrines he proclaimed about the nature of 'Alī, now see Friedländer's " 'Abdallāh b. Sabā," pp. 296ff. For the belief in 'Alī's return, see Jāḥiẓ, *Ḥayawān*, V, 134 [V, 450f.]. For the belief in *raj'a*, cf. Ibn Sa'd, III, i, 26:16; VI, 159:13.

In (non-Shī'ī) Sufi circles, too, the idea of 'Alī's continued existence and future reappearance found occasional expression, in connection with the apotheosis of 'Alī that was current among them. Sha'rānī reports that the saint 'Alī Wafā' said: " 'Alī ibn Abī Ṭālib was carried up (to heaven) as Jesus had been; like Jesus, he will once descend from there." To this Sha'rānī adds: "Sayyidī 'Alī al-Khawwāṣ (my master) taught the same. I heard him say: 'Noah kept one of the boards of the Ark, in the name of 'Alī ibn Abī Ṭālib. Upon it 'Alī would one day be assumed to heaven. This board was stored in the care of divine omnipotence until 'Alī was raised up on it to heaven.' " See *Lawāqiḥ al-anwār fī ṭabaqāt al-akhyār* (Cairo, A.H. 1299), II, 59. This Sufi legend is, incidentally, a further elaboration of the Islamic legend about the construction of the Ark. God bid Noah prepare 124,000 boards for building it; on each God caused to appear the name of one of the prophets, beginning with Adam and ending with Muhammad. In the end it turned out that four more boards were needed to complete the Ark. Noah prepared these, and on them the names of four Companions appeared. (The first four Sunnī caliphs are meant, the fourth of them being 'Alī.) So fitted out, the Ark could now hold up in the flood. The legend is related at length in Muḥammad ibn 'Abd al-Raḥmān al-Hamadānī's book about the days of the week, *Kitāb al-sub'īyāt fī mawā'iẓ al-barīyāt* (Bulaq, A.H. 1292, on the margin of Fashnī's commentary to the Forty Traditions of Nawawī), pp. 8-9.

and would return was 'Alī's son Muḥammad ibn al-Ḥanafīya, whose partisans were convinced of his continued life and future reappearance.

The idea of "the return" did not originate among the Shī'īs. Judaeo-Christian influence probably contributed this belief to Islam.[80] The prophet Elias, who was carried off to heaven and will at the end of time reappear on earth to establish again the rule of righteousness, is the most likely prototype of the Hidden *Imāms* who have been taken from earth, live unseen, and will one day reappear as *Mahdīs*, saviors of the world.

Similar religious ideas, and eschatological hopes related to such ideas, can also be found in many other environments. The Dosithean sect did not believe in the death of its founder, Dositheos, and fostered a conviction of his continued life.[81] In the belief of the Indian Vaishnavas, at the end of the present world-cycle Vishnu will appear incarnated as Kalkhi, to liberate the land of the Arians from their oppressors (by whom the Muslim conquerors are meant). The Ethiopian Christians await the return of their messianic king Theodoros.[82] Among the Mongols the belief is widespread to this day that Genghis Khan, at whose tomb sacrifices are offered, promised before his death that after eight or ten centuries he would reappear on earth and help the Mongols throw off the Chinese yoke.[83] After the failure of the movements they had called forth, Islamic heresies attached similar hopes to the reappearance of their founders. After the execution of Bihafrīd (one of those who at the beginning of the 'Abbāsid period tried to stir up a Zoroastrian reaction against Islam), his followers believed that the founder had ascended to heaven and would one day reappear on earth to wreak vengeance on his enemies.[84] The followers of al-Muqanna', "The Veiled One," entertained the same notion

[80] Wellhausen, *Die religiös-politischen Oppositionsparteien*, p. 93 [= *The Religio-political Factions*, pp. 153f.]. An attempt has been made to trace this belief to older sources. Pinches concludes ("The Early Babylonian King-Lists," *Proceedings of the Society of Biblical Archaeology*, VII, 1885, 71) from cuneiform texts that in ancient Babylon there already existed a belief in the future reappearance of the ancient king Sargon I, who would reestablish the old might of the empire (*dadrum*, "the twofold king"). But Assyriological critique has rejected both reading and interpretation.

[81] Adolf Hilgenfeld, *Die Ketzergeschichte des Urchristentums* (Leipzig, 1884), p. 158 (following Origen).

[82] Cf., most recently, René Basset's introduction to *Fekkaré Iyasous* (Paris, 1909; Les Apocryphes éthiopiens, XI), pp. 4-12.

[83] René Basset, "Contes et légendes de l'Extrême-Orient," *Revue des traditions populaires*, XX (1905), 416.

[84] Bīrūnī, *Chronology of Ancient Nations*, translated by E. Sachau (London, 1879), p. 194. About Bihafrīd, see M. T. Houtsma, "Bih'afrid," *WZKM*, III (1889), 30ff.

about their leader, even after this man, who had presented himself as a divine incarnation, had burned himself to death.[85]

Until relatively modern times this religious conception has continued productive among the Islamic peoples, and not only among Shīʿīs. The Muslims of the Caucasus believe in the future return of Elijah Manṣūr, the hero of their struggle for freedom and a forerunner of Shāmil (1791), who will reappear among them one hundred years after the expulsion of the Russians.[86] In Samarkand people believe in the reappearance of the holy persons Shāh-zindeh and Qāsim ibn ʿAbbās[87] in the same way. Among the Kurds the belief is attested from at least the eighth century of the Hijra that the executed Tāj al-ʿĀrifīn (Ḥasan b. ʿAdī) will some day come back.[88]

Of all eschatological expectations of this kind—fostered by peoples of East or West, sprung from hopes of a political or religious restoration—the Shīʿī belief in the Hidden *Imām* who will return was most vigorously elaborated.[i] The theological groundwork for this belief, and its defense against the scorn of skeptics and adversaries, form a prominent part of the Shīʿī religious literature. Quite recently a work was published in Persia whose object is to secure the belief in the hidden "*Imām* of the Age" against steadily increasing skepticism.

Just as many Jewish mystics and theologians undertook, mostly on the basis of the book of Daniel, to calculate the precise time at which the Messiah would appear, so Sufis and Shīʿīs with a speculative bent undertook, on the basis of a kabbalistic use of Qurʾān passages and the numerical values of combinations of letters, to calculate the time when the reappearance of the Hidden *Imām* would take place. Treatises concerned with such calculations are listed in the bibliographic reference works of early Shīʿī literature. However, just as in Judaism the "reckoners of the End" (*meḥashshebhē qiṣṣīn*) were subjected to the severest censure,[89] so the "fix-

[85] Barhebraeus, *Taʾrīkh mukhtaṣar al-duwal*, edited by A. Ṣāliḥānī (Beirut, 1890), p. 218. Cf. "Neuplatonische und gnostische Elemente im Ḥadīṯ," pp. 337ff. [= *Gesammelte Schriften*, V, 127ff.; partial French translation in *Arabica*, VII (1960), 11f.].

[86] R. Bosworth Smith, *Mohammed and Mohammedanism*, 2nd ed. (London, 1876), p. 32.

[87] Henry Landsdell, *Russian Central Asia* (London, 1885), I, 572.

[88] *Muhammedanische Studien*, II, 324 [= *Muslim Studies*, II, 295].

[i] For a useful survey of Islamic and other political messianic movements, see Emanuel Sarkisyanz, *Russland und der Messianismus des Orient, Sendungsbewusstsein und politischer Chiliasmus des Ostens* (Tübingen, 1955).

[89] Bab. Talmud. *Sanhedrin* 97b. About the computation of the coming of the Messiah, based on the numerical value of the words *hastēr astīr* in Deuteronomy 31:18, and on Daniel

ers of the Time" (*waqqātūn*) were branded as liars by the orthodox authorities of the moderate Shī'a. Sayings were put into the mouths of *Imāms* forbidding people from engagement in these speculations.[90] The facts had proved the reckonings delusive. It is easy to understand the mood of annoyance that these promises, made with an air of assurance, must have elicited.

12. So far we have been considering the belief in the future appearance

---

12:11-13, see Bīrūnī, *Al-Āthār al-bāqiya*, edited by E. Sachau (Leipzig, 1878), pp. 15-17 (Martin Schreiner, "Zur Geschichte der Polemik zwischen Juden und Muhammedanern," *ZDMG*, XLII, 1888, 600). For this literature, see the bibliography in M. Steinschneider, "Apocalypsen mit polemischer Tendenz," *ZDMG*, XXVIII (1874), 628 n. 2; S. Poznanski, "Miscellen über Saadja III," *Monatsschrift für Geschichte und Wissenschaft des Judentums*, XLIV (1900), 400ff., 508ff.

[90] *Kadhaba al-waqqātūna*, "the fixers of the time lie." To the *Imāms*' sayings about this a special chapter (*Bāb karāhiyat al-tawqīt*, "Chapter on the reprehensibility of fixing the time") is devoted by Kulīnī, *Uṣūl al-kāfī*, pp. 232-33. Further material is added in a Shī'ī theological work by Dildār 'Alī, *Mir'āt al-'uqūl fī 'ilm al-uṣūl* (Lucknow, A.H. 1318-1319, also known as *'Imād al-islām fī 'ilm al-kalām*), I, 115f. Ṭūsī (*Fihrist kutub al-shī'a*, edited by Aloys Sprenger et al., Calcutta, 1853-1855, no. 617) lists a *Kitāb waqt khurūj al-qā'im*, "The time of the *Mahdī*'s appearance," by Muḥammad ibn Ḥasan ibn Jumhūr al-Qummī, a man notorious as a Shī'ī extremist (*ghālī*) and a fabricator of false traditions. It is presumably in this context that it is said of a Shī'ī theologian that he was an extremist *fī'l-waqt*, "in the (computation of the) time (of the *Mahdī's* appearance);" cf. Najāshī, *Kitāb al-rijāl*, p. 64:8. A computation by Ibn 'Arabī regarding the *Mahdī* is criticized at length by Ibn Khaldūn, *Muqaddima*, edited by E. M. Quatremère (Paris, 1858), II, 167. The Ḥurūfīs (Sec. 18 below) also repudiate such computations, although one would expect as a matter of course that they would engage in such kabbalistic practices; Clément Huart, *Textes persans relatifs à la secte des Houroûfîs*, pp. 70ff. Related to computations of the time of the *Mahdī* are the kabbalistic calculations concerning the *sā'a* ("hour," that is, the end of the world, the hour of the Resurrection). Correct orthodoxy rejected such calculations as being contrary to the Qur'ān, on the ground of Sura 6, vs. 59 ("He keeps the keys of that which is hidden, none but He knows them) and Sura 7, vs. 187 ("They will ask you about the time fixed for the hour. Say: 'My Lord has the knowledge of it; none but He will reveal it when the time has arrived.' " Cf. Matt. 24:36.) The material for this theological topic may be found, in great detail, in Qasṭallānī's commentary on Bukhārī, *Ijārāt* no. 11 (IV, 150), *Tafsīr* no. 88 (VII, 232), no. 335 (VII, 458f.), *Riqāq* no. 39 (IX, 323).

Muslim astronomers were much occupied with calculating, from the constellations, the duration of the Islamic empire. The philosopher Kindī devoted a monograph to the subject; it has been studied by Otto Loth, "Al-Kindī als Astrolog," *Morgenländische Forschungen* (Fleischer Festschrift; Leipzig, 1875), pp. 263-309. Besides astrological theories, Kindī uses occult, kabbalistic interpretations of letters and numbers (*ibid.*, p. 297). He extols the Arabic script for its suitability for such operations (Balawī, *Kitāb alif-bā*, Cairo, A.H. 1287, I, 99:6). The Ikhwān al-ṣafā' (*Rasā'il*, IV, 225) also teach that the appearance of the *ṣāḥib al-amr*, in whose behalf they conduct their propaganda, is determined by the conjunctions of the stars.

[For another presentation of these doctrines, in the context of a treatise on magic, see *"Picatrix": das Ziel des Weisen von Pseudo-Mağrīṭī*, German translation by Hellmut Ritter and Martin Plessner (London, 1962), chapter 4.]

of a messianic figure as a doctrine of Shīʿī Islam. We must now add, to round out our discussion, that among followers of the orthodox *sunna* as well the belief is current that at the end of time God will send into the world one who will correct its evils. They too call him the *Imām-Mahdī*, the one guided aright by God.[91] This devout hope carried an urgency among pious Muslims; it was like a sigh of longing in the midst of a political and social system against which their religious consciousness constantly rebelled.

The circumstances of public life struck them, after all, as a violation of the ideals they upheld, as a continued offense against religion and social justice. They embraced the position, it is true, that in the interest of a united community a good Muslim must not "split the staff" but must, for the common good, resign himself to steadfast endurance (*ṣabr*) of the injustice that by God's decree prevails, and to patient perseverance in the face of evil. All the more intense was their emotional need for a reconcilement of reality with the demands of their devout convictions. Such reconcilement was offered by the firm hope for a *Mahdī*.[92] It has been

---

[91] In its early religious use, the word *mahdī* did not yet have the eschatological sense that was later associated with it. Jarīr (*Naqāʾiḍ Jarīr wa'l-Farazdaq*, II, 994, vs. 29) gives this epithet to Abraham. When Ḥassān ibn Thābit in his elegy for Muhammad (*Dīwān*, Tunis, A.H. 1281, p. 24:4 [edited by Walīd ʿArafāt (London, 1971), I, 269, vs. 2]) celebrates him as *mahdī*, he has no messianic associations in mind; his intention is to praise the Prophet as a man who always walked in the right path (cf. also *al-muhtadī* in vs. 5 of the same poem, or *al-murshad* in another poem of mourning for the Prophet, Ibn Saʿd, II, ii, 94:9). Among the early caliphs, ʿAlī was, in Sunnī circles as well, frequently distinguished with this epithet. The Prophet is represented as describing, in a comparison of his immediate successors, Abū Bakr as a pious ascetic, ʿUmar as a vigorous man of unerring judgment, and ʿAlī as *hādiyan mahdīyan*, one who guides and is guided aright (Ibn al-Athīr, *Usd al-ghāba*, IV, 31:3). Sulaymān ibn Ṣurad, Ḥusayn's avenger, calls him (after his death) *Ḥusayn . . . al-mahdī ibn al-mahdī* (Ṭabarī, II, 546:11).

The Umayyad caliphs' panegyrists also conferred this epithet on their princes. Farazdaq accords it alike to the Umayyads (*Naqāʾid*, I, 374, vs. 60) and to the Prophet (*ibid.*, p. 349, vs. 40). The same is frequent in Jarīr (*Dīwān*, I, 58:16 [I, 288, vs. 12], of ʿAbd al-Malik [actually of Hishām]; II, 40:7 from bottom [II, 717, vs. 13], of Sulaymān; 94:5 [I, 225, vs. 43], of Hishām; cf. *imām al-hudā*, Ch. III, n. 3). Pious people did, however, regard one Umayyad, ʿUmar II, as the real *Mahdī* (Ibn Saʿd, V, 245:5ff.). It is only much later (576/1180) that a flattering poet, Ibn al-Taʿāwīdhī, gives this epithet to his caliph (al-Nāṣir) in the heightened sense: he celebrates al-Nāṣir as the *Mahdī*; to await another messianic *Mahdī* besides him has become superfluous (*Dīwān*, edited by D. S. Margoliouth, Cairo, 1903, p. 158, vss. 5–6).

The word is commonly used with reference to converts to Islam (the Turks use the form *mühtedi*). Two rectors of the al-Azhar mosque bore, as converts, the surname al-Mahdī: the Copt Muḥammad (originally Hibat Allāh) al-Ḥifnī (1812-1815) and Shaykh Muḥammad al-ʿAbbāsī al-Mahdī (in the seventies and eighties of the last century; C. Snouck Hurgronje, "Berichtigung" in *ZDMG*, LIII, 1899, 703f. [= *Verspreide Geschriften*, II, 417f.])

[92] On the idea of the *mahdī* in Islam, and associated subjects, see James Darmesteter, *Le*

shown that in the first stage of its history, this hope coincided with the awaiting of the second coming of Jesus, who, as *Mahdī*, was to establish the rule of righteousness. As belief in the *Mahdī* developed, however, this motif was soon joined by others, next to which Jesus' eschatological activity came to be seen as an accessory event. People of a more realistic bent occasionally supposed the hope for the *Mahdī* to be near fulfillment by certain princes who, so they thought, were about to establish the rule of divine law and righteousness. After the fall of the Umayyads, much was expected from certain rulers of the 'Abbāsid dynasty. But in due course people awoke from these happy but deceptive hopes. The world as the pious saw it remained as evil as it had been. The idea of the *Mahdī* became more and more a utopian idea, whose realization was put off into a dim future, and which proved suited to steady enrichment with crude eschatological fables. When the time comes, God will awaken a man from the Prophet's family who will restore the Prophet's ruined work and "fill the world with righteousness as it is now filled with oppression." Features of the Zoroastrian idea of Saoshyant were combined with the Judaeo-Christian motifs to which the belief in the *Mahdī* owes its origin. Irresponsible fancy and idle speculation contributed their share to the emergence in time of a luxuriant mythology. The hadith also took possession of these beliefs, which were much discussed among the believers. The Prophet was represented as giving an exact personal description of the one who, he promised, would deliver the world. This description was not admitted into the rigorous collections, but was repeated in less scrupulous works.

In the course of Islamic history, this belief could also serve as justification for religio-political rebels who aspired to the overthrow of the existing order. It gained them popularity as embodiments of the idea of the *Mahdī*; it helped them precipitate vast areas of the Islamic world into turmoil and war. Everybody remembers such occurrences from the most recent history of Islam. Even in our own time aspirants to the role of *Mahdī* have appeared in various Islamic areas,[j] mostly in order to counter

---

Mahdi depuis les origines de l'Islam jusqu'à nos jours (Paris, 1885); C. Snouck Hurgronje, "Der Mahdi," *Revue coloniale internationale*, I (1886), 25ff. [= *Verspreide Geschriften*, I, 147ff.]; G. van Vloten, "Les Croyances messianiques," in his *Recherches sur la domination arabe*, pp. 54ff.; *idem*, "Zur Abbasidengeschichte," *ZDMG*, LII (1898), 218ff.; E. Blochet, *Le Messianisme dans l'hétérodoxie musulmane* (Paris, 1903); I. Friedländer, "Die Messiasidee im Islam," *Berliner Festschrift* (Frankfurt-am-Main, 1903), pp. 116-30. [See further the EI^1 article "Mahdī" (by D. B. MacDonald).]

[j] By far the best known of modern *Mahdis* is Muḥammad Aḥmad, who manifested him-

the increasing influence of European states on Muslim territories.[93] We learn from Martin Hartmann's interesting communications about modern Turkish trends that in our own day the confidence is nurtured among many Turkish Muslims that soon (in the year 1355/1936) the true *Mahdī* will appear "who will bring the whole world to submit to Islam, and whose coming will inaugurate the golden age."[94]

Shī'ī Islam was—as its very principle would lead us to expect—the most fertile soil for the cultivation of Mahdist hopes. For, from the outset, Shī'ism has been a protest against the violent suppression of divine right: the usurpation of the rights of the 'Alids, who alone had a legiti-

---

self in the Sudan in March 1881. On his movement, its background, and its consequences see P. M. Holt, *The Mahdist State in the Sudan 1881-1889, A Study of its Origins, Development and Overthrow*, 2nd ed. (Oxford, 1970). On other messianic movements, see Sarkisyanz, *Russland*.

[93] Such movements appeared especially frequently in Maghribī (North African) Islam. The Maghribīs entertain a traditional belief that the *Mahdī* will appear on Moroccan soil (Doutté, *Les Marabouts*, p. 74); hadiths have been brought to bear in support of this ("Materialien zur Kenntnis der Almohadenbewegung in Nordafrika," pp. 116f. [= *Gesammelte Schriften*, II, 277f.]). In the Maghrib, at various times, there also appeared men who claimed to be Jesus come again to earth, and who, in that capacity, incited their followers to combat foreign rule (Doutté, *Les Marabouts*, p. 68). While some of these Mahdist movements (as, for example, the one that led to the foundation of the Almohad empire in the Maghrib) had, after the overthrow of the political structures they had erected, next to no influence on posterity, in Shī'ism the traces of such movements have endured to this day. In recent centuries, a number of such sectarian developments occurred in various parts of Muslim India. They were called forth by men each of whom set himself up as the awaited *Mahdī*. The followers of these men are grouped in separate sects to this day, and each sect believes that its *Mahdī* was the one in whom the messianic hopes of Islam were fulfilled. Such sects are called *Ghayr-Mahdī*, that is, people who no longer need to believe in the future appearance of the *Mahdī*. Some of them (the Mahdawī sect) harbor a fiercely fanatic disposition against those who do not share their beliefs. For more about these sects, see Edward Sell, *The Faith of Islam* (London, 1880), pp. 81-83. In the Kirmān district (Baluchistan) the memory still lives of an Indian *Mahdī* of the late fifteenth century. Here the *Dhikrī* sect survives, and is in opposition to the Sunnīs (who are called *namāzī* because they practice the *ṣalāt* ritual, Persian *namāz*, as prescribed by the law). Most Dhikrīs belong to the nomadic population. They trace back their doctrines and practices—which differ from those of orthodox Islam—to a *Mahdī*, Muḥammad of Jawnpur, who had been driven from India, wandered from place to place, and died in the Hilmand Valley in 1505 ("Le Béloutchistan d'après l'administration britannique," *RMM*, V [1908], 142). On the "night of fate" (*laylat al-qadr*, 27 Ramaḍān)—a night sacred in orthodox Islam—they erect a circle of stones (*dā'ira*, "circular wall"; cf. Ja'far Sharīf, *Qanoon-e Islam*, translated by G. A. Herklots, London, 1832, p. 259) within which they practice their heretical rites. The sect is consequently called *Dā'ire wālī*, that is, "people of the circle." Josef Horovitz, Aligarh, to whom I owe this last piece of information, is preparing a publication devoted to the *Dā'ire wālī*. [This work was apparently never published.]

[94] Hartmann, *Der islamische Orient*, III, 152.

mate claim to rule. Belief in the *Mahdī* could here unfold and reach its fullest growth, for it was the vital nerve of the entire Shīʿī system.

In Sunnī Islam the pious awaiting of the *Mahdī* never took the fixed form of dogma, despite its theological treatment and documentation in the hadith.[95] It never seems to be more than a mythological adornment of an ideal of the future, a supplement to the orthodox system of envisioning the world. Moreover, Sunnī Islam is resolute in its rejection of the Shīʿī form of this belief. The Hidden *Imām* and his longevity are ridiculed. The Sunnīs find the Twelvers' Hidden *Imām* absurd to begin with, because Sunnī tradition demands that the *Mahdī* must bear the same name as the Prophet (Muḥammad ibn ʿAbdallāh), but the eleventh visible *Imām*, the father of the *Imām* in occultation, was called Ḥasan.[96] Besides, the future *Mahdī* of the Shīʿa vanished as a small child, at an age when he was not yet legally competent to assume the office of *Imām*, which can devolve only upon persons of age (*bāligh*). Others dispute the very existence of a surviving son of Ḥasan al-ʿAskarī.

In contrast, Shīʿī Islam assigns a central theological importance to belief in the future fulfillment of the hope that the *Mahdī* will come. It is the backbone of the Shīʿī system and one with the belief in the return (*rajʿa*) of the Hidden *Imām* into the visible world, whose new lawgiver he will be, and where he will resume the Prophet's work and restore the usurped rights of his family. He alone is able to "fill the world with justice and

[95] For example, *GAL*, I, 431, no. 25 [cf. *GAL*, SI, 767]. There is a critique of hadiths relating to the *Mahdī* in Ibn Khaldūn, *Muqaddima* (Bulaq, A.H. 1284), p. 261. Among orthodox theological authorities, the Meccan scholar Shihāb al-Dīn Aḥmad ibn Ḥajar al-Haytamī (d. 973/1565) collected, in several works, the *Mahdī* traditions of Sunnī Islam. He wrote a special work on the subject (*GAL*, II, 388, no. 6 [*GAL*, SII, 528, no. 6]). He refers to this work in a *fatwā* (*Al-Fatāwā al-ḥadīthīya*, pp. 27-32) in which he sums up the Sunnī doctrine on belief in the *Mahdī*, on the events that will accompany the appearance of this savior, and on false *Mahdīs*. This *fatwā* was elicited by an inquiry concerning "people who believe that a man, forty years dead, was the *Mahdī* whose coming at the end of time was foretold, and who declare all who do not believe in him to be unbelievers." It is likely that this belief was associated with one of the men, mentioned in n. 93 above, who in the tenth Islamic century claimed to be *Mahdīs*. Ibn Ḥajar also assembled the orthodox traditions relating to the *Mahdī* in one of the addresses he delivered in Mecca, in A.H. 1543, to combat Shīʿism. See *Al-Ṣawāʿiq al-muḥriqa* (Cairo, A.H. 1312), pp. 97-100.

[96] To invalidate this objection, the Twelvers assert that the text of the hadith stating the name of the *Mahdī* is corrupt (*muṣaḥḥaf*). In the place of "and the name of his father matches with that of my (the Prophet's) father (*abī*)," the text originally read "with that of my son (*ibnī*)," meaning that the name of the *Mahdī*'s father, Ḥasan, is identical with that of the Prophet's grandson. The use of *ibn* to refer to a grandson is not, so their argument runs, a cause for doubt. (Introduction to Manīnī's commentary on the panegyric to the *Mahdī* by Bahā' al-Dīn al-ʿĀmilī, in the appendix to the *Kashkūl*, Bulaq, A.H. 1288, p. 395.)

righteousness." Serious Shī'ī scholars have taken pains to demonstrate, in the face of Sunnī derision, the physiological and historical possibility of the *Imām*'s uncommonly long life.[97]

Even during his bodily absence (*ghayba*) the *Imām* is the true "Chief of the Age" (*qā'im al-zamān*), and he is not incapable of communicating his will to the believers.[98] He is the subject of extravagant hymns of praise by his faithful. They do not merely extol him as flattering subjects might extol their living ruler, but ascribe to him the superhuman epithets that go with the doctrine of the imamate: his high spiritual rank surpasses the lofty intelligences of the celestial spheres; he is the source of all knowledge and the goal of all longing. Shī'ī poets maintain the conviction that such poems of praise reach the hidden throne of the sublime person for whom they are meant.[99]

We can see in our own time how thoroughly the belief in the Hidden *Imam*'s active participation in the events of the world governs and orders the Shī'īs' religious and political world view, and how among Shī'ī peoples every institution, if it is to be effective, must be subordinated at

[97] Cf. my *Abhandlungen zur arabischen Philologie*, II, lxii ff.

[98] It is believed that a few chosen men had personal intercourse with the hidden *Imām*; examples may be found in Ṭūsī, *Fihrist kutub al-shī'a*, p. 353; Kāẓimī, *Kashf al-qinā'*, pp. 230f. The Egyptian Sufi 'Abd al-Wahhāb al-Sha'rānī (d. 973/1565), who was himself given to extravagant hallucinations of mystical encounters, relates in his book of the lives of Sufis that an older fellow Sufi, Ḥasan al-'Irāqī (d. 930/1522), told him that he had in his youth lodged the *Mahdī* for a whole week in his house in Damascus and had been instructed by the *Mahdī* in Sufi devotions. It was to the *Mahdī*'s blessing that he owed his long life; at the time of this communication with Sha'rānī, Ḥasan was, by his own account, 127 years old. He had spent fifty years in long journeys to China and India, then settled in Cairo, where he suffered much from the jealousy of other Sufis. They probably knew him for a fraud and an adventurer. (*Lawāqiḥ al-anwār*, II, 191.)

There are also fables about written communication with the hidden *Mahdī*. It is related that the father of the famous Shī'ī theologian Abū Ja'far Muḥammad ibn 'Alī ibn Bābūya al-Qummī (d. 351/991) sent, by a certain 'Alī ibn Ja'far ibn al-Aswad, a written petition to the "Master of the Age," requesting that the *Mahdī* intercede with God to have his childless state corrected. Soon after, he received from the *Mahdī* a written acknowledgment, in which he was promised the birth of two sons. The firstborn was none other than Abū Ja'far, who is said to have boasted his life long that he owed his existence to the good offices of the *ṣāḥib al-amr* (Najāshī, *Rijāl*, p. 184).

About an *'ālim* who claimed that he and the hidden *Imām* had discussed legal questions (*masā'il fī abwāb al-sharī'a*) in writing, see *ibid.*, p. 251 bottom.

[99] Such a *qaṣīda* to the Hidden *Imām* was composed, for example, by Bahā' al-Dīn al-'Āmilī (d. 1031/1622), a scholar at the court of the Persian Shāh 'Abbās. It is published in his *Kashkūl*, pp. 87–89. The text of the *qaṣīda* together with a commentary by Aḥmad (not Muḥammad, *GAL*, I, 415:18) al-Manīnī (d. 1108/1696, for his biography see Murādī, *Silk al-durar*, I, 133–45) are printed in the appendix to the *Kashkūl*, pp. 394–435. Cf. also "La Onzième Intelligence," *Revue Africaine*, L (1906), 243.

least ostensibly to the authority of that invisible power. So, for example, when the institution of parliament was introduced in Persia, in the new constitution reference was made to the "consent and concurrence of the *Imām* of the Age." Similar language is used in the manifesto (October 1908) that the revolutionary party published after Shāh Muḥammad 'Alī's antiparliamentary coup d'état, demanding the reinstatement of the parliamentary constitution: "Perhaps you have not been apprised of the decision of the *'ulamā'* of the holy city of Najaf, a clear decision that admits of no ambiguity, according to which he who sets himself against the constitution is like him who takes up the sword against the *Imām* of the Age (that is, the hidden *Mahdī*)—may Allah grant you the joy of his return!"[100]

Here the idea of the *Imām* has an enduring and always relevant force. It has attained an essential theological significance and is an active, effective, and indispensable element in the religious and political system.

13. We have acquainted ourselves with the doctrine of the imamate, its nature and its significance. We have seen that it is the most important root of Shī'ī belief where that belief differs from the Sunnī. To round out our acquaintance with Shī'ism, one more question must be considered.

Adherence to Islam means not only an act of actual or theoretical submission to a particular political system. It also requires the acceptance of certain articles of faith. These are variously formulated by disputing parties. It also means the performance of strictly defined ritual acts and the observance of laws that regulate the believer's life. Modalities of ritual and law are matters on which the coexistent and equally recognized schools differ. The question arises: apart from the theory of the imamate, did the Shī'ī system of theology and the Shī'ī practice of law develop any special features that constitute an essential difference between Shī'ī and Sunnī Islam?

Our answer must be that the basic doctrine of Shī'ī Islam entails, by its

[100] "Le Club national de Tauris," *RMM*, VI (1908), 535. The *fatwā* of the *'ulamā'* of Najaf is published in translation in *RMM*, VI (1908), 681f. It reads in part: "We must make every effort to strengthen the constitution by a holy war, keeping near the stirrups of the *Imām* of the Age—may our lives be his ransom. The slightest infraction, the slightest negligence (in the fulfillment of this duty) would be tantamount to abandoning and combating his majestic person." This last phrase does not, as the translator explains, refer to the Prophet Muḥammad but to the "*Imām* of the Age" mentioned in the previous sentence, that is to say to the hidden *Mahdī-Imām*. The partisans of the anticonstitutionalist reaction also refer, in a document supporting the withdrawal of the constitution, to the fact that the Shah's action was "inspired by God and the *Imām* of the Age"; *RMM*, VII (1909), 151.

very nature, a way of thinking that essentially differs from Sunnī thinking on fundamental theological issues as well. The Shī'ī conception of the nature of the *Imāms* had to have an effect on the formation of their ideas of God, law, and prophecy.

One more thing must be taken into account. Among the various currents within the many branches of the Shī'a, various theological positions came to prevail. In some Shī'ī schools of thought, even a flagrantly anthropomorphistic tendency has asserted itself. Nonetheless, it can be observed that, on questions that can be answered without involving the doctrine of the imamate, the line of thought that came to predominate within Shī'ism is very close to the Mu'tazila[101] (whom we studied in Chapter III). The Shī'ī theologians even understood—we shall presently see an example—how to press Mu'tazilite ideas into the service of their own doctrines. They liked to call themselves *al-'adlīya*, "those who profess justice." This is one half of the designation that the Mu'tazilites, as we have seen (Ch. III, Sec. 5) applied to themselves. The congeniality of the Shī'a with the Mu'tazila appears also from the Shī'ī assertion that 'Alī and the *Imāms* were the first founders of Mu'tazilite theology, and that later *mutakallimūn* did no more than elaborate doctrines whose groundwork had been laid by the *Imāms*.[102] Therefore in Shī'ī theological works we often find that when a Mu'tazilite proposition is described, one *Imām* or another is named as its original author.

As a vivid example of this, we may mention the following doctrinal statement, recorded in the name of the *Imām* Abū Ja'far al-Bāqir. Its second half brings to mind a well-known dictum by a Greek philosopher.[k]

> God is called Knowing and Capable in the sense that He gives knowledge to the knowing and capacity to the capable. All that you in your imagination distinguish as subtle dispositions of His essence is created and produced and is (insofar as these attributes are seen as distinct from His essence that admits of no multiplicity) your own (intellectual) act. It is as if the minuscule ants imagined that God has two feelers because, after all, such things are part of their own kind of perfection, and the lack of them, as they see it, would be a shortcoming. Rational creatures

[101] Muqaddasī already observed this; *Aḥsan al-taqāsīm*, p. 238:6.

[102] *ZDMG*, LIII (1899), 381.

[k] Goldziher is presumably referring to the pre-Socratic philosopher Xenophanes. See W.K.C. Guthrie, *A History of Greek Philosophy, the Earlier Pre-Socratics and the Pythagoreans*, I (Cambridge, 1964), 360ff., especially p. 371.

do the same thing when they ascribe their own characteristics to God.[103]

When we examine the prevalent Shīʿī theology, we have to regard its connection with Muʿtazilite thought as proven. It appears quite unambiguously in the assertion of the Shīʿī authorities that the Hidden *Imām* belongs to the school of *ʿadl* and *tawḥīd*—that is to say, the Muʿtazila.[104] It is in particular the Zaydī branch of the Shīʿa that is related, even more closely and consistently than the Imāmī branch, to the Muʿtazila in matters of detail.

In Shīʿī works the Muʿtazila has endured to this day. Thus it is a bad mistake of both religious and literary history to assert that after the sweeping victory of Ashʿarite theology there was no longer an active Muʿtazila. The assertion is refuted by an abundant Shīʿī theological literature, still fostered in our own time. Shīʿī dogmatic works betray the character of Muʿtazilite textbooks by their division into two main parts, one of which contains the chapters about God's unity, and the other the chapters about God's justice (Ch. III, Sec. 5). Naturally, the latter must have room for setting forth the theories regarding the *Imāms* and their infallibility. But in this respect as well it is not immaterial that on the question of infallibility al-Naẓẓām, one of the most radical Muʿtazilites, concurs with the Shīʿīs. It is further especially characteristic of the orientation of Shīʿī theology that it has built the proofs for its theory of the imamate on purely Muʿtazilite principles. The indispensable presence of an *Imām* in every age, and his infallibility, are linked to the assumption, proper to the Muʿtazila, that God's wisdom and justice necessitate that He provide guidance (*luṭf wājib*, Ch. III, Sec. 5). In every age God must furnish mankind with a leader who is not susceptible to error. In this fashion Shīʿī theology used the theories of Muʿtazilite dogmatics to strengthen its most important foundations.[105]

[103] Muḥammad Bāqir Dāmād, *Al-Rawāshiḥ al-samawīya fī sharḥ al-aḥādīth al-imāmīya* (Bombay, A.H. 1311), p. 133.

[104] Kāẓimī, *Kashf al-qināʿ*, p. 99. The Fāṭimid caliph al-Mustanṣir explicitly says in a short poem attributed to him that the faith he professes is *al-tawḥīd wa'l-ʿadl*; see Ibn al-Qalānisī, *Dhayl ta'rīkh Dimashq*, p. 95:11.

[105] To demonstrate this, let me only refer to a few printed works of Shīʿī theological literature, which throw into clear relief the method of Shīʿī theology mentioned above, including its application to issues associated with the doctrine of *Imāms*. A concise statement of the doctrine of *Imāms* is furnished by Naṣīr al-Dīn al-Ṭūṣī (d. 672/1273) in his *Tajrīd al-ʿaqā'id*, printed, with a commentary by ʿAlī ibn Muḥammad al-Qūshjī (d. 879/1474; *GAL*, I, 509 [SI, 925f.]) in Bombay, A.H. 1301; see pp. 399ff. In addition, Naṣīr al-Dīn al-Ṭūṣī gives a brief explanation of the Shīʿī position, as it contrasts with the Sunnī, on the question of

14. In its ritual and legal aspects, the Shīʿī religious doctrine differs from the Sunnī only in petty formalities that rarely touch essentials.

Shīʿī ritual and legal practice does not vary more widely from that of the rest of Islam than one ritual *madhhab* varies from another within orthodoxy. There are only petty, formal differences of modality, similar to the divergences that occur, for example, between Ḥanafites and Mālikites.[106] It has been observed that Shīʿī ritual shows the closest kinship to Shāfiʿite ritual. Fundamental laws are not affected. The Sunnī considers the Shīʿī a dissenter neither because of peculiarities in his legal practice, nor because of the orientation of his theology, but chiefly because of his deviation from the accepted constitutional law of the *sunna*.

To realize how minute the ritual differences are between the Shīʿī and Sunnī communities, it is most helpful to examine the regulations for the changes that a Sunnī society must make if, on being conquered, it must adapt to Shīʿī ways. For this purpose, we have selected from an available collection of examples the following instructions issued by a Shīʿī conqueror in A.D. 866. They prescribe the changes by means of which public order in Ṭabaristān was to be established according to Shīʿī principles:

> You must direct your subordinates to regard as their guideline the Book of Allah and the *sunna* of His Messenger as well as all authentic traditions of the Commander of the Faithful, ʿAlī ibn Abī Ṭālib, concerning fundamental doctrines of religion (*uṣūl*) and the branches (*furūʿ*) derived from these; moreover, to make public confession of the

---

Imāms, in his glosses to Fakhr al-Dīn al-Rāzī's *Muḥaṣṣal* (Cairo, A.H. 1323; *Takhlīṣ al-muḥaṣṣal*, *GAL*, I, 507, no. 22 [SI, 923]), pp. 176ff. Further: Ḥasan ibn Yūsuf ibn al-Muṭahhar al-Ḥillī (d. 726/1326), *Kitāb al-alfayn al-fāriq bayn al-ṣidq wa'l-mayn* ("The Book of 2,000, that Separates Truth and Falsehood," that is, a book of 1,000 proofs for the truth of the Shīʿī doctrine of *Imāms* and 1,000 refutations of objections from opponents; Bombay, A.H. 1298); the same author's *Al-Bāb al-ḥādī ʿashar*, "The Eleventh Chapter." Ḥillī joined this compendium of dogmatics, as an independent complement, to his abridgment of Abū Jaʿfar al-Ṭūṣī's *Miṣbāḥ al-mutahajjid*—a book of ten chapters (*GAL*, I, 405 [SI, 707]) dealing only with matters of ritual. It has been published with a commentary by Miqdād ibn ʿAbdallāh al-Ḥillī (*GAL*, II, 199), Naul-Kashwar Press, 1315/1898. In the recent literature, particularly noteworthy is Dildār ʿAlī's *Mir'āt al-ʿuqūl fī ʿilm al-uṣūl*, an excellent exposition of Shīʿī dogmatics. It is in two volumes, one dealing with *tawḥīd*, one with *ʿadl*; ʿImād al-Islām Press, Lucknow, A.H. 1319.

106 The book *Al-Intiṣār* by the Shīʿī scholar ʿAlī al-Murtaḍā ʿAlam al-Hudā (d. 436/1044 in Baghdad) gives a thorough survey of such points of disagreement. The book is available in a lithographic edition (Bombay, A.H. 1315). It examines the ritual and legal differences between Shīʿism and the Sunnī *madhāhib*, in all chapters of jurisprudence. It is the best resource for learning about such problems. In the European scholarly literature, the Shīʿī form of Islamic law is described by Amédée Querry, *Droit musulman* (Paris, 1871-1872).

superiority of ʻAlī to all the rest of the community of believers (*umma*). You must most strictly forbid them to believe in absolute determinism (*jabr*) and in anthropomorphic notions, and to rebel against belief in God's unity and justice. They must be forbidden to transmit reports in which superior qualities are ascribed to the enemies of God and the enemies of the Commander of the Faithful (ʻAlī). You must command them to recite aloud the *bismillāh* formula (from the first sura, at the beginning of prayer); to recite the *qunūt* invocation as part of the morning prayer;[107] to repeat the *Allāh akbar* formula five times in the funeral prayer; to cease from wiping their shoes (instead of washing their feet before prayer):[108] to add to the *adhān* (call to prayer) and the *iqāma* (the announcement of the beginning of the rite of prayer, which follows the *adhān* and consists in an abridged repetition of its text) the sentence 'Come to the best of good works,'[109] and to recite the *iqāma* twice.

[107] "Zauberelemente im islamischen Gebet," p. 323 [= *Gesammelte Schriften*, V, 52; partial French translation in *Arabica*, VII (1960), 24].

[108] For this disagreement, we refer to the vivid anecdote in the autobiography of ʻUmāra al-Yamanī, *Al-Nukat al-ʻaṣrīya*, edited by H. Derenbourg (Paris, 1897-1904), I, 126. It is a frequent topic of Sunnī-Shīʻī polemics. For example, Abū Yaḥyā al-Jurjānī (Ṭūṣī, *Fihrist kutub al-shīʻa*, p. 28:5) wrote a "Disputation between a Shīʻī and a Murji'ite (Sunnī) about the wiping of shoes, the eating of the *jirrī* fish, and other matters of controversy." The fish in question (also called *inklīs* = ἔγχελυς and *jirrīth*) is a kind of eel (*Muraena*, see Immanuel Löw, "Aramäische Fischnamen," *Nöldeke Festschrift*, I, 552 bottom). According to Shīʻī tradition ʻAlī intensely disapproved of using it for food; for interesting information on this subject see Jāḥiẓ, *Ḥayawān*, I, 111 [I, 234f.], and Kulīnī, *Uṣūl*, p. 217. Popular belief regards the *jirrī*—and also some other species of animals—as enchanted people; Jāḥiẓ, *Ḥayawān*, VI, 24:6 [VI, 77]. For the identification of the name of this fish, see further Immanuel Löw, "Lexikalische Miszellen," *ZA*, XXII (1909), 85f. (with comments by Nöldeke).

[109] E. G. Browne, *An Abridged Translation of the History of Tabaristan by Ibn Isfendiyar* (London, 1905; E.J.W. Gibb Memorial Series, II), p. 175. This alteration of the call to prayer publicly attests the Shīʻī occupation of a region formerly ruled by Sunnīs (cf. Maqrīzī, *Khiṭaṭ*, Bulaq, A.H. 1270, II, 270ff.). This is how the general Jawhar, for example, proclaims the triumph of the Fāṭimid regime in the Ibn Ṭūlūn and ʻAmr Mosques of the capital city of Egypt (Richard Gottheil, "A Distinguished Family of Fatimide Cadis (al-Nuʻmān) in the Tenth Century," *JAOS*, XXVII, 1906, 220 n. 3). In Baghdad the rebel Basāsīrī had the Shīʻī formula added to the *adhān*, in order to make known the acknowledgment of the Fāṭimid caliphate (Ibn al-Qalānisī, *Dhayl ta'rīkh Dimashq*, p. 88:5 from bottom). There is a South Arabian example in Khazrajī, *The Pearl-Strings . . .* , translated by Sir J. W. Redhouse (London, 1906-1907; E.J.W. Gibb Memorial Series, III), I, 182. In turn, the repudiation of Fāṭimid, and the return to ʻAbbāsid, authority is signaled, in Damascus and other Syrian localities, by the dropping of that formula (Ibn al-Qalānisī, *Dhayl ta'rīkh Dimashq*, p. 301:14; Amedroz's note from Fāriqī in the same work, p. 109). The mad Fāṭimid al-Ḥākim, too, ordered the formula abandoned when in one of his fits of insanity he ordered the reintroduction of Sunnī ritual customs (Ibn Taghrī Birdī, *Al-Nujūm al-zāhira*, II, 599:10). When

Thus, apart from theological principles there are only minimal differences in ritual, of a kind frequent among the orthodox *madhāhib*.[110] It is said that there are seventeen points of detail on which Shīʿī law takes a position peculiar to itself and agrees with none of the orthodox *madhāhib*.[111]

15. The most serious difference between Sunnī and Shīʿī legal practice appears in marriage law. For our examination and evaluation of Shīʿism, at

---

in the year 307/919 North Africa came under Shīʿī supremacy, the new ruler had the tongue of the devout muezzin ʿArūs ripped out and then had him put to death under fierce torture, on the testimony of witnesses that ʿArūs had failed to add to the call to prayer the supplemental phrase required by the Shīʿīs (Ibn al-ʿIdhārī, *Al-Bayān al-mughrib*, edited by R.P.A. Dozy, Leiden, 1848-1851, I, 186 [new ed. revised by G. S. Colin and É. Lévi-Provençal (Leiden, 1948-1951), I, 182f.]). Cf. the decrees of the Shīʿī conquerors in the region after the fall of the Aghlabids (*ibid.*, I, 148, 231 [I, 151, 223]).

[110] The triviality of ritual differences becomes all the clearer when we examine the various old creedal statements (*ʿaqāʾid*) by Sunnī authorities. A number of such *ʿaqāʾid* are collected, in English translation, in D. B. MacDonald, *Development of Muslim Theology, Jurisprudence and Constitutional Theory* (New York, 1903), pp. 293ff. One of the highly respected old creedal statements in Sunnī Islam is that of Abū Jaʿfar Aḥmad al-Ṭaḥāwī (d. 321/933), *Bayān al-sunna wa'l-jamāʿa* (printed in Kazan, 1902, with a commentary by Sirāj al-Dīn ʿUmar al-Hindī, d. 773/1371). This document duly refers to the chief points on which the two sects are at variance (the order of caliphs, the estimation of the Companions), and defines the Sunnī position on them. But of the points of difference in ritual, only one is taken up: whether, when preparing for prayer in certain circumstances that render washing one's feet difficult, one is allowed to be satisfied with "wiping one's shoes" (*al-masḥ ʿalā'l-khuffayn*). The Shīʿīs are not prepared to accept such a substitution. In the *Al-Fiqh al-akbar*, ascribed to Abū Ḥanīfa, after the injunction to honor all Companions and to declare no one a *kāfir* on account of his sinful acts, only the following is stressed as regards ritual: "The wiping of the shoes is *sunna*, the *tarāwīḥ* ritual during the nights of Ramaḍān is *sunna*, and it is permissible to pray behind pious or sinful (*imāms*) if they are of the believers" (cf. Ch. III, n. 2 [for the quotation, see *Al-Fiqh al-akbar* (Haydarabad, A.H. 1342), p. 9]). In another document of religious instruction, called *Waṣīya* and also ascribed to Abū Ḥanīfa, the only matter of ritual that is mentioned is the *masḥ ʿalā'l-khuffayn*. "If a person denies its permissibility, there is reason to fear that he is an unbeliever" [*Al-Waṣīya* (with the commentary of al-Bābartī, Cairo, A.H. 1289), p. 53]. In the same vein, Ghazālī reports the reputed saying by the ascetic Dhū'l-Nūn: "Three things characterize the people of the *sunna*: the wiping of the shoes, scrupulous participation in the congregational prayer, and love for the forefathers (the Companions); *Kitāb al-iqtiṣād fī'l-iʿtiqād*, edited by Muṣṭafā al-Qabbānī (Cairo, n.d.), p. 221. It is not easy to see why this trifle, of all things, was invested with so much importance and placed, as being of nearly equal value, next to theological principles. "He who is averse to the *masḥ* is averse to the *sunna*, and I know this only as a characteristic of Satan"; Ibn Saʿd, VI, 192:5ff. This view allows us to understand the reason for the minute detail in which the precedents attesting the permissibility of *masḥ* are reported in the biographical traditions in Ibn Saʿd, VI, 34:20, 75:10; cf. especially 83:12, 162:4, 166:14, 168:6, 10. These last traditions were all the more suited to serve as justification of the Sunnī acceptance of *masḥ*, as in them ʿAlī himself approves of this practice that the Shīʿīs repudiate.

[111] Cf. my *Beiträge zur Literaturgeschichte der Śīʿa*, p. 49 [= *Gesammelte Schriften*, I, 307].

any rate, it carries more weight than the minute ritual differences that may be observed in religious practices.

In this respect, one question of marriage law in particular deserves our attention: the validity or invalidity of a temporary marriage, entered upon in the understanding that it will be of limited duration.[112]

In Plato's Republic, too—although owing to essentially different viewpoints from those prevailing in Muslim life—temporary marriage has a legitimate role to play among the social elite, the people Plato calls the "guardians." Theodor Gomperz has cited analogies from social movements in New England: the sect of the "Perfectionists," founded by John Humphrey Noyes, which for a whole generation maintained its chief settlement in Oneida[113] and whose views on marriage have since been reproduced in narrative literature (trial marriage).

It was upon different considerations, naturally, that at the beginning of his career as lawgiver Muhammad tolerated a form of limited marriage that had been common among the pagan Arabs, as is attested by Ammianus Marcellinus.[1] *Mut'a* is the term used to refer to this institution. It is literally translated as "marriage of pleasure," but it is more properly called a temporary marriage. Upon the lapse of the period fixed in such a marriage agreement (*ṣīgha*), the validity of the marriage automatically ceases, in accordance with the agreement and without any formalities of divorce.[114] The validity of this form of marriage was, however, abrogated after a few years. Reports differ whether it was the Prophet himself or, which is more likely, only his second successor 'Umar who declared such temporary marriage "a sister of fornication" and forbade it to the believers. But even after this prohibition, it occurred to a limited degree (on the occasion of journeys of pilgrimage, for instance). Since the au-

[112] About this type of marriage see Edward Westermarck, *The History of Human Marriage*, 2nd ed. (London, 1894), chapter 23, pp. 517ff.

[113] Theodor Gomperz, *Griechische Denker*, 2nd ed. (Leipzig, 1903-1909), II, 417 [translated as *Greek Thinkers* (New York, 1901-1912), III, 123f.].

[1] Ammianus Marcellinus, *Histories*, edited and translated by J. C. Rolfe, rev. ed. (London and Cambridge, Mass., 1963), I, 27-28.

[114] Cf. Caetani, *Annali dell'Islam*, III, 894ff.; Robertson Smith, *Kinship and Marriage in Early Arabia*, 2nd ed. (London, 1903), pp. 83ff.; J. Wellhausen, "Die Ehe bei den Arabern," *Nachrichten von der Königlichen Gesellschaft der Wissenschaften und der Georg-Augusts-Universität zu Göttingen*, 1893, pp. 464f.; Lammens, *Mo'āwia*, p. 409 (= *MFO*, III, 273). About the abrogation of the *mut'a* marriage, see G. A. Wilken, *Het Matriarchaat bij de oude Arabieren* (Amsterdam, 1884), pp. 10ff. [= *De Verspreide Geschriften* (Semerang, 1912), II, 9ff.; German translation, *Das Matriarchat bei den alten Arabern* (Leipzig, 1884), pp. 10ff.; Arabic translation, *Al-Umūma 'inda'l-'arab* (Kazan, 1902), pp. 11ff.].

thorization of the *mut'a* marriage relies on a hadith that goes back to Ibn 'Abbās, it has been ironically called "a marriage according to the *fatwā* of Ibn 'Abbās."[115] In time, as Islamic institutions acquired their definitive form, the Sunnīs acquiesced in the prohibition of temporary marriages. The Shī'īs refer to Qur'ān 4:24[116] and still to this day consider such a marriage valid.[117] In their view there is no reliable evidence for its repeal by the Prophet; it was improperly repealed by 'Umar.[118] For, even supposing that the reports of 'Umar's decree are reliable, 'Umar was not, the Shī'īs argue, an authority in matters of the law.

We must regard the *mut'a*-marriage as the subject of the sharpest legal dispute between Sunnī and Shī'ī Islam.[m]

16. In this connection we must also mention some customs and practices in which history is remembered: they commemorate the 'Alids, and express the Shī'īs' mourning for the martyred members of this holy family. The Būyid rulers, under whose protection Shī'ism was freer to venture into the light of day, established a religious feast day of their own (*'īd al-ghadīr*) to commemorate the act of investiture by which, at the pool of Khumm, the Prophet designated 'Alī as his successor. This is an event to which the partisans of 'Alī had long referred in order to support the legitimacy of their Shī'ī belief.[119] Older is the celebration of the *'āshūrā* (the tenth day of Muḥarram) as a day of mourning and repentance in

[115] Abū'l-'Abbās al-Jurjānī, *Al-Muntakhab min kināyāt al-udabā'* (Cairo, 1908), p. 108.

[116] After some verses that enumerate the degrees of kinship that bar marriage, verse 24 reads: "Apart from these, you are permitted to desire your possessions (wives), honorably and not in the manner of fornication, and as for those of them that you have enjoyed (*istamta'tum*, hence *mut'a*), give them their reward (dowry) in the measure prescribed by law. It will not be considered sinful if you agree on a sum in excess of the lawful measure." It is on this text, supported by a series of traditions, that the arguments for the legitimacy of the *mut'a* marriage rest. According to a statement in Ḥāzimī, *Kitāb al-i'tibār fī bayān al-nāsikh wa'l-mansūkh min al-āthār* (Haydarabad, A.H. 1319), p. 179, in the original text of the Qur'ān the words "you have enjoyed" were followed by the phrase *ilā ajalin musamman*, "until a fixed term." This additional phrase is said in particular to have been Ibn 'Abbās' reading; it gives special support to those who refer the text to temporary marriage. For a concise statement of the disagreement, from the Shī'ī point of view, see Murtaḍā, *Intiṣār*, p. 42.

[117] About such marriages in Persia, see E. G. Browne, *A Year Amongst the Persians* (London, 1893), p. 462. A striking observation by Jāḥiẓ about the laxity of the conception of marriage among some Shī'īs is quoted in al-Rāghib al-Iṣfahānī, *Muḥāḍarāt al-udabā'* (Cairo, A.H. 1287), II, 140 (*wiqāya*).

[118] For the Shī'ī point of view, cf. Paul Kitabgi Khan, *Droit musulman shyite: le mariage et le divorce* (Lausanne dissertation, 1904), pp. 79ff.

[m] For further information on *mut'a*, see Francesco Castro, *Materiali e ricerche sul nikāḥ al-mut'a*; I, *Fonti Imamite* (Rome, 1974).

[119] Kumayt, *Hāshimīyāt*, no. VI, vs. 9.

memory of the catastrophe at Karbalā' which, according to tradition, took place on that day. Further, pilgrimages to places and graves in Iraq[120] hallowed by 'Alid memories give the Shī'ī cult of saints and burial places a particular, individual character that elevates it in spiritual meaning far above the cult of saints that had developed, just as richly, in Sunnī Islam.

17. So far we have examined the political, theological, and legal characteristics peculiar to the Shī'a. We must next turn to religious composites in which Shī'ī doctrine played a fundamental role. But first it is important to point out a few fallacious views on the nature of Shī'ism. These views were widespread until quite recently, and still cannot be regarded as completely dislodged.

I wish to call attention very briefly to three of these fallacies. In a work concerned with the history of religions, they cannot be passed over in silence.

A. There is a fallacy that the difference between Sunnī and Shī'ī Islam consists chiefly in the fact that in Sunnī Islam the *sunna* of the Prophet is recognized besides the Qur'ān as a source of religious belief and conduct, while the Shī'īs confine themselves to the Qur'ān and reject the *sunna*.[121]

This is a fundamental error, completely mistaking the nature of Shī'ism. It was probably brought into being by the terminological contrast between "*sunna*" and "Shī'a." No Shī'ī will tolerate being considered an opponent of the principle of the *sunna*. He represents, so he will say, the true *sunna*, the holy tradition transmitted by members of the Prophet's family, while his adversaries base their *sunna* on the authority of the "Companions," usurpers of the rights of others, whose credibility the Shī'īs impugn on principle.

There are countless traditions common to both groups, and varying only in the names of the authorities attesting to them. When Sunnī hadiths are supportive of Shī'ī lines of thought, or at least do not stand in

[120] About the most important of these holy places we now have Arnold Nöldeke's monograph, *Das Heiligtum al-Husains zu Kerbelā* (Berlin, 1909; Türkische Bibliothek XI).

[121] Leaving aside earlier erroneous statements, I will cite only two recent examples of the stubborn persistence of this error. H. Derenbourg still says in his lecture *La Science des religions et l'Islamisme* (Paris, 1886), p. 76: "La sounna . . . est rejetée par les schī'ites." And Sir J. W. Redhouse writes in his note 417 to Khazrajī's *Pearl-Strings*, p. 71: "The Shī'a and other heterodox Muslims pay little or no regard to tradition." It is even more remarkable that quite recently a Muslim jurist from Cairo made the same error in a description of the difference between the Sunnī and Shī'ī positions regarding tradition. See Dr. Riad Ghali, *De la tradition considérée comme source du droit musulman* (Paris, 1909), pp. 25-27.

their way, Shīʿī theologians have no scruples about referring to the canonical hadith collections of their opponents. We even know of an instance where the collections of Bukhārī and Muslim, as well as other works of hadith, served as the subject of pious readings at devout Friday night gatherings at the court of a fanatic Shīʿī vizier, Ṭalāʾiʿ ibn Ruzzīk.[122]

Thus in the Shīʿa, too, the tradition is an essential source of religious life. The doctors of Shīʿī Islam were intensely conscious of it, as is shown by the fact that ʿAlī's maxim about Qurʾān and *sunna* (Ch. II, Sec. 3) comes from a Shīʿī collection of ʿAlī's solemn speeches and sayings. Thus Shīʿism demands reverence for the *sunna* no less than does the form of Islam named after the *sunna*. This appears also from the extensive Shīʿī *sunna* literature and the works of research related to it: from the great zeal with which scholars of pro-ʿAlid sympathies invented hadiths, or disseminated already invented ones, in order to serve the cause of the Shīʿa.[123]

Thus it is completely false that the Shīʿīs on principle do not have a *sunna*.[124] They do not see themselves as people who reject the *sunna*, in contrast to their opponents who follow it. Rather, they see themselves as "people loyal to the Prophet's family" and as its supporters—that is the meaning of the word *shīʿa*—or as the elite (*khāṣṣa*), in contrast to all those swept along with the generality of people (*al-ʿāmma*), engulfed in blindness and error.

B. There is a fallacy that the emergence and development of the Shīʿa represents a modification of Islam by ideas of the Iranian peoples that conquest or missionary activity had brought into the Muslim community.

This widespread view is based on a historical misunderstanding that

[122] Abūʾl-Ḥasan ʿAlī ibn Ẓāfir al-Azdī, *Badāʾiʿ al-badāʾih* (Cairo, A.H. 1316, on the margin of the *Maʿāhid al-tanṣīṣ*), I, 176.

[123] It is reported that ʿUbaydallāh ibn Mūsā, who died in Kufa during the reign of al-Maʾmūn (213/828), transmitted tendentious Shīʿī hadiths (Ibn Saʿd, VI, 279:13). His contemporary, Khālid ibn Makhlad (*ibid.*, 283:24) is accused of the same thing.

[124] Whether other sources for the derivation of laws have a normative force like that of the prescriptions in recognized hadiths is a question that also divides the Shīʿī theologians into two parties: the *akhbārīyūn*, those who derive their law exclusively from reliable traditional reports (*akhbār*) and reject the application of speculative methods, and, opposed to them, the *uṣūlīyūn*, who also admit *qiyās* (analogy) and other subjective methods as "roots," *uṣūl*. The Shīʿism prevalent in Persia belongs to the latter trend. The same methodological controversy was carried on on Sunnī soil. Cf. Shahrastānī, p. 131:7 from bottom, where mention is made of the *akhbārīya* and *kalāmīya*, parties that fought "with the sword and with denunciations of one another as unbelievers" (*sayf wa-takfīr*).

Wellhausen, in his *Religiös-politische Oppositionsparteien im alten Islam*, has conclusively refuted. The pro-'Alid movement originated on genuine Arab soil; not until al-Mukhtār's rebellion did it spread among Muslims of non-Semitic stock.[125] Moreover, as we have seen, the roots of the theory of the imamate, the theocratic opposition to the secular view of the power of the state, the messianism into which the theory of the imamate flows, and the belief in a *parousia* which gives that messianism its form, are to be traced to Judaeo-Christian influences. Even the extremist apotheosis of 'Alī was first proclaimed by 'Abdallāh ibn Sabā[n]—before there could be any question of an influx of such ideas from an Aryan environment—and Arabs joined this movement in large numbers.[126] The most extravagant results of an anthropomorphic doctrine of incarnation (Sec. 8 above) have also, in part, authors of unmistakably Arab extraction. Shī'ism as a sectarian doctrine was embraced by Arab tribesmen with legitimist or theocratic leanings quite as fervently as by Iranians. To be sure, the Shī'ī form of opposition was most welcome among the latter, and they cheerfully joined it. It is also true that with their ancestral concepts of divine kingship, the Iranians could exert an influence on its further development. But the beginnings of Shī'ī ideas do not presuppose Iranian influence. Shī'ism is quite as Arab in its roots as Islam itself.[o]

C. There is a fallacy that Shī'ism represents a reaction in favor of intellectual freedom, against Semitic ossification.

In our time Carra de Vaux in particular has regarded the opposition of the Shī'a to Sunnī Islam as "the reaction of broad and free thinking against narrow and rigid orthodoxy."[127]

No one familiar with Shī'ī legal doctrines will be able to accept this view. Their adversaries could, it is true, reasonably accuse the Shī'īs of placing the cult of 'Alī so much at the center of their religious life that next to it the other elements of religion retreated into the background (Sec. 6 above). But this is an observation about Shī'ī society, and irrelevant to a characterization of Shī'ī legal principles. These are no less strict than their Sunnī counterparts. Nor must the laxer attitude that prevails

[125] It appears that Shī'ism was first introduced into Persian territory (Qumm) by Arab settlers; cf. Yāqūt, *Mu'jam al-buldān*, IV, 176:4ff.

[n] This has since been questioned by other scholars. See above, Ch. 5, Sec. 7.

[126] Ṭabarī, I, 3081:10, 14.

[o] On ethnic, social and other interpretations of Shī'ism, see B. Lewis, *Islam in History: Ideas, Men and Events in the Middle East* (London, 1973), pp. 217ff.

[127] Carra de Vaux, *Le Mahométisme; le génie sémitique et le génie aryen dans l'Islam* (Paris, 1897), p. 142.

among Iranian Shīʿīs toward certain restrictions imposed by the ritual law[128] mislead us in our historical evaluation of the principles of Shīʿism. By their very repudiation of all elements of collective judgment in favor of an infallible personal authority, the Shīʿīs rejected the liberal, facultative aspects of the Sunnī form of Islam.[129] It is, in fact, the spirit of absolutism that pervades the Shīʿī conception of religion.

If we admit, further, that liberalism and illiberalism in religion are best measured by the degree of toleration accorded to people with divergent opinions, then Shīʿism must be ranked lower than the Sunnī version of Islam. Naturally we have in mind not the contemporary practice of Shīʿī peoples, but the religious and legal institutions defined in the documents of Shīʿī doctrine. Today these institutions have been in many respects allowed to lapse everywhere, owing to the concrete demands of life in the modern age. Only among those strata of the populace remote from the rest of the world do they retain their full rigor in social intercourse.

On examining the legal documents, we find that the Shīʿī legal position toward other faiths is much harsher and stiffer than that taken by Sunnī Muslims. Their law reveals a heightened intolerance to people of other beliefs. The Shīʿī interpretation of the law had no use for the orthodox Sunnī mitigation of certain narrow-minded old conceptions. Of the severe rule in the Qur'ān (9:28) that "unbelievers are unclean," Sunnī Islam has accepted an interpretation that is as good as a repeal. Shīʿī law, on the other hand, has maintained the literal sense of the rule; it declares the bodily substance of an unbeliever to be ritually unclean, and lists the touching of an unbeliever among the ten things that produce *najāsa*, ritual impurity.[130] Life is faithfully reflected in the astonishment of Morier's Hajji Baba (*Hajji Baba . . . in England*, chapter 16) to whom "the most extraordinary feature of the character of the English is that they seem to look upon nothing as impure. They will touch a Jew as soon as one of their own tribe." From the viewpoint of Shīʿī law, such a liberal attitude toward people of other faiths is indeed anything but natural. In works by Europeans who have lived among Shīʿīs, there are many examples showing the Shīʿī attitude. I will cite only a few remarks from the work of a

[128] Shāhfūr ibn Ṭāhir al-Isfarā'inī, a polemicist who died in 1078, already censured the Imāmīs (in what is undoubtedly an extravagant generalization) for their indifference to the ritual law. See the excerpt in Friedländer, "Heterodoxies," *JAOS*, XXIX (1908), 61:20.

[129] "Die Religion des Islams," p. 122:14 from bottom.

[130] *Die Ẓāhiriten*, pp. 61ff. [= *The Ẓāhirīs*, pp. 58ff.]; *ZDMG*, LIII, 382. Cf. Querry, *Droit musulman*, I, 44, in the chapter about "Les Êtres impurs et les substances impures"; no. 10 is: "L'infidèle . . . tels sont les sectateurs des ennemis de l'imam ʿAli et les hérétiques."

reliable observer of the Persian popular mentality, Dr. J. E. Polak, who lived many years in Shīʿī Persia as personal physician to Shāh Nāṣir al-Dīn. "Should a European arrive at the beginning of a meal, a Persian is thrown into embarrassment. Good manners forbid sending the European away, but to invite him in is fraught with difficulty because food touched by an unbeliever is considered unclean."[131] "Remnants of food from the table of Europeans are scorned by the servants and left to the dogs." Speaking of trips undertaken in Persia: "A European must not fail to carry with him a drinking vessel. Nowhere will he be offered one, because according to Persian belief every vessel becomes unclean immediately an unbeliever has used it."[132] Dr. Polak relates about Mīrzā Sayyid Khān, then foreign minister, that "after seeing a European, he washes his eyes to guard them from defilement." This minister was a very pious Muslim who could not, except with great reluctance, and only for reasons of health, bring himself to take wine as a medication. At length, however, he came to enjoy the medication so much that "despite his undamaged piety he never could be found sober."[133] The Shīʿīs show the same intolerance toward the Zoroastrians living in their midst. Edward G. Browne relates a number of experiences of it, from his year's stay in Yazd. A Zoroastrian was given the bastinado because his clothes accidentally touched some fruit displayed for sale in the bazaar. Contact with the unbeliever had rendered the fruit unclean, and it could no longer be eaten by a true (Shīʿī) believer.[134]

This mentality is often encountered among uneducated Shīʿī groups outside Persia. In villages in southern Lebanon, between Baalbek and Safad and eastward to Coelesyria and the Antilebanon, there are Shīʿī peasants known by the name of *Metāwile*. The singular is *Mitwālī*, for the standard Arabic *mutawālī*, "a loyal adherent of the house of ʿAlī"—an attribute of the Shīʿī spirit that serves in this region to designate the sect. They number fifty to sixty thousand souls.[p] According to a report—wholly unsubstantiated—they are descended from Kurdish settlers transplanted, in Saladin's time, from Iraq to Syria. They would then be of Iranian origin;[135] but this seems a completely groundless assumption.

131 J. E. Polak, *Persien. Das Land und seine Bewohner* (Leipzig, 1865), I, 128:13.

132 *Ibid.*, II, 55; cf. p. 356:8.

133 *Ibid.*, II, 271:2.

134 Browne, *A Year Amongst the Persians*, p. 371 bottom.

p Since then, the Matāwila have increased greatly in numbers. The Shīʿa are now one of the largest communities—some indeed claim the largest single community—in Lebanon.

135 Ernest Renan, *Mission de Phénicie* (Paris, 1864), p. 633. Cf. also H. Lammens, "Sur la

Their largest communities are in Baalbek and the surrounding villages. The Ḥarfūsh family of emirs came from among them. Toward people of other faiths, these peasants share with other Shī'īs the feelings described above. Although they practice the virtue of hospitality toward everyone, they regard as polluted the dishes in which they have offered food and drink to outsiders. The American scholar Selah Merrill, who traveled a great deal in this region between the years 1875 and 1877, on commission from the American Palestine Exploration Society, reports that they "consider that they are polluted by the touch of Christians. Even a vessel from which a Christian has drunk, and anything from which he may have eaten, or even handled while eating, they never use again but destroy at once."[136]

We had to reject as erroneous the assumption that the rise of Shī'ism was the result of Iranian influence on Arab Islam. But Persian influences did play a secondary part in the historical development of Shī'ī ideas, and in this rigid attitude toward the believers of other religions we may see an effect of that Persian influence.[137] The treatment of non-Shī'īs in Shī'ī law reminds us immediately of the ancient rules in Persian religious texts. These rules are mostly obsolete among modern Zoroastrians. The Shī'ī attitude may be regarded as their Islamic echo. For example: "A Zoroastrian must purify himself with *nīrang* if he has touched a non-Zoroastrian." "A Zoroastrian must not eat any food, including butter

frontière nord de la Terre Promise," in the journal *Les Études*, LXXVIII (1899), 5ff. of the offprint. It is an error to include the Matāwila among the extremist groups of the Shī'a (such as the Nuṣayrī). They are regular Imāmīs; their religious leaders occasionally receive their education in Persia.

[136] *East of the Jordan* (London, 1881), p. 306. The same is reported of them by Louis Lortet, *La Syrie d'aujourd'hui* (Paris, 1884), p. 115, with the nonsensical explanation, "à ces minuties intolérantes on reconnaît les pratiques de l'ancien judaisme." In the older literature, we can refer to the description of the Metwālī-Shī'īs by C. F. Volney who traveled in Syria in 1783-1785: "Ils se réputent souillés par l'attouchement des étrangers; et contre l'usage général du Levant, ils ne boivent ni ne mangent dans le vase qui a servi à une personne qui n'est pas de leur secte, ils ne s'asseyent même pas à la même table," *Voyage en Syrie et en Égypte*, 2nd ed. (Paris, 1787), p. 79. Similar views are reportedly held by a Shī'ī group settled in the surroundings of Medina, the *Nakhāwla* (properly *Nakhāwila*, "date-palm planters") who trace their genealogy to the ancient *Anṣār*. "They count both Jew and Christian as unclean, being as scrupulous in this particular as the Persians, whose rules they follow in the discharge of their religious purifications." See Gazanfar Ali Khan and Wilfrid Sparroy, *With the Pilgrims to Mecca: the Great Pilgrimage of A.H. 1319, A.D. 1902* (London, 1905), p. 233.

[137] For further details see my article, "Islamisme et Parsisme," *Actes du premier Congrès International d'Histoire des Religions*, I (Paris, 1900), 119-47 [= *Gesammelte Schriften*, IV, 232ff.].

and honey, prepared by a non-Zoroastrian. He must not do so even on a journey."[138]

Adoption of this last Persian rule in particular has created a ritual difference between the two branches of Islam. Despite the explicit permission given in the Qur'ān (5:5), Shī'ī law regards food prepared by Christians and Jews as forbidden food, and the meat of animals slaughtered by them as forbidden meat.[139] In this matter, too, the Sunnīs follow the less illiberal practice, to which the Qur'ān itself opens the door.[140]

There is yet another area of religious law in which the Shī'īs do not take advantage of a freedom allowed in the Qur'ān, but in contradiction of their holy scripture, draw the consequences of their intolerant views. The Qur'ān allows a Muslim to marry virtuous Jewish or Christian women (5:5). From the Sunnī point of view such mixed marriages may be regarded, according to the theory of early Islam, as unobjectionable.[141] The caliph 'Uthmān married the Christian woman Nā'ila.[142] The Shī'īs, on the other hand, rest their opinion of such marriages on the law in Sura 2, verse 221, which forbids marriage with polytheists (*mushrikāt*). The Qur'ān verse favorable to marriage with non-Muslim monotheists is, by exegesis, divested of its original sense.[143]

[138] See D. Menant, "Les Zoroastriens de Perse," *RMM*, III (1907), 219.

[139] Murtaḍā, *Intiṣār*, pp. 155, 157. This question of Shī'ī law is also dealt with in the work listed in *GAL*, I, 188:15, by the author whom the Imāmīs celebrate as al-Shaykh al-Mufīd. The translation "über die Schlachtopfer" in Brockelmann is misleading; the subject is the ordinary secular slaughtering of animals. Bahā' al-Dīn al-'Āmilī wrote a special work on the "Prohibition of the flesh of animals slaughtered by the *ahl al-kitāb*" (Berlin ms., Petermann 247). At the court of the Safavid Shāh 'Abbās, the Shī'ī theologians held a disputation over this vexed question with Shaykh Khiḍr al-Māridīnī, ambassador of the Turkish Sultan Aḥmad (Muḥibbī, *Khulāṣat al-athar*, II, 130). In their interpretation of the dietary laws the Shī'īs practice their intolerance even toward Muslims whom they consider *kāfirs* (Ibn Taymīya, *Rasā'il*, I, 278:6).

[140] 'Umar II explicitly allowed the consumption even of animals slaughtered by Samaritans (Ibn Sa'd, V, 260:15), but this was not generally conceded. About Sabians, see August Müller, "Aus einem Briefe . . . an Dr. Steinschneider," *ZDMG*, XXXII (1878), 392. In the course of the later, darker, development of religious practice, some Sunnī doctors also endeavored to put a prohibition on the *dhabā'iḥ ahl al-kitāb*, but their efforts were countered by reference to the unambiguous text of Sura 5, vs. 5. Cf. Steinschneider, *Polemische und apologetische Literatur in arabischer Sprache* (Leipzig, 1877), p. 151.

[141] On marrying women of the *ahl al-kitāb*, see Caetani, *Annali dell'Islam*, III, 787. On this issue, too, later development seems, among Sunnīs as well, to have been favorable to more exclusive views. See Juynboll, *Handbuch des islamischen Gesetzes*, p. 221.

[142] Cf. Lammens, *Mo'āwia*, p. 293 (*MFO*, III, 157).

[143] Murtaḍā, *Intiṣār*, p. 45. We should add that Shī'ī law excludes only standard, permanent marriage (*nikāḥ dā'im*) with such women. For *mut'a*-marriage (Ch. V, Sec. 15), which is in lower esteem, they are rather more acceptable.

But the intolerant disposition of the true Shī'īs extends not only to non-Muslims but also to Muslims of a different persuasion. In this intolerance their literature is richly steeped. The Shī'ī community has suffered the hardships of an *ecclesia oppressa*, having from the outset struggled against persecution and repression. It has on the whole lacked the freedom to make open profession of its beliefs, and could disclose and practice them only in the conspiratorial secrecy of its members. Its mood therefore tends toward rage against the adversaries who prevailed. The Shī'īs regard the *taqīya* forced upon them as a form of martyrdom, which constantly feeds their hatred against the authors of the actual state of affairs. We have already seen that their theologians managed to raise the cursing of enemies to an outright religious duty (Sec. 5 above). Some of their theologians go so far in lacking charity for the members of other faiths as to add a restriction to the Qur'ān verse that prescribes almsgiving. In their view, unbelievers and opponents of the 'Alid cause are to be excluded from all acts of kindness. They relate that the Prophet said: "He who gives alms to our enemies is like one who steals from God's sanctuaries."[144] The Sunnīs have the authority of the caliph 'Umar for taking a more humane position: on entering Syria, he issued an order that the *ṣadaqāt*—taxes collected for the general needs of the Muslim community—must be used to support also helpless and sick Christians.[145] The Shī'ī traditions are almost more hostile toward non-Shī'ī Muslims than toward non-Muslims. In one of their maxims the Syrians (that is, the Sunnī adversaries) are ranked below the Christians, and the Medinese (who had accepted the caliphate of Abū Bakr and 'Umar) below the pagans of Mecca.[146] Here is no soil for tolerance and forbearance toward people who think differently. The following detail may illustrate the degree of irrationality to which their contempt for their opponents rises. One of their standard authorities teaches that in doubtful cases, where the sources of religious law furnish no criterion for a firm decision, one must on principle do the opposite of what the Sunnīs hold to be correct. "Correctness lies in what is contrary to the *'āmma* (that is, the Sunnī view)."[147] This is a theology of hate and intolerance.

18. Of the many branches of Shī'ism besides the Twelvers, most of

[144] 'Askarī, commentary to Sura 2, vs. 218.

[145] Balādhurī, *Futūḥ al-buldān*, p. 129.

[146] Kulīnī, *Uṣūl*, p. 568. The *Imām* Ja'far al-Ṣādiq is reported to have said: "It is better to have one's child nursed by a Jewish or Christian woman than to entrust it to a nurse who is of the *Nāṣibīya* (enemies of 'Alī)"; Najāshī, *Kitāb al-rijāl*, p. 219.

[147] Kulīnī, *Uṣūl*, p. 39: *mā khālafa al-'āmma fa-fīhi al-rashād.*

which have completely vanished with the passage of time, two sects in particular played prominent roles: the Zaydīs and the Ismāʿīlīs.[q]

A. The Zaydīs diverge from the Twelvers in the chain of *Imāms* after the fourth. Their fifth, after whom they are named, is Zayd ibn ʿAlī, a great-grandson of Ḥusayn. In the year 122/740 in Kufa, he set himself up as ʿAlid pretender to the throne, as rival to his nephew Jaʿfar al-Ṣādiq, whom the majority of Shīʿīs recognized as the legitimate heir to the imamate. Zayd perished fighting against the Umayyad caliphate. His son Yaḥyā took up the struggle, but with no greater success; he fell in Khurāsān, in 125/743. Among those Shīʿīs who did not recognize the imamate of the Twelvers and regarded Zayd's ambitions as the watchword of their schism, the office of *Imām* was, after Yaḥyā's death, no longer passed down by direct transmission from father to son within a single line. Thus they differed from the Twelvers, who considered the line of Ḥusayn ibn ʿAlī exclusively destined to hold that office. Instead, the Zaydīs ignored lines of descent and acknowledged as their *Imām* any ʿAlid who not only possessed the spiritual powers required of a religious leader but also took up the fight for the sacred cause and thus obtained the homage of the community. They conceived of an active imamate, unlike the passive one of the Twelvers, with the hidden *Mahdī* as its conclusion. They also rejected fables about the *Imāms'* supernatural knowledge and godlike qualities. In the place of such fancies, the real principal feature of the *Imām* appears: he is the leader and teacher of the community of believers, active in life and openly fighting for his cause. Following their founder's view, the Zaydīs are tolerant in their judgment of the Sunnī caliphate of the early Islamic age. They do not concur with the absolute damnation of Abū Bakr and ʿUmar and the Prophet's other Companions who failed to confer the immediate succession upon ʿAlī. These men failed to recognize ʿAlī's surpassing merits, but their shortsightedness does not brand them as evildoers, nor the persons of their choice as usurpers. In this respect the Zaydīs constitute, in relation to the Sunnīs, the moderate wing of the Shīʿī groups. Like the Idrīsid dynasty in Northwest Africa (A.D. 791-926), the Zaydī ruling houses came from the Ḥasanid branch of ʿAlī's descendants. The Shīʿī dynasty, claiming descent from Ḥasan ibn ʿAlī, which succeeded in establishing its rule in Ṭabaristān,

[q] Both the Zaydīs and the Ismāʿīlīs have been the subject of a considerable scholarly literature since Goldziher's time. Surveys, with bibliographies, will be found in the relevant articles in the *Encyclopaedia of Islam*, "Zaidīya" (by R. Strothmann) in the 1st edition; "Ismāʿīliyya" (by W. Madelung) in the 2nd edition.

A.D. 863–928, as well as the similarly Ḥasanid imamate in South Arabia (since the ninth century), based their legitimacy on Zaydī claims. This branch of the Shī'ī sect is still widespread today in south Arabia (and is popularly known as *al-zuyūd*).

B. The Ismā'īlīs end their line of visible *Imāms*, in contrast to the Twelvers, with the seventh. To this they owe their name. Their seventh *Imām*—unrecognized by the Twelvers—is Ismā'īl, son of the sixth *Imām* Ja'far (d. A.D. 762). For reasons that are variously given, Ismā'īl did not in fact assume the office of *Imām* but passed it to his son Muḥammad. Muḥammad, thus in effect the seventh *Imām*, acted as his father's representative. His descendants followed him in an uninterrupted line as hidden, latent *Imāms*, in seclusion from public view, until prolonged secret Ismā'īlī propaganda bore fruit, and in the person of 'Ubayd Allāh—the founder of the Fāṭimid empire in North Africa (A.D. 910)—the rightful *Imām* made his public appearance as *Mahdī*. The followers of this Shī'ī system are therefore also distinguished from the ordinary Imāmīs as "Seveners."

In itself this distinction would only have a formal significance, and would not prompt us to single out the Ismā'īlīs from the many divisions within Shī'ism. But Ismā'īlī propaganda supplied the framework for a movement of prime importance in the religious history of Islam, and the success of secret Ismā'īlī subversion led to the establishment of a state that played a memorable part in the political history of Islam.

The people who made propaganda for the Ismā'īlī form of the doctrine of the imamate also put their Ismā'īlī convictions to a further use: they fused it with theories that called into question traditional Islam, even in its Shī'ī form, and were leading to its complete disintegration.

Neoplatonic philosophy exerted one of the most powerful influences on the internal evolution of Islamic ideas. The ideas of this philosophical system affected Muslims of the most varied descriptions, and even found their way into documents in which the unassailably orthodox doctrines of Islam were put forward.[148] In Chapter IV we learned that Neoplatonic ideas found their most persistent Islamic application in Sufism. In Shī'ī circles, too, there was no lack of attempts to weave into a single fabric theories about *Imām* and *Mahdī*, and Neoplatonic theories of emanations.[149]

[148] "Neuplatonische und gnostische Elemente im Ḥadīṯ," pp. 317ff. [= *Gesammelte Schriften*, V, 107ff.; partial French translation in *Arabica*, VII (1960), 8ff.].

[149] Especially remarkable is the system of Aḥmad ibn al-Kayyāl; see Shahrastānī, p. 138.

This influence is most obvious in the use that Ismā'īlī propaganda made of Neoplatonic ideas. Sufism aimed only at a spiritual restructuring of religious life, but in Ismā'īlism the function of Neoplatonic ideas was to take hold of the whole organism of Islam and to modify it. The idea of the imamate is a mere cloak over this destructive work, an ostensibly Islamic point of leverage on which the movement could gain a purchase. The Ismā'īlīs started with the Neoplatonic theory of emanations. The so-called "Sincere Brethren"[r] of Basra had, in a systematic encyclopedia, elaborated that theory into a religio-philosophical structure, which the Ismā'īlīs now followed out to its extreme consequences. They constructed a historical reflection of the cosmic emanations posited by Neoplatonism: a theory of periodical manifestations of the Universal Intellect. The sequence of these manifestations begins with Adam, continues through Noah, Abraham, Moses, Jesus, and Muhammad, and concludes with the *Imām* following the sixth *Imām* of the Shī'īs (these are Ismā'īl and his son Muḥammad b. Ismā'īl), forming a cycle of seven "Speakers" (*nāṭiq*). The interval between any two of these "Speakers" is filled by a series of seven persons, also emanations of transcendental powers, who reinforce the work of the Speaker they follow and prepare the work of the Speaker to come. This is a well-defined, artificially constructed hierarchy in whose progressive unfolding since the beginning of the world the divine mind has been revealing itself to mankind in ever more perfect manifestations. Each manifestation perfects the work of the one before it. Divine revelation did not conclude at a particular date in the history of the world. With the same cyclical regularity, the seventh *nāṭiq* is followed by the *Mahdī* who, as an even more perfect manifestation of the Universal Intellect, is destined to pass beyond the work of his predecessors, including that of the Prophet Muhammad.

With this twist in the concept of the *Mahdī*, one of the basic principles of Islam was destroyed, one that ordinary Shī'ism had not dared to undermine. To a Muslim, Muhammad was the "seal of the prophets." This is an attribute that the Qur'ān had conferred on Muhammad, although probably in a different sense (33:40). Sunnī and Shī'ī theology alike understood it to mean that Muhammad ended the series of Prophets

[r] On the name "Sincere Brethren" (*Ikhwān al-Ṣafā*), see I. Goldziher, "Über die Benennung der Ichwān al-Safā," *Der Islam*, X (1910), 22-26 (= *Gesammelte Schriften*, V, 197ff.); a series of articles was devoted to the topic by Y. Marquet and published in the *Revue des Etudes Islamiques*, 1962-1964, in *Arabica*, 1961-1964, and in *Studia Islamica*, parts 24 and 25. The subject is examined at greater length by Yves Marquet in his thesis, "La Philosophie des Ihwan Safa de Dieu à l'homme" (Lille, 1973, Service de Reproduction des Thèses).

forever, that he had accomplished for all eternity what his predecessors had prepared, that he was God's last messenger delivering God's last message to mankind. The "awaited *Mahdī*," in this view, will do no more than reestablish the work of the last prophet, squandered by the corruption of mankind. He will "follow in the tracks," and bear the name, of that last prophet. He will not himself be a prophet, much less a teacher who transcends Muhammad's revelation and passes to a higher evolutionary stage in the history of the divine plan of salvation.[150] In the Ismāʿīlīs' system of emanations, Muhammad's prophetic character and the law Muhammad brought in the name of God lose the significance they have in the rest of Islam, including Shīʿism.

Under the flag of the Shīʿī party of the Ismāʿīlīya—which served as pretext—these doctrines, so destructive of Islam, were disseminated by secret propaganda, and by gradual initiation into successive degrees of knowledge.[s] As the higher degrees of initiation are reached, it becomes clear that the profession of adherence to the religion of Muhammad is form devoid of content. In the end Ismāʿīlism is a destruction of all positive law and doctrine in Islam. But even in the preparatory stages, Islamic law and tradition, as well as the sacred history in the Qur'ān, are understood allegorically. The literal sense is forced into the background, as mere husk around the true spiritual essence. Just as Neoplatonic doctrine inculcates the aspiration to strip away the corporeal husk and enter the heavenly home of the Universal Soul, so the Ismāʿīlī initiate must remove the bodily husk of the law by rising to ever higher and purer knowledge, and he must soar to the world of pure spirituality. The law is only a pedagogical tool that has a temporary, relative value for the imma-

[150] It is, however, noteworthy that in an old description of the events that will accompany, and the results that will follow, the appearance of the *Mahdī*, it is stressed that from that time on the enjoyment of wine will be permitted to Muslims. See Jāḥiẓ, *Ḥayawān*, V, 75:4 [V, 237].

[s] Goldziher's presentation of Ismāʿīlī doctrines, with his stress on their antinomian and destructive character and on the system of initiation by which converts were gradually led to complete nihilism, reflects the state of knowledge of his time, based largely on anti-Ismāʿīlī polemics. The discovery of Ismāʿīlī sources in considerable quantity and the studies based on them have made possible a more accurate interpretation of Ismāʿīlī doctrine and history. It is now seen that extreme antinomianism was only one trend within the Ismāʿīlī camp and, moreover, one that only prevailed very briefly. The quasi-masonic system of initiation ascribed to the sectaries by their enemies is also now treated with some reserve. A major contribution to the study of Ismāʿīlī doctrines was made by Goldziher himself, in his book *Streitschrift des Ġazālī gegen die Bāṭinijja-Sekte* (Leiden, 1916). This consists of a detailed analysis of a treatise by Ghazālī refuting the doctrines of the Ismāʿīlīs, together with excerpts from the unpublished Arabic text of the *Mustaẓhirī* (see below, n. 157).

ture.[151] It is a symbol whose real meaning is to be sought in the spiritual assets one strives to attain by it. They go so far as to recognize as true believers only those who follow these destructive doctrines. Those who understand the laws and the narratives of the Qur'ān according to their literal sense are unbelievers.

The allegorical understanding of the law and the unbinding character of the literal sense of the law were no doubt foreshadowed in the fact that Ismā'īl, whose name the sect bears, was rejected by the opposing Imāmīs because he was guilty of drinking wine and had thus rendered himself unworthy of succession to the imamate. A person in whom the sanctity of the *Imām*-to-be has inhered from birth—so answer those who consider Ismā'īl's name their watchword—cannot commit a sinful act. For Ismā'īl, and therefore for his followers, the prohibition of wine had only an allegorical sense. It is just so with the other laws: fasting, pilgrimage, and so on. Their opponents asserted that this Ismā'īlī view of religion also included the throwing off of moral laws and the permission of all manner of infamy.[152] There is no reason to believe that malicious descriptions of this sort correspond to the facts.

Because of its initiatory character and its hierarchy of degrees of knowledge, the Ismā'īlī system was particularly well suited for clandestine propaganda. Astute calculation made skillful use of it to stir up movements that affected large parts of the Islamic world. The establishment of the Fāṭimid empire in North Africa, and then in Egypt and the areas under Egyptian control (909-1171), was on the foundation of Ismā'īlī subversion. Consistent Ismā'īlīs could not be content with the ultimate manifestation of the Universal Intellect in the Fāṭimid *Imām*. The circle must be closed. In the year 1017 they thought the time had come for the Fāṭimid caliph Ḥākim to reveal himself as an incarnation of God. When in the year 1021 Ḥākim vanished, presumably by assassination, his few followers refused to believe that he was really dead. He must be alive, in occultation, and would return (*raj'a*, Sec. 11 above). To this day belief in the divinity of Ḥākim has endured among the Druzes of Lebanon. The group that the history of the Crusades knows by the name of Assassins is also an offshoot of the Ismā'īlī movement.[t]

[151] "Die Religion des Islams," p. 126:7-32.

[152] A hate-filled description of this sort is given by the pseudo-Balhkī, *Al-Bad' wa'l-ta'rīkh*, edited and translated by Clément Huart (Paris, 1899-1919), IV, 8.

[t] The Druzes, estimated to number about a quarter of a million, are now divided between Lebanon, Syria, and Israel. Their doctrines, though allegedly secret, are fairly well known, thanks to the presence of large numbers of Druze manuscripts in Western public collec-

The relation of this religious revolution to Islam proper is best understood in the light of its essential aspect: the allegorical interpretation of basic religious material. Truth is contained in the esoteric sense (*bāṭin*). The outward meaning (*ẓāhir*) is an insubstantial veil meant for the uninitiated. In proportion as they are prepared, the veil is drawn aside to let them glimpse the undisguised truth face to face. Hence the name *Bāṭinīya*, which the theologians applied to the supporters of these theories.

Such theories were fostered by Ismāʿīlīs and Sufis alike. In Sufism, too, as a result of the same Neoplatonic principles, the doctrine of the "esoteric meaning" gained central importance.[153] An Ismāʿīlī Bāṭinī might have written, word for word, the following passage by the mystical poet Jalāl al-Dīn Rūmī, expressing the true thrust of the allegorical view:

> Know that the words of the Qur'ān are simple, but they conceal beneath the outward meaning an inner, secret one;
> Besides this secret meaning there is yet a third that bewilders the subtlest intelligence;
> The fourth meaning none has discerned but God, who is beyond comparison and is the source of sufficiency for all.
> In this way one can advance to seven meanings, one after the other.
> So, my son, do not confine your view to the outward sense as the demons did who saw only clay in Adam;
> The outward sense of the Qur'ān is like Adam's body; only its exterior is visible but its soul is hidden.[154]

In their gradually increasing subtlety, these levels of a profound, secret meaning concealed beneath the outward wrap of literal expression remind one of what the Ismāʿīlīya calls the *ta'wīl al-ta'wīl*, the secret interpretation of the secret interpretation. With each advance to the next higher level, the mystical and symbolic content of the previous level becomes a material substratum for an even subtler interpretation,[155] until

---

tions. On the history and doctrines of the Druzes, see the article "Durūz" in *EI*² (by M.G.S. Hodgson, M. C. Şihabeddin Tekindag, and M. Tayyib Gökbilgin). On the Assassins, see M.G.S. Hodgson, *The Order of Assassins: The Struggle of the Early Nizārī Ismāʿīlīs against the Islamic World* (The Hague, 1955), and B. Lewis, *The Assassins: a Radical Sect in Islam* (London, 1967).

[153] M. J. de Goeje, *Mémoire sur les Carmathes du Bahraïn et les Fatimides*, 2nd ed. (Leiden, 1886), esp. pp. 158-70.

[154] *Masnavī* (Whinfield), p. 169.

[155] Masʿūdī, *Al-Tanbīh wa'l-ishrāf*, edited by M. J. de Goeje (Leiden, 1894), p. 395:11.

the originally Islamic object of the exegetical process has dissolved into thin air.

Ismā'īlism, with its boundless extravagance in *ta'wīl*, inspired a number of less influential offshoots. The most important among them is the secret doctrine of the so-called Ḥurūfīs ("those who interpret the letters of the alphabet"), founded in 800/1397-1398 by a certain Faḍl Allāh from Astarābād. It, too, is based on the theory of the cyclical evolution of the World Spirit. Faḍl Allāh represented himself as a manifestation of the godhead, and his message as the most perfect revelation of the truth. For this he suffered at Timur's hands a martyr's death. He combined his doctrine with a particularly ingenious symbolic interpretation of the letters of the alphabet and their numerical values, to which he ascribed cosmic meanings and effects. Using this kabbalistic method, ever more extensively elaborated by his followers, the Ḥurūfīs practiced a *ta'wīl* of the Qur'ān that retained hardly anything from the original intent of the book. Their pantheism offered many points of contact with the doctrines of the Sufis, among whom the order of the Bektashis espoused the Ḥurūfī system.[156]

The numbering of the *Imāms* became a matter of secondary importance to these groups that developed out of, and modeled themselves on, Ismā'īlism. Their views were quite compatible with recognition of the Twelvers' line. The essential was that they rejected the literal understanding of the facts of Muslim belief and made extravagant use of 'Alid traditions. These traditions served as vehicles for their gnostic mysteries touching the ever-increasing perfection of revelation, visible in ever new manifestations of the godhead.

19. The philosophizing streak in their system did not free the Ismā'īlīs from the narrow views characteristic of the ordinary Shī'a. This is chiefly seen in two aspects.

First, they carried to an extreme the doctrine, related to the theory of the imamate, that belief must be dictated by an authority. For this reason the Ismā'īlīs were given the name *ta'līmīya*, "those who receive instruction." The name refers to their absolute dependence on the doctrinal authority of the *Imām*, contrasting that dependence with the right of individual investigation and with the collective contribution of the *ijmā'*. Calling them by the name *ta'līmīya*, Ghazālī attacks them in several

[156] About this system and its literature, see the publication by Clément Huart and Dr. Riza Tawfiq, *Textes persans relatifs à la secte des Houroûfîs*; G. Jacob, *Die Bektaschijje in ihrem Verhältnis zu verwandten Erscheinungen*.

polemical writings,[u] including one in the form of a Platonic dialogue in which he engages one of their representatives.[157] Ismā'īlī allegorization considered the Qur'ānic laws mere forms under which submission was demanded to the authority of the *Imām*.[158] Hand in hand with this cult of authority went the duty of unconditional obedience to one's superiors. It was particularly in evidence among the Assassins. This offshoot of the Ismā'īlī movement manifested it in acts of outright terrorism.[159]

Second, the Ismā'īlīya shares with the ordinary Shī'a an intense intolerance toward people who think differently from them. Let it suffice to cite, instead of many examples, a short passage from an interesting Ismā'īlī book about the alms tax and its allegorical interpretation, available in a Leyden manuscript: "He who considers another authority the equal of his *Imām* (lit. associates it with him, *ashraka*), or doubts his *Imām*, is like him who considers someone to be of the same rank as the Prophet, and doubts the Prophet. By doing so he becomes like him who recognizes another God besides Allah. Whoever associates someone (with the *Imām* as the *Imām*'s equal) or doubts or denies the *Imām*, is *najas* (unclean), not *ṭāhir* (pure). It is forbidden to make use of anything that has come into the possession of such a person."[160] Aside from the Druzes—the Ismā'īlīs who deified Ḥākim and went their own way—there are still Ismā'īlīs today, scattered in central Syria[161] and various other areas of the Islamic world, especially in Persia and India, where they are known as Khojas.[162] Quite recently, an Ismā'īlī meeting-house was built in Zan-

[u] On one of these texts, studied by Goldziher, see above, note *s*.

[157] In his Confessions (*Munqidh*), Ghazālī enumerates the polemical works that he has directed against this sect. One of them bears the name of the caliph to whom he dedicated it (*al-Mustaẓhirī*). [See *Al-Munqidh min al-ḍalāl*, edited by Jamīl Ṣalībā and Kāmil 'Ayyād, 5th ed. (Damascus, 1376/1956), pp. 92f.] The most interesting of these works, in form and content, is the *Just Balance* (*Al-Qusṭās al-mustaqīm*), the polemical dialogue, mentioned above, between the author and an Ismā'īlī (edited by Muṣṭafā al-Qabbānī, Cairo, 1318/1900).

[158] Cf. de Goeje, *Mémoire sur les Carmathes*, p. 171.

[159] On the position of the Assassins within the Ismā'īlī movements, see Stanislas Guyard, "Un Grand Maître des Assassins au temps de Saladin," *JA*, 7th Series, IX (1877), 324ff. Cf. Ibn Jubayr, *Riḥla*, p. 255:3ff. [The work of Stanislas Guyard, cited by Goldziher, has been superseded by a considerable body of later work. For details, see the books by Hodgson and Lewis cited in note *t* above.]

[160] Cf. my essay "Lā Misāsa," *Revue Africaine*, LII (1908), 25.

[161] There are about nine thousand of them there. About their Syrian settlements see Lammens, "Au Pays des Nosairis," *ROC*, V (1900), p. 54 of the offprint [see *ROC*, V (1900), 312ff.], where additional bibliography is furnished.

[162] Cf. Freiherr von Oppenheim, *Vom Mittelmeer zum Persischen Golf* (Berlin, 1899-1900), I, 133 n. In the same book there is a survey of the branches of the Ismā'īlīya. The Khojas do not, however, follow the sevener-system of the Ismā'īlī doctrine of *Imāms*; cf. the association *Khoja ithnā 'asharī jamā'at* (that is, Twelvers), *RMM*, VIII (1909), 491.

zibar.[163] These Ismāʿīlīs of today recognize as their chief a man with the title Agha Khan.[v] This dignitary traces his family tree to the Nizārī branch of the Fāṭimid dynasty, as a descendant of the Assassin princes who had laid claim to Nizārī ancestry.[164]

To the Agha Khan, who resides at present in Bombay and in other places in India, his faithful pay homage in the form of *zakāt* taxes and rich donations. The present Agha Khan is a man of abundant means, rather worldly, imbued with the ideas of modern civilization, and given to using his wealth for extensive travel. He has been in London, Paris, the United States, and also at the Japanese court in Tokyo. He shows scarcely a trace of the principles of the system that it is his office to represent. He spends his wealth generously to encourage modern cultural movements in Indian Islam, which we will examine in the further course of this work. He has a leading share in the creation of such movements.[165] Only recently, the All-India Moslem League chose him as their president.[166] He is a stalwart advocate of English rule, which he considers beneficial for the peoples of India. During the latest home-rule movements, he addressed a warning to the Muslims of India—also meant for the Hindus—demonstrating the folly and immaturity of the desire for independence and calling attention to the necessary and salutary character of English rule, arguing that it is a unifying and equalizing principle among the disparate peoples with divergent aspirations who compose the population of India.[167]

[163] *RMM*, II (1907), 373.

[v] The Ismāʿīlīs of the present day are divided into several subgroups of which one, probably the largest and most important, recognizes the Agha Khan as its chief, and the remainder do not. The followers of the Agha Khan are to be found in India and Pakistan, where they are known as Khojas, in Iran, Afghanistan, and Soviet Central Asia, and in central Syria east and west of the town of Hama. Non-Agha-Khani Ismāʿīlīs are also to be found in India and Pakistan, where they are known as Bohoras, and in the Yemen. Indian and Pakistani Ismāʿīlīs of both persuasions have settled in numbers in East Africa. The title Agha Khan was conferred on the head of the sect by the Shah of Persia in the early nineteenth century, and retained thereafter. After an unsuccessful revolt against Iranian rule in 1838, the Agha Khan fled to Sind in British India, and later moved to Bombay, which remained his residence and the headquarters of the sect. The present Agha Khan (1980) is the grandson of the Agha Khan described by Goldziher.

[164] See A. Chatelier's article "Aga Khan" in *RMM*, I (1906-1907), 48-85. On the rank of Agha Khan and its prehistory (in Persia, with their residence in Kahk), see Guyard, "Un Grand Maître des Assassins," pp. 378ff.

[165] Cf. M. Hartmann, "Der Islam 1907," *MSOS*, XI (1908), ii, 25 [apparently an offprint is meant; see p. 231 of the issue cited]. The name of Lady Agha Khan is also encountered among those who further the Indian movement for the education of women; *RMM*, VII (1909), 483:20.

[166] *RMM*, IV (1908), 852.

[167] Translated *ibid.*, VI (1908), 548-51. [The attitudes ascribed to the Agha Khan and ex-

20. The Shī'ī form of belief endowed 'Alī and his descendants with superhuman attributes. In doing so it enabled them to serve as vehicles for the remnants of atrophied mythological traditions. Stories about persons at once human and divine—fables that had existed in the traditions of the peoples converted to Islam but that had lost their hold with the overthrow of the old religions—could easily take refuge among the 'Alid legends and, reinterpreted, continue alive. The members of the 'Alid family assumed the attributes of mythological figures, and these attributes could fit without difficulty into the Shī'ī realm of ideas. It raised few scruples if venerated figures were elevated above the earthly sphere and made to share in superhuman powers.

How far even moderate Shī'ism goes in this respect, we have already had occasion to see: the luminous substances of 'Alī and his family are imprinted upon God's throne. According to a legend, Ḥasan and Ḥusayn wore amulets filled with down from the wings of the angel Gabriel.[168] In this environment mythological features could thus very easily attach themselves to figures of the house of 'Alī. For example, 'Alī becomes a god of thunder; 'Alī appears in the clouds and causes thunder and lightning; lightning is the wand he brandishes. Just as in Greek myth the red that suffuses the sky at sunset is the blood of Adonis killed by the boar, in Shī'ī legend the same red is the blood of the murdered Ḥusayn. Before his death the red flush of sunset had not existed.[169] The cosmographer Qazwīnī (d. 682/1283) tells of the Baghrāj, a Turkic people, that it is ruled by a dynasty that traces its origin to the 'Alid Yaḥyā ibn Zayd. They have in their keeping a gilded book, on the outside of which is inscribed an elegy on Zayd's death. They look upon this book with a religious veneration. They call Zayd "King of the Arabs," 'Alī "God of the Arabs." When they look up at the sky they look fixedly, with their mouths open, and say: "There is the God of the Arabs going up and down."[170]

It was in particular the Neoplatonic and Gnostic elements, superimposed on Islamic belief by Ismā'īlī sectarianism, that enabled some forms of Shī'ī Islam to serve as a cover under which the wreckage of ancient

---

pressed by Goldziher were not unusual among Indian Muslim leaders and European scholars in 1910. For the Agha Khan's own version of these events, written after the partition and independence of India, see *The Memoirs of Agha Khan: World Enough and Time* (London, 1954). For two varying modern interpretations of these events, see Wilfred Cantwell Smith, *Modern Islam in India* (London, 1946), especially pp. 246ff., and P. Hardy, *The Muslims of British India* (Cambridge, 1972), especially pp. 164ff.]

[168] *Aghānī*, XIV, 163:20.

[169] *Muhammedanische Studien*, II, 331 [= *Muslim Studies*, II, 301].

[170] Qazwīnī, *Āthār al-bilād*, p. 390.

pagan religions was preserved. As the persons of the holy family were elevated to the sphere of divinity, they could easily serve as hypostases for old gods masked under a nomenclature with an Islamic ring.

In this fashion, in the valleys of Lebanon (between Tripoli and Antioch), ancient Syrian paganism survived in ostensibly Shī'ī-Islamic form, in the sect of the Nuṣayrīs. In their Twelver cult unmistakably pagan conceptions predominate. In the regions where this Shī'ī sect is represented, the ancient pagan religion was still vigorous shortly before the penetration of Islam, and Christianity, too, was very late in gaining a foothold.[171] Thus it is all the easier to account for the interweaving of Islamic conceptions with ancient pagan elements. This religion is Islam only in appearance. The soul of these people has in reality preserved the pagan traditions of their ancestors, and quite superficially transferred them to the new apparent objects of the cult. In the resulting amalgam of paganism, gnosticism, and Islam, the Islamic component does no more than give a distinct form to a pagan nature-cult, a mere name to pagan religious ideas. 'Alī is, as they say in a prayer, "eternal in his divine nature; in his inner reality he is our God, although outwardly he is our *Imām*."[172] In the various Nuṣayrī sects 'Alī is identified with various divine forces of nature. Heightening a Shī'ī title of him as "emir of the bees," that is, the stars, most regard him as a moon god. We have mentioned that next to 'Alī, Muhammad himself is reduced to the subordinate role of the "Veil." Muhammad, 'Alī, and Salmān form a divine triad that remains attached, with all its trimmings, to the pagan nature cult.

It is really the cult of sky, sun, moon, and other forces of nature that appears in the cult of 'Alī and his family, the persons connected with the 'Alid legends, and the *Imāms*. These transferences are made palatable with the help of the gnosticism that pervades all such vestigial paganism. Their true character is gradually disclosed to the novice as he advances from degree to degree of initiation. Even at the lower stages Islamic law is allowed no more than a symbolic meaning—as among the Ismā'īlīs, to whom, by the way, the Nuṣayrīs are hostile. For the adept, all Islam proper completely evaporates. The Qur'ān itself takes a position subordinate to another holy book. In spite of the mystifying ways of such sectarian groups, this book has been made public by a Nuṣayrī convert to

[171] Harnack, *Die Mission und Ausbreitung des Christentums*, p. 429 [4th ed., II, 658f. = *The Mission and Expansion of Christianity*, II, 123].

[172] Sulaymān al-Adhanī, *Al-Bākūra al-sulaymānīya* (Beirut, 1863), p. 10:14; René Dussaud, *Histoire et religion des Noṣairis* (Paris, 1900), p. 164:1.

Christianity. Its significance for the history of religions has been examined several times in the European and American literature.[173] In their own opinion, the Nuṣayrīs are, of course, in contrast to the rest of the Muslims, the true believers in the unity of God (*ahl al-tawḥīd*), and the correct interpreters of the Shī'ī idea. They regard the ordinary Shī'a as *Ẓāhirīya*, people who maintain a superficial understanding of religion and have failed to penetrate to the profound reaches of true monotheism, or as *muqaṣṣira*, people who in their cult of 'Alī fall short of the required measure.[174]

These disguises of ancient Asian paganism are Islamic only in name. In the course of their development they also incorporated several Christian elements, as for example the consecration of bread and wine, a kind of communion, and the celebration of feast days proper to Christianity. The history of religions often shows that such sects with atrophied beliefs are especially prone to syncretism.

We have examined the forms of dissent that influenced the development of Islam before its orthodox conception was conclusively fixed.

But even after it had been fixed, not all minds were at rest. We must now discuss subsequent movements, whose effects are still felt in the modern age.

[173] Dussaud, *Histoire et religion des Noṣairis*, with bibliography. Cf. *Archiv für Religionswissenschaft*, III (1900), 85ff.

[174] *Archiv für Religionswissenschaft*, III (1900), 90. [Since Goldziher's day, Western scholarship has devoted a good deal of attention to the Nuṣayrīs. A bibliography was published in 1939 by Louis Massignon, "Esquisse d'une bibliographie Nuṣayrie" *Mélanges Dussaud* (Paris, 1939), pp. 913-22. See further, Claude Cahen, "Note sur les origines de la communauté syrienne des Nuṣayri," *REI*, XXXVIII (1970), 243-49. Rudolf Strothmann published a number of texts and studies relating to the doctrines and scriptures of the Nuṣayrīs. See in particular his *Esoterische Sonderthemen bei den Nusairi: Geschichten und Traditionen von den Heiligen Meistern aus dem Prophetenhaus* (Berlin, 1958). The Nuṣayrīs are also called 'Alawīs, and it is by this latter name that they are commonly known in modern Syria. In recent years, members of the 'Alawī sect have played an important and, at times, a dominant role in Syrian politics.]

VI. *Later Developments*

1. In the seventh chapter of his work, *The Origin and Development of the Moral Ideas*, Edward Westermarck examines how custom affects the basic formation of opinions about morality and legality. "In primitive society custom stands for law, and even where social organisation has made some progress it may still remain the sole rule for conduct."[1]

Drawing on diverse literary and historical references, he demonstrates, more amply than his predecessors in this much-discussed field of the history of civilization and law, the importance of custom as a standard of legality and a basis for all ethical and juridical rules. In passing he touches on the ideas of the Arab and Turkoman nomads (p. 164), but he misses the opportunity to inquire more closely into one of the most prominent instances of his object of study: the concept of the *sunna* and its role first among the Arabs and then in Islam.

From time immemorial, the Arabs' chief criterion for determining propriety and lawfulness in any aspect of life had been conformity in word and deed to ancestral norm and usage. Whatever is true and just must accord with, and be rooted in, inherited opinion and custom. These constitute the *sunna*. The *sunna* was their law and their *sacra*. It was the sole source of their legal practice and their religion; to forsake it was to transgress against the inviolable rules of hallowed custom. This applied to actions and, for the same reasons, to inherited ideas. In the sphere of

[1] Westermarck, *The Origin and Development of the Moral Ideas*, I, 161. In vol. II of the same work, pp. 519f., there are examples relevant to the subject at hand, drawn from primitive cultures and considered in connection with the cult of the dead.

[Even in this chapter dealing with "later events," Goldziher's pages have stood up remarkably well to the passage of time. Inevitably, however, there is much to add to what he said, in relation both to developments within Islam and to the study of these developments from outside. Among a number of books and studies dealing with modern Islam, mention may be made of the following: Wilfred Cantwell Smith, *Islam in Modern History* (Princeton, 1957); Walther Braune, *Der islamische Orient zwischen Vergangenheit und Zukunft, eine geschichtstheologische Analyse seiner Stellung in der Weltsituation* (Bern and Munich, 1960); Pierre Rondot, *L'Islam et les musulmans d'aujourd'hui* (Paris, 1958); G. E. von Grunebaum, *Modern Islam: the Search for Cultural Identity* (Berkeley and Los Angeles, 1962); B. Lewis, *The Middle East and the West* (London and New York, 1966), especially chapter V, "The Revolt of Islam."]

ideas, too, the group could accept nothing new that was not in harmony with the views of its ancestors.[2] From this we can understand the objections of the Meccans, whose most frequent argument against the Prophet preaching to them of Paradise, Hell, and Judgment Day was that their ancestors had known nothing about such things and that they themselves could only walk in the way of their ancestors.[3] In contrast with their ancient traditions, Muhammad's prophecy was in their view a *dīn muḥdath*, a brand new—and consequently reprehensible—faith.[4]

Consciousness of the *sunna* may be regarded as one of the phenomena Herbert Spencer calls "representative feelings," that is, "organic results that a segment of mankind has gathered through the course of centuries, that become condensed into an inherited instinct and constitute an object of heredity in the individual."[5]

When the Arabs accepted Islam—which had commanded them to break with their authentic *sunna*—they brought the concept of *sunna* with them. From that time forth it became the main pillar of the Islamic view of law and religion. There was, naturally, one essential modification: in Islam one could not draw one's precedents from the pagan *sunna*. Its point of departure was shifted; its source now consisted in the doctrines, conceptions, and practices of the oldest generation of Muslims, founders of an entirely different *sunna* from what the original Arab one had been. Henceforth the norm was the demonstrable usage and view first of the Prophet and then of his Companions. People did not so much ask what was, in a given situation, good or proper in itself, as what the Prophet and his Companions had said about the matter, how they had acted,[6] and what had accordingly been passed down as the proper view and the proper action. These were attested and made known to later generations by the hadith, which preserved reports of the words and deeds of these models of truth and lawfulness. It is true that in the course of the earliest developments of Islamic law, a tendency made itself felt to grant jurists

[2] "Die Religion des Islams," p. 100. This feeling prevails even today among those Arabs who remained unaffected by historic cultural influences. In various parts of the land they inhabit, they use the word *silf*, ancestral custom, to denote this conception of *sunna*. See C. Landberg, *Études sur les dialectes de l'Arabie méridionale* (Leiden, 1901-1913), II, 743.

[3] See *Muhammedanische Studien*, I, 9-12 [= *Muslim Studies*, I, 18-21].

[4] Ibn Sa'd, III, i, 37:3; VIII, 29:10. The Qur'ān too refers to its admonition as *dhikr muḥdath* (21:2, 26:5). The commentators, however, take the phrase to mean "repeated (renewed) admonition."

[5] I have unfortunately lost the page reference to this quotation.

[6] Cf. D. B. MacDonald, "Moral Education of the Young among Muslims," *International Journal of Ethics*, XV (1904-1905), 290.

broad authority to make free use of opinion and deductive reasoning in deriving legal rules, whenever they were faced with suspicious hadiths or the lack of trustworthy and explicit hadiths (Ch. II, Sec. 5). But no one went so far as to deny the primacy of the *sunna* whenever an undoubtedly authentic tradition was available, rendering the application of speculative reasoning superfluous.

It was in this fashion that the need for a *sunna* became a "representative emotion" in Islam. The whole concern of the pious and faithful was to conform to the *sunna* of the Companions, to act only as the *sunna* prescribed, and to shun all that might contradict it or that had no foundation in it. If anything contradicted—or, in a stricter view, was not identical with—ancient usage (the *sunna*), they called it *bid'a*, "innovation," whether it had to do with belief or with the most trivial aspects of daily life.[7] The proponents of rigor rejected all forms of *bid'a*: everything that could not be attested among the views and practices of the ancients.

2. It was all very well in theory to demand such rigor. No one questioned the theory, but at every step the practice of daily life inevitably collided with it. With new lands and times came changed ways of life and new experiences. They presented needs and led to situations quite foreign to the simple life and thought of the age of the Companions. Moreover, the diverse foreign antecedents and influences that had to be assimilated and digested were bound to make a breach in the consistent maintenance of the rigid concept of the *sunna* as the sole criterion of truth and justice. One had to compromise. Soon fine distinctions were made that could invest certain innovations with legitimacy and bring them into the pale of adherence to the *sunna*. Theories were devised for the circumstances in which a *bid'a* might be considered acceptable, or even as good and praiseworthy. The ingenuity of theologian and casuist found a rich field of action. This has continued to our own time.

Amid these tendencies, the concept of the *ijmā'* proved a balancing element. When a custom had taken root by having been long tolerated and recognized, it finally became *sunna* by virtue of the fact that it had so taken root. For a few generations the pious theologians would rail against the *bid'a*, but with the passage of time it would come to be tolerated, and

[7] Before the tribunal of the stringent followers of the *sunna*, even a conventional phrase of social courtesy must be proved traditionally correct before it is accepted as legitimate. "Where did he take it from?" (Ibn Sa'd, VI, 121:6). In this manner, quite indifferent phrases of greeting are rejected as contrary to the *sunna*. See " 'Alī b. Mejmūn al-Maġribī," p. 310 [= *Gesammelte Schriften*, VI, 18; partial French translation in *Arabica*, VIII (1961), 246]; Makkī, *Qūt al-qulūb*, I, 163. Cf. also *RMM*, III (1907), p. 130.

finally required as a matter on which consensus had been reached. It was then considered *bid'a* to oppose it; he who called for the ancient custom was now censured as an innovator, *mubtadi'*.

An illuminating example is offered by the *mawlid al-nabī*, the celebration of the Prophet's birthday. This folk holiday, kept in all regions of the orthodox Islamic world, is celebrated at the beginning of the month Rabī' al-awwal, with the participation of the religious authorities. As late as the eighth century of the Hijra, it was a point of controversy among Muslim theologians whether this holiday was justified by *sunna*. Many rejected it as *bid'a*. *Fatwās* were issued in favor and against. It has since become, on the strength of popular sanction, an indispensable part of Muslim life. It would now occur to no one to think of it as *bid'a*, in the bad sense of the word.[8] The same is true of other religious feast days and liturgical ceremonies that arose in late centuries; they were not recognized without a struggle, and only after having long been branded as *bid'a*.[9] The history of Islam proves that Muslim theologians, no matter how rigid their initial attitude was to newly adopted customs, were not averse, once those customs had become established, to giving up their resistance and to extending the sanction of *ijmā'* to what shortly before they had considered *bid'a*.

3. The evidence allows us to say that on the whole the religious leaders of Islam, despite all pious upholding of the concept of the *sunna*, did not always stubbornly ignore changing needs and new circumstances that arose with the passage of time. Thus it would be wrong to describe Islamic law as immutable from the first to the last.

Even in the early period of Islam, political and economic institutions had to be developed beyond the usage of primitive Islam. Not everyone refused to take new circumstances into account; not everyone felt that to take them into account was a laxity incompatible with the spirit of the *sunna*.

One of the four orthodox rites—the rite attached to the name of Mālik ibn Anas (Ch. II, Sec. 5)—recognizes *maṣlaḥa* (*utilitas publica*, that which is required for the benefit of the community) as a guiding consideration in the application of the law. One may depart from the norms established in the law if it is proved that the interest of the community requires a judg-

[8] Cf. the bibliography in Muḥammad Tawfīq al-Bakrī, *Bayt al-ṣiddīq* (Cairo, A.H. 1323), pp. 404ff.

[9] "Ueber den Brauch der Maḥjā-Versammlungen im Islam," *WZKM*, XV (1901), 33ff. [= *Gesammelte Schriften*, IV, 277ff.; partial French translation in *Arabica*, VIII (1961), 238ff.].

ment that differs from the law. (This is in Roman law the principle of *corrigere ius propter utilitatem publicam.*) To be sure, this freedom applies only to extraordinary cases. It must not lead to a definitive abrogation of the law, but the statement of the principle is itself a sign that some flexibility is admissible within the law. We ought not overlook an important statement by the highly regarded theologian al-Zurqānī (d. 1122/1710 in Cairo) who, in a passage of his commentary on Mālik's codex (*al-Muwaṭṭa'*) quite unambiguously declares that one may, in keeping with new circumstances, arrive at new legal decisions. "It is nothing strange"—he says in conclusion—"that laws should be adapted to circumstances."[10]

Thus from the viewpoint of religious law, the gate of "innovation" and reform is not closed to Islam. Under the protection of this freedom, new institutions, borrowed from Western civilization, were granted entry into Muslim life. In certain cases, it is true, they called forth the opposition of the obscurantists, but they were ultimately sanctioned by the formal *fatwās* of acknowledged scholars of the law, and thus secured against extreme orthodox attacks. It is, to be sure, rather repugnant that salutary institutions with a purely practical and secular role must have their entrance into life justified by a *fatwā*, after discussion of their admissibility under the religious law.

It was under the protection of such theological patents that the innovations adopted in Islamic society since the eighteenth century (the first being perhaps the introduction of the printing press in 1729, in Istanbul)[a] acquired an untroubled title to legitimate existence. In the economic sphere, as well, there was need for the ingenuity of the religious lawyers: they had to find means of circumventing the apparent obstacles to the admission into Islamic society of certain institutions required by the

[10] Zurqānī's commentary on the *Muwaṭṭa'*, I, 360.

[a] On these matters, see *EI*[2] articles "Bid'a" (by J. Robson) and "Istiḥsān and Istiṣlāḥ" (by R. Paret). The first printing presses in Turkey were set up by Jewish refugees from Spain before the end of the fifteenth century. They were authorized to do so on condition that they did not print any books in Turkish or Arabic and confined themselves to Hebrew and European languages. The Jews were followed by the Armenians and Greeks, who set up presses in 1567 and 1627, respectively. The ban on printing in Turkish or Arabic remained effective until the eighteenth century when, after some argument, Shaykh al-Islām 'Abdallah Efendi issued a ruling authorizing the printing of books in Turkish provided that they dealt with subjects other than religion. An imperial decree giving permission for the establishment of a Turkish printing press was issued in 1727, and the first book was published in February 1729. For further details and bibliographies, see B. Lewis, *The Emergence of Modern Turkey*, 2nd ed. (London, 1968), pp. 41–42, 50–51.

modern age. For example, insurance contracts are suspect to rigorous Islam, since they may be regarded as a form of gambling. The jurists are now toiling to establish distinctions that will allow scrupulous Muslims to avail themselves of insurance.[b] Theological learning had to remove similar obstacles to the institution of savings banks. Such an institution is theoretically not admissible in a society whose law prohibits the charging not only of usurious, but of all forms of interest.[11] Nonetheless, in a learned *fatwā* dealing with this matter, Shaykh Muḥammad ʿAbduh, the Egyptian *muftī* who died in 1905, found ways to show that under the religious law savings banks and the drawing of dividends were admissible in Islamic society. Similarly, his colleagues in Istanbul had handed down earlier *fatwās* that made it religiously possible for the Ottoman state to issue government bonds bearing interest.[12]

The same phenomenon could most recently be seen in the domain of the great constitutional issues. We have witnessed, in the course of the most recent upheavals in Muslim states,[c] that the introduction of con-

[b] For discussions of the views of Muslim jurists on insurance, see C. A. Nallino, "Delle assicurazioni in diritto musulmano ḥanafita," *Oriente Moderno*, VII (1927), 446–61, reprinted in Nallino, *Raccolta di scritti editi e inediti*, IV (Rome, 1942), 63–84; E. Klingmüller, "The Concept and Development of Insurance in Islamic Countries," *Islamic Culture*, XLIII (1969), 27-37. On interest, see *EI*¹ article "Ribā" (by J. Schacht); J. Schacht, *An Introduction to Islamic Law*, pp. 145ff.; Fazlur Rahman, "Ribā and Interest," *Islamic Studies*, III (1964), 1–43; N. Cağatay, "Ribā and Interest Concept and Banking in the Ottoman Empire," *Studia Islamica*, XXXII (1970), 53–68.

[11] ʿAbdul-Hakīm Hikmet, "La Médecine en Turquie," *RMM*, III (1907), 60. [Sic. This passage contains nothing relevant to the subject of interest and usury. In the volumes published up until 1910, these matters are discussed in *RMM*, VII (1909), 186–88; VIII (1909), 514-16.]

[12] Among the reasons given for the deposition of the Moroccan Sultan ʿAbd al-ʿAzīz was, together with other charges of actions contrary to Islam, his acceptance of a bank, "which causes interest to accrue on money, which is a great sin"; E. Michaux-Bellaire, "Proclamation de la déchéance de Moulay Abd el Aziz . . . par les ouléma de Fes," *RMM*, V (1908), 428. About the religious anxiety that this question causes among modern Indian Muslims, see now M. Hartmann, "Der Islam 1908," *MSOS*, XII (1909), ii, 101. Cf. Ben Ali Fakar, *L'Usure en droit musulman* (Lyon, 1908), esp. pp. 119, 128. About the Islamic law concerning usury, see Th. W. Juynboll, *Handbuch des islamischen Gesetzes*, pp. 270ff., and the bibliography, *ibid.*, p. 358:12 from bottom ff. [On Ottoman bonds and assignats, see *EI*² articles "Ashām" (by B. Lewis) and "Ḳāʾime" (by R. H. Davison).]

[c] Goldziher is here referring to the constitutional revolutions that took place in Iran in 1906 and in Turkey in 1908. On these and other similar movements in Muslim countries, see *Dustur, A Survey of the Constitutions of the Arab and Muslim States, reprinted, with additional material, from the 2nd edition of the Encyclopaedia of Islam* (Leiden, 1966), where further bibliographical indications are given. On the development of libertarian and constitutional political thought, see B. Lewis, *The Middle East and the West*, chapter 3, "The Quest for Freedom"; idem, *Islam in History*, section 6.

stitutional government, in both Sunnī and Shī'ī Islam, received better than a forced approbation from the orthodox jurists; they brought the Qur'ān itself to bear, demonstrating from it that the parliamentary form of government alone conforms to the law (*shūrā* in Sura 42, vs. 38, and elsewhere, is so interpreted).[13] We have seen that the Shī'ī mollahs, following the *mujtahids* of the holy places Najaf and Karbalā—whose authority is greatest in the religious life of Shī'ī Persia—supplied the revolutionaries with a religious warrant, referring in their parliamentary demands to the "Hidden *Imām*" himself (Ch. V, Sec. 12). Authoritative doctors of Islam are making efforts, in a large number of theological tractates, to find support in Qur'ān and hadith for the requirements of modern political life, as also for the requirements of progress in civil life (the question of women, etc.).[14]

4. Our examples have been drawn from modern developments in the Islamic world, but they illustrate a tendency that also existed in earlier centuries.

To this, however, we must add at once this limitation: during all those centuries, there always existed minorities who were less inclined to such give-and-take in the matter of *sunna* and *bid'a*, who delimited the domain of the good *bid'a* as narrowly as possible, who endeavored to keep Islam altogether unadulterated by *bid'a*, and who fought with all possible means, often including fanatical ones, against flexible theory and practice. They severely condemned, as unauthorized and reprehensible innovations, not only legal usages with which ancient Islam could not yet be familiar, but also theological speculations unknown to the early age. They reprobated the resulting dogmatic statements, even those of the Ash'arites who advanced the claim that their doctrines should be recognized as *sunna* (Ch. III, Sec. 12).

In the internal history of Islamic movements we witness a continual struggle of *sunna* against *bid'a*, of intransigent traditionalism against the

[13] The speech with which the Turkish sultan opened a new session of Parliament on November 14, 1909, began with a reference to "parliamentary government prescribed by the *shar'* (religious law)."

[14] Modern Muslim scholars regard it as axiomatic that one should recognize "dans ce réveil un retour à l'ancien état de choses établi par le Prophète et préconisé par lui" (Dr. Riad Ghali, *De la tradition considérée comme source du droit musulman*, p. 5). This tendency has, in recent years, brought into existence a large quantity of apologetic works by Muslim theologians.

[For a guide to the now extensive literature on women, see John Gulick and Margaret E. Gulick, *An Annotated Bibliography of Sources Concerned with Women in the Modern Muslim Middle East*, Princeton Near East Paper No. 17 (Princeton, 1974).]

steady extension of the borders of tradition and the breaching of its original limits. This conflict persisted throughout the history of Islam, in both its dogmatic and legal development. The fact that this struggle was necessary, that in every age it found objects that were then of concern, is the best refutation of the very widespread view that Kuenen expressed in his Hibbert Lectures: "Islam was destined, after a very brief period of growth and development, to stereotype itself once and for all and assume its inalterable shape."[15] Now Kuenen himself linked this statement to a relation of the fact, which I am about to discuss, that in the middle of the eighteenth century the desire to purge Islam from all innovations manifested itself in a powerful reaction. But what follows from this fact is that Islam could not be stereotyped, even at that time, without a bloody struggle.

5. Among the various currents within Islamic theology, none was or is animated by a spirit as consistent and vigorous in the condemnation and persecution of *bid'a* as the school that honors the celebrated *Imām* Aḥmad ibn Ḥanbal (Ch. II, Sec. 5; Ch. IV, Sec. 17) as its patriarch and founder, and bears his name. It is from this group that the most fanatic zealots of the *sunna* have come, those who have been shrillest in the condemnation of all *bid'a* in theology, in ritual, and in the customs of daily life. Had things gone as the Ḥanbalites wished, all Islam would have been reduced in content to what it had been in the earliest Medinese period and recast in the form that, according to their reconstruction, it had had in the age of the Companions. It would be a mistake to think that their disposition has been governed by a romantic impulse, a sentimental yearning for a past beautiful in its naive immediacy. Effects of deep emotion upon these literalists are not much in evidence; it is nothing but a consistent and formal adherence to the principle of the *sunna* that animates their protests.

There was, to be sure, enough to protest about over the course of centuries. The prime example is spiritualist theology with its attendant method of scriptural exegesis, at which the followers of Aḥmad ibn Ḥanbal pointed their finger. We have seen that even in their Ash'arite form these things were heresy to the Ḥanbalites. The Ḥanbalites would not depart from the literal text, not by a hair's breadth; they would interpret nothing into it and nothing out of it. Religious life offered further subjects for Ḥanbalite protests. We must do here without a discussion of

[15] *National Religions and Universal Religions*, p. 54.

minor details, and limit ourselves to a single example. It is one, however, that concerns the religious life of Islam more profoundly than any other.

6. For reasons in part psychological and in part historical, a cultic phenomenon evolved in Islam that soon made itself at home in all of the Islamic world, no matter how contrary it was to the Islamic idea of God, and no matter how repugnant it was to the genuine *sunna*. Among some classes of Muslims its importance exceeds that of the core of the religion, and is in effect the form which the religious consciousness of the people takes. Allah is remote from mankind; close to people's souls are the local saints (*walī*). To these saints they address their religious cult; on them their fears and hopes, their veneration and devotion hang. Saints' tombs and other sacred places connected with this cult are their places of worship, occasionally linked to a crudely fetishistic veneration of relics and concrete cultic objects. The varieties of this cult of saints differ in matter and manner according to geographic and ethnographic conditions, and according to the pre-Islamic past of the peoples who embraced Islam. In the cult of saints, the residues of cults supplanted by Islam come into their own, in more or less abundant measure, in more or less powerful and direct form.[d] With its peculiarities varying from province to province, the cult of saints adds to the uniform, catholic system of universal Islam a popular character determined by local circumstances.[16]

Besides the ethnological conditions, the already intimated psychological need, too, was favorable to the cult of saints in Islam: the need to bridge the gulf that divides the simple believer, with his everyday wishes, from the unapproachable and unreachable divinity, the need to find powers of mediation with which he feels more at home and that seem more accessible to his heart than the godhead enthroned in infinite altitudes, above all human and earthly things. The people acknowledge and fear the exalted Allah as ruler of the world who governs the vast events of the cosmos, and they do not expect Him to care about the petty needs of a

[d] The cult of saints in Islam has given rise to a considerable literature, much of it dealing with particular regions or individual saints. Goldziher himself devoted a general article to the subject in "The Cult of Saints in Islam," *Muslim World*, I (1911), 302-12. For two important studies, see Ernest Gellner, *Saints of the Atlas* (London, 1969), and Clifford Geertz, *Islam Observed: Religious Development in Morocco and Indonesia* (New Haven and London, 1968). A general account will be found in the article "Saints and Martyrs (Mohammedan)," in Hastings, *Encyclopaedia of Religion and Ethics*.

[16] *Muhammedanische Studien*, II, 277ff. [= *Muslim Studies*, II, 255ff.]; E. Doutté, *Les Marabouts* (Paris, 1900; reprinted from *RHR*, XL (1899), 342ff.; XLI (1900), 22ff., 289ff.). Cf. also my lecture "Die Fortschritte der Islamwissenschaft in den letzten drei Jahrzehnten," *Preussische Jahrbücher*, CXXI (1905), 292-98 = *Congress of Arts and Science-Universal Exposition, St. Louis 1904*, II, 508-15 [= *Gesammelte Schriften*, IV, 461-67].

small group, much less a single individual. That the fields in a certain locality or the herds of a certain tribe should thrive, that a particular man should recover from disease or be blessed with many children—such matters are, rather, the concern of the familiar local saint. People offer sacrifices and address vows to him, in order to obtain his good will or—if we prefer to stick to the Islamic language and the ideas embodied in it—"to ensure his intercession with Allah." He is also the guardian and protector of justice and truth among those who venerate him. People are more afraid to swear falsely by his name or in a place sacred to him than to take a false oath by the name of Allah. He dwells among his faithful and watches over their weal and woe, over the righteousness of their ways, and their virtue. In large areas of the Islamic world (for example, among the Beduins of the Arabian steppe and the Kabyles of North Africa) the population's adherence to Islam is reduced mainly to the cult of the local *walī*, and to the rituals and offerings connected with it.

This need was also favorable to those ethnographic processes by which many elements of pre-Islamic religious life were preserved and, under the innumerable local forms of the cult of saints, outwardly clothed in Islamic dress.

The systematic study of the phenomena related to this religio-historical process is one of the most important areas in the religious history of Islam. Here we can only touch on it in a general way. What we stress is that for centuries these forms of the cult have been theoretically tolerated by the authorities of the official religion. They have been content to bar instances of flagrant paganism from these manifestations of the religious spirit—a limitation whose practical extent could never be precisely determined. The official theology had not from the first been quite so tolerant to the needs of popular religious consciousness. For there can hardly be a sharper break with the old *sunna* than this extension of the cult, which distorts the very essence of Islam, and which a true follower of the *sunna* had to condemn, relegating it to the domain of *shirk*, the association of other divine powers with the one God. Moreover, in keeping with this cult of saints, a change was also suffered in the traditional view of the Prophet's character. The Prophet, too, was drawn into the realm of hagiology and hagiolatry, and thus an image of him was developed that is absolutely contrary to the human one offered by Qur'ān and *sunna*.[e]

[e] For a fuller development of this point, see Tor Andrae, *Die Person Muhammeds in Lehre und Glauben seiner Gemeinde.*

Nothing could more justify the call for eradicating the *bid'a* that had stolen into religious doctrine and practice than the goings-on, entirely contrary to the *sunna*, that accompanied the cult of the saints and the Prophet. After some resistance, however, official Islam bowed to the universally prevalent religious ideas that had gained recognition from the popular *ijmā'*. With certain doctrinal reservations, and with the imposition of some theological discipline and moderation, it admitted this result of historical development into the system of orthodoxy.

7. But the zeal of the Ḥanbalites had no use for toleration of innovations. They saw it as their vocation to be the heralds of the *sunna* against all dogmatic, ritual, or social *bid'a*. This handful of zealots stood in powerless opposition to the prevailing spirit. But at the beginning of the fourteenth century there arose in Syria a powerful spokesman for their views, in the person of a bold theologian, Taqī al-Dīn ibn Taymīya,[f] who in his sermons and writings subjected the current state of Islam to scrutiny, sorting *sunna* from *bid'a*. He turned against all "innovations" that had altered, in doctrine or practice, the original concept of Islam. He fought with equal zeal against the influences of philosophy that had found their way into Islam (including the formulas of Ash'arite *kalām*, long accepted by orthodoxy, and Sufism with its pantheistic doctrines) and against the cult of the Prophet and the saints. He condemned as contrary to the faith the high religious value set on pilgrimage to the tomb of the Prophet, which pious Muslims had long considered the complement to the pilgrimage to Mecca. He turned ruthlessly against the theological authorities that had accorded the legitimacy of *ijmā'* to various outgrowths of the cult. He relied on the *sunna* and on the *sunna* alone.

The Islamic empire was then suffering the aftermath of the Mongol onslaught; the time was right for rousing the conscience of the people. There had to be a regeneration of Islam in the spirit of the *sunna*, the distortion of which had called down the wrath of God. But the secular rulers and authoritative theological leaders showed no favor to the zealot. *Quieta non movere.* After all, where Ibn Taymīya demanded a return to the beginnings, people had been for centuries living with the results of history, in both faith and practice, and the results of history now had to be respected as *sunna*. The last ecclesiastic authority in Islam had been Ghazālī, who had found the formula for reconciling ritualism, rationalism, dogmatism, and mysticism, and whose system had since become the

[f] Ibn Taymīya has been the subject of a major work by Henri Laoust, *Essai sur les doctrines sociales et politiques de Taḳi-d-Dīn Aḥmad b. Taimīya* (Cairo, 1939).

common property of orthodox-Sunnī Islam. Ghazālī was also the one who, so to speak, made the neo-Ḥanbalites see red in their inclination to fight against every form of historical development.

Ibn Taymīya had little success. He was dragged from one ecclesiastic[g] tribunal to another, and died in prison (1328). In the age immediately following, the salient theme of theological literature was whether he had been a heretic or a devout zealot of the *sunna*. His handful of followers surrounded his memory with a nimbus of holiness, and his opponents were soon appeased and brought to a more favorable view of him by the lasting impression of earnest religiosity that the writings of the dead enthusiast made on them. For four centuries his influence was latent but felt. His works were read and studied. In many Islamic milieus they were a mute force that from time to time released outbreaks of hostility to *bid'a*.

It was the influence of Ibn Taymīya's teachings that called forth, around the middle of the eighteenth century, one of the recent religious movements in Islam: that of the Wahhābīs.

8. The history of Arab Islam did not lack for examples of leaders whose vigorous personalities combined the virtues of the learned theologian with those of the gallant warrior.

As "lyre and sword" had been joined in paganism, so in Islam religious learning and military valor were joined in fight against unbelief and heresy. The early history of Islam is very rich in examples of this; at least religious tradition—which, to be sure, is quite unhistorical—was much given to enriching a warrior's triumphal crown with the laurels of theological knowledge.

The prototype for this is the sword of 'Alī, wielded, as religious legend has it, by a man who was also regarded as a high authority in all religious questions that theological knowledge had to resolve. But even when we reach firmer historical ground, we often see a combination of martial and scholarly virtues in the men who stand at the head of the fighting masses. A few examples will suffice to show the continuity of this phenomenon to the most recent times. In the twelfth century, 'Abd al-Mu'min emerged from the schools of theology to take his place at the head of the

[g] The term "ecclesiastic" (German: kirchlich) may seem somewhat strange as applied to Muslim judicial procedures. There were, of course, no special courts charged with specifically religious cases. The ordinary judiciary—the courts of the *qāḍīs*—were in principle responsible for administering the Holy Law in all its aspects, and could be empowered to deal with the discovery and punishment of religious error.

Almohad movement, and in many heroically fought battles, to which the masses had followed his call, he founded a great empire in the western Islamic world. The most recent Muslim hero was ʿAbd al-Qādir. During the exile in Damascus that followed his heroic military resistance to the French conquest of his Algerian homeland, he gathered around himself eager disciples who listened avidly to his lectures on Mālikite law and other subjects of Islamic theology. Shāmil, the hero of Caucasian independence, and the warrior-*Mahdīs* in the Sudan and in Somaliland, of whom we have heard so much in recent times, are, it is true, less illustrious examples of this phenomenon in the history of Islam; nonetheless, these warriors, too, came from among the disciples of Islamic theology.[h]

One of the most remarkable theological and military movements in the history of the Arab people came into being in modern times in Central Arabia under the leadership of Muḥammad ibn ʿAbd al-Wahhāb (d. 1787).[i] Inspired by assiduous study of the writings of Ibn Taymīya, this man sparked a theologically based movement among his compatriots; it soon burst into high flame, swept along a warlike populace, and, after important successes in the field—in the peninsula and as far as Iraq—led to the establishment of a political commonwealth. After various ups and downs, and weakened by internal confusion and rivalries, this commonwealth still exists in central Arabia, and is an influential factor in the politics of the Arabian peninsula. While Ibn ʿAbd al-Wahhāb differs from the just-mentioned warlike theologians in that he did not himself, at the head of his followers, flourish a champion's sword, his theology spurred his son-in-law and protector, the tribal chief Muḥammad ibn Saʿūd, to undertake military campaigns for the restitution of the *sunna*. He drew the sword, so it appears on the outside, for the sake of theological doctrines and their practical application.

[h] Most of these figures have been studied in detail since Goldziher's day. See, for example, Roger Le Tourneau, *The Almohad Movement in North Africa in the 12th and 13th Centuries* (about ʿAbd al-Mu'min; Princeton, 1969); Raphael Danziger, *Abd al-Qadir and the Algerians: Resistance to the French and Internal Consolidation* (New York, 1977); P. M. Holt, *The Mahdist State in the Sudan 1881-1898* (2nd ed. Oxford, 1970). There still appear to be no critical monographs based on original sources on Shamil, the leader of Caucasian resistance to the Russian conquest, and Muḥammad ibn ʿAbdallāh Ḥasan al-Mahdī (1864-1920/21) the Somali leader who fought against the Ethiopians and the British. Both are the subjects of articles in *EI*[1], by W. Barthold and Enrico Cerulli, respectively.

[i] On the development of Wahhābī doctrines, see Laoust, *Essai*, pp. 506-40, where the Arabic sources are cited. A biography of Muḥammad ibn ʿAbd al-Wahhāb, together with a history of the movement, will be found in H. St. J.B. Philby, *Arabia* (London, 1930). For a shorter account, see *EI*[1] article "Wahhābiya" (by D. S. Margoliouth).

Later Developments

Preceded by some other travelers, Julius Euting was a most recent eyewitness to the internal life of this religious state, in which he had occasion, on one of his Arabian travels, to make a lengthy stop.[17]

The Wahhābī movement carried into effect Ibn Taymīya's Ḥanbalite protests against the innovations that had gained the recognition of the *ijmā'* but were contrary to the *sunna*. These included dogmatic formulas established in the course of historical development, as well as innovations in everyday life. Suffice it to say that Wahhābī doctrine is consistent enough to extend the protest against all *bid'a* to such things as the use of tobacco and coffee, which naturally cannot be attested in the *sunna* of the "Companions." Their use is prohibited, as a grave sin, in the territory of the Wahhābī state of our day.[j]

Sword in hand, their bands fell upon the most venerated sanctuaries of the cult of saints, Sunnī and Shī'ī alike, and could only be halted by the troops that Muḥammad 'Alī, the sultan's Egyptian vassal, dispatched to the aid of the Turks, the peninsula's nominal rulers. In the Wahhābī view, such sanctuaries were the places of the most reprehensible *shirk*, and the cults and related customs associated with them were no better than idolatry. True to the teaching of Ibn Taymīya, they regarded in the same light the cult addressed to the Prophet's tomb in Medina. All this was thought and done in the name of restitution of the *sunna*. In their struggle, the examples of devout ancestors shone before their eyes. Reputedly, when the Umayyad 'Umar II, a caliph faithful to the *sunna*, built a monument over the Prophet's grave, he intentionally did not orient the building according to the correct *qibla*, "for fear that people might regard the monument as a place of prayer." He wished to guard against this

[17] Julius Euting, *Tagbuch einer Reise in Inner-Arabien* (Leiden, 1896–1914), I, 157ff. For further bibliography about the Wahhābīs, see Juynboll, *Handbuch des islamischen Gesetzes*, p. 28 n. 2. The Wahhābīs' opposition to all innovations that are not founded on ancient Islamic custom has occasionally given rise to the misunderstanding that their form of Islam is founded exclusively on the Qur'ān. This error occurs, for example, in the otherwise sound characterization of the Wahhābīs' aspirations in Charles Didier [*Séjour chez le grand-chérif de la Mekke* (Paris, 1857), pp. 178ff.; German translation], *Ein Aufenthalt bei dem Gross-Scherif von Mekka* (Leipzig, 1862), pp. 222-255. Baron Eduard Nolde makes the same mistake in his *Reise nach Innerarabien, Kurdistan und Armenien* (Braunschweig, 1895) when he reports that the Wahhābīs "reject all tradition, and so, most importantly, also the *sunna*." The opposite is the case.

[j] The acceptance of tobacco and coffee by the Sunnī *'ulamā'* was not accomplished without considerable difficulty. See *EI*² article "Ḳahwa" (by C. van Arendonck). On tobacco, see Snouck Hurgronje, *Verspreide Geschriften*, VI. Tobacco was declared licit by the Ottoman jurist Bahā'ī Mehmed Efendi (died 1654), on whom see *EI*², s.v. (by B. Lewis).

danger by not having the building oriented in the manner of a mosque.[18] Besides the cult of graves and relics, the Wahhābīs rejected and combatted other innovations in the ritual, such as the joining of minarets to mosques, and the use of the rosary, which had been unknown to early Islam (Ch. IV, Sec. 10). The cult was to reflect faithfully the conditions of the age of the Companions.

So it was with daily life, as well. The utmost puritanical simplicity was reestablished, such as had been practiced, according to the testimony of hundreds of hadiths, by the Companions and even the caliphs. All luxury was rejected. The conditions of seventh-century Medina were to serve, half a millennium later, as model and norm in the state the Wahhābīs erected on the foundation of the *sunna*.

From the Wahhābī attitude toward the cult of saints, which was the salient target of their struggle, we may conclude that there is good reason for the name *Tempelstürmer in Hocharabien* ("*Assailants of Sanctuaries in High Arabia*"), which Karl v. Vincenti gave them in his novel describing their social life. The novel, in agreement with other reports, also describes the spirit of hypocrisy and sanctimoniousness that is an inward consequence of an outwardly stringent puritanism.

The great impact of the Wahhābīs' convictions is also clear from the analogous phenomena that arose in far-flung parts of the Islamic world, under the unmistakable influence of the Arabian movement.

9. Upon examining the relation of standard Islam to this movement, the following fact in particular strikes the attention of the historian of religions. Any objective observer of Islam must regard the Wahhābīs as fighters for the form of religion established by Muhammad and his Companions. Their aim and vocation is the restoration of early Islam. In theoretical discussions, the *'ulamā'*, too, often admit this much.[19] Nonetheless, in the practical judgment of the orthodox Muslim, the Wahhābīs must be rejected as sectaries. To abandon the *ijmā'*, to cast aside what the consensus of the community of believers—as it has historically evolved—acknowledges as sound and true, is to forsake orthodox belief. One is not to look for warrants from the ancient *sunna*. *Ijmā'* makes *sunna*; there is no need for further examination. Only that is *Sunnī*, orthodox, which conforms to the acknowledged common belief and practice of the Muslims. Whatever is opposed to this *ijmā'* is heterodox. From these premises the orthodox Muslim can draw only one conclusion: al-

[18] Ibn Jubayr, *Riḥla*, p. 190:13.

[19] J. G. Wetzstein, *Reisebericht über Hauran und die Trachonen* (Berlin, 1860), p. 150.

though their loyalty to the *sunna* is not in question, the Wahhābīs, by opposing and reprobating things that are permitted, and in part required, by the four orthodox rites, have left the pale of orthodox Islam, no less than had the ancient Khārijites. For orthodox Islam, since the twelfth century, Ghazālī has been the final authority. In their literary struggles against the Meccan orthodoxy—which have not halted to this day[k]—the Wahhābīs advance against Ghazālī the doctrines of the man whom the ruling theology rejected: Ibn Taymīya. The names of Ghazālī and Ibn Taymīya have been the rallying cries in this struggle. The *ijmā'* had accepted Ghazālī's work and rendered it sacrosanct. Those who hold a different opinion have breached the *ijmā'*; despite their consistent and truly Muslim faithfulness to the *sunna*, they must be regarded as heterodox and condemned as such.[20]

10. The movement born in the Arabian Peninsula, whose ideas and effects we have just described, fixed its gaze on the past, denied the legitimacy of the results and achievements of historical development, and insisted that true Islam must have the form of a fossil from the seventh century. But another Islamic movement of recent origin had its point of departure in, and has been animated by, a belief in the religious evolution of mankind. This is the Bābī movement that arose in Persia.[1]

It undoubtedly sprang from the form of Shī'ism prevalent in that country, but its fundamental ideas are related in their development to the principle we have encountered as the guiding thought of the Ismā'īlī sect: that the divine revelation renders itself more and more perfect through the gradual manifestation of the Universal Intellect.

At the beginning of the nineteenth century the doctrine of the imamate in the Twelver Shī'a put forth a new branch: the school of the Shaykhīs, whose followers practice a fervent cult of the "Hidden *Mahdī*" and of the *Imāms* who preceded him. In Gnostic fashion, they regard these persons

[k] The long struggle between the Wahhābīs and the rulers of Mecca ended in 1925 when Ibn Sa'ūd, the ruler of the Wahhābī state in northeastern Arabia, conquered the Hijaz. In 1926 he was proclaimed King of the Hijaz and Sultan of Najd. In 1932 the kingdom was renamed Saudi Arabia, after the name of the dynasty. Doctrinal disagreements between the Wahhābīs and the more common forms of Sunnī belief remain in existence, but have become less acute.

[20] A Maghribī zealot of the *sunna*, Muḥammad al-'Abdarī (d. 737/1336-1337), notes the phenomenon that once a *bid'a* has taken firm root in common practice, resistance to it is usually regarded as rebellion against the *sunna*. For various examples from the domain of ritual, and al-'Abdarī's critique of the process, see his *Madkhal al-shar' al-sharīf*, I, 54:15, 249:6 from bottom; II, 75:10.

[1] The Bābīs and Bahā'īs are the subject of articles in *EI*[2] (both by A. Bausani).

as hypostases of divine attributes, and creative forces. In so doing, they expand the scope of the *Imām*-mythology of the standard Imāmīya, and follow in the footsteps of the "extremists" (*ghulāt*, Ch. V, Sec. 8).

Such was the milieu in which Mīrzā Muḥammad 'Alī grew up, a young religious enthusiast born in Shiraz in 1820. Because of his zeal and outstanding abilities, his companions recognized him as destined for a sublime calling. Such recognition by his fellow enthusiasts exercised a powerful suggestion upon the mind of the meditative young man. At length he came to regard himself as the embodiment of an exalted, superhuman mission that formed part of the evolution of Islam, and would reveal the role that Islam is to play in the history of the world. From the conviction that he was the *Bāb*, "gate," through which the unerring will of the Hidden *Imām*, the highest source of all truth, manifested itself to the world, he soon advanced to the belief that he was, in the economy of the evolution of the spirit, something more than the mouthpiece of the *Imām* of the age living and teaching in occultation. He was himself the new *Mahdī* making himself known at the precise turn of the millennium following the appearance of the twelfth *Imām* (A.H. 260–1260). But he no longer conceived of the office of *Mahdī* as the standard Shī'a did. Rather, he thought of the *Mahdī*—and here he crossed over to Ismā'īlī ground—as a manifestation of the World Spirit, as the "point of manifestation," as the highest truth, which had taken corporeal form in him. The *Mahdī* was different only in appearance from the previous manifestations of the spiritual substance radiating from God, and was identical with them in essence. He was Moses and Jesus reappearing on earth, as well as the reincarnation of all other prophets in whose bodily form, in previous ages of the world, the divine world spirit had manifested itself. To his followers he preached aversion to the *mollahs*—in Persia particularly, this term is used for the *'ulamā'*—to their sanctimoniousness and hypocrisy, to their worldly aspirations. He sought to raise the revelations of Muhammad, most of which he interpreted in an allegorical manner, to a higher degree of maturity. The practices of Islam, the punctilious laws of ritual purity and the like, were little esteemed in his teaching, and were in part supplanted by others. To Last Judgment, Paradise, Hell, and Resurrection new meanings were assigned.[21] In this he had predecessors in previous spiritualist systems. Resurrection is each new periodic manifestation of the divine spirit, in relation to an earlier one. The first one is

[21] "Die Religion des Islams," p. 128:14-28.

raised to a new life by the next. This is the meaning of the phrase "meeting God" that the Qur'ān uses to refer to the afterlife.

But it was not only in his dogmatic and legal ideas that the young Persian enthusiast set himself against the ossified theology of the *mollahs*. His message was also profoundly concerned with the social conditions of his coreligionists. His thoughtful ethics demanded, in place of the walls dividing classes and religions, the brotherhood of mankind. He wished to grant full equality to women, and so to raise them from the low position in which, in the name of tradition, they had in practice been placed. He began by abolishing the obligatory veil, and rejected the crude conception of marriage that had come to prevail, although by no means as a necessary consequence of religious principles, in Islamic society. He advanced a nobler conception of marriage, along with ideas about the tasks of the family and educational reform.

Thus the Bāb's intended religious reforms touched the foundations of social life. He was not only a religious, but also a social reformer. But the gnostic and mystical ideas he had begun with remained a pervasive element of the system that he constructed from his views. He combined ideas of modern enlightenment with Pythagorean ingenuities. Like the Ḥurūfīs (Ch. V, Sec. 18), he played with combinations of letters and ascribed great significance to the numerical values of the letters of the alphabet. The number nineteen has the highest importance in his construction of ideas, and serves as the focus of the exercises in numerology that play a prominent role in his speculations.

Just as he advanced the idea of his own essential identity with the prophets of previous ages[22]—an idea rooted in Gnosticism and also put forward by previous schismatic movements in Islam—so he proclaimed that the divine spirit, embodied in him in his lifetime, would continue in the future to manifest itself again and again. Revelation did not reach its definitive conclusion either in Muhammad or in the Bāb himself. In an endless unfolding, the divine spirit makes itself known in periodically renewed manifestations. In these, the divine will appears in ever greater perfection and fullness, in keeping with the progress of history. By advancing such ideas, Mīrzā Muḥammad 'Alī also prepared the change that was to occur in his community soon after his death.

He set down the sum of his doctrines in a religious book entitled *Bayān* (*Explanation*). His sect regards it as holy. These doctrines must have

[22] Cf. "Neuplatonische und gnostische Elemente im Ḥadīṯ," p. 337 [= *Gesammelte Schriften*, V, 127; partial French translation in *Arabica*, VII (1960), 11].

struck the ruling authorities as extremely dangerous, from both the religious and political points of view. Founder and followers who had gathered around him—among whom a woman, the heroic Qurrat al-'Ayn ("Solace of the Eye") attracts our sympathy—were mercilessly persecuted and proscribed, hunted down and delivered to the executioner. Muḥammad 'Alī was himself executed in July 1850. The disciples who were spared martyrdom, and whose fervor was only intensified by the persecution they had endured, found refuge on Turkish soil.

Soon after the founder's death, a cleavage occurred in the community of the Bāb's believers. He had appointed two disciples to guide the community, and some believers recognized one, some the other, as the more faithful interpreter of the Bāb's will. The smaller faction gathered around Ṣubḥ-i Azal ("Dawn of Eternity"), who resided in Famagusta, in Cyprus. This man wanted to maintain the work of the Bāb in the form that the master had given it; his followers are the conservative Bābīs. The majority of the believers adopted the view of the other apostle, Bahā' Allāh ("Splendor of God") who, at the beginning of the sixties, during the Bābī exiles' stay in Adrianople (Edirne), declared—somewhat beforehand with the cyclical system—that he was the more perfect manifestation prophesied by the master, the one that would raise the Bāb's own work to a higher state. Muḥammad 'Alī was his precursor, his John the Baptist, so to speak. In Bahā' Allāh himself the divine spirit reappeared, to accomplish truly what his precursor's work had prepared. Bahā' was to be regarded as greater than the Bāb. The Bāb had been the *Qā'im* ("the one who rises up"): Bahā' was the *Qayyūm* ("the one who subsists"). "The one who will appear in days to come"—this was the Bāb's expression for the person who would at some future time succeed him—"is greater than the one who has already appeared."[23] He had a predilection for calling himself *maẓhar*, or *manẓar*, the palpable manifestation of God, in which the beauty of God could be seen as in a mirror. He was himself "the beauty (*jamāl*) of Allah" whose face shone as a precious, polished pearl between heaven and earth.[24] Only through him could one come to know God's essence, of which he was himself an emanation.[25] His followers regarded him, in fact, as a superhuman being, and endowed him

[23] *Rasā'il Bahā' Allāh*, edited by Victor Rosen (St. Petersburg, 1908), I, 112:2-5.

[24] *Ibid.*, pp. 19:7, 94:24.

[25] E. G. Browne, "Some Remarks on the Bābī Texts Edited by Baron Victor Rosen," *JRAS* (1892), pp. 326-35.

with divine attributes. One has only to read the rapturous hymns, published by E. G. Browne, that they addressed to him.[26]

Because of the dispute that broke out between Bahā's new party and the conservative Bābīs, Bahā' and his community were banished to Acre. Here he developed his teaching into a self-contained system, which he opposed not only to the *millat al-furqān*, the community of the Qur'ān, but also to the *millat al-bayān*, the conservative Bābīs who had not accepted his reform and refused to go beyond the book *Bayān*. His teachings are contained in a series of books and letters in Arabic and Persian. Most important among them is the *Kitāb-i aqdas* (*Holy Book*).[27] He claimed a divine origin for the teachings set forth in his writings. "This tablet itself"—meaning one of his letters—"is a hidden writing that has been stored among the treasures of divine immunity through all eternity, and whose signs, if you would know it, were written by the fingers of (divine) power."

Moreover, he promoted the impression that he had not wholly revealed the riches of his redemptive doctrine. He appears to have kept some esoteric ideas for a chosen few, the elect among the elect. He also sought to conceal certain doctrines from his antagonists. "We do not wish," he writes in one passage, "to explain this stage in detail, for the ears of our enemies are inclined toward us, to overhear things in return for which they contradict the truthful and enduring God. For they do not attain to the mystery of the knowledge and wisdom of the one who has appeared in the orient of the splendor of Divine Unity."

The manifestation of the universal spirit in Bahā' Allāh—which alone was supposed to bring the teachings of the original founder to their real completion—did away with essential particulars of the Bāb's revelation. That revelation had been, in reality, no more than a reform of Islam. Bahā' advanced to the broad conception of a world religion and so the brotherhood of all mankind. In his political doctrines he professed cosmopolitanism: "It is not love of one's country, but love of the world, that constitutes superior merit."[28] In the same vein, his religion puts an end to all narrow confessionalism.

[26] *Rasā'il Bahā' Allāh*, pp. 71:15, 82:22, 84 bottom. In particular, all of letter no. 34 is a polemic against the adherents of the *Bayān*.

[27] Edited by A. H. Toumansky (Mémoires de l'Académie Imp. de St. Pétersbourg, 8th Series, vol. III, no. 6, 1899).

[28] *Rasā'il Bahā' Allāh*, pp. 18:21, 20:14ff., 94 bottom, 93:20.

He regarded himself as the manifestation of the world spirit for all mankind. Accordingly, he sent apostolic letters, which form part of his book of revelations, to the nations and rulers of Europe and Asia. He himself already looked also toward America. He proclaimed also "to the kings of America and the chiefs of the Republic" "what the dove in the branches of eternity coos." In a letter to Napoleon III, written four years before Sedan, he prophesied the emperor's impending fall. This raised him considerably in the eyes of his followers as a prophetically inspired divine-and-human being.

In keeping with his cosmopolitan tendency, he recommended to his followers that they should learn foreign languages and prepare themselves for a mission as apostles of the world religion that would unite all mankind and all nations, "so that the master of languages might bring God's cause to the whole world, East and West, and that he might proclaim it among the states and nations in such a manner that people's hearts should be drawn to it and mouldering bones should revive." "This is the means of unification, and the foremost cause of understanding and of civilization."[29] The ideal means to world-wide understanding was, he considered, a single universal language. He requested of kings and their ministers that they agree to recognize one of the existing languages, or one to be created artificially, as a universal language to be taught in all schools of the world.[30]

He threw off all restrictions, of Islam and of the old Bābism alike. He did not, it is true, free his prophecy of all the mystical speculation, of all the juggling with letters and numbers, that had clung to the original Bābism. Nevertheless, his chief concern was with ethical and social improvement. War was condemned; the use of weapons was allowed only "in an emergency." Slavery was strictly forbidden. The equality of all mankind was taught, as the essential point of the new prophecy.[31] In a revelation entitled *sūrat al-mulūk*, "the sura of kings," he severely reproved the sultan of Turkey for permitting such great differences of wealth to exist among the inhabitants of Istanbul.[32] He instituted marital reforms—a matter to which the Bāb had already devoted much attention. Monogamy was his ideal; he made concessions to bigamy, but two wives were to be the limit. Divorce was permissible, but it was surrounded

[29] *Al-Kitāb al-aqdas*, nos. 212, 276, 468.

[30] Ethel Rosenberg, "Bahaism, Its Ethical and Social Teachings," *Transactions of the Third International Congress for the History of Religions* (Oxford, 1908), I, 324.

[31] *Al-Kitāb al-aqdas*, nos. 164, 385.

[32] *Rasā'il Bahā' Allāh*, p. 54:21ff.

with humane requirements. Remarriage to a person one had divorced was permitted, provided the person had not in the meantime entered into a new marriage. This was the precise contrary of Islamic usage. Islamic law was regarded as obsolete in its entirety. New forms of prayer and ritual were laid down. The congregational prayer with its liturgical forms (*ṣalāt al-jamā'a*) was abolished; everyone was to pray by himself individually (*furādā*). Congregation was retained only for the prayer over the dead. The *qibla* (the direction one faces at prayer) was not toward Mecca but toward wherever resided the one whom God had caused to appear (meaning God's manifestation): if he moved, the *qibla* moved, until he took up permanent residence somewhere. Bodily purity, ablutions, and baths were most emphatically recommended as matters of religion, but not without warnings against the Persians' bathing establishments, which were represented as particularly impure.

With a stroke of the pen, without mention of details (except for some laws of dress he specifically rejected), Bahā' annulled the restrictions Islam imposed on the believers: "You may do all that is not contrary to sound human reason."[33] Like his precursor, he was tireless in his fight against the *'ulamā'* who distorted and slighted the will of God. One was, however, to refrain from dispute with religious adversaries. The Bahā'ī religion was to have no professional clergy. Each member of this universal religious community should have a productive occupation useful to society, and those capable of it should also function, without remuneration, as spiritual leaders of the community.[34] To instruct was no longer to be the office of a guild-like special group. This was rendered palpable by the abolition of the pulpit (*minbar*) in the places of assembly.[35]

One would expect that in politics Bahā' Allāh would be in the liberal camp. The expectation is disappointed. He surprises us, rather, by attacking political liberty. "We see that some people want liberty and glory in it: they are in evident error. Liberty leads to disorder whose flames cannot be extinguished. You must learn that liberty springs from and reflects man's animal character; man must be under laws that guard him against his own brutality and against hurt from the treacherous. Indeed, liberty turns man away from the demands of morality and decency"—and so forth, in a frankly reactionary vein.[36] Bahā's followers also did not ap-

[33] *Al-Kitāb al-aqdas*, nos. 145, 155ff., 324, 179, 252, 371, 386.

[34] Rosenberg, "Bahaism," p. 323.

[35] See Hippolyte Dreyfus, "Une Institution Béhaïe: Le Machreqou'l-Aẕkār d''Achqābād," *Mélanges Hartwig Derenbourg* (Paris, 1909), p. 421.

[36] *Al-Kitāb al-aqdas*, nos. 284-92.

prove of the liberal political developments in Turkey and Persia; they disapproved of the deposition of the sultan and the shah.[37]

After Bahā' Allāh's death (May 16, 1892) his mission passed to his son and successor 'Abbās Efendi, called 'Abd al-Bahā' or *ghuṣn-i a'ẓam,* "the great branch."[38] The succession was disputed by only a few among Bahā's friends (*aḥbāb*). At his hands, his father's ideas have undergone far-reaching developments. They are ever more adapted to the forms and goals of educated thought in the West. The fantastic speculations that still clung to the previous states are tempered as much as possible, if not yet completely eliminated. 'Abbās has made extensive use of the books of the Old and New Testaments, citing them in support of his cause, in an effort to extend his influence beyond the circle of his father's followers.

Propaganda since the accession of 'Abd al-Bahā' has indeed achieved spectacular results. A large number of American ladies (some of whose names will be found in the notes) have undertaken the pilgrimage to the Persian prophet at the foot of Mt. Carmel, in order to carry to their home in the West the words of salvation that they heard from the prophet's own mouth, when they were with him face to face. We owe the best exposition of 'Abbās Efendi's doctrines to a lady, Miss Laura Clifford Barney. During a lengthy stay in 'Abbās's entourage, she took down his pronouncements in shorthand, in order to transmit them reliably to the Western world as the quintessence of the new Bahā'ī doctrine.[39]

The movement set afoot by the Bāb could no longer bear the name of its founder. It is justly preferred nowadays to use the name *Bahā'īya* for this offshoot of the teaching of Mīrzā Muḥammad 'Alī, which has been steadily expanding and relegating its rival to the background. *Bahā'īya* is the name that the believers have assumed, as well, to distinguish themselves from the insignificant remnant of conservative adherents of the *Bayān* who are under a different leadership.

[37] Cf. the information on this point in *RMM*, IX (1909), 339-41.

[38] One can find portraits of Bahā' and 'Abbās, as well as a picture of Bahā' 's tomb in Acre, in the otherwise anti-Bābī book *Zustände im heutigen Persien, wie sie das Reisebuch Ibrahim Bejs enthüllt*, translated by Walter Schulz (Leipzig, 1903). There is a picture of the Ṣubḥ-i Azal in E. G. Browne, *The Tárikh-i Jadíd, or, New History of Meírzá 'Alí Muḥammad the Báb* (Cambridge, 1893).

['Abbās Efendi, otherwise 'Abd al-Bahā, headed the sect until his death in 1920. By his will he appointed his grandson, Shoghi (Arabic: Shawqī) Efendi Rabbani as "Guardian of the Cause of God." On his death in 1957, the Guardianship of the sect passed to an elected committee.]

[39] Her book [*Some Answered Questions, Collected and Translated from the Persian of 'Abdu'l-Baha* (London, 1908)] is discussed (with an outline of its contents) by Oscar Mann, *OLZ*, XII (1909), 36ff.

The broad universalism that characterizes the Bahā'īs brought to them adherents not only from mosques, but from churches, synagogues, and fire-temples. Recently they built in Ashkabad, in Russian Turkestan near the Persian border, a public meeting house for religious services.[m] Hippolyte Dreyfus, an ardent European interpreter of the Bahā'ī faith, has quite recently described it.[40]

In other quarters, the term Bahā'ism has been used to mean religious freethinking, the repudiation of the positive contents of Islamic belief. Just as once the term *zindīq* (which had originally meant Muslims whose religious views approached Zoroastrian and Manichean beliefs), as later the name *faylasūf* (philosopher), and as most recently also *farmaṣūn* (franc-maçon) have been used to refer to freethought in general, without distinguishing specific forms of apostasy from correct Islam, so in Persia today the name Bahā'ī is used not only to denote adherence to this latest development of the Bābī religion, but often—as the Reverend F. M. Jordan observed—to refer to people who are in fact nothing more than simple irreligious rationalists.[41] Since in Persia, as also in other Muslim countries, those who hold Bahā'ī beliefs still have good reason to conceal from the public their completely anti-Islamic convictions and to avail themselves of the practice of *taqīya* (Ch. V, Sec. 5), it would be difficult to furnish even approximately correct figures for the adherents of Bābism in its two forms. The Rev. Isaac Adams, author of one of the most recent descriptions of Bābism, probably errs on the high side in setting their number at three million in Persia alone; that would be nearly one-third of the entire population of the country.[n]

Thus Bābism, as it moved forward into Bahā'ism, entered a phase of earnest propaganda. Its teachers and followers acted on their conviction that they were not an Islamic sect but representatives of a teaching that was to encompass the whole world. Their propaganda has not only touched many Muslims—even as far as Indochina—but has been steadily, and with remarkable success, spreading beyond the pale of Islam. The prophet of Acre has found ardent followers in America—and reputedly

[m] Ashkabad is now the capital of the Soviet Republic of Turkmenistan. The Bahā'ī meeting house was taken over by the state and turned into a museum.

[40] Dreyfus, "Une Institution Béhaïe," pp. 415ff.

[41] In the collection *The Muhammedan World of To-day*, p. 129.

[n] Bausani, writing in about 1958, estimated the number of Bahā'īs as follows: in Iran, estimates varying from "more than a million down to about five hundred thousand"; in the United States, about ten thousand; in Europe, about one thousand; in other countries, some hundreds; in Africa, more than three thousand.

in Europe as well—even among Christians.[42] In Chicago preparations have already been made for the building of a religious meeting-house for the Bahā'īs of that city. By the time these pages are in print, this design may have been carried into execution.[43]

Jewish enthusiasts have also rummaged in the prophetic books of the Old Testament until they found predictions of Bahā' and 'Abbās. Wherever the "splendor of Yahweh" is mentioned, it is taken by them to mean the appearance of the savior of the world, Bahā' Allāh. They profited greatly from all references to Mt. Carmel, in the vicinity of which, at the end of the nineteenth century, the light of God shone forth for the whole world. Nor did they lack ingenuity for finding, in the visions in the book of Daniel,[44] the prophecy and predicted date of the movement that the Bāb ushered in. According to their calculations, the 2,300 days (anniversaries) in Daniel 8:14, after whose passing "the sanctuary will be purified," came to an end with the year 1844 of the common era, the year in which Mīrzā Muḥammad 'Alī proclaimed himself as Bāb, at which time the world spirit entered the new phase of its manifestation.

With the accession of 'Abbās Efendi, the use of the Bible advanced a step further. The text "unto us a child is born, unto us a son is given: and the government shall be upon his shoulder" is thought to be a prophecy of him; to him refer the marvelous epithets that follow, in Isaiah 9:6. During the writing of these pages, I have had occasion to hear such Biblical proofs from the mouth of a Bahā'ī zealot. This man, originally a doctor from Teheran, has been staying for the last two years or so in the city where I live, in an effort to gain converts to his religion. He feels that he has a particular mission in my country: one more proof that it is not only American soil that the extra-Islamic propaganda of the new Bahā'īs has in view.

11. India demands a place all to itself in the study of the historical de-

[42] I can now refer to E. G. Browne's comprehensive description of Bābism and its history, which appeared, after completion of my text, in Hastings' *Encyclopaedia of Religion and Ethics*, II, 299-308. The article includes a bibliography of works by Western adepts of Bahā'ism. Further, see Hippolyte Dreyfus, *Essai sur le Béhaïsme, son histoire, sa portée sociale* (Paris, 1909).

[43] Jean Masson reports in the February 1909 issue of the *American Review of Reviews* of the extraordinary progress made by Bahā'ism, and advances the claim that it is destined to be the "ultimate religion." [The foundation stone of the Bahā'ī temple at Wilmette, Illinois, near Chicago, was laid on May 10, 1912. The building was officially consecrated in the presence of Shoghi Rabbani's wife in June 1953.]

[44] Cf. the manuscript tractate noted by E. G. Browne, "Catalogue and Description of 27 Bābī Manuscripts," *JRAS*, 1892, p. 701.

velopment of Islam.[o] The phenomena produced by the ethnographic conditions peculiar to this province of Islam lead the historian of religions to very fruitful considerations, to which, however, in the present context we can only pay limited attention.

Although the Ghaznavid conquest in the eleventh century dealt palpable wounds to the old Indian culture, in Muslim-dominated India the ancient forms of religion have endured in their primitive form to this day. Islam was greatly enriched by its numerous converts from Hinduism; the Qur'ān could not make serious inroads upon the Vedas. On the contrary, in no country was Islam compelled to practice its toleration of alien cults to the same degree as in India. Here demography forced Islam to go beyond its fundamental law that grants extensive toleration to monotheistic religions but commands the ruthless extirpation of idolatrous cults in conquered lands. In India the temples of idols remained standing under Muslim rule, despite the war that Maḥmūd of Ghazna, a vigorous ruler and a zealous Muslim, waged to annihilate them. Adherents of the Hindu religions had to be tacitly granted the legal status of *ahl al-dhimma* (those who enjoy the protection of Islam).[45]

In the kaleidoscopic variety of the religious world of India, it was in turn inevitable that Islam, the new arrival, and Indian religion should in diverse ways influence each other.[46] As masses of Hindus converted to Islam, some of their social views now and then were carried along into their lives as Muslims.[47] We encounter most peculiar phenomena in the

[o] The development of Islam in India has given rise to an immense literature. For general surveys, see Wilfred Cantwell Smith, *Modern Islam in India*; Aziz Ahmad, *Islamic Modernism in India and Pakistan, 1857-1964* (London, 1967); *idem, Studies in Islamic Culture in the Indian Environment* (Oxford, 1964); P. Hardy, *The Muslims of British India* (Cambridge, 1972). Wm. Theodore de Bary, Stephen N. Hay, Royal Weiler, and Andrew Yarrow, eds., *Sources of Indian Tradition* (New York, 1958), offers a well-chosen selection of religious and other texts representing the main religions of India.

[45] Ibn Baṭṭūṭa, *Riḥla*, edited and translated by C. Defrémery and B. R. Sanguinetti (Paris, 1853-1858), IV, 29. On p. 223, about Indian provinces: "Most of their inhabitants are unbelievers (that is, pagans, *kuffār*) under protection (of the Muslims, *taḥt al-dhimma*)." Thus they are *ahl al-dhimma*, "those under protection," which is normally used to refer only to Jews and Christians who pay the *jizya*. In the fourteenth century, a Muslim prince in India permitted the Chinese to erect a pagoda in a Muslim region, against payment of the *jizya* (Ibn Baṭṭūṭa, IV, 2).

[46] M. C. Westcott published in 1908 a lecture on the influences of Hinduism and Islam on each other. It is not, unfortunately, available to me. [The study intended here seems to be G. H. Westcott's *Kabīr and the Kabīrpanth* (Cawnpore, 1907)].

[47] For example, the influence of the institution of castes, see J. Kohler, "Die Gewohnheitsrechte der Provinz Bombay," *Zeitschrift für vergleichende Rechtswissenschaft*, X (1892), 83ff. For aversion to the remarriage of widows, see *Muhammedanische Studien*, II, 333 [=

sphere of religious life. Fundamental Islamic concepts are re-formed in accordance with Indian ideas. An astonishing example—not demonstrative, to be sure, of the general spirit—is the version in which the two-part Muslim creed occasionally appears on the coins of Muslim rulers in India: "The Undefinable is one, and Muhammad is its avatar."[48] The Islamic cult of saints allows extensive scope for popular manifestations of Hindu influence upon the *sacra* of Islam. In that cult Indian elements daily assert themselves. Especially in Indian Shī'ism, they have produced some extraordinary phenomena. Indian divinities became Muslim saints; Indian holy places were automatically reinterpreted in the light of Islam.

Of all the territories Islam has conquered, none offers such conspicuous examples of the preservation of pagan elements as India and the Malay Archipelago. Here at every step we are struck by evidence of a real religious mixture between Islam and paganism. There is a wholly external cult of Allah, a wholly superficial use of the Qur'ān, an uncomprehending performance of Islamic practices—and hard by all this the persistence of the cult of demons and the dead, and other practices of animistic religion. Islamic phenomena among the peoples of the Malay Archipelago offer abundant material for the observation of this syncretism. They have been thoroughly described, from this point of view, in important books by C. Snouck Hurgronje and R. J. Wilkinson.[49] Concerning the Indian subcontinent, T. W. Arnold has recently reported instructive findings about the survival of the worship of Hindu gods and the practice of Hindu rituals among the lower classes of the Muslim populace in the most varied parts of India.[50]

Thus to zealous partisans of the *sunna*, stirred by Wahhābī ideas and

---

Muslim Studies, II, 303]; incidentally, this feeling has been observed outside India in the province of Jurjān (Muqaddasī, *Aḥsan al-taqāsīm*, p. 370:9). About such phenomena, cf. also John Campbell Oman, *The Mystics, Ascetics and Saints of India* (London, 1905), pp. 135f.

[48] T. Bloch, "Über einige bildliche Darstellungen altindischer Gottheiten," *ZDMG*, LXII (1908), 654 n. 2.

[49] C. Snouck Hurgronje, *De Atjèhers*, 2 vols. (Batavia and Leiden, 1893-1894), English translation, *The Achehnese*, by A.W.S. Sullivan, 2 vols. (Leiden, 1906); the same author's *Het Gayōland en zejne bewoners* (Batavia, 1903); R. J. Wilkinson, *Papers on Malay Subjects. Life and Customs* (Kuala Lumpur, 1908). Cf. *RMM*, VIII (1909), 45ff., 94ff., 180-97 [see the Bibliography under Cabaton, Antoine. To the works cited by Goldziher on Malay and Indonesian Islam, the following may be added: G. H. Bousquet, "Introduction à l'étude de l'Islam Indonesien," *REI*, II-III (1938), 133-259; C.A.O. van Nieuwenhuijze, *Aspects of Islam in Post-Colonial Indonesia* (The Hague and Bandung, 1958); R. O. Winstedt, *The Malays, a Cultural History*, 6th ed. (London, 1961); Clifford Geertz, *Islam Observed*.]

[50] T. W. Arnold, "Survivals of Hinduism among the Muhammadans of India," *Transactions of the Third International Congress for the History of Religions* (Oxford, 1908), I, 314ff.

bent upon the purification of Islam, Indian Islam offered a rich field of action. They were prompted to undertake extensive tasks of two kinds: first, to purge Islam from saints who were only Hindu religious figures reinterpreted, and to eliminate the religious practices related to the cult of such saints; second, to engage in missionary activity among those strata of the Indian population that Islam had only superficially touched.

Indian Islam has been experiencing such movements for the last hundred years. The ideas of the Wahhābī movement streamed out of Arabia into this Islamic land, as well. Contacts and experiences gained during the pilgrimage to Mecca have always proved a powerful means for the awakening of religious forces, for the adoption of new tendencies, and for their transplantation to remote areas of Islam. After a period of quiet theoretical preparation, the Wahhābī stimulus found in India a man who acted on it with vigor. This was Sayyid Aḥmad Brēlwī, who spread the Wahhābī ideas in the first quarter of the nineteenth century, in various regions of Muslim India. He combined purging Islam from *shirk*—so starkly in evidence here in the cult of saints and in superstitious practices—with a mission to the Hindus. His followers have described his missionary work as extremely successful.

In his zeal to bring back the early Islamic way of life, he also led his numerous followers into holy war, *jihād*. Suppression of the Sikh sect, widespread in northern India—and about which we shall soon have a few words to say—presented itself as an immediate aim. In this unsuccessful war he met his death, in 1831. Although the adventurous undertaking of the *jihād* and the related political attempts came to an end with Aḥmad's death, the intra-Islamic religious movement that he had set afoot continued to be effective in Indian Islam.

Although not under the Wahhābī flag, the apostles of Aḥmad's teachings worked in India, under various religious appellations, for the complete Islamization of the nominal Muslims who were still given to Indian practices. They won them over to the observance of Islamic law, and gathered bands of adherents to the *sunna*. Their various divisions augmented the number of Islamic sects in India. An important group of these bears the name, characteristic of their aspirations, of *Farā'iḍīya*, that is, "adherents to the religious duties (of Islam)."[51] This reform movement, rooted in Wahhābī ideas about the *sunna*, has its literary epitome in a

[51] Hubert Jansen, *Verbreitung des Islams* (Friedrichshagen, 1897), pp. 25-30, has a bibliography of these widely ramified movements, information about their geographic extension, and statistics about their results.

book written by a faithful comrade of Aḥmad Brēlwī, the Mawlawī Ismā'īl of Delhi. It is still read today. Under the title *Taqwiyat al-Īmān*, "the strengthening of belief," it vigorously combats all *shirk* and guides Muslims back to *tawḥīd* (the profession of Unity).[52]

12. Just as Indian Islam could not escape the influence of the native religions, the adherents of Indian cults did not remain unaffected by the Islamic conception of God. There are highly conspicuous signs of a syncretism of this latter kind. They are important mainly for the development of Hinduism, but since they were produced by Islam, the historian of Islam cannot disregard them.

It has been noted that at the end of the fourteenth and beginning of the fifteenth centuries Islamic elements passed into the religious world of the Hindus. Such influences made themselves felt especially through the teachings of a weaver named Kabīr, one of the twelve apostles of the Rāmananda school, who was regarded as a saint both by Indian Muslims and by his Hindu followers.[53] As part of this influence, Islamic Sufi ideas also flowed back into the milieu that had been one of their original sources.

We must not, however, pass in silence over the fact that the precise nature of these influences is as yet a matter of controversy. Professor Grierson, one of the scholars most knowledgeable about India, explains these phenomena as due to the effect of Christian ideas, and rejects the hypothesis of an Islamic influence. We cannot, naturally, take a stand in this dispute that provided the most interesting topic of discussion at the annual meeting of the Royal Asiatic Society in 1907.[54] But the present context demands that we should note that a theory of Islamic influence has been advanced by scholars whose views merit consideration.[55]

Further, the religion of the Sikhs of northern India, founded by Nānak (d. 1538), a disciple of Kabīr, is also regarded as an instance of Hindu-Islamic syncretism. The literature about the Sikh religion has recently been enriched by the great work of M. A. Macauliffe.[56] Under the influ-

[52] About this book, see Mir Shahamat Ali, "Translation of the *Takwiyat-ul-Imām*," *JRAS*, XIII (1852), 310-72. On Aḥmad, now see the article in *EI*[1], [I, 190, "Aḥmed b. Muḥammad 'Irfān"; also *EI*[2], I, 282f. "Aḥmad Brēlwī"].

[53] Oman, *The Mystics, Ascetics and Saints of India*, p. 126.

[54] George A. Grierson, "Modern Hinduism and Its Debt to the Nestorians," *JRAS* (1907), pp. 325, 485, 501-503. Cf. Grierson in *JRAS* (1908), p. 248.

[55] Oman, *The Mystics, Ascetics and Saints of India*, also regards Kabīr's doctrine as influenced by Islam.

[56] *The Sikh Religion, its Gurus, Sacred Writings and Authors*, 6 vols. (Oxford, 1909).

ence of Islamic mysticism, and with some additional inspiration from Buddhism, the author of the *Ādi Granth* devised a religious world view in which Hinduism and Islam were to be united. This, as Frederic Pincott describes it, "was meant to serve as the means to bridge the abyss dividing the Hindus from the believers of the Prophet."[57] The most important element in this work was the repudiation of polytheism and its replacement by the monist world view of the Sufis. To be sure, under his successors, Nānak's work was obscured also in its social aspect. The struggles that subsequently flared between Sikhs and Muslims[58] no longer show any sign that the original goal of the founder of the Sikh religion had been to bring about an accommodation between religions in conflict.[p]

Islamic influence on Indian sects remains noticeable in later times. In the first half of the eighteenth century there arose a Hindu sect, Ram Sanaki, that combatted idolatry, and whose cult resembled, in a variety of ways, the religious services of Islam.[59]

13. Once more we return to the consideration that India, with its diversity of religious phenomena, recommends itself to the scholar as a school for the comparative study of religions. It has indeed served as such a school.

The occasion that India offered for the observation and comparison of religions could easily serve also as a stimulus for the establishment of new forms of religion. As historians of Islam, we must mention one in particular, which sprang from thoughtful contemplation of the religious world of India.

Its founder is the Indian monarch Abū 'l-Fatḥ Jalāl al-Dīn Muḥammad, known to history by his honorific title as Akbar (The Great). In the European scholarly literature, his reign found a historian in Friedrich August von Schleswig-Holstein, count of Noer (1881), and was again discussed most recently by Professor R. Garbe in a *Rektoratsrede* at the

[57] This view is taken also by Oman, *The Mystics, Ascetics and Saints of India*, p. 132. Maurice Bloomfield, in his *The Religion of the Veda, the Ancient Religion of India* (New York, 1908; American Lectures on the History of Religions, Series VII, 1906-1907), p. 10, characterizes this religious system as "Mohammedanism fused with Hinduism in the hybrid religion of the Sikhs." This view is opposed by A. Berriedale Keith in *JRAS* (1908), p. 884. Now see also Antoine Cabaton, "Les Sikhs de l'Inde et le sikhisme," *RMM*, IV (1908), 681ff.; and Julien Vinson, "La Religion des sikhs," *RMM*, IX (1909), 361-ff.

[58] M. Macauliffe, "How the Sikhs Became a Militant People," *Actes du XIVe Congrès International des Orientalistes* (Paris, 1906), I, 137-63.

[p] For more recent literature on the Sikhs, see the relevant articles in Hastings, *Encyclopaedia of Religion and Ethics* and the *Encyclopaedia of Islam*.

[59] Oman, *The Mystics, Ascetics and Saints of India*, p. 133.

University of Tübingen. Max Müller once praised the Emperor Akbar as the first proponent of the comparative study of religions.[q] At all events, the ground had been prepared for him by the man who later became his minister, Abū 'l-Faḍl al-'Allāmī, who in his book, the *Akbar-nāmeh*, raised a monument to the prince he had served. He had preceded Akbar to the study of the different forms of religion, and had pondered the formation of a religion that would go beyond standard Islam.[60] But only Akbar had the power to embody the results of such comparative thinking in an institution enjoying the patronage of the state. Because of a deficient early education he had seemed little suited for occupation with matters of high culture.[61] Nevertheless the name of this prince of the Mughal dynasty (which claimed descent from Timur, and whose rule, 1525-1707, marked the efflorescence of Islamic culture in India) is linked to one of the most remarkable episodes in the history of Indian Islam, toward the end of the sixteenth century. This talented prince had an interest in, and susceptibility to, the deeper stirrings of religious feeling. He showed this disposition by undertaking a long journey, in the disguise of a lowly servant, in order to listen to the religious poems of the sweet Hindu singer Haridāsa. With such a cast of mind, Akbar naturally did not fail to avail himself of the opportunity, which the religious diversity of his realm offered in abundance, to receive instruction from the learned representatives of the various faiths. He arranged disputations among theologians of various persuasions. Such disputations aroused the conviction in his mind that no one religion had more than a relative value. Above all, he was also shaken in the belief that his own religion, Islam, possessed the value of being the sole means to salvation. Incidentally, the

[q] The three works intended here are, respectively, Noer, *Kaiser Akbar: Ein Versuch über die Geschichte Indiens im sechzehten Jahrhundert*, 2 vols. (Leiden, 1880-1885), English translation: *The Emperor Akbar: a Contribution towards the History of India in the 16th Century*, 2 vols. (London and Calcutta, 1890); Garbe, *Kaiser Akbar von Indien; ein Lebens- und Kulturbild aus dem sechzehnten Jahrhundert* (Tübingen, 1909), English translation: "Akbar, Emperor of India: A Picture of Life and Customs from the Sixteenth Century," *The Monist*, XIX (1909), 161ff.; Müller, *Introduction to the Science of Religion* (London, 1873), p. 68.

[60] *EI*[1], I, 84, "Abū'l-Faḍl 'Allāmī"; [cf. also *EI*[2], I, 117f.]. The "ascetics of Lebanon" (*EI*[1], I, 84b:11f.) does not refer to the Druzes, but to Muslim ascetics whose preeminent place of residence Mt. Lebanon is said to be (Yāqūt, *Mu'jam al-buldān*, IV, 348:1). The part of the mountains called al-Lukkām (= Amanus, see Lammens, *Mo'āwia*, I, 15)—the region of Antioch and Maṣṣīṣa—is particularly celebrated as the place of abode of great saints; cf. Yāfi'ī, *Rawḍ al-rayāḥīn*, pp. 49:5, 54:14, 156:1. For Syria as a place of saints and penitents, see " 'Alī b. Mejmūn al-Maġribī," p. 295 [= *Gesammelte Schriften*, VI, 3].

[61] Cf. T. Bloch, "Eine Sammlung persischer und arabischer Handschriften in Indien," *ZDMG*, LXIII (1909), 101:22ff.

Sufi form of Islam was the only one in which he still personally participated.

Around the year 1578, he promised unlimited freedom of religion to the adherents of the various faiths in his broad realm. But for himself, he set about devising a new religion that was outwardly related to Islam but in fact meant its complete overthrow. The monarch had accommodating scholars at court declare him a *mujtahid*, that is, a theologian who had, in the Islamic sense of the term, the authority to advance doctrines of his own. Armed with this right, he erected a system of beliefs in which the dogmas and formal requirements of Islam seem to have been denied all value. The imperial religion—called *tawḥīd ilāhī*, "monotheism,"—centered instead on an ethical rationalism whose ultimate ideal was the Sufi union of the soul with the divine. In matters of ritual, one notes the strong influence of the prince's Zoroastrian advisors, whose religion, after suffering oppression in its Persian homeland, had found refuge on Indian soil, and completed the rich diversity of the religious world of India. The most conspicuous and unmistakable feature of the new religion, whose high priest was the emperor himself, was the cult of light, sun, and fire.[r]

The religion of Akbar cannot be called a reform of Islam. It is a negation of it; it is so sharp a break with Islamic tradition that even in Ismā'īlism nothing comparable ventured to appear. But there is no sign that it had any profound effect on the development of Islam. It appears not to have spread beyond the court and the intellectual elite. Nor did it outlive its founder. As in antiquity the reform of the Egyptian religion that the enlightened Pharaoh Amenophis IV bestowed on his realm was bound to his presence and yielded, after his death, to the ancestral cult, so Akbar's religious achievement failed to endure after him. After his death in 1605 orthodox Islam regained its former hegemony, without upheaval. It was only in the course of the recent rationalist movements among Hindus and Muslims in British India that Akbar came to be called a precursor of the effort to bring Hinduism, Parsism, and Islam nearer to one another.[62]

[r] A good deal has been written since Goldziher's time on the Emperor Akbar and the religious movement that he launched. On the latter, known as *Din-i Ilahi*, see Aziz Ahmad, "Akbar, heretique ou apostat?" *JA*, CCXLIX (1961), 21-38; Makhanlal Roychoudhury, *The Din-i Ilahi* (Calcutta, 1941). Reference may also be made to a Swedish thesis by Gudmar Aneer, "Akbar the Great Mogul and His Religious Thoughts" (Skriv Service AB, Uppsala, 1973).

[62] G. Bonet-Maury, "La Religion d'Akbar et ses rapports avec l'Islamisme et le Parsisme," *RHR*, LI (1905), 153ff.

Later Developments

14. This brings us to a fully modern phase in the development of Indian Islam.[s]

In India, contacts with Western civilization had been close. European colonization and conquest subjected millions of Muslims to non-Muslim government, and caused Muslims to participate in the modern forms of social life. Inevitably these experiences had a profound effect on the attitude of educated Muslims toward inherited religious views and practices that were in ever more urgent need of accommodation to new circumstances. They set about critically separating fundamentals from historical accretions: the latter could be more easily sacrificed to the demands of civilization. On the other hand, they sensed a need to stand up as apologists of the fundamental doctrines of Islam, to defend them against the alien world view, to refute the accusation that the doctrines of Islam were contrary to civilization, and to demonstrate the adaptability of its precepts to all times and nations.

This apologetic activity has always been accompanied by the noble endeavor to separate the wheat from the chaff. But it is also shot through with a tendentious rationalism that cannot always do justice to the demands of historical inquiry. These rationalist aspirations, aiming at the reconciliation of Islamic thought and life with the demands of the Western civilization impinging upon them, have mostly been expressed and promoted in India by the fruitful social and literary work of enlightened Muslim intellectuals. Sayyid Amīr ʻAlī, Sir Sayyid Aḥmad Khān Bahādur, together with other highly esteemed personalities of the Islamic world, have been the leaders of this spiritual movement for the reorganization of Islam. Its results are proved by the new intellectual life of Indian Islam, ever more sturdily advancing along the road of culture. They are meant to demonstrate that Islam—in the rationalist form, to be sure, which these men represent—has a right to life amidst the currents of modern civilization.

These trends, which the upholders of the past like to refer to as the new Muʻtazila, have found expression in an abundant literature of theological and historical monographs, books, and periodicals in English and in Indian languages. They have led to the establishment of highly respected

[s] On the Indian modernists, reference may be made to the works cited above by Wilfred Cantwell Smith, Aziz Ahmad, and Peter Hardy; also, Aziz Ahmad, *An Intellectual History of Islam in India* (Edinburgh, 1969), and Bashir Ahmad Dar, *Religious Thought of Sayyid Ahmad Khan* (Lahore, 1957). Sample texts and further bibliographical guidance will be found in Aziz Ahmad and G. E. von Grunebaum, *Muslim Self-Statement in India and Pakistan, 1857-1968* (Wiesbaden, 1970).

Muslim associations in which this reformed Islam has its embodiment and public representation. They have prompted the founding of numerous schools at all levels, among which pride of place belongs to the University of Aligarh,[t] supported by the munificence of Muslim princes. The already mentioned Agha Khan, the present chief of the remaining Isma'īlīs, is also among the supporters of this and many other educational activities.

Through Indian or other influences, this Islamic modernism that first appeared in India has also affected, although less extensively at first, the religious thought of Muslims in other countries: in Egypt, Algeria, Tunis,[u] and particularly in the territories of the Tatars under Russian rule.[63]

These cultural tendencies, intimately related to religious life, that are making themselves felt in various parts of the Muslim world carry the seeds of a new phase in the evolution of Islam. Under their influence, perhaps the theology of Islam will reach an objective, historical view of its sources.

[t] On Aligarh, see David Lelyveld, *Aligarh's First Generation* (Princeton, 1978).

[u] The Islamic modernist movements in the Middle East and North Africa, thus summarily dismissed by Goldziher, have formed the subject of a vast literature. For an introduction, see H.A.R. Gibb, *Modern Trends in Islam* (Chicago, 1947); E.I.J. Rosenthal, *Islam in the Modern National State* (Cambridge, 1965); Hichem Djait, *La Personalité et le devenir arabo-islamiques* (Paris, 1974), and the works by von Grunebaum, Smith, and Braune cited above. For two conflicting views of some of the major figures, see Malcolm H. Kerr, *Islamic Reform: the Political and Legal Theories of Muhammad Abduh and Rashid Rida* (Berkeley and Los Angeles, 1966), and Elie Kedourie, *Afghani and Abduh: an Essay on Religious Belief and Political Activism in Modern Islam* (London, 1966).

[63] About this last movement, see H. Vámbéry, "Die Kulturbestrebungen der Tataren," *Deutsche Rundschau*, XXXIII (1907), 72-91. On the favorable progress in education in these regions, see Molla Aminoff, "Les Progrès de l'instruction chez les Musulmans russes," *RMM*, IX (1909), 247-63, 295.

[Much less attention has been given to the intellectual and indeed to the general history of the Muslim subjects of the Russian Empire and later of the Soviet Union than to the Middle East. For introductory accounts, see A. Zenkovsky, *Pan-Turkism and Islam in Russia* (Cambridge, Mass., 1960); A. Bennigsen and C. Quelquejay, *Histoire des mouvements nationaux chez les musulmans de Russie: le sultangalievisme au Tatarstan* (Paris and The Hague, 1960); *idem, La Presse et le mouvement national des musulmans de Russie avant 1920* (Paris and The Hague, 1964); Chantal Lemercier Quelquejay, "Un Reformateur Tatar au XIXe siècle; Abdul Kajjum al-Nasyri," *Cahiers de monde russe et sovietique*, IV (1973), 117-42; Bennigsen and Quelquejay, *The Evolution of the Muslim Nationalities of the USSR and Their Linguistic Problems* (London, 1961); A. A. Bennigsen and C. Quelquejay, *Islam in the Soviet Union* (London, 1967, translated from the French); Vincent Monteil, *Les Musulmans sovietiques* (Paris, 1957); A. A. Bennigsen and S. Enders Wimbush, *Muslim National Communism in the Soviet Union* (Chicago, 1979). The fullest source of information on Soviet Muslim affairs is the *Central Asian Review*.]

15. It was amid such intellectual currents, also in India, that the most recent Islamic sect was born. Its serious study is as yet somewhat difficult. The founder of the Aḥmadīya,[v] as the sect is called, Mīrzā Ghulām Aḥmad of Qādiān in the Punjab, linked its origin to his discovery that the genuine tomb of Jesus was in Khānjār Street in Srinagar in Kashmir: it was the same as the grave known by the name of Yuz-Asaf, an otherwise unknown saint. (Incidentally, it is probably of Buddhist origin.) Jesus escaped his persecutors in Jerusalem, and in the course of his wanderings in the East, he came here, where he died. By means of this discovery, supported by written evidence, Ghulām Aḥmad wishes to combat both the Christian and Islamic traditions about the continued life of Jesus. He is himself the Messiah who has appeared "in the spirit and power" of Jesus to the seventh millennium of the world, as he is also the *Mahdī* awaited by the Muslims.

According to an Islamic tradition, at the beginning of each century God raises up, to strengthen the faith, a man who renews the religion of Islam. Sunnīs and Shī'īs zealously enumerate the men who are regarded, each for his century, as "renewers." The last of them will be the *Mahdī* himself. He is that man, Aḥmad claims; he is the renewer of religion sent by God at the onset of the fourteenth Islamic century. With this twofold claim of being both Jesus come again and the *Mahdī*—to which, for the benefit of the Hindus, he adds the title of avatar—he means not only to embody the hopes of Islam for its universal triumph in time to come, but also to express the universal mission of Islam to all mankind.

His first public appearance took place in the year 1880, but only since 1889 has he been earnestly recruiting followers and referring, to confirm his prophetic mission, to signs and miracles and predictions come true. The occurence of a solar and a lunar eclipse in the Ramaḍān of 1894 served to prove that he was the *Mahdī*, for according to Islamic tradition the appearance of the *Mahdī* will be heralded by such celestial phenomena. But the office of *Mahdī* he lays claim to differs from that of the standard Islamic idea, for his mission is of a peaceful character. The *Mahdī* of Islamic orthodoxy is a warrior who combats the unbelievers, sword in hand, and whose path is marked in blood. The Shī'īs give him the title, among others, of *ṣāḥib al-sayf*, "Man of the Sword."[64] The new prophet is a prince of peace. He has eliminated *jihād* (holy war) from the obligations of Muslim men. He inculcates upon his followers peace and tolerance, condemns fanaticism, and in general strives to awaken in them

[v] See further *EI*² article "Aḥmadiyya" (by W. Cantwell Smith).
[64] Kulīnī, *Uṣūl al-kāfī*, p. 350.

a spirit receptive and favorable to culture.[65] In the creed that he has laid down for his community, great emphasis is placed on the ethical virtues of the Muslim. He aspires to bring about the regeneration of mankind by strengthening man's belief in God and releasing him from the bondage of sin. He does insist, however, on performance of the essential Muslim obligations. In his preaching he draws for support on the Old and New Testaments, the Qur'ān, and reliable hadith. Outwardly he seeks to be in constant conformity to the Qur'ān, but he is very skeptical about the traditions, whose reliability he subjects to scrutiny. From this there result a number of deviations from formal aspects of orthodox Islam, insofar as these are based on hadith.

An educational activity is also linked to his propaganda, in which even instruction in the Hebrew language has a place. At the time of this writing (1907), the new *Mahdī*'s community is estimated to have grown to 70,000 souls.[w] Of those within range of his activity, he has gained many followers, especially among Muslims influenced by European civilization. The *Mahdī* is a prolific writer. In more than sixty theological works in Arabic and Urdu, he has expounded his doctrines to the Muslims, and has offered proofs for the authenticity of his mission. He tries to have an impact outside the Eastern world by publishing an English monthly periodical, the *Review of Religions*.[66] This, then, appears to be the most recent sectarian development within Islam.[67]

16. In conclusion we must mention one more trend in certain Muslim circles.

[65] Cf. M. Hartmann, "Der Islam 1907," p. 231:7ff.

[w] Ghulām Aḥmad, the founder of the sect, died in May 1908. At the present time, the Aḥmadīya claim some half million members, of whom about half are in Pakistan, a quarter in India, and the rest in a variety of other countries, the most important communities of these being in West Africa.

[66] M. Th. Houtsma, "Le Mouvement religieux des Ahmadiyya aux Indes anglaises," *RMM*, I (1906–1907), 533ff., makes available a description of the movement and its goals by one of its members, in his own words.

[67] Mention should be made here also of the Chaiherinye. This sectarian movement has existed since the sixties of the last century. It came into being in connection with the rebellion of the Muslims in their Chinese region (Kansu), and was called forth by the self-proclaimed Prophet Ma Hua-lung. But the available information about the prehistory, nature, and tendencies of this Sino-Islamic sect (*hsin chiao*, "the new religion," as opposed to *lao chiao*, "the old religion") is still so uncertain that it is unadvisable to attempt a comprehensive description of it in the present context. The French Mission d'Ollone has most recently investigated these phenomena in *RMM*, V (1908), 93, 459, and especially in "Recherches sur les musulmans chinois," *RMM*, IX (1909), 538, 561ff. On earlier religious movements in Chinese Islam, cf. J. J. de Groot, "Over de Wahabietenbewegung in Kansoeh 1781-1789," *Verslagen en Mededeelingen der Koninklijke Akademie van Wetenschappen*, Afdeeling Letterkunde IV, 6 (Amsterdam, 1904), 130–33.

Even in the past there was no lack of effort to bridge the gulf between Sunnīs and Shī'īs. Given the many transitional stages that exist between the two forms of Islam, this sectarian division had important public consequences only where Shī'ism succeeded in organizing itself into a ruling state religion, in other words, in Shī'ī states. Of these there were not many in the history of Islam. Where such a political organization existed (Ch. V, Sec. 18), Shī'ism could assert itself, over against the Sunnī orientation of other lands, as a closed ecclesiastic community, resistant to the outside world.

That in our time Persia is the foremost power in Shī'ism is the result of the rise of the Ṣafavid dynasty (1501-1721) in that country. Where previous attempts had failed,[68] the Ṣafavids raised Shī'ism to the rank of state religion in their Persian empire, by way of contrast to the Turkish state across their border. However, after the fall of that dynasty, the great conqueror Nādir Shāh worked, after his peace treaty with Turkey, to bring about the unification of the two sects. His undertaking was brought to nought by his death shortly afterward, in 1747. In the notes—now available in print—of the Sunnī theologian 'Abdallāh ibn Ḥusayn al-Suwaydī (b. 1104/1692, died 1174/1760)[69] we possess an interesting comtemporary document about a synod of the theologians of both sides, convoked by Nādir Shāh. In this synod a compromise was reached by which Shī'ism was to be added as a fifth orthodox *madhhab* to the four orthodox rites of Sunnī Islam.[70] According to the compromise, there would soon have followed the highest token of the reception of Shī'ī Islam into the system of orthodoxy: in the sacred precinct of Mecca, next to the stations (*maqām*) of the four orthodox rites, a fifth *maqām* would have been established for the Ja'farī rite, henceforth to be recognized as orthodox. But all this soon proved itself a visionary's utopia. The inher-

[68] As such an attempt, the following deserves notice. In the fourteenth century, the government of the province of Fārs wished to introduce Shī'ism as the official form of Islam. It was only the obstinate resistance of the *Qāḍī al-quḍāt* of Shiraz, Majd al-Dīn Abū Ibrāhīm al-Bālī (d. 756/1355 in Shiraz, at the age of ninety-four) that frustrated this intention. His convictions exposed him to severe trials. This Majd al-Dīn was in his fifteenth year already appointed chief *qāḍī*; deposed soon after, his successor was Bayḍāwī, famous as Qur'ān commentator and theologian. Six months later he was reinstated in his position, only to have soon to return it again to Bayḍāwī. After yet another deposition of Bayḍāwī, Majd al-Dīn held the position without interruption to the end of his life. See Subkī, *Ṭabaqāt*, VI, 83, where the statement that Majd al-Dīn administered that office for seventy-five years must be due to a slip of the pen.

[69] On Suwaydī, see Louis Cheikho, "Al-Ādāb al-'arabīya fī'l-qarn al-tāsi' 'ashar," *Al-Mashriq*, XI (1908), 275, where 1170/1756 is given as the year of his death. The document under discussion is not mentioned.

[70] *Kitāb al-ḥujaj al-qaṭ'īya li-ittifāq al-firaq al-islāmīya* (Cairo, A.H. 1323).

ited hatred that theologians of both sides harbored for each other did not incline them to keep alive the shah's tolerant aspirations after his death.

Later (in the first half of the last century) we witness once more an ephemeral alliance of the two sects, in their common struggle for freedom against the oppressor in the Caucasus. They were led by Shāmil (the correct pronunciation is Shamvīl, that is, Samuel) and his Murīds. This, however, was a patriotic, rather than theological, phenomenon.

During recent decades there has been much talk about a movement that people have become accustomed to call Pan-Islamism and to regard now as a danger, now as a phantom. In Muslim circles this movement has frequently cast up the idea of smoothing over sectarian differences in order to achieve a homogeneous union. Independently of Pan-Islamic tendencies, but rather in the service of modern cultural aspirations, such ideas of concord have been expressed in the Islamic territories under Russian rule, where in recent times many signs of a healthy progress have appeared among the Muslim population. Sunnīs have been participating in services at Shī'ī mosques; in Astrakhan they could hear it said from the pulpit that "there is but one Islam, and it was only by the regrettable influence of the philosophers and of Greek habits (?) that the controversies of commentators in the 'Abbāsid age called forth the schism." In the same service, the *imām* conducting the prayer could combine a eulogy of Ḥasan and Ḥusayn, the martyrs of the Shī'a, with praise of the caliphs whose names it had been sound Shī'ī practice to accompany with phrases of malediction and feelings of a fanatic hate.[71]

On August 23, 1906 a Muslim congress in Kazan discussed the question of the religious instruction of school children. It was resolved that a single textbook would be used for Sunnīs and Shī'īs and that teachers could be chosen indifferently from both sects.[72] Common religious instruction for Shī'ī and Sunnī children has since prevailed in practice. In Iraq similar signs of a rapprochement between the two hostile sects have recently appeared in the social sphere, with the approval of the Shī'ī authorities of Najaf.[73]

But as yet these are only isolated signs. In view of other phenomena, it is still very much in question whether the way of thinking that they reflect will gain a more extensive following.

[71] *RMM*, I (1906-1907), 116; cf. II (1907), 389f.

[72] A. Chatelier, "Les Musulmans russes," *RMM*, I (1906-1907), 160; cf. *RMM*, II (1907), 534.

[73] *RMM*, IX (1909), 311.

Bibliography

al-ʻAbdarī, Muḥammad ibn al-Ḥājj. *Kitāb madkhal al-sharʻ al-sharīf.* Alexandria, A.H. 1293.

[Abdel Razek, M. "Le Mot Islam, son sense primitif et son évolution." In *Actes du 18e Congrès International des Orientalistes.* Leiden, 1932, pp. 225ff.]

ʻAbduh, Muḥammad. *Al-Islām wa'l-naṣrānīya ma'a'l-ʻilm wa'l-madanīya.* Cairo, n.d.

Abū Dāwūd Sulaymān ibn al-Ashʻath al-Sijistānī. *Sunan Abī Dāwūd.* 2 vols. Cairo, A.H. 1280.

[Abū Ḥanīfa al-Nuʻmān ibn Thābit (attr.). *Al-Fiqh al-akbar.* Haydarabad, A.H. 1342].

———. *Al-Waṣīya.* With the commentary of al-Bārbartī. Cairo, A.H. 1289.

al-ʻAdawī, Ḥasan. *Al-Nafaḥāt al-shādhalīya fī sharḥ al-burdah al-būṣīrīya.* 3 vols. Cairo, A.H. 1297.

al-Adhanī, Sulaymān. *Al-Bākūra al-sulaymānīya.* Beirut, 1863.

Aghānī, see al-Iṣbahānī.

[Ahmad, Aziz. "Akbar, hérétique ou apostat?" *JA,* CCXLIX (1961), 21ff.]

[———. *An Intellectual History of Islam in India.* Edinburgh, 1969.]

[———. *Islamic Modernism in India and Pakistan, 1857-1964.* London, 1967.]

[———. *Studies in Islamic Culture in the Indian Environment.* Oxford, 1964.]

[———, and G. E. von Grunebaum. *Muslim Self-Statement in India and Pakistan, 1857-1968.* Wiesbaden, 1970.]

[Ahmad, Maqbul. *Indo-Arab Relations: An Account of India's Relations with the Arab World from Ancient up to Modern Times.* New Delhi, 1969.]

al-ʻAjjāj, Abū'l-Shaʻthā' ʻAbdallāh ibn Ru'ba. *Dīwān.* Edited by Wilhelm Ahlwardt in *Sammlungen alter arabischer Dichter,* II. Berlin, 1903.

ʻAlī, Moulavi Cherágh. *The Proposed Political, Legal and Social Reforms in the Ottoman Empire.* Bombay, 1883.

Ali, Mir Shahamat. "Translation of the *Takwiyat-ul-Imān,*" *JRAS,* XIII (1852), 310ff.

Ali Khan, Gazanfar, and Wilfrid Sparroy. *With the Pilgrims to Mecca: the Great Pilgrimage of A.H. 1319, A.D. 1902.* London, 1905.

al-ʻĀmilī, Bahā' al-Dīn. *Al-Kashkūl.* To which is appended a panegyric to the Mahdi with a commentary by al-Manīnī. 2 vols. Cairo, A.H. 1288.

———. *Al-Mikhlāt.* Cairo, A.H. 1317.

Aminoff, Molla. "Les Progrès de l'instruction chez les Musulmans russes," *RMM,* IX (1909), 247ff.

[Ammianus Marcellinus. *Histories.* Edited and translated by J. C. Rolfe. Rev. ed. London and Cambridge, Mass., 1963.]

[Anawati, G. C., and Louis Gardet. *Mystique musulmane.* Paris, 1961.]

[Anderson, J.N.D. *Islamic Law in the Modern World.* London, 1959.]
[Andrae, Tor. *Mohammed, the Man and His Faith.* Translated by Theophil Menzel. London, 1936.]
[———. *Die Person Muhammeds in Lehre und Glauben seiner Gemeinde.* Stockholm, 1917.]
[Aneer, Gudmar. "Akbar the Great Mogul and His Religious Thoughts." Skriv Service AB, Uppsala, 1973.]
[Aptowitzer, V. "Arabisch-Jüdische Schöpfungstheorien," *Hebrew Union College Annual*, VI (1929), 205ff.]
[Arberry, A. J. *Introduction to the History of Sufism.* London, 1942.]
[——— (ed.). *Religion in the Middle East: Three Religions in Concord and Conflict.* 2 vols. Cambridge, 1969.]
[———. *Revelation and Reason in Islam.* London, 1957.]
[———. *Sufism: An Account of the Mystics of Islam.* London, 1950.]
Arnold, T. W. "Survivals of Hinduism among the Muhammadans of India." In *Transactions of the Third International Congress for the History of Religions.* Oxford, 1908. I, 314ff.
al-Ash'arī, Abū'l-Ḥasan 'Alī ibn Ismā'īl. *Kitāb al-ibāna 'an uṣūl al-diyāna.* Haydarabad, A.H. 1321.
Asín Palacios, Miguel. "La psicologia según Mohidin Abenarabi." In *Actes du XIVe Congrès International des Orientalistes.* Paris, 1908, III, 79ff.
al-'Askarī, Ḥasan. *Tafsīr* [cf. *GAL* SI, 333].
'Aṭṭār, Farīd al-Dīn. *Tadhkirat al-awliyā'.* Edited by R. A. Nicholson. 2 vols. London, 1905-1907.
Avicenna, *see* Ibn Sīnā.
al-Azdī, Abū'l-Ḥasan 'Alī ibn Ẓāfir. *Badā'i' al-badā'ih* (on the margin of the *Ma'āhid al-tanṣīṣ*). Cairo, A.H. 1316.
Bab. Talmud = *The Babylonian Talmud.* Goldziher's references are standard for all editions.
Badshah Husain, *A. F. Ḥusain in the Philosophy of History.* Lucknow, 1905.
al-Baghawī, Abū Muḥammad al-Ḥusayn ibn Mas'ūd. *Maṣābīḥ al-sunna.* 2 vols. Cairo, A.H. 1294.
al-Baghdādī, 'Abd al-Qādir ibn 'Umar. *Khizānat al-adab.* 4 vols. Cairo, A.H. 1299.
Bahā' Allāh. *Al-Kitāb al-aqdas.* Edited by A. H. Toumansky. St. Petersburg, 1899.
———. *Rasā'il Bahā' Allāh.* Edited by Victor Rosen. St. Petersburg, 1908.
Bahgat, Aly bey. "Note sur deux bronzes du Musée Arabe," *Bulletin de l'Institut Égyptien*, 4th Series, VII (1906), 57ff.
Baḥya ibn Paquda, *Kitāb ma'ānī al-nafs (Buch vom Wesen der Seele).* Edited by Ignaz Goldziher. Abhandlungen der Königlichen Gesellschaft der Wissenschaften zu Göttingen, Philologisch-Historische Klasse, New Series, IX, 1. Berlin, 1907.
al-Bakrī, Muḥammad Tawfīq. *Bayt al-ṣiddīq.* Cairo, A.H. 1323.
al-Balādhurī, Aḥmad ibn Yaḥyā. *Futūḥ al-buldān (Liber Expugnationis Regionum).* Edited by M. J. de Goeje. Leiden, 1866.
al-Balawī, Abū'l-Ḥajjāj Yūsuf ibn Muḥammad. *Kitāb alif-bā.* Cairo, A.H. 1287.
pseudo-Balkhī, *see* al-Maqdisī.

[Baneth, D.Z.H. "What Did Muhammad Mean when He Called His Religion 'Islam'? The Original Meaning of Aslama and Its Derivatives," *Israel Oriental Studies*, I (1971), 183ff.]

Banning, Hubert. *Muḥammad ibn al-Ḥanafīja*. Erlangen, 1909.

Barhebraeus (Ibn al-'Ibrī, Abū'l-Faraj). *Ta'rīkh mukhtaṣar al-duwal.* Edited by A. Ṣāliḥānī. Beirut, 1890.

Barney, Laura Clifford. *Some Answered Questions, collected and translated from the Persian of 'Abdu'l-Baha*. London, 1908.

Barth, J. "Midraschische Elemente in der muslimischen Tradition." In Berliner *Festschrift*, pp. 33ff.

[de Bary, Wm. Theodore, et al., eds. *Sources of Indian Tradition.* New York, 1958.]

Basset, René. "Contes et légendes de l'Extrême-Orient," *Revue des traditions populaires*. XX (1905), 416ff.

———. "Recherches bibliographiques sur les sources de la Salouat el-Anfâs." In *Recueil de mémoires et de textes publié en l'honneur du XIVe Congrès des Orientalistes*. Algiers, 1905, 1ff.

al-Baṭalyawsī, Abū Muḥammad 'Abdallāh ibn Muḥammad ibn al-Sīd. *Al-Inṣāf fī'l-tanbīh*. Edited by Aḥmad 'Umar al-Maḥmaṣānī. Cairo, A.H. 1319.

al-Bayḍāwī, Abū'l-Khayr 'Abdallāh ibn 'Umar. *Anwār al-tanzīl wa-asrār al-ta'wil (Commentarius in Coranum).* Edited by H. O. Fleischer. 2 vols. Leipzig, 1846-1848.

al-Bayhaqī, Ibrāhīm ibn Muḥammad. *Al-Maḥāsin wa'l-masāwī*. Edited by Friedrich Schwally. Giessen, 1902.

Becker, C. H. *Christentum und Islam*. Tübingen, 1907. Reprinted in *Islamstudien*, I, 386ff. Translated as *Christianity and Islam*. London, 1909.

[———. *Islamstudien*. 2 vols. Leipzig, 1924-32.]

———, "Ist der Islam eine Gefahr für unsere Kolonien?" *Koloniale Rundschau*, I (1909), 266ff. Reprinted in *Islamstudien*, II, 156ff.

———. *Papyri Schott-Reinhardt I.* Heidelberg, 1906.

Bel, Alfred. "La Population musulmane de Tlemcen," *Revue des études ethnographiques et sociologiques*, I (1908), 200ff., 417ff.

"Le Béloutchistan d'après l'administration britannique," *RMM*, V (1908), 121ff.

[Belyaev, E. A. *Arabs, Islam and the Arab Caliphate in the Early Middle Ages.* Translated by Adolphe Gourevitch. New York and London, 1969.]

[Bennigsen, A., and C. Quelquejay. *The Evolution of the Muslim Nationalities of the USSR and Their Linguistic Problems*. London, 1961.]

[———. *Histoire des mouvements nationaux chez les musulmans de Russie: le sultangalievisme au Tatarstan*. Paris and The Hague, 1960.]

[———. *Islam in the Soviet Union*. London, 1967.]

[———. *La Presse et le mouvement national des musulmans de Russie avant 1920.* Paris and The Hague, 1964.]

van Berchem, Max. "Titres califiens d'Occident," *JA*, 10th Series, IX (1907), 245ff.

Berliner Festschrift-Festschrift zum siebzigsten Geburtstage A. Berliner's. Edited by A. Freimann and M. Hildesheimer. Frankfurt-am-Main, 1903.

Besse, Jean. "Les Diverses Sortes de moines en Orient avant le Concile de Chalcédoine (451)," *RHR*, XL (1899), 159ff.

Beveridge, H. "Ibrāhīm b. Adham," *JRAS*, 1909, pp. 751f.

BGA = *Bibliotheca Geographorum Arabicorum.*

[Birge, J. K. *The Bektashi Order of Dervishes.* London and Hartford, Conn., 1937.]

al-Bīrūnī, Abū'l-Rayḥān Muḥammad ibn Aḥmad. *Al-Āthār al-bāqiya (Chronologie orientalischer Völker).* Edited by Eduard Sachau. Leipzig, 1878. Translated by Eduard Sachau as *Chronology of Ancient Nations.* London, 1879.

[Blachère, R. *Introduction au Coran.* 2nd ed. Paris, 1959.]

Bloch, T. "Eine Sammlung persischer und arabischer Handschriften in Indien," *ZDMG*, LXIII (1909), 98ff.

———. "Über einige bildliche Darstellungen altindischer Gottheiten," *ZDMG*, LXII (1908), 648ff.

Blochet, E. *Le Messianisme dans l'hétérodoxie musulmane.* Paris, 1903.

Bloomfield, Maurice. *The Religion of the Veda, the Ancient Religion of India.* New York, 1908.

Böckenhoff, Karl. *Speisegesetze mosaischer Art in mittelalterlichen Kirchenrechtsquellen.* Münster, 1907.

Bonet-Maury, G. "Les Confréries religieuses dans l'Islamisme et les ordres militaires dans le Catholicisme." In *Transactions of the Third International Congress for the History of Religions.* Oxford, 1908. II, 339ff.

———. "La Religion d'Akbar et ses rapports avec l'Islamisme et le Parsisme," *RHR*, LI (1905), 153ff.

[Bousquet, G. H. *Du Droit Musulman et de son application effective dans le monde.* Algiers, 1949.]

[———. "Introduction à l'étude de l'Islam Indonesien," *REI*, II-III (1938), 133ff.]

[———. "Observations sur la nature et les causes de la conquête Arabe," *Studia Islamica*, VI (1956), 37ff.]

[Braune, Walther. *Der islamische Orient zwischen Vergangenheit und Zukunft: eine geschichtstheologische Analyse seiner Stellung in der Weltsituation.* Bern and Munich, 1960.]

[Bravmann, M. M. *The Spiritual Background of Early Islam: Studies in Ancient Arab Concepts.* Leiden, 1972.]

Brockelmann, Carl. *Geschichte der arabischen Litteratur.* 1st ed. 2 vols. Weimar, 1898-1902; 2nd ed. 2 vols. Leiden, 1943-1949; *Supplementbände.* 3 vols. Leiden, 1937-1942.

Browne, Edward G. *An Abridged Translation of the History of Tabaristan by Ibn Isfendiyar.* E.J.W. Gibb Memorial Series, II. London, 1905.

———. "Bab, Babis." In *Encyclopaedia of Religion and Ethics.* Edited by James Hastings. New York, 1908-1927. II, 299ff.

———. "Catalogue and Description of 27 Bābī Manuscripts," *JRAS*, 1892, pp. 433ff., 637ff.

———. *A Catalogue of the Persian Manuscripts in the Library of the University of Cambridge.* Cambridge, 1896.

———. *A Literary History of Persia.* 4 vols. London, 1902-1924.

———. "Some Remarks on the Bābī Texts Edited by Baron Victor Rosen," *JRAS*, 1892, pp. 259ff.
———. *The Tárīkh-i Jadíd, or, New History of Mírzá 'Alí Muḥammad the Báb.* Cambridge, 1893.
———. *A Year amongst the Persians.* London, 1893.
[Brunschvig, Robert. *Études d'Islamologie.* Paris, 1976.]
al-Bukhārī, Abū 'Abdallāh Muḥammad ibn Ismā'īl. *Al-Jāmi' al-ṣaḥīḥ (Le recueil des traditions mahométanes).* Edited by Ludolf Krehl and T. W. Juynboll. 4 vols. Leiden, 1862-1908.
[Burton, John. *The Collection of the Qur'ān.* Cambridge, 1977.]
[Butzer, K. W. "Late Glacial and Post Glacial Climatic Variations in the Near East," *Erdkunde*, II (1957), 21ff.]
[———. "Der Umweltfaktor in der grossen arabischen Expansion," *Saeculum*, VIII (1957), 359ff.]
Cabaton, Antoine. "Quelques Groupes islamiques dans les possessions extérieures des Indes Néerlandaises," *RMM*, VIII (1909), 180ff.
———. Review of Wilkinson, *Papers on Malay Subjects*, in *RMM*, VIII (1909), 45ff.
———. "Les Sikhs de l'Inde et le sikhisme," *RMM*, IV (1908), 681ff.
Caetani, Leone. *Annali dell'Islam.* 10 vols. Milan, 1905-1926.
———. "Das historische Studium des Islams." Lecture held at the International Historical Congress. Berlin, 1908.
[Cağatay, N. "Ribā and Interest Concept and Banking in the Ottoman Empire," *Studia Islamica*, XXXII (1970), 53ff.]
[Cahen, Claude. *L'Islam des origines au debut de l'empire Ottoman.* Paris, 1970.]
[———. "Note sur les origines de la communauté syrienne des Nuṣayri," *REI*, XXXVIII (1970), 243ff.]
[Calverley, E. E. "Sumaniyyah," *Muslim World*, LIV (1964), 200ff.]
Carra de Vaux, Bernard. *La Doctrine de l'Islam.* Paris, 1909.
———. *Le Mahométisme; le génie sémitique et le génie aryen dans l'Islam.* Paris, 1897.
[Castro, Francesco. *Materiali e Recerche sul Nikāḥ al-Mut'a.* Rome, 1974.]
Chatelier, A. "Aga Khan," *RMM*, I (1906-1907), 48ff.
———. "Les Musulmans russes," *RMM*, I (1906-1907), 145ff.
Cheikho, Louis. "Al-Ādāb al-'arabīya fī'l-qarn al-tāsi' 'ashar," *Al-Mashriq*, XI (1908), 273ff.
———. " 'Uhūd Nabī al-Islām wa'l-khulafā' al-rāshidīn li'l-naṣārā," *Al-Mashriq*, XII (1909), 609ff., 674ff.
Clement of Alexandria. *Stromata.* [Edited by Otto Stählin; new edition revised by Ludwig Früchtel. 2 vols. Berlin, 1960-1970.]
"Le Club national de Tauris," *RMM,* VI (1908), 534ff.
[Corbin, Henry. *L'Homme de lumière dans le soufisme Iranien.* Paris, 1971. Translated as *The Man of Light in Iranian Sufism* by Nancy Pearson. Boulder, Colo. and London, 1978.]
[Coulson, N. J. *A History of Islamic Law.* Edinburgh, 1964.]
al-Dabbūsī, Abū Zayd. *Ta'sīs al-naẓar.* Cairo, n.d.

Dāmād, Muḥammad Bāqir. *Al-Rawāshiḥ al-samawīya fī sharḥ al-aḥādīth al-imāmīya*. Bombay, A.H. 1311.

al-Damīrī, Muḥammad ibn Mūsā. *Ḥayāt al-ḥayawān al-kubrā*. 2 vols. Cairo, A.H. 1319.

[Daniel, Norman. *Islam and the West: The Making of an Image*. Edinburgh, 1958.]

[Danziger, Raphael. *Abd al-Qadir and the Algerians: Resistance to the French and Internal Consolidation*. New York, 1977.]

[Dar, Bashir Ahmad. *Religious Thought of Sayyid Ahmad Khan*. Lahore, 1957.]

al-Dārimī, Abū Muḥammad 'Abdallāh ibn 'Abd al-Raḥmān. *Sunan al-Dārimī*. Cawnpore, A.H. 1293.

Darmesteter, James. *Le Mahdi depuis les origines de l'Islam jusqu'à nos jours*. Paris, 1885.

Darwīsh al-Maḥrūqī. *Kitāb al-dalā'il fī'l-lawāzim wa'l-wasā'il*. Cairo, A.H. 1320.

Derenbourg, Hartwig. *La Science des religions et l'Islamisme*. Paris, 1886.

al-Dhahabī, Abū 'Abdallāh Muḥammad ibn 'Uthmān. *Mīzān al-i'tidāl*. 2 vols. Lucknow, A.H. 1301. [Edited by 'Alī Muḥammad al-Bajāwī. 4 vols. Cairo, 1382/1963.]

———. *Tadhkirat al-ḥuffāẓ*. 4 vols. Haydarabad, A.H. 1315. [Edited in 4 vols. Haydarabad, 1375/1955.]

Didier, Charles. [*Séjour chez le grand-chérif de la Mekke*. Paris, 1857.] German translation, *Ein Aufenthalt bei dem Gross-Scherif von Mekka*. Leipzig, 1862.

Dildār 'Alī. *Mir'āt al-'uqūl fī 'ilm al-uṣūl*. 2 vols. Lucknow, A.H. 1319.

[Djait, Hichem. *La Personalité et le devenir arabo-islamiques*. Paris, 1974.]

Doutté, Edmond. *Les Marabouts*. Paris, 1900. Reprinted from *RHR*, XL (1899), 342ff.; XLI (1900), 22ff., 289ff.

———. "Un Texte arabe en dialecte oranais," *Mémoires de la Société de Linguistique*, XII (1903), 335ff., 373ff.

Dreyfus, Hippolyte. *Essai sur le Béhaïsme, son histoire, sa portée sociale*. Paris, 1909.

———. "Une Institution Béhaïe: Le Machreqou'l-Aẓkār d''Achqābād." In *Mélanges Hartwig Derenbourg*. Paris, 1909, pp. 415ff.

Dussaud, René. *Histoire et religion des Noṣairis*. Paris, 1900.

[*Dustur: A Survey of the Constitutions of the Arab and Muslim States*. Leiden, 1966.]

[Eaton, Richard. *Sufis of Bijapur, 1300-1700*. Princeton, 1978.]

EI[1], *EI*[2], *see Encyclopaedia of Islam*.

Eliot, Sir Charles, *see under the pseudonym* Odysseus.

Encyclopaedia of Islam. 1st edition edited by M. T. Houtsma et al. 4 vols. Leiden and London, 1913-1934. New edition edited by H.A.R. Gibb et al. Leiden and London, 1960-proceeding.

[Ende, Werner. *Arabische Nation und islamische Geschichte: die Umayyaden im Urteil arabischer Autoren des 20 Jahrhunderts*. Beirut, 1977.]

[van Ess, Josef. *Anfänge muslimischer Theologie*. Beirut, 1974.]

[———. *Zwischen Ḥadīṯ und Theologie: Studien zum Entstehen prädestinatianischer Überlieferung*. Berlin, 1975.]

Ethé, Hermann. *Die Rubā'is des Abū Sa'īd Abulkhair*. Sitzungsberichte der Bayerischen Akademie der Wissenschaften, Philosophisch-philologische Klasse. II.

Euting, Julius. *Tagbuch einer Reise in Inner-Arabien.* 2 vols. Leiden, 1896–1914.
Fakar, Ben Ali. *L'Usure en droit musulman.* Lyon, 1908.
[Fakhry, Majid. *Islamic Occasionalism and Its Critique by Averroes and Aquinas.* London, 1958.]
al-Fārābī, Abū Naṣr Muḥammad ibn Muḥammad. *Alfārābīs philosophische Abhandlungen.* Edited by Friedrich Dieterici. Leiden, 1890.
al-Fārābī (attrib.). *Al-Fuṣūṣ fī'l-ḥikma (Das Buch der Ringsteine Fārābī's).* With the Commentary of al-Fārīnī. Edited by Max Horten in *ZA*, XVIII (1904), 257ff.; XX (1907), 16ff., 303ff.
al-Fārīnī, *see* al-Fārābī (attrib.).
Fekkaré Iyasous. Edited by René Basset. Les apocryphes éthiopiens, XI. Paris, 1909.
Fihrist al-kutub al-'arabīya al-maḥfūẓa bi'l-kutubkhāna al-khidiwīya al-miṣrīya. 7 vols. Cairo, A.H. 1306–1309.
Fischer, August. "Eine Qorān-Interpolation." In *Nöldeke Festschrift.* I, 33ff.
———. "Zu Musil's zwei arabischen Inschriften aus Arabia Petraea," *ZDMG*, LXII (1908), 280ff.
Fraenkel, Siegmund. Review of Bedjan's edition of the *Nomocanon* of Barhebraeus, in *Deutsche Literaturzeitung*, XXI (1900), 187ff.
Friedländer, Israel. " 'Abdallāh b. Sabā, der Begründer des Šī'a, und sein jüdischer Ursprung," *ZA*, XXIII (1909), 296ff.
———. "The Heterodoxies of the Shiites in the Presentation of Ibn Ḥazm," *JAOS*, XXVIII (1907), 1ff.; XXIX (1908), 1ff.
———. "Die Mesiasidee im Islam." In *Berliner Festschrift*, pp. 116ff.
[Fück, Johannes. "Die Originalität des arabischen Propheten," *ZDMG*, XC (1936), 509ff.]
[Gabrieli, Francesco. *Arabeschi e studi Islamici.* Naples, 1973.]
GAL = Carl Brockelmann. *Geschichte der arabischen Litteratur.*
GAL, S = Carl Brockelmann. *Geschichte der arabischen Litteratur, Supplementbände.*
Galland, Henri. *Essai sur les Mo'tazélites: les rationalistes de l'Islam.* Geneva, 1906.
Galtier, Émile. *Foutouḥ al-bahnasâ.* Mémoires publiés par les membres de l'Institut français d'archéologie orientale du Caire, XXII. Cairo, 1909.
[von Garbe, Richard. *Kaiser Akbar von Indien; ein Lebens- und Kulturbild aus dem sechzehnten Jahrhundert.* Tübingen, 1909. English translation, "Akbar, Emperor of India: A Picture of Life and Customs from the Sixteenth Century," *The Monist*, XIX (1909), 161ff.]
[Gardet, Louis, and M. W. Anawati. *Introduction à la théologie Musulmane: essai de théologie comparée.* Paris, 1948.]
[Geertz, Clifford. *Islam Observed: Religious Development in Morocco and Indonesia.* New Haven and London, 1968.]
[Gellner, Ernest. *Saints of the Atlas.* London, 1969.]
Geyer, Rudolf. Review of H. Reckendorf, *Mohammed und die Seinen,* in *WZKM*, XXI (1907), 399ff.
———. Review of K. Vollers, *Volkssprache und Schriftsprache im alten Arabien*, in *Göttingische gelehrte Anzeigen*, CLXXI (1909), pt. 1, 10ff.
Ghali, Riad. *De la tradition considérée comme source du droit musulman.* Paris, 1909.

al-Ghazālī, Abū Ḥāmid Muḥammad ibn Muḥammad. *Fātiḥat al-'ulūm*. Cairo, A.H. 1322.

———. *Iḥyā' 'ulūm al-dīn*. 4 vols. Cairo, A.H. 1289.

———. *Al-Iqtiṣād fī'l-i'tiqād*. Edited by Muṣṭafā al-Qabbānī. Cairo, n.d.

———. *Al-Maqṣad al-asnā*. Cairo, A.H. 1322.

———. [*Mīzān al-'amal*. Edited by Sulaymān Dunyā. Cairo, 1964.] Hebrew translation, *Mōznē ṣedeq (Compendium doctrinae ethicae)*. Edited by Jacob Goldenthal. Leipzig and Paris, 1839.

[———. *Al-Munqidh min al-ḍalāl*. Edited by Jamīl Ṣalībā and Kāmil 'Ayyād. 5th ed. Damascus, 1376/1956.]

———. *Al-Qusṭās al-mustaqīm*. Edited by Muṣṭafā al-Qabbānī. Cairo, 1318/1900.

[Gibb, H.A.R. *Modern Trends in Islam*. Chicago, 1947.]

[———. *Mohammedanism, an Historical Survey*. 2nd ed. New York, 1962.]

[———. "Pre-Islamic Monotheism in Arabia," *Harvard Theological Review*, LV (1962), 269ff.]

[———. *Studies in the Civilization of Islam*. Edited by S. J. Shaw and W. J. Polk. Boston, 1962.]

[Gimaret, Daniel, ed. and trans. *Le Livre de Bilawhar et Būḏās selon la version arabe ismaélienne*. Geneva and Paris, 1971.]

Ginzberg, Louis, *Geonica*. 2 vols. New York, 1909.

de Goeje, M. J. "Al-Belādhorī's Ansāb al-aschrāf," *ZDMG*, XXXVIII (1884), 382ff.

———. "Kitāb al-imāma wa'l-siyāsa," *RSO*, I (1907), 415ff.

———. *Mémoire sur la conquête de la Syrie*. 2nd ed. Leiden, 1900.

———. *Mémoire sur les Carmathes du Bahraïn et les Fatimides*. 2nd ed. Leiden, 1886.

[Goitein, S.D.F. *Studies In Islamic History and Institutions*. Leiden, 1966.]

Goldziher, Ignaz. *Abhandlungen zur arabischen Philologie*. 2 vols. Leiden, 1896-1899.

———. " 'Alī b. Mejmūn al-Maġribī und sein Sittenspiegel des östlichen Islam," *ZDMG*, XXVIII (1874), 293ff. [= *Gesammelte Schriften*, VI, 1ff. Partial French translation in *Arabica*, VIII (1961), 245ff.]

———. *Beiträge zur Literaturgeschichte der Schī'a und der sunnitischen Polemik*. Sitzungsberichte der Philosophisch-historischen Classe der Kaiserlichen Akademie der Wissenschaften, LXXVIII. Vienna, 1874. [= *Gesammelte Schriften*, I, 261ff.]

———. "Bismillāh." In *Encyclopaedia of Religion and Ethics*. Edited by James Hastings. New York, 1908-1927. II, 666ff. [= *Gesammelte Schriften*, V, 167ff.]

[———. "The Cult of Saints in Islam," *Muslim World*, I (1911). 302ff.]

———. "De l'ascétisme aux premiers temps de l'Islam," *RHR*, XXXVII (1898), 314ff. [= *Gesammelte Schriften*, IV, 159ff.]

———. "Le Dénombrement des sectes mohamétanes," *RHR*, XXVI (1892), 129ff. [= *Gesammelte Schriften*, II, 406ff.]

———. "Die dogmatische Partie der Sālimijja," *ZDMG*, LXI (1907), 73ff. [= *Gesammelte Schriften*, V, 76ff.]

———. "L'École Superieure des Lettres et les médersas d'Alger au XIVe. Congrès des Orientalistes," *RHR*, LII (1905), 219ff.

———. "Einige arabische Ausrufe und Formeln," *WZKM*, XVI (1902), 131ff. [= *Gesammelte Schriften*, IV, 345ff.]

———. "Die Fortschritte der Islamwissenschaft in den letzten drei Jahrzehnten," *Preussische Jahrbücher*, CXXI (1905), 274ff. [= *Gesammelte Schriften*, IV, 443ff.]

[———. *Gesammelte Schriften*. Edited by Joseph DeSomogyi. 6 vols. Hildesheim, 1967-1973.]

———. "Die Handwerke bei den Arabern," *Globus*, LXVI (1894), 203ff. [= *Gesammelte Schriften*, III, 316ff.]

———. "Die islamische und die jüdische Philosophie," *Allgemeine Geschichte der Philosophie* (Berlin and Leipzig, 1909; Part I, Section v, of Paul Hinneberg's *Die Kultur der Gegenwart*), pp. 45ff.

———. "Islamisme et Parsisme." In *Actes du premier Congrès International d'Histoire des Religions*, I (Paris, 1900), 119ff. [= *Gesammelte Schriften*, IV, 232ff.]

———. "Kämpfe um die Stellung des Ḥadīṯ im Islam," *ZDMG*, LXI (1907), 860ff. [= *Gesammelte Schriften*, V, 86ff. Partial French translation in *Arabica*, VII (1960), 5ff.]

———. "Lā Misāsa," *Revue Africaine*, LII (1908), 23ff.

———. "Materialien zur Entwicklungsgeschichte des Ṣūfismus," *WZKM*, XIII (1899), 35ff. [= *Gesammelte Schriften*, IV, 173ff. Partial French translation in *Arabica*, VIII (1961), 240ff.]

———. "Materialien zur Kenntniss der Almohadenbewegung in Nordafrika," *ZDMG*, XLI (1887), 30ff. [= *Gesammelte Schriften*, II, 191ff.]

———. *Muhammedanische Studien*. 2 vols. Halle, 1889-1890. [Translated as *Muslim Studies*. Edited by S. M. Stern. 2 vols. London, 1967-1971.]

———. "Neuplatonische und gnostische Elemente im Ḥadīṯ," *ZA*, XXII (1909), 317ff. [= *Gesammelte Schriften*, V, 107ff. Partial French translation in *Arabica*, VII (1960), 8ff.]

———. "Neutestamentliche Elemente in der Traditionslitteratur des Islām," *Oriens Christianus*, II (1902), 390ff. [= *Gesammelte Schriften*, IV, 315ff.]

———. "L' Onzième Intelligence," *Revue Africaine*, L (1906), 242f.

———. "Das Prinzip der *Taḳijja* im Islam," *ZDMG*, LX (1906), 213ff. [= *Gesammelte Schriften*, V, 59ff. Partial French translation in *Arabica*, VII (1960), 134.]

———. "Die Religion des Islams," *Die orientalischen Religionen*. (Berlin and Leipzig, 1906; Part I, Section iii, 1, of Paul Hinneberg, *Die Kultur der Gegenwart*), 87ff.

———. Review of Carra de Vaux, *Le mahométisme*, in *ZDMG*, LIII (1899), 380ff.

———. Review of de Vlieger, *Kitāb al-Qadr*, in *ZDMG*, LVII (1903), 392ff.

———. Review of Nallino, *Chrestomathia Qorani arabica*, in *RHR*, XXVIII (1893), 378ff.

———. Review of Patton, *Aḥmed ibn Ḥanbal and the Mihna*, in *ZDMG*, LII (1898), 155ff.

———. Review of Yahuda, *Prolegomena zu . . . des Kitāb al-Hidāja ilā farā'iḍ al-qulūb*, in *REJ*, XLIX (1904), 154ff.

Goldziher, Ignaz. "Le Rosaire dans l'Islam," *RHR*, XXI (1890). 295ff. [= *Gesammelte Shriften*, II, 374ff.]

———. "Die Sabbathinstitution im Islam." In *Gedenkbuch zur Erinnerung an David Kaufmann*. Edited by M. Brann and F. Rosenthal. Breslau, 1900. I, 86ff. [Partial French translation in *Arabica*, VII (1960), 237ff.]

———. "Ṣāliḥ b. 'Abd-al-Ḳuddūs und das Zindīḳthum während der Regierung des Chalifen al-Mahdī." In *Transactions of the Ninth International Congress of Orientalists*. London, 1893. I, 104ff. [= *Gesammelte Schriften*, III, 1ff.]

———. " 'Säulenmänner' im Arabischen," *ZDMG*, LV (1901), 503ff. [= *Gesammelte Schriften*, IV, 309ff. Partial French translation in *Arabica*, VII (1960), 252.]

———. "Spottnamen der ersten Chalifen bei den Schī'iten," *WZKM*, XV (1901), 321ff. [= *Gesammelte Schriften*, IV, 295ff. Partial French translation in *Arabica*, VIII (1961), 267ff.]

[———. *Streitschrift des Ġazālī gegen die Bāṭinijja-Sekte*. Leiden, 1916.]

———. "Die Śu'ūbijja unter den Muhammedanern in Spanien," *ZDMG*, LIII (1899), 601ff. [= *Gesammelte Schriften*, IV, 204ff.]

[———. *Tagebuch*. Edited by Alexander Scheiber. Leiden, 1978.]

———. "Ueber Bibelcitate in muhammedanischen Schriften," *ZATW*, XIII (1893), 315ff. [= *Gesammelte Schriften*, III, 309ff.]

———. "Ueber den Brauch der Maḥjā-Versammlungen im Islam," *WZKM*, XV (1901), 33ff. [= *Gesammelte Schriften*, IV, 277ff. Partial French translation in *Arabica*, VIII (1961), 238ff.]

———. "Ueber eine rituelle Formel der Muhammedaner," *ZDMG*, XLVIII (1894), 95ff. [= *Gesammelte Schriften*, III, 342ff. Partial French translation in *Arabica*, VII (1960), 249f.]

———. *Die Ẓâhiriten: Ihr Lehrsystem und ihre Geschichte*. Leipzig, 1884. [Translated as *The Ẓāhirīs; Their Doctrine and Their History*. Leiden, 1971.]

———. "Zauberelemente im islamischen Gebet." In *Nöldeke Festschrift*. I, 303ff. [= *Gesammelte Schriften*, V, 32ff. Partial French translation in *Arabica*, VII (1960), 18ff.]

———. "Zur Geschichte der ḥanbalitischen Bewegungen," *ZDMG*, LXII (1908), 1ff. [= *Gesammelte Schriften*, V, 135ff. Partial French translation in *Arabica*, VII (1960), 135ff.]

———. "Zur Literatur des Ichtilāf al-maḏâhib," *ZDMG*, XXXVIII (1884), 669ff. [= *Gesammelte Schriften*, II, 137ff.]

Gomperz, Theodor. *Griechische Denker*. 2nd ed. 3 vols. Leipzig, 1903-1909. [Translated as *Greek Thinkers*. 4 vols. New York, 1901-1912.]

Gottheil, Richard. "A Distinguished Family of Fatimide Cadis (al-Nu'mān) in the Tenth Century," *JAOS*, XXVII (1906), 217ff.

Grierson, George A. "Modern Hinduism and Its Debt to the Nestorians," *JRAS*, 1907, pp. 311ff. Discussants' comments and Grierson's reply, 477ff.

———. Review of Westcott's *Kabīr and Kabīrpanth*, in *JRAS*, 1908, pp. 245ff.

Grimme, Hubert, "Der Logos in Südarabien." In *Nöldeke Festschrift*. I, 453ff.

———. *Mohammed*. 2 vols. Münster, 1892-1895.

———. *Mohammed*. Weltgeschichte in Karakterbildern, Part II. Munich, 1904.

de Groot, J. J. "Over de Wahabietenbewegung in Kansoeh 1781-1789." In *Verslagen en Mededeelingen der Koninklijke Akademie van Wetenschappen.* Afdeeling Letterkunde IV, 6. Amsterdam, 1904, 130ff.

Grünbaum, Max. *Gesammelte Aufsätze zur Sprach- und Sagenkunde.* Berlin, 1901.

[von Grunebaum, G. E. *Modern Islam: the Search for Cultural Identity.* Berkeley and Los Angeles, 1962.]

[———. "Von Mohammeds Wirkung und Originalität," *WZKM,* XXIV (1937), 29ff.]

[Guidi, Michelangelo. *La Religione dell'Islam.* In *Storia delle Religioni.* Edited by P. Pietro Tacchi-Venturi. Turin, 1949. II, 303ff.]

[Gulick, John, and Margaret E. Gulick. *An Annotated Bibliography of Sources Concerned with Women in the Modern Muslim Middle East.* Princeton, 1974.]

[Guthrie, W.K.C. *A History of Greek Philosophy, the Earlier Pre-Socratics and the Pythagoreans.* Cambridge, 1964.]

Guyard, Stanislas. "Un Grand Maître des Assassins au temps de Saladin," *JA*, 7th Series, IX (1877), 324ff.

Ḥāfiẓ, Shams al-Dīn Muḥammad. *Der Diwan des grossen lyrischen Dichters Hafis.* Edited and translated by Vincenz, ritter v. Rosenzweig-Schwannau. 3 vols. Vienna, 1858-1864.

al-Ḥafnāwī, Abū'l-Qāsim. *Ta'rīf al-khalaf bi-rijāl al-salaf* (*Biographies des savants musulmans de l'Algérie*). I. Algiers, 1325/1907.

al-Hamadānī, Muḥammad ibn 'Abd al-Raḥmān. *Kitāb al-sub'īyāt fī mawā'iẓ al-barīyāt.* Bulaq, A.H. 1292.

[Hardy, P. *The Muslims of British India.* Cambridge, 1972.]

von Harnack, Adolf. *Die Mission und Ausbreitung des Christentums in den ersten drei Jahrhunderten.* 1st edition. Leipzig, 1902. [4th edition. 2 vols. Leipzig, 1924. Translated as *The Mission and Expansion of Christianity in the First Three Centuries.* 2 vols. London and New York, 1908.]

Hartmann, Martin. "Die arabisch-islamischen Handschriften der Universitäts-Bibliothek zu Leipzig und der Sammlungen Hartmann und Haupt," *ZA*, XXIII (1909), 235ff.

———. "Die École Supérieure des Lettres in Alger und die Medersas Algeriens auf dem XIV. Orientalistenkongress," *ZA*, XIX (1905), 342ff.

———. *Der Islam.* Leipzig, 1909.

———. "Der Islam 1907," *MSOS*, XI (1908), ii, 207ff.

———. "Der Islam 1908," *MSOS*, XII (1909), ii, 33ff.

———. *Der islamische Orient.* 3 vols. Berlin, 1905-1910.

Ḥassān ibn Thābit. *Dīwān.* Tunis, A.H. 1281. [Edited by Walīd 'Arafāt. 2 vols. E.J.W. Gibb Memorial, New Series, XXV. London, 1971.]

Haupt, Rudolf. *Orientalischer Literaturbericht.* Leipzig, 1908-1909.

al-Ḥāzimī, Muḥammad ibn Mūsā. *Kitāb al-i'tibār fī bayān al-nāsikh wa'l-mansūkh min al-āthār.* Haydarabad, A.H. 1319.

Hell, Joseph. "Al-Farazdaḳ's Lieder auf die Muhallabiten," *ZDMG*, LX (1906), 1ff.

Hikmet, 'Abdul-Hakīm. "La Médecine en Turquie," *RMM*, III (1907), 38ff.

Hilgenfeld, Adolf. *Die Ketzergeschichte des Urchristentums.* Leipzig, 1884.

al-Ḥillī, Ḥasan ibn Yūsuf. *Al-Bāb al-ḥādī 'ashar.* (Appended to al-Ḥillī's abridgment of Abū Ja'far al-Ṭūṣī's *Miṣbāḥ al-mutahajjid*, with a commentary by Miqdād ibn 'Abdallāh al-Ḥillī.) Naul-Kashwar Press, 1315/1898.

———. *Kitāb al-alfayn al-fāriq bayn al-ṣidq wa'l-mayn.* Bombay, A.H. 1298.

al-Hindī, *see* al-Ṭaḥāwī.

[Hinds, Martin. "Kufan Political Alignments and Their Background in the Mid-Seventh Century A.D.," *IJMES*, II (1971), 346ff.]

[Hodgson, Marshall G. S. "How Did the Early Shī'a Become Sectarian?" *JAOS*, LXXV (1955), 1ff.]

[———. *The Order of Assassins: the Struggle of the Early Nizārī Ismā'īlīs against the Islamic World.* The Hague, 1955.]

[Holt, P. M. *The Mahdist State in the Sudan 1881-1898: A Study of Its Origins, Development and Overthrow.* 2nd ed. Oxford, 1970.]

Hommel, Fritz, "Die älteste arabische Barlaam-Version." In *Verhandlungen des VII. Internationalen Orientalisten-Congresses*, Semitic Section (Vienna 1888), 115ff.

Horovitz, Josef. *Spuren griechischer Mimen im Orient.* Berlin, 1905.

Horovitz, Saul. *Über den Einfluss der griechischen Philosophie auf die Entwicklung des Kalām.* Breslau, 1909.

Horten, Max J. H. "Die Lehre vom Kumūn bei Naẓẓām," *ZDMG*, LXIII (1909), 774ff.

———. *Die philosophischen Probleme der spekulativen Theologie im Islam.* Renaissance und Philosophie, III. Bonn, 1910.

———. Review of Horovitz, *Über den Einfluss der griechischen Philosophie . . .*, in *OLZ*, XII (1909), 391ff.

Houtsma, M. T. "Bih'afrid," *WZKM*, III (1889), 30ff.

———. "Le Mouvement religieux des Ahmadiyya aux Indes anglaises," *RMM*, I (1906-1907), 533ff.

Huart, Clément. *Textes persans relatifs à la secte des Houroûfîs.* E.J.W. Gibb Memorial Series, IX. Leiden and London, 1909.

Hupfeld, Hermann. *Die Psalmen.* 2nd ed. Edited by Eduard Riehm. 2 vols. Gotha, 1867-1871.

al-Ḥurayfīsh, Abū Maydān Shu'ayb. *Kitāb al-rawḍ al-fā'iq fī'l-mawā'iẓ wa'l-raqā'iq.* Cairo, A.H. 1310.

al-Ḥuṭay'a, Jarwal ibn Aws. "Der Dīwān des Ǧarwal b. Aus al-Ḥuṭej'a." Edited by Ignaz Goldziher. *ZDMG*, XLVI (1892), 1ff., 173ff., 471ff.; XLVII (1893), 43ff., 163ff. [= *Gesammelte Schriften*, III, 50ff.]

Ibn 'Abd al-Barr al-Namarī. *Jāmi' bayān al-'ilm wa-faḍlihi.* Edited by Aḥmad 'Umar al-Maḥmaṣānī. Cairo, A.H. 1326.

———. *Jāmi' bayān al-'ilm wa-faḍlihi.* Abridged edition. Cairo, A.H. 1320.

[Ibn Abī'l-Ḥadīd, Abū Ḥāmid 'Abd al-Ḥamīd ibn Abī'l-Ḥusayn. *Sharḥ nahj al-balāgha.* Edited by Muḥammad Abū'l-Faḍl Ibrāhīm. 20 vols. Cairo, 1959-1964.]

Ibn Abī Ṭāhir Ṭayfūr. *Kitāb Baghdād.* Edited by Hans Keller. Leipzig, 1908.

Ibn 'Arabshāh, Abū'l-'Abbās Aḥmad ibn Muḥammad. *Fākihat al-khulafā' (Fructus imperatorum).* Edited by Georg Freytag. 2 vols. Bonn, 1832.

Ibn 'Asākir, Abū'l-Qāsim 'Alī ibn al-Ḥasan. *Ta'rīkh Dimashq*. New Haven, Yale University Library Ms. no. 1182.

Ibn al-Athīr, 'Izz al-Dīn Abū'l-Ḥasan 'Alī ibn Muḥammad. *Usd al-ghāba fī ma'rifat al-ṣaḥāba*. 5 vols. Cairo, A.H. 1285-1286.

Ibn al-Athīr, Majd al-Dīn Abū Sa'ādāt al-Mubārak ibn Muḥammad. *Al-Nihāya fī gharīb al-ḥadīth*. 4 vols. Cairo, A.H. 1322.

Ibn Baṭūṭa, Abū 'Abdallāh Muḥammad ibn 'Abdallāh. *Riḥla (Voyages d'Ibn Batoutah)*. Edited and translated by C. Defrémery and B. R. Sanguinetti. 4 vols. Paris, 1853-1858.

Ibn al-Faqīh al-Hamadānī. *Kitāb al-buldān*. Edited by M. J. de Goeje. *BGA* V. Leiden, 1885.

Ibn al-Fāriḍ, Abū'l-Qāsim 'Umar ibn 'Alī, *Jalā' al-ghāmiḍ fī sharḥ dīwān al-fārid*. Beirut, 1894.

Ibn Ḥajar al-'Asqalānī Abū'l-Faḍl Aḥmad ibn 'Alī. *Al-Iṣāba fī tamyīz al-ṣaḥāba* (*A Biographical Dictionary of Persons Who Knew Mohammed*). Edited by Aloys Sprenger et al. 4 vols. Calcutta, 1856-1888. [Edited in 8 vols. Cairo, A.H. 1323-1325.]

———. *Al-Qawl al-musaddad fī'l-dhabb 'an al-Musnad*. Haydarabad, A.H. 1319.

Ibn Ḥajar al-Haytamī, Abū'l-'Abbās Aḥmad ibn Muḥammad. *Al-Fatāwā al-ḥadīthīya*. Cairo, A.H. 1307.

———. *Al-Ṣawā'iq al-muḥriqa*. Cairo, A.H. 1312.

Ibn Ḥanbal, Aḥmad. *Al-Musnad*. 6 vols. Cairo, A.H. 1311.

Ibn Ḥazm, Abū Muḥammad 'Alī ibn Aḥmad. *Al-Akhlāq wa'l-siyar fī mudāwāt al-nufūs*. Edited by Aḥmad 'Umar al-Maḥmaṣānī. Cairo, 1908.

———. *Al-Faṣl fī'l-milal wa'l-ahwā' wa'l-niḥal*. 5 vols. Cairo, A.H. 1317-1321.

Ibn Hishām, Abū Muḥammad 'Abd al-Malik. *Sīrat Rasūl Allāh* (*Das Leben Muhammed's*). Edited by Ferdinand Wüstenfeld. 2 vols. Göttingen, 1858-1860.

Ibn 'Idhārī, Abū'l-'Abbās Aḥmad ibn Muḥammad. *Al-Bayān al-mughrib* (*Histoire de l'Afrique et de l'Espagne*). Edited by R.P.A. Dozy. 2 vols. Leiden, 1848-1851. [New ed. revised by G. S. Colin and É. Lévi-Provençal. 2 vols. Leiden, 1948-1951.]

[Ibn al-'Imād, 'Abd al-Ḥayy ibn Aḥmad. *Shadharāt al-dhahab fī akhbār ramz dhahab*. 8 vols. Cairo, A.H. 1350-1351.

Ibn Jubayr, Abū'l-Ḥusayn Muḥammad ibn Aḥmad. *Riḥlat Ibn Jubayr* (*The Travels of Ibn Jubayr*). Edited by William Wright. 2nd ed. revised by M. J. de Goeje. E.J.W. Gibb Memorial Series, V. Leiden and London, 1907.

Ibn Khaldūn, 'Abd al-Raḥman ibn Muḥammad. *Al-Muqaddima* (*Prolégomènes d'Ebn Khaldoun*). Edited by E. M. Quatremère. 3 vols. Notices et Extraits des manuscrits de la Bibliothèque Impériale, XVI, XVII, XVIII. Paris, 1858. Also printed as Vol. I of Ibn Khaldūn's *Kitāb al-'ibar*. 7 vols. Bulaq, A.H. 1284.

Ibn Khallikān, Abū'l-'Abbās Aḥmad ibn Muḥammad. *Wafayāt al-a'yān* (*Vitae illustrium virorum*). Edited by Ferdinand Wüstenfeld. 12 pts. Göttingen 1835-1850. [Edited by Iḥsān 'Abbās. 8 vols. Beirut, n.d.]

Ibn Manẓur, Abū'l-Faḍl Muḥammad ibn Mukarram. *Lisān al-'arab*. 20 vols. Cairo, A.H. 1300-1308.

Ibn al-Muqaffa'. *Risāla fī'l-ṣaḥāba*. Edited by Muḥammad Kurd 'Alī in *Al-Muqtabas*, III (1908), 220ff., and in his *Rasā'il al-bulaghā'* (Cairo, 1908), 49ff. [Edited and translated by Charles Pellat. Paris, 1976.]

Ibn al-Murtaḍā, Aḥmad ibn Yaḥyā. *Kitāb al-milal wa'l-niḥal (The Mu'tazilah)*. Edited by Thomas W. Arnold. Leipzig, 1902. [= *Ṭabaqāt al-mu'tazila* (*Die Klassen der Mu'taziliten*). Edited by Susanna Diwald-Wilzer. Wiesbaden, 1961.]

Ibn al-Qalānisī, Abū Ya'lā Ḥamza ibn Asad. *Dhayl ta'rīkh Dimashq* (*History of Damascus*). Edited by H. F. Amedroz. Beirut, 1908.

Ibn Qays al-Ruqayyāt, 'Ubayd Allāh ibn Qays. *Dīwān*. Edited and translated by N. Rhodokanakis. Vienna, 1902. [Edited by Muḥammad Yūsuf Najm. Beirut, 1378/1958.]

Ibn Qayyim al-Jawzīya, Abū Bakr Muḥammad ibn Abī Bakr. *Al-Jawāb al-kāfī li-man sa'ala 'an al-dawā' al-shāfī*. Cairo: Taqaddum Press, n.d.

———. *Kitāb al-rūḥ*. Haydarabad, A.H. 1318.

———. *Kitāb al-ṣalāt wa-aḥkām tārikihā*. Cairo, A.H. 1313.

Ibn Qutayba, Abū Muḥammad 'Abdallāh ibn Muslim. *Kitāb al-ashriba*. Edited by A. Guy in *Al-Muqtabas*, II (1325/1907), 234ff., 387ff., 529ff. [Edited by Muḥammad Kurd 'Alī. Damascus, 1366/1947.]

———. *Kitāb al-ma'ārif*. Edited by Ferdinand Wüstenfeld. Göttingen, 1850. [Edited by Tharwat 'Ukāsha. Cairo, 1960.]

———. *'Uyūn al-akhbār*. Edited by Carl Brockelmann. 4 pts. Berlin, 1900-1908. [Edited in 4 vols. Cairo, 1343-1349/1925-1930.]

Ibn Sa'd, Abū 'Abdallāh Muḥammad. *Kitāb al-ṭabaqāt al-kabīr (Biographien)*. Edited by Eduard Sachau et al. 9 vols. Leiden, 1904-1940.

Ibn al-Ṣaghīr. *Chronique*. Edited and translated by A. de C. Motylinski in *Actes du XIVe Congrès International des Orientalistes*. Paris, 1908. III, ii, 3ff.

Ibn Sīnā, Abū 'Alī al-Ḥusayn ibn 'Abdallāh. *Die Metaphysik Avicennas*. Translation and commentary by Max Horten. Halle, 1907.

Ibn al-Ta'āwīdhī, Abū'l-Fatḥ Muḥammad ibn 'Ubayd Allāh. *Dīwān*. Edited by D. S. Margoliouth. Cairo, 1903.

Ibn Taghrī Birdī, Abū'l-Maḥāsin. *Al-Nujūm al-zāhira (Annals)*. Edited by William Popper. 7 vols. Berkeley, 1909-1936.

Ibn Taymīya, Taqī al-Dīn Aḥmad. *Jawāb ahl al-īmān fī tafāḍul āy al-Qur'ān*. Cairo, A.H. 1322.

———. *Majmū'at al-rasā'il al-kubrā*. 2 vols. Cairo, A.H. 1323.

———. *Tafsīr Sūrat al-Ikhlāṣ*. Edited by Muḥammad al-Na'asānī. Cairo, A.H. 1323.

Ibn al-Ṭiqṭaqā, Muḥammad ibn 'Alī. *Al-Fakhrī*. Edited by Wilhelm Ahlwardt. Gotha, 1860. [Edited by Hartwig Derenbourg. Paris, 1895.]

Ibn Ṭufayl, Abū Bakr Muḥammad ibn 'Abd al-Malik. *Ḥayy ibn. Yaqẓān*. Edited by Léon Gauthier. Algiers, 1900. [2nd ed. Beirut, 1936.]

Ibn Tūmart, Muḥammad. *Kitāb Muḥammad ibn Tūmart mahdī al-muwaḥḥidīn* (*Le Livre de Mohammed ibn Toumert*). Edited by Ignaz Goldziher. Algiers, 1903.

al-Ījī, ʻAḍud al-Dīn ʻAbd al-Raḥmān. *Al-Mawāqif fī ʻilm al-kalām.* With the Commentary of al-Jurjānī. Istanbul, A.H. 1239.

IJMES = International Journal of Middle Eastern Studies.

Ikhwān al-Ṣafā'. [*Rasā'il*] *Ikhwān al-Ṣafā'.* 4 vols. Bombay, A.H. 1305-1306.

Al-Imāma wa'l-siyāsa (falsely attributed to Ibn Qutayba). 2 vols. Cairo, 1904.

al-Iṣbahānī, Abū'l-Faraj ʻAlī ibn al-Ḥusayn. *Kitāb al-aghānī.* 20 vols. Cairo, A.H. 1285.

JA = Journal Asiatique.

Jacob, Georg. *Beiträge zur Kenntnis des Derwisch-Ordens der Bektaschis.* Türkische Bibliothek, IX. Berlin, 1908.

———. *Die Bektaschijje in ihrem Verhältnis zu verwandten Erscheinungen.* Abhandlungen der Philosophisch-philologischen Klasse der Königlich Bayerischen Akademie der Wissenschaften, XXIV, pt. iii, no. 2. Munich, 1909.

[Jafri, S.H.M. *The Origins and Early Development of Shiʻa Islam.* London, 1979.]

al-Jāḥiẓ, Abū ʻUthmān ʻAmr ibn Baḥr. *Al-Bayān wa'l-tabyīn.* 2 vols. Cairo, A.H. 1311-1313. [Edited by ʻAbd al-Salām Muḥammad Hārūn. 4 vols. Cairo, 1367-1370/1948-1950.]

———. *Kitāb al-bukhalā'* (*Le Livre des avares*). Edited by G. van Vloten. Leiden, 1900. [Edited by Ṭaha al-Ḥājirī. 4th ed. Cairo, 1971.]

———. *Kitāb al-ḥayawān.* 7 vols. Cairo, A.H. 1323-1325. [Edited by ʻAbd al-Salām Muḥammad Hārūn. 2nd ed. 8 vols. Cairo, 1385/1389/1965-1969.]

———. *Rasā'il.* Cairo, A.H. 1324.

———. *Al-Tarbīʻ wa'l-tadwīr.* Edited by G. van Vloten in *Tria Opuscula.* Leiden, 1903, pp. 86ff. [Edited by Charles Pellat. Damascus, 1955.]

Pseudo-Jāḥiẓ. *Al-Maḥāsin wa'l-aḍdād (Le livre des beautés et des antithèses).* Edited by G. van Vloten. Leiden, 1898.

Jalāl al-Dīn Rūmī. *Masnavī-i Maʻnavī, the Spiritual Couplets of Maulāna Jalalu-'d-Dīn Muḥammad-i Rūmī.* Translated by E. H. Whinfield. London, 1887.

———. *Rubāʻīyāt ḥaḍrat-i Mawlānā.* Translated into Hungarian by Alexander Kégl in *Abhandlungen der ungarischen Akademie der Wissenschaften, I. Kl.*, XIX. Budapest, 1907, no. 10.

———. *Selected Poems from the Dīvāni Shamsi Tabriz.* Edited and translated by R. A. Nicholson. Cambridge, 1898.

Jansen, Hubert. *Verbreitung des Islams.* Friedrichshagen, 1897.

[Jansen, J.J.G. *The Interpretation of the Koran in Modern Egypt.* Leiden, 1974.]

JAOS = Journal of the American Oriental Society.

Jarīr ibn ʻAṭīya. *Dīwān.* 2 vols. Cairo, A.H. 1313. [Edited by Nuʻmān Muḥammad Amīn Ṭaha. 2 vols. Cairo, 1969-1971.]

[Jeffery, Arthur. *Islam, Muhammad and His Religion.* New York, 1958.]

[———. *Materials for the History of the Text of the Qur'ān.* Leiden, 1937.]

JESHO = Journal of the Economic and Social History of the Orient.

al-Jīlānī, ʻAbd al-Qādir. *Al-Ghunya li-ṭālib ṭarīqat al-ḥaqq.* 2 vols. Mecca, A.H. 1314.

———. *Sirr al-asrār,* on the margin of his *Al-Ghunya.* Mecca, A.H. 1314.

Jordan, S. M. Appendix to W. St. Clair Tisdall, "Islam in Persia," in *The Muham-*

medan World of To-day. Edited by S. M. Zwemer et al. New York, 1906, pp. 129f.

JRAS = *Journal of the Royal Asiatic Society*.

al-Jurjānī, Abū'l-'Abbās Aḥmad ibn Muḥammad. *Al-Muntakhab min kināyāt al-udabā'*. Cairo, 1908.

[Juynboll, G.H.A. *The Authenticity of the Tradition Literature: Discussions in Modern Egypt*. Leiden, 1969.]

[———. "The *qurrā'* in Early Islamic History," *JESHO*, XVI (1973), 113ff.]

Juynboll, T. W. "Akdarīya." In *Encyclopaedia of Islam*. 1st ed. Leiden, 1913-1936. I, 229f.

———. *Handbuch des islamischen Gesetzes*. Leiden, 1908-1910.

[al-Kashshī, Abū 'Amr Muḥammad ibn 'Umar. *Ma'rifat akhbār al-rijāl*. Bombay, A.H. 1317.]

al-Kāẓimī, Asad Allāh. *Kashf al-qinā' 'an wujūb ḥujīyat al-ijmā'*. Bombay, A.H. 1316.

[Kedourie, Elie. *Afghani and Abduh: an Essay on Religious Belief and Political Activism in Modern Islam*. London, 1966.]

Keith, A. Berriedale. Review of Bloomfield, *The Religion of the Veda*, in *JRAS*, 1908, pp. 883ff.

Kern, Friedrich. Review of K. Vollers, *Katalog der islamischen . . . Handschriften*, in *MSOS*, XI (1908), 258ff.

———. "Ṭabarī's Ihtilāf alfuqahā'," *ZDMG*, LV (1901), 61ff.

[Kerr, Malcolm H. *Islamic Reform: the Political and Legal Theories of Muhammad Abduh and Rashid Rida*. Berkeley and Los Angeles, 1966.]

[Khadduri, M., and H. J. Liebesny, editors. *Law in the Middle East: I, Origin and Development of Islamic Law*. Washington, D.C., 1955.]

Khan, Paul Kitabgi. *Droit musulman shyite: le mariage et le divorce*. Lausanne, 1904.

al-Khaṣṣāf, Aḥmad ibn 'Umar. *Kitāb al-Khaṣṣāf fī'l-ḥiyal*. Cairo, A.H. 1314.

al-Khazrajī, 'Alī ibn Ḥasan. *The Pearl-Strings, A History of the Resúliyy Dynasty of Yemen*. Translated by Sir J.W. Redhouse. E.J.W. Gibb Memorial Series, III. 2 vols. Leiden and London, 1906-1907.

al-Khwārizmī, Abū Bakr Muḥammad ibn al-'Abbās. *Rasā'il Abī Bakr al-Khuwārizmī*. Istanbul, A.H. 1297.

Kitāb uthūlūjiyā Arisṭāṭālīs (*Die sogenannte Theologie des Aristoteles*). Edited by Friedrich H. Dieterici. Leipzig, 1882. [Edited by 'Abd al-Raḥmān Badawī in *Aflūṭīn 'inda'l-'arab*. Cairo, 1955.]

Klein, F. A. *The Religion of Islam*. London, 1906.

[Klingmüller, E. "The Concept and Development of Insurance in Islamic Countries," *Islamic Culture*, XLIII (1969), 27ff.]

Kohler, J. "Die Gewohnheitsrechte der Provinz Bombay," *Zeitschrift für vergleichende Rechtswissenschaft*, X (1892), 64ff.

von Kremer, Alfred. *Culturgeschichte des Orients unter den Chalifen*. 2 vols. Vienna, 1875-1877. [Vol. I translated as *The Orient under the Caliphs*. Calcutta, 1920.]

———. *Culturgeschichtliche Streifzüge auf dem Gebiete des Islams*. Leipzig, 1873. [Translated in S. Khuda Bukhsh. *Contributions to the History of Islamic Civilization*. Calcutta, 1929-1930. I, 43ff.]

———. *Geschichte der herrschenden Ideen des Islams*. Leipzig, 1868.

———. *Über die philosophischen Gedichte des Abū-l-'Alā al-Ma'arry*. Sitzungsberichte der Philosophisch-historischen Classe der Kaiserlichen Akademie der Wissenschaften, CXVII, no. 6. Vienna, 1888.

Kuenen, Abraham. *National Religions and Universal Religions*. Hibbert Lectures. London, 1882.

al-Kulīnī, Muḥammad ibn Ya'qūb. *Al-Uṣūl min al-jāmi' al-kāfī*. Bombay, A.H. 1302.

al-Kumayt ibn Zayd. *Al-Hāshimīyāt*. Edited by Josef Horovitz. Leiden, 1904.

Kurd 'Alī, Muḥammad, ed. *Rasā'il al-bulaghā'*. Cairo, 1908.

Lammens, Henri. "Au pays des Nosairis," *ROC*, IV (1899), 572ff.; V (1900), 99ff., 303ff., 423ff.

[———. *Le Califat de Yazīd Ier*. Beirut, 1910-1919. Also in *MFO*, IV (1910), 233ff.; V (1911), 79ff., 589ff.; VI (1913), 401ff.; VII (1921), 211ff.]

———. *Études sur le règne du calife omaiyade Mo'āwia Ier*. Beirut, 1908. Also in *MFO*, I (1906), 1ff.; II (1907), 1ff.; III (1908), 145ff.

———. "Sur la frontière nord de la Terre Promise," *Les Études*, LXXVIII (1899), 497ff., 601ff.

Landberg, Carlo, comte de. *Études sur les dialectes de l'Arabie méridionale*. 4 vols. Leiden, 1901-1913.

Landsdell, Henry. *Russian Central Asia*. 2 vols. London, 1885.

[Laoust, Henri. *Essai sur les doctrines sociales et politiques de Taḳī-d-Dīn Aḥmad b. Taimīya*. Cairo, 1939.]

[———. *Les Schismes dans l'Islam: Introduction à une étude de la religion musulmane*. Paris, 1965.]

[Lelyveld, David. *Aligarh's First Generation*. Princeton, 1978.]

[Le Tourneau, Roger. *The Almohad Movement in North Africa in the 12th and 13th Centuries*. Princeton, 1969.]

[Lewis, Bernard. *The Assassins: A Radical Sect in Islam*. London, 1967.]

[———. *The Emergence of Modern Turkey*. 2nd ed. London, 1968.]

[———. *Islam in History: Ideas, Men and Events in the Middle East*. London, 1973.]

[———. *The Middle East and the West*. London and New York, 1966.]

[———. *Race and Color in Islam*. New York, 1971.]

[Lidzbarski, M. "Salām und Islām," *Zeitschrift für Semitistik*. I (1922), 85ff.]

Lisān al-'arab, *see* Ibn Manẓūr.

List of Arabic and Persian Mss. acquired on behalf of the Government of India by the Asiatic Society of Bengal during 1903-7. Calcutta, 1908.

Loisy, Alfred. Review of four studies on early Christianity, in *Revue critique d'histoire et de littérature*. New series, LXII (1906), 306ff.

Lortet, Louis. *La Syrie d'aujourd'hui*. Paris, 1884.

Loth, Otto. "Al-Kindī als Astrolog." In *Morgenländische Forschungen: Festschrift . . . H. L. Fleischer*. Leipzig, 1875.

Löw, Immanuel. "Aramäische Fischnamen." In *Nöldeke Festschrift*. I, 549ff.

———. "Lexikalische Miszellen," *ZA*, XXII (1909), 79ff.

[Lyall, Sir Charles. "The Meaning of *'Alā ḥubbihi* in Qur. II, 172," *JRAS*, 1914, pp. 158ff.]

Macauliffe, Max Arthur. "How the Sikhs Became a Militant People." In *Actes du XIVe Congrès International des Orientalistes.* Paris, 1906. I, 137ff.

———. *The Sikh Religion, its Gurus, Sacred Writings and Authors.* 6 vols. Oxford, 1909.

[MacDonald, Duncan B. *Aspects of Islam.* New York, 1911.]

———. *Development of Muslim Theology, Jurisprudence and Constitutional Theory.* New York, 1903.

———. "Moral Education of the Young among Muslims," *International Journal of Ethics,* XV (1904-1905), 286ff.

———. *The Religious Attitude and Life in Islam.* Chicago, 1909.

[Madelung, W. "The Origins of the Controversy Concerning the Creation of the Koran." In *Orientalia Hispanica.* Edited by J. M. Barral, I, i. Leiden, 1974, 504ff.]

Maimonides (Moses ben Maimon). *Dalālat al-ḥā'irīn (Le Guide des égarés).* Edited and translated by Salomon Munk. 3 vols. Paris, 1856-66.

al-Makkī, Abū Ṭālib. *Qūt al-qulūb.* Cairo, A.H. 1310.

Mālik ibn Anas. *Al-Muwaṭṭa'.* With the Commentary of al-Zurqānī. 4 vols. Cairo, A.H. 1279-1280.

al-Manīnī, *see* al-'Āmilī, *Al-Kashkūl.*

Mann, Oscar. Review of the French version of Barney, *Some Answered Questions . . . ,* in *OLZ,* XII (1909), 33ff.

al-Maqdisī, Muṭahhar ibn Ṭāhir (pseudo-Balkhī). *Al-Bad' wa'l-ta'rīkh* (*Le Livre de la création et de l'histoire*). Edited and translated by Clément Huart. 6 vols. Paris, 1899-1919.

al-Maqrīzī, Abū'l-'Abbās Aḥmad ibn 'Alī. *Al-Mawā'iẓ wa'l-i'tibār bi-dhikr al-khiṭaṭ wa'l-āthār.* 2 vols. Bulaq, A.H. 1270.

Margoliouth, D. S. "Notice of the Writings of Abū 'Abdallah al-Ḥārith b. Asad al-Muḥāsibī, the First Ṣūfī Author." In *Transactions of the Third International Congress for the History of Religions* (Oxford, 1908), I, 292f.

[Marquet, Yves. "La Philosophie des Ihwan Safa de Dieu à l'homme." Lille, 1973. Service de reproduction des thèses.]

Masnavī, see under Jalāl al-Dīn Rūmī.

[Massignon, Louis. "Esquisse d'une bibliographie Nuṣayrie." In *Mélanges Dussaud.* Paris, 1939, pp. 913ff.]

[———. *La Passion d'al-Hosayn-ibn-Mansour al-Hallaj: Martyr mystique d'Islam.* Paris, 1922. Revised ed. 1975. Translated by Herbert Mason as *The Passion of al-Ḥallāj.* Bollingen Series XCVIII. 4 vols. Princeton, 1980.]

Masson, Jean. "The Bahaï Revelation: Its Western Advance," *American Review of Reviews,* XXXIX (January-June 1909), 214ff.

al-Mas'ūdī, Abū'l-Ḥasan 'Alī ibn al-Ḥusayn. *Murūj al-dhahab (Les Prairies d'or).* Edited by Barbier de Meynard and Pavet de Courteille. 9 vols. Paris, 1861-1877. [Edited by Charles Pellat. 5 vols. Beirut, 1966-1974].

———. *Al-Tanbīh wa'l-ishrāf.* Edited by M. J. de Goeje. *BGA* VIII. Leiden, 1894.

al-Māturīdī, Abū Manṣūr Muḥammad ibn Muḥammad. *Sharḥ al-fiqh al-akbar.* Haydarabad, A.H. 1321.

al-Māwardī, Abū'l-Ḥasan 'Alī ibn Muḥammad. *Al-Aḥkām al-sulṭānīya (Constitutiones Politicae)*. Edited by Maximilian Enger. Bonn, 1853.

———. *A'lām al-nubūwa*. Cairo, A.H. 1319.

al-Maydānī, Abū'l-Faḍl Aḥmad ibn Muḥammad. *Majma' al-amthāl*. 2 vols. Cairo, A.H. 1284. [Edited by Muḥammad Muḥyī al-Dīn 'Abd al-Ḥamīd. 2 vols. Cairo, 1379/1959.]

Mehren, M.A.F. "Correspondance du philosophe Soufi Ibn Sab'īn Abd Oul-Haqq avec l'empereur Frédéric II de Hohenstaufen," *JA*, 7th Series, XIV (1879), 341ff.

[Meier, Fritz. "The Mystic Path." In *Islam and the Arab World*. Edited by B. Lewis. New York, 1976, pp 117ff.]

[*The Memoirs of Agha Khan: World Enough and Time*. London, 1954.]

Menant, D. "Les Zoroastriens de Perse," *RMM*, III (1907), 193ff., 421ff.

Merrill, Selah. *East of the Jordan*. London, 1881.

Meyer, Richard M. Review of Müller, *Rāmakrishna: His Life and Sayings*, in *Archiv für Religionswissenschaft*, III (1900), 85ff.

MFO = *Mélanges de la Faculté Orientale de l'Université Saint-Joseph*.

Michaux-Bellaire, ed. "L'Islam et l'état marocain," *RMM*, VIII (1909), 313ff.

———. "La Maison d'Ouezzan," *RMM*, V (1909), 23ff.

———. "Proclamation de la déchéance de Moulay Abd el Aziz . . . par les ouléma de Fes," *RMM*, V (1908), 424ff.

Mission d'Ollone. "Recherches sur les musulmans chinois," *RMM*, IX (1909), 521ff.

[Monteil, Vincent. *Les Musulmans soviétiques*. Paris, 1957.]

Montet, E. *Le Culte des saints musulmans dans l'Afrique du Nord et plus spécialment au Maroc*. Mémoires publiés a l'occasion du Jubilé de l'Université de Genève. Geneva, 1909.

[Moscati, S. "Per una storia dell'antica Šī'a," *RSO*, XXX (1955), 251ff.]

Motylinski, A. de C., *see* Ibn al-Ṣaghīr.

MSOS = *Mitteilungen des Seminars für Orientalische Sprachen*.

Muhammedanische Studien, see under Goldziher.

al-Muḥibbī, Muḥammad al-Amīn ibn Faḍl Allāh. *Khulāṣat al-athar fī a'yān al-qarn al-ḥādī 'ashar*. 4 vols. Cairo, A.H. 1284.

von Mülinen, Eberhard. "Bemerkungen zum 10. Band." In Georg Jacob, *Türkische Bibliothek,* XI (Berlin, 1909), 67ff.

Müller, August. "Aus einem Briefe . . . an Dr. Steinschneider," *ZDMG*, XXXII (1878), 388ff.

———. *Der Islam im Morgen- und Abendlande*. 2 vols. Berlin, 1885-1887.

[Müller, F. Max. *Introduction to the Science of Religion*. London, 1873.]

al-Muqaddasī, Abū 'Abdallāh Muḥammad ibn Aḥmad. *Aḥsan al-taqāsīm fī ma'rifat al-aqālīm (Descriptio Imperii Moslemici)*. Edited by M. J. de Goeje. *BGA* III. Leiden, 1877.

al-Murādī, Muḥammad Khalīl ibn 'Alī. *Silk al-durar*. 4 vols. Bulaq, A.H. 1291-1301.

al-Murtaḍā 'Alam al-Hudā, 'Alī, *Al-Intiṣār*. Bombay, A.H. 1315.

Muslim ibn al-Ḥajjāj. *Ṣaḥīḥ Muslim*. With the commentary of al-Nawawī. 5 vols. Cairo, A.H. 1283.

al-Muttaqī, 'Alī ibn 'Abd al-Malik. *Kanz al-'ummāl fī sunan al-aqwāl wa'l-af'āl*. 8 vols. Haydarabad, A.H. 1312-1314.

Muwaṭṭa', *see* Mālik ibn Anas.

al-Nadīm, Abū'l-Faraj Muḥammad ibn Isḥāq. *Al-Fihrist*. Edited by Gustav Flügel. Leipzig, 1871. [Edited by Riḍā-Tajaddud. Tehran, 1391/1971.]

Nahj al-balāgha. Edited by Muḥammad 'Abduh. 2 vols. Beirut, A.H. 1307.

al-Najāshī, Aḥmad ibn 'Alī. *Kitāb al-rijāl*. Bombay, A.H. 1317.

[Nallino, C. A. "Delle assicurazioni in diritto musulmano ḥanafita," *Oriente Moderno*, VII (1927), pp. 446ff. Reprinted in his *Raccolta di scritti editi e inediti* . IV. Rome, 1942, 63ff.]

Naqā'iḍ Jarīr wa'l-Farazdaq. Edited by A. A. Bevan. 3 vols. Leiden, 1905-1912.

al-Nasā'ī, Abū 'Abd al-Raḥmān Aḥmad ibn Shu'ayb. *Al-Sunan*. 2 vols. Shāhdara, A.H. 1282.

al-Nawawī, Abū Zakarīyā' Yaḥyā ibn Sharaf. *Al-Adhkār*. Cairo, A.H. 1312.

———. *Al-Arba'ūn ḥadīthan*. Various numbered editions.

———. *Tahdhīb al-asmā' (Biographical Dictionary)*. Edited by Ferdinand Wüstenfeld. Göttingen, 1842-1847.

[al-Nawbakhtī, Ḥasan ibn Mūsā. *Kitāb firaq al-shī'a (Die Sekten der Schī'a)*. Edited by Helmut Ritter. Bibliotheca Islamica, IV. Leipzig, 1931.]

Neander, August. *Genetische Entwicklung der vornehmsten gnostischen Systeme*. Berlin, 1818.

[Nemoy, Leon. *Arabic Manuscripts in the Yale University Library*. New Haven, 1956.]

Nicholson, R. A. "A Historical Enquiry Concerning the Origin and Development of Sufism," *JRAS*, 1906, pp. 303ff.

[———. *The Idea of Personality in Sufism*. Cambridge, 1923.]

———. "The Lives of 'Umar Ibnu'l-Farid and Muhiyyu'ddin Ibnu'l-'Arabi," *JRAS*, 1906, pp. 797ff.

[———. *The Mystics of Islam*. London, 1914.]

———. "The Oldest Persian Manual of Sufism." In *Transactions of the Third International Congress for the History of Religions*. Oxford, 1908. I, 293ff.

[———. *Studies in Islamic Mysticism*. Cambridge, 1921.]

[van Nieuwenhuijze, C.A.O. *Aspects of Islam in Post-Colonial Indonesia*. The Hague and Bandung, 1958.]

[Noer, Friedrich August, Graf von. *Kaiser Akbar: Ein Versuch über die Geschichte Indiens im sechzehnten Jahrhundert*. 2 vols. Leiden, 1880-1885. English translation, *The Emperor Akbar: a Contribution towards the History of India in the 16th Century*. 2 vols. London and Calcutta, 1890.]

Nolde, Eduard. *Reise nach Innerarabien, Kurdistan und Armenien*. Braunschweig, 1895.

Nöldeke, Arnold. *Das Heiligtum al-Husains zu Kerbelā*. Türkische Bibliothek XI. Berlin, 1909.

Nöldeke, Theodor. *Geschichte des Qorāns*. 1st ed. Göttingen, 1860. 2nd ed., edited by Friedrich Schwally, G. Bergsträsser, and O. Pretzl. 3 vols. Leipzig, 1909-1938.

———. Review of vol. I of Caetani, *Annali dell'Islam*, in *WZKM*, XXI (1907), 297ff.

———. "Ṣūfī," *ZDMG*, XLVIII (1894), 45ff.

Nöldeke Festschrift = *Orientalische Studien Theodor Nöldeke gewidmet*. Edited by Carl Bezold. 2 vols. Gieszen, 1906.

[Obermann, J. "Political Theology in Early Islam: Ḥasan al-Baṣrī's Treatise on Qadar," *JAOS*, LV (1955), 138ff.]

Odysseus (pseud.). *Turkey in Europe*. London, 1900.

Oldenberg, Hermann. *Die Religion des Veda*. Berlin 1894. [Translated as *La Religion du Véda*. Paris, 1903.]

Oltramare, Paul. *L'Histoire des idées théosophiques dans l'Inde*. 2 vols. Annales du Musée Guimet, Bibliothèque d'études, XXIII. Paris, 1906-1923.

OLZ = *Orientalistische Literaturzeitung*.

Oman, John Campbell. *The Mystics, Ascetics and Saints of India*. London, 1905.

Opitz, Karl. *Die Medizin im Koran*. Stuttgart, 1906.

Oppenheim, Max, Freiherr von. *Vom Mittelmeer zum Persischen Golf*. 2 vols. Berlin, 1899-1900.

Pal. Talmud = *The Palestinian (Jerusalem) Talmud*; Goldziher's references are standard for all editions.

Palmer, E. H., trans. *The Koran*. London, 1900.

[Paret, Rudi. *Der Koran: Kommentar und Konkordanz*. Stuttgart, 1971.]

[———. "Sure 2, 256: *Lā ikrāha fī d-dīni*, Toleranz oder Resignation?" *Der Islam*, XLV (1969), 299ff.]

[———. "Toleranz und Intoleranz im Islam," *Saeculum*, XXI (1970), 344ff.]

Patton, Walter M. *Aḥmed ibn Ḥanbal and the Miḥna*. Leiden, 1897.

[Pellat, Charles. "Le Culte de Mu'āwiya au IIIe siècle de l'hégire," *Studia Islamica*, VI (1956), 53ff.]

[———. "Essai d'inventaire de l'oeuvre Ǧāḥiẓienne," *Arabica*, III (1956), 147ff.]

Pertsch, W. *Die arabischen Handschriften der Herzoglichen Bibliothek zu Gotha*. 5 vols. Gotha, 1877-1892.

[Petersen, Erling Ladewig. *'Alī and Mu'āwiya in Early Arabic Tradition*. Odense, 1974.]

[Philby, H. St. J.B. *Arabia*. London, 1930.]

Phillott, D. C., and R. F. Azoo, "The Birds' Complaint before Solomon," *Journal of the Asiatic Society of Bengal*, New Series, III (1907), 173ff.

[*"Picatrix": das Ziel des Weisen von Pseudo-Mağrīṭī*. Translated by Helmut Ritter and Martin Plessner. London, 1962.]

Pinches, Theo. G. "The Early Babylonian King-Lists," *Proceedings of the Society of Biblical Archaeology*, VI (1884), 193ff.; VII (1885), 65ff.

[Pines, S. *Beiträge zur islamischen Atomenlehre*. Berlin, 1936.]

Polak, J. E. *Persien: das Land und seine Bewohner*. 2 vols. Leipzig, 1865.

Porter, Josias L. *Five Years in Damascus*. 2nd ed. London, 1870.

Poznanski, S. "Miscellen über Saadja III," *Monatsschrift für Geschichte und Wissenschaft des Judentums*, XLIV (1900), 400ff., 508ff.

Prasad, Rama. *The Science of Breath and the Philosophy of the Tatwas, translated from Sanskrit*. London, 1890.

al-Qālī, Abū 'Alī Ismā'īl ibn al-Qāsim. *Al-Amālī*. 2 vols. Cairo, A.H. 1324.

al-Qārī, 'Alī ibn Sulṭān. *Sharḥ al-fiqh al-akbar*. Cairo, A.H. 1323.

———. *Sharḥ al-shifā'*. 2 vols. Istanbul, A.H. 1299.

al-Qasṭallānī, Abū'l-'Abbās Aḥmad ibn Muḥammad. *Irshād al-sārī ilā sharḥ ṣaḥīḥ al-Bukhārī*. 10 vols. Cairo, A.H. 1285.

al-Qazwīnī, Abū Yaḥyā Zakarīyā' ibn Muḥammad. *Āthār al-bilād wa-akhbār al-'ibād*. Edited by Ferdinand Wüstenfeld. El-Cazwini's Kosmographie, II. Göttingen, 1848.

al-Qifṭī, 'Alī ibn Yūsuf. *Ta'rīkh al-ḥukamā'*. Edited by Julius Lippert. Leipzig, 1903.

[Quelquejay, C. "Un Reformateur Tatar au XIXe siècle; Abdul Kajjum al-Nasyri," *Cahiers de monde russe et sovietique*, IV (1973), 117ff.]

Querry, Amédée. *Droit musulman*. 2 vols. Paris, 1871-1872.

al-Qushayrī, Abū'l-Qāsim 'Abd al-Karīm ibn Hawāzin. *Risāla fī 'ilm al-taṣawwuf*. Cairo, A.H. 1304.

al-Qūshjī, 'Alī ibn Muḥammad, *see* al-Ṭūṣī, *Tajrīd*.

al-Rāghib al-Iṣfahānī, Abū'l-Qāsim al-Ḥusayn ibn Muḥammad. *Muḥāḍarāt al-udabā'*. Cairo, A.H. 1287.

[Rahman, Fazlur. *Islam*. London, 1966.]

[———. "Riba and Interest," *Islamic Studies*, III (1964), 1ff.]

[———. "Sunnah and Hadith," *Islamic Studies*, I (1962), 33ff.]

al-Rāzī, Fakhr al-Dīn. *Ma'ālim uṣūl al-dīn* (on the margin of his *Muḥaṣṣal afkār al-mutaqaddimīn wa'l-muta'akhkhirīn*). Cairo, A.H. 1323.

———. *Mafātīḥ al-ghayb*. 6 vols. Cairo, A.H. 1278.

———. *Muḥaṣṣal afkār al-mutaqaddimīn wa'l-muta'akhkhirīn*. With glosses by Naṣīr al-Dīn al-Ṭūṣī, *Takhlīṣ al-muḥaṣṣal*. Cairo, A.H. 1323.

REI = Revue des études islamiques.

Reitzenstein, Richard. *Hellenistische Wundererzählungen*. Leipzig, 1906.

REJ = Revue des études juives.

Renan, Ernest. *Mission de Phénicie*. Paris, 1864.

[Rescher, Oscar, "Eine Bemerkung zu Goldziher's *Vorlesungen über den Islam*," *Der Islam*, XVI (1927), 156.]

RHR = Revue de l'histoire des religions.

[Ringgren, H. *Islam, 'Aslama and Muslim*. Lund, 1949.]

Rinkes, D. A. *Abdoerraoef van Singkel; Bijdrage tot de kennis van de mystiek op Sumatra en Java*. Heerenveen, 1909.

[Ritter, Helmut. *Das Meer der Seele*. Leiden, 1955.]

RMM = Revue du monde musulman.

Robert, Achille. "Fanatisme et légendes arabes," *Revue des traditions populaires*, XIX (1904), 110.

ROC = Revue de l'orient chrétien.

[Rodinson, Maxime. "Bilan des études mohammadiennes," *Revue historique*, CCXXIX (1963), 169ff.]

[Rondot, Pierre. *L'Islam et les musulmans d'aujourd'hui*. 2 vols. Paris, 1958-60.]

da la Roque, Jean. *Voyage de Syrie et du Mont Libanon*. Paris, 1722.

Rosen, Friedrich. *Die Sinnsprüche Omars des Zeltmachers*. Stuttgart and Leipzig, 1909.

Rosenberg, Ethel. "Bahaism, Its Ethical and Social Teachings." In *Transactions of the Third International Congress for the History of Religions*. Oxford, 1908. I, 321ff.

[Rosenthal, E.I.J. *Islam in the Modern National State*. Cambridge, 1965.]

[Roychoudhury, Makhanlal. *The Din-i Ilahi*. Calcutta, 1941.]

RSO = *Rivista degli studi orientali*.

[Runge, Hans-Joachim. *Über Gazālī's Faiṣal-al-tafriqa baina-l-Islām wa-l-zandaqa: Untersuchung über die Unterscheidung von Islam und Ketzerei*. Kiel, 1938.]

Sachau, Eduard. "Über die religiöse Anschauungen der ibaditischen Muhammedaner in Oman und Ostafrika," *MSOS*, II (1899), ii, 47–82.

Al-Ṣaḥīfa al-kāmila. Lucknow, A.H. 1312.

[Santillana, David. *Istituzioni di diritto musulmano malichita con riguardo anche al sistema sciafiita*. 2 vols. Rome, 1926-1938.]

al-Sanūsī, Abū 'Abdallāh Muḥammad ibn Yūsuf. *Al-Muqaddima (Les Prolégomènes théologiques de Senoussi)*. Edited and translated by J. D. Luciani. Algiers, 1908.

Sarkīs, Yūsuf. "Tarjama 'arabīya qadīma min al-Anjīl al-Ṭāhir." *Al-Mashriq*, XI (1908), 902ff.

[Sarkisyanz, Emanuel. *Russland und der Messianismus des Orients, Sendungsbewusstsein und politischer Chiliasmus des Ostens*. Tübingen, 1955.]

The Satapatha-Brāhmana. Translated by Julius Eggeling. The Sacred Books of the East, XII. Oxford, 1882.

Sayce, A. H. "Cairene Folklore," *Folklore*, XI (1900), 354ff.

Sayyid 'Alī Muḥammad. *Zād qalīl*. Lucknow, 1290/1873.

[Schacht, Joseph. *An Introduction to Islamic Law*. Oxford, 1964.]

[———. *The Origins of Muhammedan Jurisprudence*. 4th ed. Oxford, 1967.]

Schreiner, Martin. *Beiträge zur Geschichte der theologischen Bewegungen im Islam*. Leipzig, 1899.

———. "Zur Geschichte der Polemik zwischen Juden und Muhammedanern," *ZDMG*, XLII (1888), 591ff.

———. "Zur Geschichte des Aš'aritenthums." In *Actes du huitième Congrès International des Orientalistes*. Leiden, 1892-1893. II, 1A, 79ff.

Seder Eliyyāhū Rabbā. Edited by Meir Friedmann. Vienna, 1900.

Sell, Edward. *The Faith of Islam*. London, 1880.

[Sezgin, Fuat. *Geschichte des arabischen Schrifttums*. Leiden, 1967—proceeding.]

[Shaban, M. A. *Islamic History A.D. 600-750 (A.H. 132): A New Interpretation*. Cambridge, 1971.]

al-Shādhilī, Aḥmad ibn Muḥammad. *Al-Futūḥāt al-ilāhīya*. 2 vols. Cairo, 1324/1906.

al-Shahrastānī, Muḥammad ibn 'Abd al-Karīm. *Kitāb al-milal wa'l-niḥal (Book of Religious and Philosophical Sects).* Edited by William Cureton. London, 1842-1846.

al-Sha'rānī, Abū 'Abd al-Raḥmān 'Abd al-Wahhāb ibn Aḥmad. *Kashf al-ghumma 'an jamī' al-umma.* 2 vols. Cairo, A.H. 1281.

———. *Kitāb al-mīzān.* Translated by Nicolas Perron as *Balance de la loi musulmane ou Esprit de la législation islamique et divergences de ses quatre rites jurisprudentiels.* Algiers, 1898.

———. *Mukhtaṣar al-tadhkira.* Cairo, A.H. 1310.

Sharīf, Ja'far. *Qanoon-e Islam.* Translated by G. A. Herklots. London, 1832.

[Siddiqi, Mazheruddin. *The Qur'anic Concept of History.* Karachi, 1965.]

Sifrē (Deuteronomy). Edited by Meir Friedmann. Vilna, 1864.

[Smirnov, N. A. *Očerki Istorii Izučeniya Islama v SSSR.* Moscow, 1954. Abridged translation and analysis in *Islam and Russia,* with an introduction by A.K.S. Lambton. London, 1956.]

Smith, R. Bosworth. *Mohammed and Mohammedanism.* 2nd ed. London, 1876.

Smith, Vincent A. "Ibrahim b. Adham," *JRAS*, 1910, p. 167.

Smith, W. Robertson. *Kinship and Marriage in Early Arabia.* 2nd ed. London, 1903.

[Smith, Wilfred Cantwell. *Islam in Modern History.* Princeton, 1957.]

[———. *Modern Islam in India.* London, 1946.]

Snouck Hurgronje, Christiaan. *Arabië en Oost Indië.* Leiden, 1907. French version, "L'Arabie et les Indes Neerlandaises," *RHR*, LVII (1908), 60ff. [= *Verspreide Geschriften*, IV, ii, 97ff.]

———. *De Atjèhers.* 2 vols. Batavia and Leiden, 1893-1894. English translation by A.W.S. Sullivan, *The Achehnese.* 2 vols. Leiden, 1906.

———. "Berichtigung" in *ZDMG*, LIII (1899), 703f. [= *Verspreide Geschriften*, II, 417f.]

———. "Le Droit musulman," *RHR*, XXXVII (1898), 1ff., 174ff. [= *Verspreide Geschriften*, II, 285ff.]

———. *Het Gayōland en zejne bewoners.* Batavia, 1903.

———. "Der Mahdi," *Revue coloniale internationale*, I (1886), 25ff. [= *Verspreide Geschriften*, I, 147ff.]

———. *Het Mekkaansche Feest.* Leiden, 1880. [= *Verspreide Geschriften*, I, 1ff. Partial translation in *Oeuvres choisies*, 171ff.]

———. *Oeuvres choisies de C. Snouck Hurgronje.* Translated by G.-H. Bousquet and Joseph Schacht. Leiden, 1957.

———. Review of van der Berg, *Beginselen van het Mohammedaansche Recht*, offprint. [= *Verspreide Geschriften*, II, 59ff.]

[———. *Verspreide Geschriften van C. Snouck Hurgronje.* Edited. by J. Wensinck. 5 vols. Bonn and Leiden, 1923-1926.]

[Speyer, Heinrich. *Die biblischen Erzählungen im Qoran.* Gräfenhainichen, n.d. Reprinted Hildesheim, 1961.]

Sprenger, Aloys. *Das Leben und die Lehre des Moḥammad.* 2nd ed. 3 vols. Berlin, 1869.

Sproat, G. M. *Scenes and Studies of Savage Life.* London, 1868.

Steinschneider, Moritz. "Apocalypsen mit polemischer Tendenz," *ZDMG*, XXVIII (1874), 627ff.

———. *Die hebräischen Übersetzungen des Mittelalters und die Juden als Dolmetscher.* Berlin, 1893.

———. *Polemische und apologetische Literatur in arabischer Sprache.* Leipzig, 1877.

———. *Rangstreit-Literatur.* Sitzungsberichte der Kaiserlichen Akademie der Wissenschaften, Philosophisch-Historische Klasse, CLV. Vienna, 1908.

[Strothmann, Rudolf. *Esoterische Sonderthemen bei den Nusairi: Geschichten und Traditionen von den Heiligen Meistern aus dem Prophetenhaus.* Berlin, 1958.]

al-Subkī, Tāj al-Dīn Abū Naṣr 'Abd al-Wahhāb. *Mu'īd al-ni'am wa-mubīd al-niqam.* Edited by David W. Myhrman. London, 1908.

———. *Ṭabaqāt al-shāfi'īya al-kubrā.* 6 vols. Cairo, A.H. 1324.

al-Suwaydī, 'Abdallāh ibn Ḥusayn. *Kitāb al-ḥujaj al-qaṭ'īya li-ittifāq al-firaq al-islāmīya.* Cairo, A.H. 1323.

al-Suyūṭī, Abū'l-Faḍl 'Abd al-Raḥmān ibn Abī Bakr. *Al-La'ālī al-maṣnū'a fī'l-aḥādīth al-mawḍū'a.* 2 vols. Cairo, A.H. 1317.

al-Ṭabarī, Abū Ja'far Muḥammad ibn Jarīr. *Ikhtilāf al-fuqahā'.* Edited by Friedrich Kern. Cairo, 1902.

———. *Tafsīr al-Ṭabarī (Al-Jāmi' al-bayān fī ta'wīl āy al-Qur'ān).* 30 vols. Cairo, A.H. 1323-1329.

———. *Ta'rīkh al-rusul wa'l-mulūk (Annales).* Edited by M. J. de Goeje et al. 15 vols. Leiden, 1879-1901.

al-Ṭabarsī, al-Ḥasan ibn. al-Faḍl. *Makārim al-akhlāq.* Cairo, A.H. 1303.

al-Ṭaḥāwī, Abū Ja'far Aḥmad ibn Muḥammad. *Bayān al-sunna wa'l-jamā'a.* With the commentary of Sirāj al-Dīn 'Umar al-Hindī. Kazan, 1902.

al-Tha'ālibī, Abū Manṣūr 'Abd al-Malik ibn Muḥammad. *Yatīmat al-dahr.* 4 vols. Damascus, A.H. 1304. [Edited by Muḥammad Muḥyī al-Dīn 'Abd al-Ḥamīd. 4 vols. Cairo, A.H. 1375-1397.]

Thompson, R. Campbell. "The Folklore of Mossoul," *Proceedings of the Society of Biblical Archaeology*, XXVIII (1906), 76ff.

Tiele, Cornelius Petrus. *Inleiding tot de Godsdienstwetenschap.* Amsterdam, 1899. [Translated as *Elements of the Science of Religion.* 2 vols. Edinburgh and London, 1897-1899.]

al-Tirmidhī, Abū 'Īsā Muḥammad ibn 'Īsā. *Ṣaḥīḥ al-Tirmidhī.* 2 vols. Cairo, A.H. 1292.

Tisdall, William. *The Religion of the Crescent.* 2nd ed. London, 1906.

Trumelet, C. *L'Algérie légendaire.* Algiers, 1892.

al-Ṭūsī, Naṣīr al-Dīn. *Fihrist kutub al-shī'a* (*Tusy's List of Shy'ah Books*). Edited by Aloys Sprenger et al. Calcutta, 1853-1855.

———. *Tajrīd al-'aqā'id.* With the commentary of 'Alī ibn Muḥammad al-Qūshjī. Bombay, A.H. 1301.

———. *Takhlīṣ al-muḥaṣṣal, see* al-Rāzī, *Muḥaṣṣal.*

Vámbéry, H. "Die Kulturbestrebungen der Tataren," *Deutsche Rundschau*, XXXIII (1907), 72ff.

Vinson, Julien. "La Religion des sikhs," *RMM*, IX (1909), 361ff.

van Vloten, Gerlof. "Irdjā," *ZDMG*, XLV (1891), 161ff.

———. *Recherches sur la domination arabe, le chiitisme et les croyances messianiques sous le khalifat des Omayades*. Amsterdam, 1894.

———. "Zur Abbasidengeschichte," *ZDMG*, LII (1898), 213ff.

Vollers, K. "Chidher," *Archiv für Religionswissenschaft*, XII (1909), 234ff.

Volney, Constantin François. *Voyage en Syrie et en Égypte*. 2nd ed. Paris, 1787.

[Wansbrough, J. *Qur'ānic Studies*. London, 1977.]

[Watt, W. Montgomery. *Free Will and Predestination in Early Islam*. London, 1948.]

[———. *Islamic Philosophy and Theology*. Edinburgh, 1962.]

[———. *Islamic Political Thought: The Basic Concepts*. Edinburgh, 1968.]

[Weber, Max. *The Sociology of Religion*. Translated by E. Fischoff. London, 1965.]

Wellhausen, Julius. *Das arabische Reich und sein Sturz*. Berlin, 1902. [Translated as *The Arab Kingdom and Its Fall*. Calcutta, 1927.]

———. "Die Ehe bei den Arabern," *Nachrichten von der Königlichen Gesellschaft der Wissenschaften und der Georg-Augusts-Universität zu Göttingen*, 1893, 431ff.

———. *Die religiös-politischen Oppositionsparteien im alten Islam*. Abhandlungen der Königlichen Gesellschaft der Wissenschaften zu Göttingen, Philologisch-Historische Klasse, V, 2. Berlin, 1901. [Translated as *The Religio-political Factions in Early Islam*. Amsterdam, 1975.]

———. *Skizzen und Vorarbeiten*. 6 vols. Berlin, 1884-1899.

Wensinck, A. J. *Concordance et indices de la tradition musulmane*. 7 vols. Leiden, 1936-1969.

———. *Mohammed en de Joden te Medina*. Leiden, 1908. [Translated as *Muhammad and the Jews of Medina*. Freiburg im Breisgau, 1975].

Westcott, G. H. *Kabīr and the Kabīrpanth*. Cawnpore, 1907.

Westermarck, Edward A. *The History of Human Marriage*. 2nd ed. London, 1894.

———. *The Origin and Development of the Moral Ideas*. 2 vols. London, 1906-1908.

Wetzstein, Johann Gottfried. *Reisebericht über Hauran und die Trachonen*. Berlin, 1860.

[Wilken, G. A. *De Verspreide Geschriften*. 4 vols. Semerang, 1912.]

———. *Het Matriarchaat bij de oude Arabieren*. Amsterdam, 1884. [= *De Verspreide Geschriften* (Semerang, 1912), II, 1ff. German translation, *Das Matriarchat bei den alten Arabern*. Leipzig, 1884. Arabic translation, *Al-Umūma 'inda'l-'arab*. Kazan, 1902.]

Wilkinson, R. J. *Papers on Malay Subjects. Life and Customs*. Kuala Lumpur, 1908.

[Winstedt, R. O. *The Malays: a Cultural History*. 6th ed. London, 1961.]

WZKM = *Wiener Zeitschrift für die Kunde des Morgenlandes*.

al-Yāfi'ī, Abū'l-Sa'āda 'Abdallāh ibn As'ad. *Rawḍ al-rayāḥīn*. Cairo, A.H. 1297.

Yahuda, A. S. *Prolegomena zu . . . Kitāb al-hidāja ilā farā'iḍ al-qulūb*. Darmstadt, 1904.

al-Yamanī, 'Umāra. *Al-Nukat al-'asrīya ('Oumāra du Yemen, sa vie et son oeuvre)*. Edited by Hartwig Derenbourg. 2 vols. Paris, 1897-1904.

al-Ya'qūbī, Aḥmad ibn Abī Ya'qūb. *Ta'rīkh* (*Historiae*). Edited by M. T. Houtsma. 2 vols. Leiden, 1883.

Yāqūt ibn 'Abdallāh al-Ḥamawī, Abū 'Abd Allāh. *Irshād al-arīb ilā ma'rifat al-adīb*

(Dictionary of Learned Men). Edited by D. S. Margoliouth. E.J.W. Gibb Memorial, VI. 7 vols. Leiden and London, 1907-1926.

———. *Mu'jam al-buldān (Jacut's geographisches Wörterbuch)*. Edited by Ferdinand Wüstenfeld. 6 vols. Leipzig, 1866-1873.

ZA = *Zeitschrift für Assyriologie und verwandte Gebiete.*

al-Zabīdī, Abū'l-Fayḍ Muḥammad Murtaḍā. ibn Muḥammad. *Itḥāf al-sāda al-muttaqīn*. 10 vols. Cairo, A.H. 1311.

[Zaehner, R. C. *Hindu and Muslim Mysticism*. London, 1960.]

ZATW = *Zeitschrift für alttestamentliche Wissenschaft.*

ZDMG = *Zeitschrift der Deutschen Morgenländischen Gesellschaft.*

[Zenkovsky, A. *Pan-Turkism and Islam in Russia*. Cambridge, Mass., 1960.]

Zurqānī, *see* Mālik ibn Anas.

Zustände im heutigen Persien, wie sie das Reisebuch Ibrahim Bejs enthüllt. Translated by Walter Schulz. Leipzig, 1903.

Zwemer, Samuel M. "Islam in Arabia." In *The Mohammedan World of To-day*, edited by S. M. Zwemer et al. New York, 1906, pp. 99ff.

Index